A High School Understanding of
Blockchain Technology

Some Dude

~~Author:~~ Jacob Owen

Copyright © 2024 by Jacob Owen. All rights reserved.

No part of this book may be reproduced in any form without permission from the author or publisher, except as permitted by U.S. copyright law.

This book offers no financial advice, and it is not endorsing any of the Alt-coins that are mentioned, always do your own research before investing in a coin or token.

This book will not teach you how to write code, nor will it help you find the next 100x coin or token. Instead, it covers the basic concepts of blockchain technology, there are simplified examples to help you better understand how a blockchain works overall, and I would suggest further research for anyone looking to understand individual aspects of this technology on a deeper level. The illustrations are not actual representations of how the technology works, they are my interpretation of the many individual aspects of a blockchain, and they are simplified so you can understand how each aspect could affect a blockchain, for better or worse.

In this book we will cover blockchains and their consensus methods, as well as decentralization and how it can affect many aspects of a blockchain, and we will look at the Bitcoin blockchain in detail. The next book will cover many blockchain use cases, exchanges, and several Alt-coins in detail.

ISBN: 9798326208941

Contents

Foreword vii
About Some Dude ix
    Form of Communication: ix
    Past to Present: xi

Basic Blockchain Encryption   1

Basic information on what a blockchain is*
    Basic Encryption: 1
    Wallet / Ledger: 3
    Transactions: 4
    Public and Private Keys: 6
    Orphan Blocks: 7
    Quantum Computing: 7
    Conclusion: 8

Blockchain / Consensus Methods 101   11

More detail on how blockchains work, based off individual aspects, that may be common between many blockchains*
    Basic Consensus Method: 11
    Validator Locations: 11
    Validators vs Nodes: 12
    Majority Control of the Consensus Method: 12
    51% Attacks: 13

Consensus Methods 202   15

Expanded information on prior concepts, bringing it together to go over consensus methods*
    Proof of Work, POW: **15**
        POW is Hardware: 15
        Mining Block Rewards: 16
        Mining Farms: 16
        Mining Farm Efficiency: 17
        Conclusion: 18
    Proof of Stake, POS: **18**
        Stake Pools: 19
        Staking to a Pool: 19
        Slashing: 20
        Epochs: 20
        Block Reward Limits: 22
        Number of Pools: 24
        POS Pros and Cons: 24
        3rd Party Staking: 25
    Nodes: **26**
        Copy of the Blockchain: 26
        Oracles: 27
    Consensus Method Vulnerabilities: **29**

Blockchain 202   31

How these blockchains work at basic generic levels, each blockchain is different, so these are still somewhat basic concepts that may or may not apply to all blockchain coins and tokens*
    Improvement Proposals, IPs: **31**
        POW IPs: 31
        POS IPs: 32
    Blockchain Users: **32**
    Blockchain Forks: **33**
        Soft Fork: 33
        Hard Fork: 35
        Two Examples of Hard Forks: 36

Simple Hard Fork Examples:	38
Coin Creation:	**39**
Consensus Methods and IPs:	**40**
Other Consensus Methods:	40
Proof of Time:	42
Proof of Authority:	42
Unique Node List:	42
Conclusion:	**43**

Decentralization 45

The many different aspects of decentralization for blockchain technology*

Introduction:	**45**
Decentralized Consensus Method:	**46**
Decentralized POW Blockchain:	46
Simple Example:	47
Large Mining Farms:	48
Mining Farm Locations:	48
Barrier to Entry:	49
Decentralized POS Blockchain:	51
Cost to Become a Validator:	53
Stake Pool Types:	53
Stakeholders:	54
Fewer Stake Pools:	55
Individually Controlled Validators:	56
Block Reward Limits:	57
Stake Pool Operators:	58
Staking as a Service:	58
Decentralization for "Trusted" and Local Stake Pools:	59
Local Stake Pools:	59
Local Pool Example:	60
"Trusted" Stake Pool:	61
Decentralized Voting Structure:	**64**
Voting on a POS Blockchain:	64
Voting Coins:	65
Voting Tokens:	67
Community Voting Tokens:	68
Other Aspects of Decentralization:	**69**
Nodes:	69
Improvement Proposals:	71
Decentralized External Factors:	**72**
External Factors, Development Team:	73
External Factors, Whale Wallets:	73
External Factors, Front Running:	74
External Factors, Exchanges and Wallets:	76
External Factors, Hard Wallets:	78
Decentralization is Not Exact:	**79**
Hard Wallets, Shades of Gray:	79
Howey Test Definitions:	82
Digital Securities:	82
"Decentralized":	85
Advantages of Decentralized Blockchains:	**86**
Minute Man Validators:	87
Advantages and Disadvantages:	89
Hope:	91
Decentralization Conclusion:	**92**
Creation of a Cage:	93
Must have the Option:	95

Bitcoin Blockchain — 99
The many decentralized aspects to Bitcoins blockchain, and how they play a part in securing the blockchain overall*

- **Blockchain Basics, Bitcoin:** — 99
  - SHA-256: — 99
  - Coin Creation: — 100
  - Bitcoin Block Rewards: — 101
  - Bitcoin Distribution: — 102
  - Bitcoin Halving and Difficulty Adjustment: — 104
  - Bitcoin Price Cycle: — 105
  - Bitcoin Demand: — 108
  - Bitcoin Nodes: — 108
- **Centralization Risks:** — 110
  - Bitcoins Creator: — 110
  - Large Bitcoin Mining Farms: — 111
  - Satoshi: — 112
  - Satoshi Wallets: — 113
- **Bitcoins History:** — 114
  - Bitcoin Pizza Day: — 115
  - Bitcoins Hash Rate History: — 116
  - China's Bitcoin Mining Ban: — 117
  - Bitcoin Hard Forks: — 118
- **Bitcoins Future:** — 119
  - Bitcoins Current and Future Developments: — 119
  - Lighting Network: — 122
  - Bitcoin Block Rewards: — 122
- **Bitcoin Validators:** — 125
  - Mining Farm Quote: — 125
  - Example Bitcoin Mining Farm: — 127
  - Do Not Think in Dollars: — 127
  - Weeding Out of Bitcoin Miners: — 128
  - Balancing the Grid with Bitcoin Mining Farms: — 129
  - Bitcoin Mining Farms in Texas: — 132
- **Renewable Energy Sources Being Used Today:** — 133
  - Nuclear: — 134
  - Hydropower in Norway: — 135
  - Geothermal: — 135
  - Flare Gas / Natural Gas: — 136
  - Solar: — 136
- **Our Bitcoin Mining Farm:** — 137
  - GPU Mining Rig: — 138
  - ASIC Hash Rate: — 139
  - Solar: — 139
  - ASIC Cooling: — 139
  - Dielectric Fluid Cooling: — 140
  - Dielectric Fluid Cooling 2.0: — 142
  - Education: — 143
  - Temperatures and Noise: — 144
  - Rough Temperature Numbers: — 145
  - Temperature Recordings: — 145
  - Mining Farm Conclusion: — 146
- **Bitcoin Conclusion:** — 147
  - Bitcoin Cycles: — 148
  - Long-Term Wealth Storage: — 149
  - Forms of Demand for Bitcoin: — 150
  - Bitcoin and Gold: — 151
  - Balancing the Power Grid: — 153
  - Alternative Blockchains: — 154
  - Decentralization is Important: — 154

Foreword

By Erica Stephens, PhD

As a clinical psychologist specializing in neurodiversity and a myriad of other mental health presentations, I have had the privilege of understanding and working with individuals who present with unique passions and interests and display remarkable dedication in their pursuits.

I have also had the pleasure of developing a close relationship with Jacob Owen, who affectionately self-identifies as "some dude." But Jacob is far more than just "some dude."

Jacob's journey is one of resilience, marked by his service as a veteran of the Iraq war and his ongoing battle with PTSD, anxiety, and likely additional neurodivergence that provides him a one of a kind understanding of his interests. It is within the intersection of these experiences that Jacob's extraordinary passion for understanding the intricate world of cryptocurrency and blockchain technology has flourished.

In this book, Jacob's unique perspective shines through, offering readers a window into the mind of someone whose innate characteristics drive an insatiable curiosity and dedication to learning. Through his lens, he illuminates the complexities of crypto and blockchain, breaking down barriers for novice learners and offering insights that only someone with his depth of understanding can provide.

As I reflect on Jacob's journey, I am reminded of the profound impact that individuality and perseverance can have in shaping our understanding of the world. His willingness to share his knowledge and experiences is a testament to his generosity and commitment to empowering others.

It is with great admiration and gratitude that I write this forward, knowing that Jacob's contributions to the field of crypto and blockchain will undoubtedly leave a lasting impression on those who have the privilege of engaging with his work.

About Some Dude

- **Form of Communication**
- **Past to Present**

Form of Communication:

In my basic training at Ft Leonard Wood Missouri, I was taught many things, from the correct form of push-ups and sit-ups, to urban combat training and room clearing. The Army, like other branches, focused a great deal of time training new soldiers on how to operate, maintain, and effectively fire a rifle. Many factors are involved in accurately firing a weapon, breathing affects your sight picture of the target, either making your round higher or lower than where you were aiming, while trigger squeeze can cause your round to hit to the left or right of your target. There are other environmental factors that can also affect your accuracy, distance to your target, high winds, extreme heat or cold etc. all these factors play a part in aiming at and hitting your target. Range days are where soldiers practice and perfect these skills, and "zero" their issued weapons, meaning they make the necessary adjustments to the front and rear sights of their weapon (or to whatever optic they have on their weapon). This allows them to line up their sights and hit the target they are aiming at, the weapon is now zeroed, and the soldier's accuracy is now only affected by the other factors such as breathing control, trigger pull, etc.

Kentucky windage is a correction made by aiming the weapon to the left or right of the target rather than adjusting the sights, this works for some and can be very accurate, however the Army looks down on this practice, they would rather the sights be adjusted, reducing the factors involved in accurately hitting the target. If you are consistently missing the target high and to the right of where you are aiming, then adjusting your aim low and to the left will bring your rounds on target, there is some guesswork involved, and this adjustment is added to all the other factors involved in accurately hitting the target, the Army would rather have you just adjust your sights and remove this additional variable.

I realize my ability to communicate the information in my mind to others is off, I was never great at English and grammar, and typing out papers and using spell check is what got me average English grades in high school, although math, history, and science came very easy to me. This has become more apparent since I started researching blockchain technologies, while talking about blockchain related topics I often talk fast and jump from topic to topic, the same is true with typing out what I am trying to communicate, sometimes it can take me hours to write out just a paragraph, and these papers are either short and not able to communicate what I want to say, or they are overly complicated and very long.

I have come to realize that illustrating what I am trying to communicate with drawings and descriptions is easier for me to do, analogies also help, using physical analogies for non-physical things like blockchain coins and tokens also makes it easier to communicate the information from myself to others. This is like my way of communicating information using Kentucky windage, it may not be the normal way, or "the right way" but it works for me, and it helps me better convey complicated information that covers many areas and has many aspects. Using these illustrations and analogies I can convey the concept of something, I can then describe each factor or detail more in depth, and the reader can see how all the information fits together through the visuals. My anxiety (or PTSD) is like a weapon that is not zeroed and cannot have its sights adjusted, if I try to communicate "the right way" I will always miss the target, however I can use this form of Kentucky windage communication to have a better shot at hitting the target and getting my information across.

Another option would be to accept the lower accuracy by increasing the volume of rounds fired at the target, this is usually done with a crew-served weapon that can fire many rounds at an area target, not all of them hit the target, but the large number fired ensures some rounds will likely hit, and at the very least it will get the attention of the target and force them to find cover. This is similar to what I do when trying to verbally

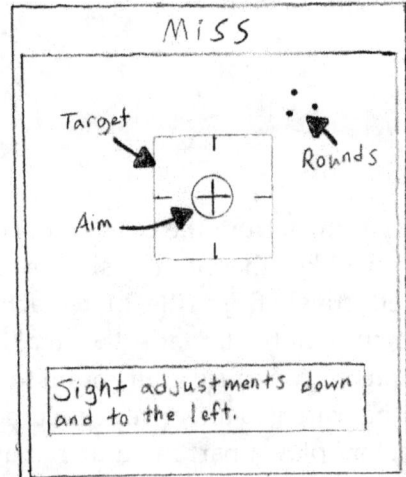
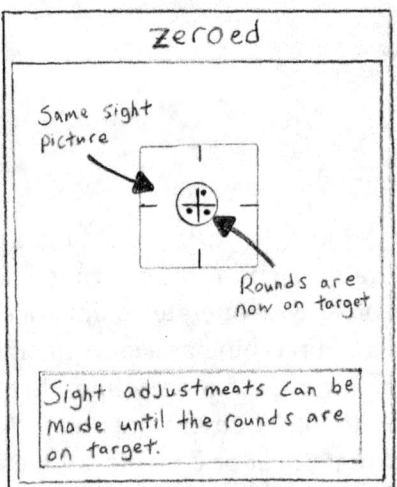
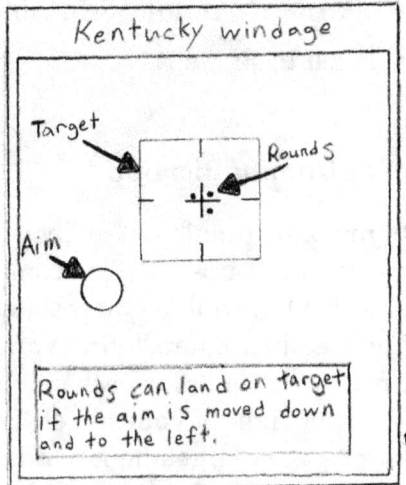

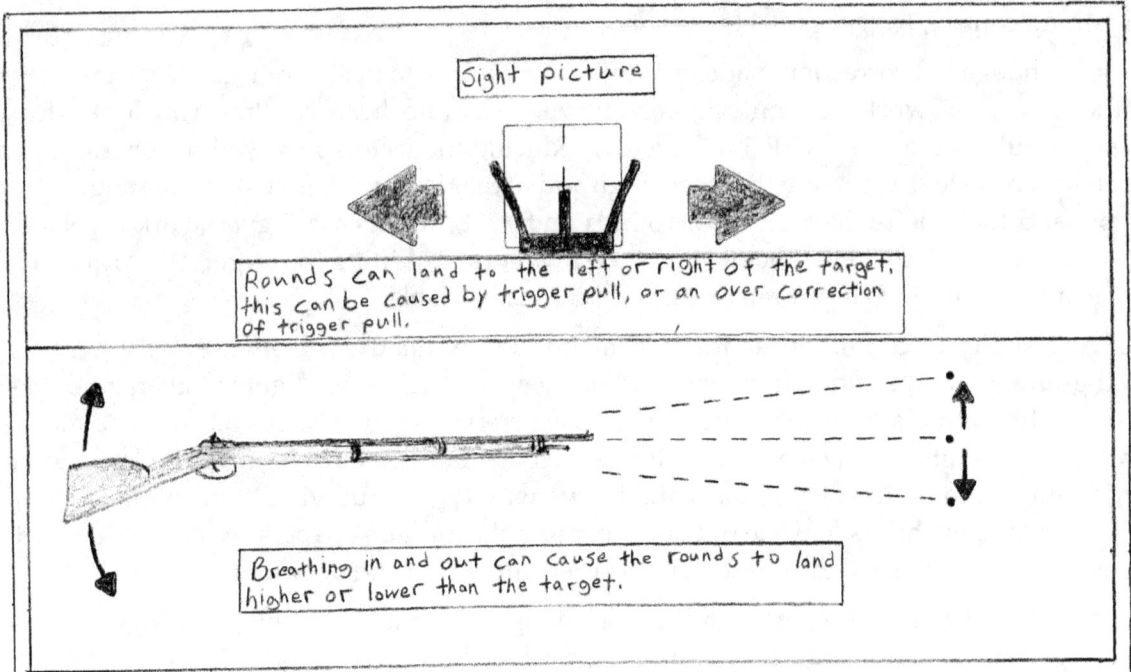

Kentucky Windage

Sights may need to be adjusted several times before the rounds are on target and the weapon is zeroed, but Kentucky windage does not involve adjusting the sights, just adjusting the aim, and this requires some guesswork. This factor would be in addition to other factors like trigger pull, basically squeezing the trigger too hard, or by over correcting this action, and this will cause the rounds to pull to the left or right of the target. Rounds landing above or below the target are usually caused by breathing, both breathing in, or out, will affect the rifle and its aim, and these are factors involved each time the weapon is fired, whether the weapon is zeroed or not.

communicate some ideas, I talk fast, sometimes I lose breath, and I jump from an important fact or topic to the next. I am rapidly sending information that I believe the person I am talking to needs to know, and even though I may not be fully, or accurately, explaining some aspects of the topic, I am sending an overwhelming amount of information to make up for the lack of accuracy. This is obviously not a normal, or a good way to communicate information, it started happening about a year into my research, I called it a mind dump back then, and it was basically me involuntary going on long rants about blockchain technology whenever someone asked about it. I believe accuracy, even if it must be achieved with some form of Kentucky windage, is a better way to communicate the information in my mind to others, simply increasing the volume of information does not work as well, and leaves most people confused after listening to me.

Past to Present:

I took AP macro and microeconomics courses in high school, I understand supply and demand, and how they interact in individual markets and global markets, I understood the concepts, but was not really interested in the topic. I was more interested in math and other subjects that were involved with mechanical engineering, that was my major at Cal Poly Pomona for 2 semesters. However, most of the classes were full, and I only took a few worthwhile classes like trigonometry and pre-calculus, I obviously don't remember much of the equations, but I do understand algorithms and many of the concepts. The lack of open classes and the college environment eventually led me to enlisting in the Army, and my recruiter said I could have just about any job in the Army, I scored 97% on my ASVAB, although I didn't want to sit behind a desk and do computer work, and this led to me joining as a 21B, combat engineer. I was stationed at Ft Campbell KY with the 101st Airborne Division, completed Air Assault School, and was deployed to Tikrit Iraq for 15 months in 2007, we conducted route clearance and sphere of influence missions in our AO. This was during the troop drawdown, and when units left, they were not replaced, their tasks and responsibilities were passed on to my company, most nights I was lucky to get 4 hours of sleep, and my platoon was cut in half from both injuries and guys being tasked to other areas of our AO. Of the 420 days I was deployed, I was on mission outside the wire for well over 300 days, days off were rotated, and we usually got 1 or 2 days off a month. These were not days off from work, just days off from missions, I had 3 vehicles I had to maintain and spent my days off at the motor pool getting them dispatched. The longest stretch of missions I had was 56 days straight, my NCO was taking my days off for "paperwork" and it took another NCO in my platoon to notice my numb zombie like state, he gave me his day off (the next day) and my NCO was chewed out.

After 3 years active duty, 5 years Army reserve, one deployment, and a joint training NATO exercise in Germany, I got out of the military, and had several jobs in retail and real estate before 2019. From 2009-2019 my anxiety got worse, first it was just chest pressure and stomach pain, but around 2015 I started having anxiety attacks, the first was after a promotion at the job I worked at, I thought I was having a heart attack and ended up in the ER. Over the next few years I would end up in the ER 3 or 4 times, and twice passed out while standing up, the last anxiety attack I had was in September 2019, I lost 15 pounds in about 2 weeks and ended up in the VA clinic, and they sent me to the ER before I could be discharged. In the months that followed I started to feel better, I was seeing a VA counselor, and they helped me focus on dealing with the anxiety, and I improved rapidly. During this time Covid was happening, and my buddy is a day trader, he got me into the GameStop and AMC pumps. I didn't make much since I was not up at 6am following the charts daily, these types of short squeezes have volatility, and I was not interested in trying to time short-term moves. Around May 2020 is when my friend suggested Bitcoin, the halving had just happened and day traders were making a lot of money buying and selling the large price swings, this plus the massive amount of QE being pumped into the economy is what led me to start looking into Bitcoin as a hedge against the dollar.

I started looking into Bitcoin and did what most people do, read the white paper, learned about the type of scams that exist, got a hard wallet, and I got research material from multiple places and platforms. I understood it enough to feel comfortable investing, and over the next few months I dollar cost averaged into Bitcoin until I reached 1 BTC, around 10k at the time, and over the next year Bitcoins price would go from 10k to about 70k. I was also in the process of selling a fixer-upper I had bought in 2018, it took a year to sell and during this time I would try to keep the place ready for showings, and this gave me a lot of time to research blockchain, I would work on my buddy's house until about 3pm, then I would research till about 9pm every night. This soon became 8, and then 10 hours a day, I would work on other things until about 1-2pm, then I would be watching YouTube videos on my TV, looking up topics they were talking about on my computer if I didn't understand something, and using platforms like Reddit and Twitter to find research that went deeper into individual topics. I would have to force myself to stop around 11pm most nights, and this was all being fueled by Bitcoin breaking 20k, 40K, then 60K (twice) over the next year or so. This research was soon not limited to just Bitcoin, I looked into all the different way's blockchain technology could be used, and even started researching the economy, the stock market, bonds, and how everything was interacting together. The more I learned about traditional markets, the dollar, the economy, etc., the more I understood how blockchain technology was going to affect the overall globally economy in the years to come, and this pushed me to learn even more about blockchain technology.

By mid-2021 I convinced 2 friends to pool some of our Bitcoin gains, and we bought 3 Bitcoin miners (Canaan Avalon 1146a), it was nothing big about 200 TH/s, however I live in the Mohave desert and summers reach 120 degrees, so we had to build very efficient cooling systems, and we ended up with a dielectric fluid cooling system. We used a horse trough, a small pond pump, and 2 car radiators, to dissipate the heat with Bitcool-888, a dielectric fluid similar to vegetable oil, it does not conduct electricity, so we were able to fully submerge the mining computers that were pulling about 9000w combine. I also had 27 solar panels installed on my roof, usually this offset our power bill by about 30%, and we ran the miners off and on for about a year, testing and adjusting our cooling systems and the pump's efficiency. We learned a lot through trial and error, and I got hands-on experience participating in a POW blockchain, and being a part (a small part) of the consensus method for the Bitcoin network. My buddy and I would joke about how the Bitcoin miners were just an experiment, we knew we could not scale up without capital, and the first quote we wrote up was going to cost over 2 million dollars for the equipment and cooling systems. So, we knew we could not scale and would not survive the next halving, we just focused on learning, having fun with it, and once we had stacked up enough Bitcoin we stopped mining in late 2022. During this year I was still doing about 5-6 hours of research a night, working on the mining farm, as it is called, whenever it needed attention, also during this time I had spent several months building up my knowledge on blockchain concepts and terminology. I had found a great class on MIT's YouTube channel, MAS.S62, Spring 2018, Cryptocurrency Engineering and Design, it took a while to build up my knowledge on just the terminology, but once you understand the basics, it is a great class. It doesn't teach the coding side of the class on YouTube, but it does a great job of breaking down how Bitcoin/blockchain works, some of my illustrations are from this class, and my limited knowledge on how quantum computing can interact with a blockchain comes from this class, it took me about a month to finish, there are about 25 videos, each one over an hour long, I would watch one video a night, and research everything they talked about in the class.

Also during this time, I met with my local city mayor, and a state senator who was the chair of a study committee in the Arizona House of Representatives (HB 2544), I was trying to help them understand how abundant renewable energy sources could be used to mine Bitcoin, and this can be thought of as a link between watts and wealth. Cities with an abundance of sunlight, like ones in the desert, could use this resource to run Bitcoin mining farms, and if set up at scale, or with a balanced block reward to cost ratio, these mining farms would be profitable for several more halving cycles taking place over the next decade. I had started writing about what I had learned around this time too, over the course of my research I had written a few things, and in 2022 I focused on balancing regulation with the realities of this new asset class and/or industry. Early on I had started writing notes for a blockchain class I was hoping to give to friends and family, it ended up being 35 pages, but I felt like I was not even touching on so many important topics, and with the few people I did explain it to, I went into much more detail, I could expand upon topics and turn a paragraph into an hour of talking. After that I wrote the Arizona Blockchain Standards, they take into account the new technology, what it is, and is not capable of, and it tries to bridge the gap between blockchain coins and tokens, and traditional rules and regulations. It consists of 7 risk category levels, and 10 plus subcategories along with disclosure information, I sent it to a few State and Federal level representatives, but I never really heard back from any of them. I also wrote an interpretation of the Howey test for blockchain, this shows how the blockchain standards could be used by existing rules and regulations to better define blockchain coins and tokens. I use the Howey test as an example and show how it could define and split these coins and tokens into several groups, digital securities, digital assets, and digital commodities, I also sent this to the same representatives I had sent the blockchain standards to, and again no reply other than their assistants confirming they would pass it along.

During my first year of research, I would draw out the new ideas I was learning, as soon as I understood something I would draw out how it works (at least how I understand it to work), blockchain being mostly digital means these interpretations were just to help me understand, not actual representations of the technology. I would use these drawings when trying to explain Bitcoin and blockchain to my family and friends, but they were not that detailed, and probably did not look very convincing. I also talked to a few people on the phone for hour plus long conversations, during these talks anything I had trouble explaining I would draw out after the conversation, and this helped me for the next time I had to explain a specific topic or concept. Many of these early drawings are what led to later more detailed illustrations, realizing this is an easier way of communicating for me was the idea behind this book, and some of these early drawings and ideas are what inspired the illustrations in this book.

All of this has led to me drawing and explaining blockchain technology in this simplified way, I understand blockchain coins and tokens are not physical, they are digital ledgers, and some of the terminology has not been settled on even by experts in the industry, for example, hard wallets, cold storage wallets, and self-custody wallets may all refer to the same thing. I will do my best to explain the concepts of many parts of this new technology (Bitcoin is over a decade old), and I use illustrations to help convey many of these concepts. Basically, I will describe how blockchain technology works in the form of hand drawn illustrations, and written explanations of blockchain topics, I apologize in advance for penmanship in the illustrations, sit back and enjoy.

Basic Blockchain Encryption

Basic information on what a blockchain is*
- Basic Encryption
- Wallet / Ledger
- Transactions
- Public / Private Keys
- Orphan Blocks
- Quantum Computing
- Conclusion

Basic Encryption:

Before we can understand what a blockchain is, we need to understand how the information, or data, is sent, received, and secured. How new blocks are created will be discussed later, for now we will look at how this information is encrypted and deciphered, this is not a new concept, and was used in WWII. The Enigma machine was used by German U-boats for encrypting their communications, these were physical boxes that resembled a typewriter, they had 3 sets of rotors with 26 wires scrambled inside each, and this type of encryption is similar to a Caesar Cipher in that the encrypted information is deciphered by reversing the way the information was scrambled. The Enigma machine has 26 wires representing the 26 letters of the alphabet, and 3 rotors that individually scrambled the 26 wires, they would be rotated each time a letter on the typewriter was pressed, and this caused further scrambling, or encryption of the information. This level of encryption is impossible for a human to decipher, we require a lot of computing power in order to even attempt this, the movie "The Imitation Game" shows the lengths Britain went through attempting to crack the Enigma encryption, and in the end it was a captured German U-boat that finally gave the allies the ability to read German communications. This is because they had captured the U-boat's Enigma machine along with its rotors, this allowed the British to decipher German messages, and change the rotors in unison with the U-boats during communication resets. This is also common in the military today, called COMSEC changeovers, the sequence used to encrypt messages is changed, and communication equipment needs to be given the new information, or it will no longer be able to read messages. Changing the sequence every few weeks or months means even if someone was able to break the encryption, it would only work until the next sequence change, and they would need to start over trying to break the encryption, unless you had the actual device like Britain, they essentially had the "keys" or password.

(Illustration, next page)

The Enigma machine was basically a physical password that allowed whoever had it, access to all the information, and the ability to send secure messages as well. The internet has allowed for the world to connect in a digital way, information is sent out across the globe for anyone to see, and even "safe" information can be hacked by those that know how to. Blockchain allows for information to be encrypted in a complex way similar to the Enigma machine, however, instead of physical "passwords" like the rotors in the Enigma machine, the password is digital, and there are a few names that refer to it, seed phrase or keys, are sometimes used, but basically it is a password that allows access to the information. We will go over wallets later, there are several types, for self-custody wallets access comes in the form of a 12 or 24 word sequence, sometimes referred to as the keys to a wallet, and this is different from a password you might make to log into the wallet app or interface. These 12 or 24 words represent a set of 4 numbers each, meaning there is a unique sequence of 48 or 96 numbers that give a user access to the contents of the wallet. These numbers can be thought of as the rotors in the Enigma machine, they are the sequence that scrambled the original message, and the only way to access the information is to know the sequence, basically you need to have the keys to the wallet.

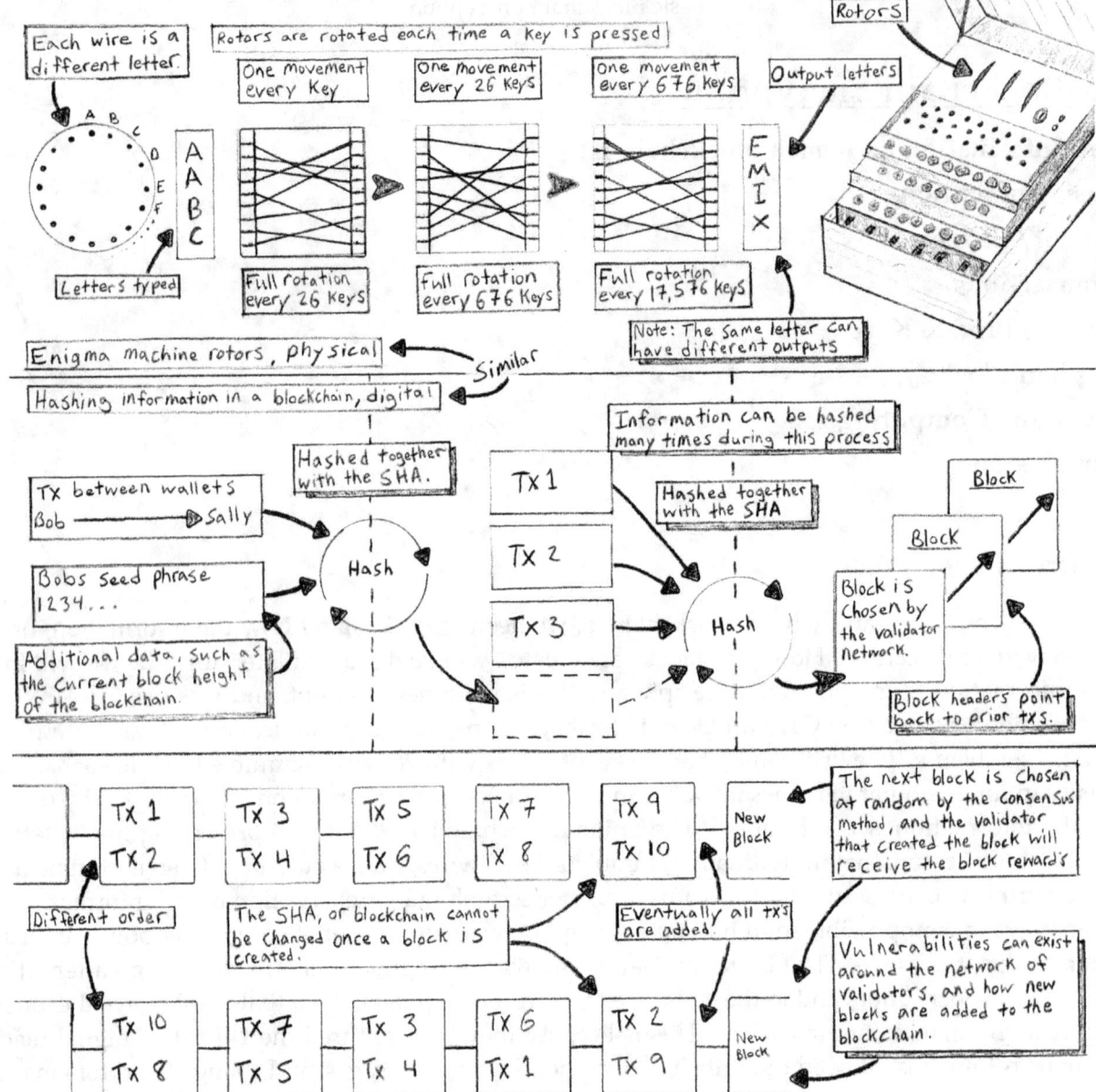

Enigma Machine

The rotors in the Enigma machine each rotate at different rates, the second rotor would not move until the first rotor had done one full rotation, and the same is true for the third rotor. This allows for the same letter that was typed twice, to be represented by different letters, this design is somewhat simple, and it allowed for messages to be created and sent fast, as well as received and decoded fast. This scrambling of information is similar to the hashing of a transaction on a blockchain, although it is purely digital, and hashing information can take place at several points during the transaction process. Valid transactions that do not violate the blockchains code are added to the blockchain by validators, even if nodes verify the transaction, it is validators that create new blocks, locking the transaction into the blockchain, and each validator may have a slightly different order of transactions in their version of the next block in the blockchain.

Pg. 3, middle section: Individual transactions and the seed phrase are hashed together, along with the SHA. Then, transactions in a block are hashed together, along with the SHA. Scrambling up this information again and again, or hashing it, adds to the encryption, and hashing information can happen at many points in this process, depending on how the blockchain is set up.

Pg. 12, middle section: Verifying a transaction is done by using the public key of the wallet, this is basically reversing the hash of the blocks and transactions, and this is done by using block headers, these will allow the transaction to be verified all the way back to its creation as a block reward.

Pg. 29, bottom section: The order of transactions can vary between validators in a consensus method, depending on the blockchain this would not necessarily violate the blockchains code, and eventually all valid transactions will be added to the blockchain, it just depends on what validators block of transactions is chosen to be the next added to the blockchain.

Pg. 51, bottom section: If there was a large part of the validator network controlled by small group, then changing the order of transactions would be easier, basically more validators would have the same manipulated order of transactions, and the small number of validators not under their control would not add blocks to the blockchain often.

Pg. 52, bottom section: "Trusted" validators usually have the ability to change the order of transactions, although it does not mean they will, and there would need to be enough validators in the consensus method participating, the greater the percent of the total validator network they control, the easier it would be.

Pg. 74, bottom section: Changing the order of transactions does not always violate the blockchains code, and these are all valid transactions that have been hashed by nodes as well, they are not invalid transactions.

Pg. 81, middle section: The seed phrase when hashed with a transaction on the blockchain will result in the movement of coins, even if the seed phrase was used by someone other than the wallet holder, and this is because it would be considered a valid transaction on the blockchain. The blockchain itself is not "hacked" or negatively affected, although the wallet holder's wealth would be.

Pg. 111, middle section: Hashing a transaction is just the scrambling of data, or numbers, and other information that is verifiable on the blockchain can be added into this hash, and this would basically make the unique data part of the seed phrase for the wallet.

The way these keys encrypt information is by hashing the transaction information and the keys together, this information is visible to everyone on the internet, however, the information has been hashed, or scrambled up, at least once and sometimes many times. *(Reference page 2)* The only way to access the information, meaning you have control over it, is with the keys to the wallet, the wallet itself is just a ledger in the blockchain, and this is visible to anyone viewing the blockchain, but there is no identification linked to the wallet. All wallets and transactions on the blockchain are public, because of this tracing transactions can allow someone to find out who the owner of a wallet is, however it is complicated, and we will go over it in more detail later. For now, think of hashing as the scrambling of the wires in the rotors of the Enigma machine, this sequence or password, is needed to decipher the message, and instead of being something physical, this sequence is purely digital. Instead of all the U-boats using one set of constantly changing sequences, these digital wallets allow for each wallet to have a unique sequence, and because the transaction information is scrambled up with the addition of the keys, or the sequence of numbers they represent, the only way to decipher the information is to have the keys that were hashed along with the transaction. The hash itself is a constant, basically the blockchain algorithm, it is a set equation that can be represented as a curved line on a graph, called a secure hash algorithm, or SHA, Bitcoin runs on SHA-256, and there are many different SHAs. They can be very different, or exactly the same in almost every way, an example would be, the addition of a constant to the equation, making it the same curved line, but higher or lower than the similar SHA.

A simple example of this is Bitcoin and Dogecoin, both use SHA-256, they are similar in many ways, with several small changes to Bitcoins original code, Dogecoin does not have a max limit for the number of coins that can exist, and has a much higher inflation rate, in the form of block rewards to miners. Both can be thought of as the same curved line (or SHA) with one small change, creating an entirely new blockchain and coin for that blockchain. This is also how some blockchains can be mined on the same mining computers, receiving dual block rewards, and we will go over this in more detail later.

Wallet / Ledger:

If we understand the SHA as a curved line on a graph, then a wallet address would be a liner line that intersects with that curve, we will go over this in more detail later, for now just understand that the two points where the two lines cross is the wallet, or ledger that was created on the blockchain with a sequence of numbers represented by the 12-24 word seed phrase. Knowing either of these points would be like knowing the seed phrase sequence, one point can be thought of as the private keys to your wallet, the other point would be your public keys, and we will go over these in a bit. Basically, the curved line is the blockchain algorithm, it extends forever, the creation of a liner line is the creation of a ledger or wallet on the blockchain, and the number sequence used to create it is considered to be the keys, and there can be a near infinite number of wallets created on a blockchain. Each of these wallets is unique because each password is unique, and the odds of guessing the correct number sequence is almost zero, for example, there are 2,048 words to choose from, 2,048 to the power of 12 (more than a decillion) is the number of possible word combinations for just a 12 word seed phrase. These wallets hold coins, and they are the units of account for the blockchain's ledger, these coins represent wealth or information and can only be moved out of the wallet by someone with the keys, and this creates a transaction on the blockchain, a credit of coins to one wallet, and a debit of coins to another wallet.

Transactions on a blockchain are like ledger updates and happen when coins move wallets, depending on the blockchain, transactions can represent other information too, such as NFTs (non-fungible tokens), and their minting (creation), or their movement between wallets. *(Reference page 28)* For now let's stick with fungible coins and tokens, these can be divided into very small amounts, for example Bitcoin is divisible to 8 decimals places (0.00000001). *(Reference page 120)* The dollar value of these coins is very volatile, so we will look at a transaction on the blockchain not in dollar terms, but by the amount of coins moved, remember the idea of coins is just a simple way to represent a unit of account, they are not physical, and they are technically created and destroyed with each transaction. The simple way to understand the process of a transaction is just to think of actual coins, and the wallets that they move between, this is easy to understand for most people, and it is not incorrect. However, the actual way blockchain ledgers move coins between each other is a little more complicated, but understanding how it works gives you a better idea of how these blockchain transactions are grouped together to form blocks, and these blocks are added together to form blockchains. A simple example is, a wallet has 1.6 coins, and someone wanted to send .6 coins to another wallet, at the transaction level, basically the inputs and outputs, the entire 1.6 coins are destroyed, .6 of a coin is credited to the other wallet, and 1 coin is credited back to the original wallet. Sometimes transaction fees are paid to the miners or stake pools during this process, and this depends on how the blockchain is set up, if say .1 was the transaction fee, then the original wallet would be credited back .9 of a coin. This process ensures there can be no double spending of coins, once a transaction is accepted into a block and added to the blockchain it cannot be changed, but there are a few exceptions to this like orphan blocks or orphan chains, and we will go over these in more detail later.

(Illustration, next page)

All coins point back to where they came from, the example of the .6 coins being sent would have the wallet address of where it came from, and this allows for even the smallest unit of account to be traced back to its creation. We will discuss the different types of coins, tokens, and consensus methods, for blockchains later, for now just understand these transactions are public and there are ways to trace them, just like there are ways to break the chain of transactions using blockchains called mixers, and we will go over these more in depth later. So, if coins can be traced back to their creation, how are they created? There are several ways depending on the blockchain, we will go over each in more detail later, generally coins are created through the consensus method and the forming of new blocks, these can be block rewards in either a proof of work (POW), or a proof of stake (POS) blockchain. The block header is what points back to prior transactions, each coin, or fraction of a coin, has a block header that basically says where it came from, all the way back to its creation as a block reward, and when these new coins are created their block header is blank. The miner that found the block can add any information they want in the header, and this is how Bitcoin was able to reference a British newspaper and the bank bailouts of 2009, the information was placed in the block header of a new block reward. This is how most layer 1 blockchains work, they can all vary in slight ways, and even other types of consensus methods can be used. The same is true for layer 2 blockchains, the token that represents the blockchain points back to prior transactions, although tokens can be created in a slightly different way, and we will go over the differences in detail later.

Transactions:

Transactions on a blockchain are part of what form blocks in a blockchain, this is basically a very detailed ledger of wallets and the movement of coins between them, invalid transactions can and are attempted with most blockchains, and they are what might create an orphan block or chain, but overall transactions on the blockchain are what form the blockchain. There can be empty blocks, that is no transactions taking place on the blockchain, and this does not affect the blockchain or its ability to function, however if the blockchain is set up with miners being paid only transaction fees, then this would affect the miners of that blockchain, Bitcoin for example uses small fees and a reducing inflation rate to compensate miners, and we will go over this in more detail later. *(Reference page 103)*

These coins and tokens are simply a unit of account on a blockchain, and they are secured through the hashing of information, basically the encryption of that information, and the unique sequence of numbers that the wallet keys represent. If the coins have value, then this ledger of wallets will be able to securely move the wealth that the coins represent, and coins can have value by being needed to pay for transaction fees on a blockchain, or one of many other use cases on a blockchain that we will go over later. This value when measured in another currency will be volatile, and there are many factors involved such as; the number of coins that exist, the rate at which new coins are created (inflation rate), the circulating supply of coins, the demand for the coin (use cases), and all these transactions are settled almost instantly, this creates the major price moves in many coins like Bitcoin. There can also be small price differences in a coin's value between

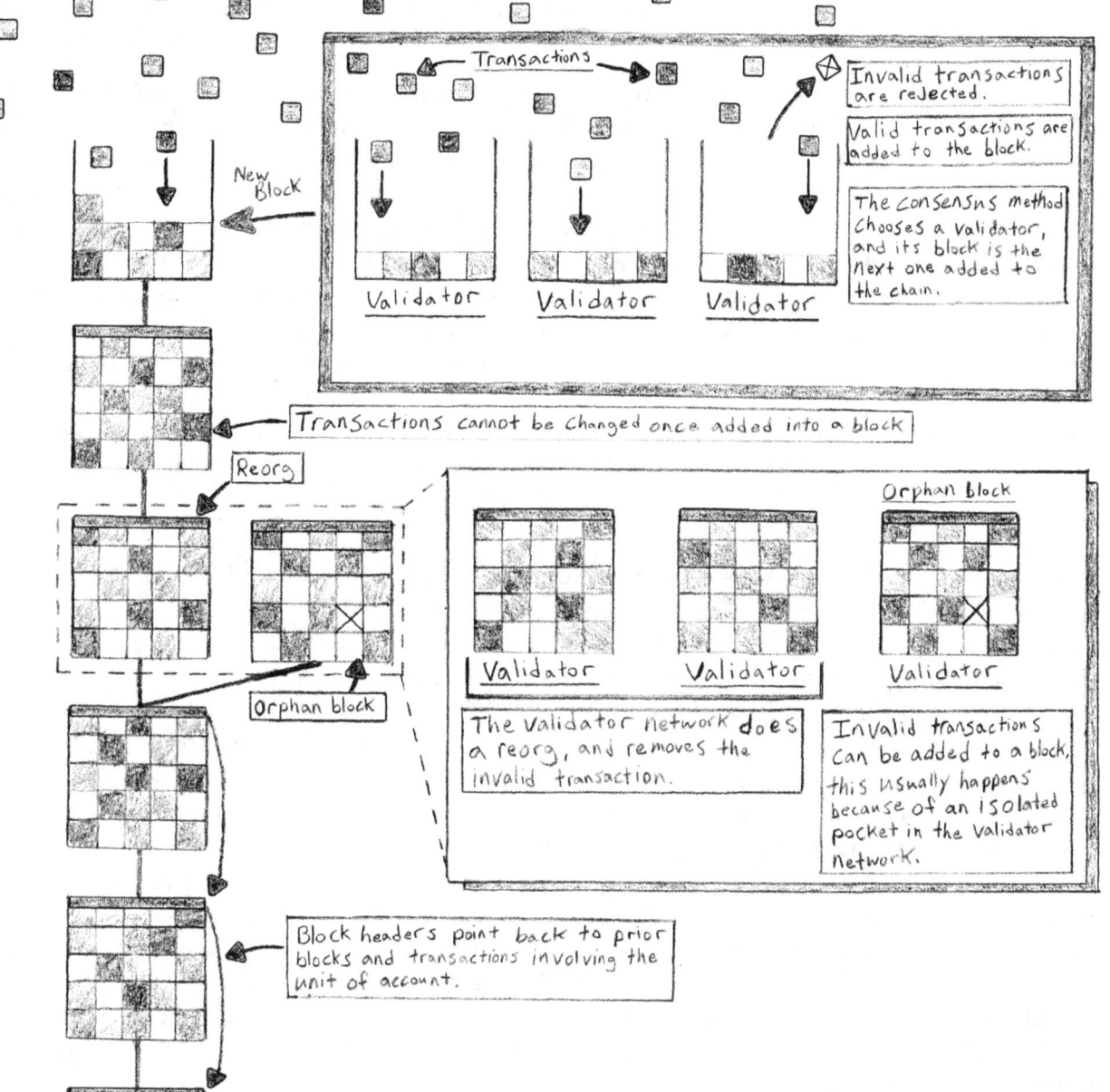

Blockchain

Each validator in the consensus method is hashing the same transactions, they add valid transactions to their version of the next block in the blockchain, and they reject invalid transactions. The consensus method will choose the next validator according to the blockchains code, basically at random, and this validators version of the next block becomes the next block in the blockchain. Once transactions are added to the blockchain, there is no changing the transactions, with the exception of orphan blocks that sometimes include an invalid transaction, and once the rest of the validator network picks up on the discrepancy, there is a reorg of the block, basically removing the invalid transaction. This process might vary depending on how the blockchains consensus method is set up, but most blockchains have the ability to remove invalid transactions from orphan blocks, and as long as they are kept short, they do not negatively affect the blockchain.

Pg. 7, bottom section: Orphan blocks are created when the validator chosen by the consensus method has an invalid transaction in their version of the next block in the blockchain, and this can be caused by several things, such as an isolated pocket in the validator network, or a malicious transaction trying to cheat the network.

Pg. 12, top section: Each validator in the consensus method is hashing the same transactions, and they should all have the same version of the next block in the blockchain, although sometimes their blocks can vary a little. Either way, the consensus method chooses the next validator more or less at random, and this validators version of the next block becomes the newest block added to the blockchain.

Pg. 13, bottom section: Orphan blocks are created when an invalid transaction is included in the newest block, and this is not always a deliberate action taken by a malicious actor, it can come from a node with an incomplete interpretation of transactions on the blockchain, basically the node does not have the full blockchain downloaded.

Pg. 49, bottom section: Orphan blocks are corrected with a reorg, basically removing the invalid transaction from the block, this happens once the rest of the validator network picks up on the discrepancy, and this usually happens fast depending on how the blockchain is set up, meaning most orphan blocks are limited to just a single block in length.

Pg. 109, bottom section: Orphan blocks are possible on the Bitcoin blockchain, this is because anyone can set up a Bitcoin node, and sometimes these nodes are pushing invalid transactions. These nodes can be ignored by validators in the consensus method by changing the list of nodes the validator receives transactions from, and this helps prevent these invalid transactions from being included in the validators version of the next block in the blockchain.

Pg. 151, top section: Each validator is hashing the same transactions, and when a group of validators tries to ignore a certain valid transaction, they might be able to prevent the transaction for several blocks. However, eventually a validator not preventing the transaction would be chosen by the consensus method, and this would allow the valid transaction to be added to the blockchain.

exchanges, and we will go deeper into exchanges later, for now just understand exchanges have wallets or ledgers on the blockchain of the coins they hold and/ or offer for sale on their exchange. Some wallets can hold many different coins and tokens, but the idea is still the same, the wallet and its seed phrase are linked to the blockchain of the coin, giving the key holder the ability to access and move the coins. Exchanges can have one or many wallets for the coins and tokens they hold, either as wealth owned by the exchange, or wealth owned by account holders on the exchange, and trades taking place on their exchange would not always need to be settled on the blockchain. *(Reference page 80)* Transactions that do need to take place on the blockchain of a coin would be coins moving from one exchange to another, since the wealth would be transferring between wallets, not being transferred within the same exchange wallet. The supply and demand of a coin is a major factor in its value as well, and just like in traditional markets there exists arbitrage opportunities for investors between exchanges, it depends on each exchange and their transaction volume, or buy and sell orders for a certain coin, and we will go over this more when we look at how exchanges work.

Public and Private Keys:

Private keys and public keys are sometimes referred to as the password and address for a wallet, the private keys being the 12-24 word sequence mentioned before, and the public keys being the address a person can give to someone so they can send coins to their wallet. This public key can be re-generated by the private key, basically meaning you can change the public key to a wallet again and again, and this public key does not give someone access to the wallet, only the ability to verify transactions from that wallet, and the ability to send coins to that wallet. This is possibly because the public keys only have some of the information regarding its location on the graph, going back to the curved and liner lines that represent the blockchain, or SHA, and the wallet or ledger on the blockchain, we know that the liner line intersects the curved line at two points. The first point is the private keys, being the sequence of numbers represented by a seed phrase, while the second point is not fully disclosed by the public keys, on a graph we can think of this as being given only one of the X,Y coordinates, and this prevents someone that has the public key to a wallet from knowing the exact point of intersection. Knowing the location of either point would be to know the seed phrase, it would allow them access to the wallet and the ability to transfer coins out of the wallet. But the public key only provides part of this information, this allows others to verify transactions and send coins to the wallet without disclosing the full sequence of numbers that represent the liner line, which is a wallet and its keys, or password. *(Reference page 9)*

So private keys need to be kept secret at all costs, they are one of the points where the two lines cross, public keys only give part of their location away, enough to verify transactions but not enough to allow access to the wallet. The main takeaway here is, knowing the exact location of where either of the two lines intersect is basically knowing the password to the wallet, and we will talk about a possibly third point of intersection in a bit. Being able to verify transactions with a public key is basically being able to trace a coin back to its creation, or as far back as you want to, the further back a coin is traced the harder it would be to create an invalid transaction, and this would be something like creating new coins, or trying to move coins from a wallet you do not have the seed phrase for. Tracing transactions is possible, but it is a very technical process, especially when following wealth from wallet to wallet and linking those wallets to people or companies in the non-digital world, and this, know your customer, or KYC, is what links a person's identity to a bank account, or in this case accounts on some crypto exchanges. The interaction of wallets that are linked to a person's identity can be used to identify other wallets that have no KYC or personal information attached, like a hard wallet or self-custody wallet, and we will go over 3rd party wallets and other wallet types later, but for now just understand most if not all transactions on a blockchain can be traced. Chainalysis is a company that provides these tracing services, they work with governments and large companies to track criminals that are moving wealth using coins and tokens, they have been working with Congress and the FBI for years tracking hackers, and making their wallet addresses known. These wallet addresses are put on a black list that regulated banking institutions cannot transact with, and they have helped identify North Korean and Russian hacker wallet addresses in recent years.

An example is the Colonial pipeline hack, in May 2021 a ransomware attack on the oil pipeline impacted computerized equipment managing the pipeline, and Bitcoin was used as payment to the hackers to regain control over the pipeline's equipment. Malware from Russia, and hardware in northern California, was used to hack the east coast pipeline, police in California executed a search warrant and were able to capture the computers running the malware, the FBI worked with companies like Chainalysis to track the Bitcoin payments to both the Russian malware providers, and the actors in northern California. The authorities were able to recover about half of the Bitcoin ransom, this is because the FBI was able to access data stored in the cloud from the hardware, the hackers had saved their seed phrase in the cloud, and then deleted it, but the FBI was still able to recover the keys to the wallet the Bitcoin had been sent to. Some media outlets said the FBI had "hacked" Bitcoin to retrieve the ransom, in reality they had the keys to the wallet, there was no hacking of Bitcoins blockchain, and the coins sent to Russia were never recovered, this is because the FBI did not have the seed phrase for that wallet, although by tracking the transactions they did know where the wealth had been sent to.

Orphan Blocks:

Invalid transactions on a blockchain are attempted on a regular basis, they are transactions that violate the blockchain code in some way, and they are normally rejected by validators and not added into new blocks. There are many types of invalid transactions, a few simple examples would be, creating "new" coins, basically attempting to send coins that did not come from a prior transaction, and this can be thought of as counterfeiting and trying to pass off fake coins as real ones. Another type of invalid transaction would be trying to move coins from a wallet that did not include the keys to that wallet, basically trying to make a transaction where coins are sent from someone's wallet to a hacker's wallet. However, without the correct sequence of numbers, or keys, included in the hash of that transaction, it will not comply with the blockchain code, and it will be rejected by validators. There are many more technical examples of invalid transactions, but the main takeaway from this part is to understand that the blockchain and its consensus method are constantly being attacked with invalid transactions. These come from hackers or bots that are trying to cheat the network in some way, most times they are rejected from blocks, but sometimes a few might get by the validator network and make it into a block, and the resulting reorg creates an orphan block. *(Reference page 5)*

An orphan block is just a block of transactions that was added to the blockchain, and not all the validators in the consensus method agree with this block. We will go deeper into the different types of consensus methods later, but an orphan block is basically created when the validators of a blockchain don't agree with some or all of the transactions in a block that was added to the blockchain. This can involve the miners or pools in a POW or POS blockchain, as well as nodes in some blockchains, even though nodes do not validate blocks, and this is because some miners or pools could pull data from these nodes and spread the invalid transaction. These are usually corrected within a few blocks, making most orphan blocks relatively short, being just one block in length. However, sometimes additional blocks are added to it, creating an orphan chain which is usually also relatively short. Reorgs are the reorganization of the blockchain, put simply it removes transactions that are invalid and recreates blocks with only valid transactions, these do not happen often, and as long as they are kept short, they do not negatively affect the blockchain overall. We will go over how orphan blocks are created in more detail later when we look at validator networks, and the factors that can affect them and lead to the creation of the orphan blocks or orphan chains. *(Reference page 50)*

Quantum Computing:

The security of a blockchain involves many things like, a unique sequence of numbers, or keys, the hashing of transactions and those numbers, and a decentralized aspect of the consensus method, which we will talk about next, but first let's look at a vulnerability in this security. Going back to understanding the blockchain, or SHA, as a curved line on a graph, and a wallet or the keys that created it, as a liner line that intersects the curved line, we can better understand where this vulnerability comes from. The two points where the lines cross, are simply put, the keys to that wallet, and knowing either point would allow you to move coins out of that wallet, but there may exist a third point where the lines cross, and if its location is found then the wallet could be accessed. This is not "hacking" the blockchain, it would be like having your car stolen because you left the key in the ignition. I by no means am an expert in quantum computing or 4th dimensional mathematics, the MIT class I watched made this third point comparison, as well as the curved and liner line example, but other simple examples can help us understand how this third point could be found.

Before we look at how mathematics in a higher dimension can warp our understanding of math in our dimension, let's look at how we, in the 3rd dimension, can manipulate the second dimension. The Mobius strip is a 2-dimensional piece of paper that has been cut into a long strip, by rotating one end of the strip and attaching it to the other end of the strip, it becomes endless, this is because the paper was rotated on a 3rd axis that does not exist in the 2-dimensional world. We here in the 3rd dimension can see and understand how this object can exist, however to anyone in the 2nd dimension it would look like an endless straight line that somehow connects back to itself, something that is impossible in this dimension. The same is true for the Klein bottle, it is a 3-dimensional tube that is manipulated in the 4th dimension, and it becomes endless, but this is not possible in our 3-dimensional world and the Klein bottle can only be partially represented in our world, it looks something like a water pitcher, but lines intersect where they do not in the 4th dimension. In both instances the objects can be viewed by the lower dimension, but they will only be able to understand them if the objects are viewed in sections, over periods of time, meaning you cannot view the full object at once from the lower dimension. If you do view these objects all at once, lines that you think would not be able to intersect would, and they would bend on an axis that does not exist in the dimension you are viewing from, this is why the Klein bottle cannot fully exist in our world, but it does exist in the 4th dimension.

Now going back to our blockchain and wallet, the SHA is a curved line that extends forever, moving ever farther away from the liner line that intersects it twice, this liner line goes straight forever, and also continues moving away from the curved line. What quantum computing is attempting to do is bend the liner line in a way where it intersects the curved line for a 3rd time, this is only math, and there is no physical coin that is being manipulated. There is only 4th dimensional mathematics gaining the sequence of numbers to a ledger on the blockchain, and this again would not be thought of as "hacking" the blockchain, it would be like leaving the key in your car and having it stolen. The blockchain would see these transactions as valid because they would include the correct sequence, or keys, just as a car would start if the key was turned in the ignition, the car does not care if it is not the owner, as long as it's the correct key, the car will start.

(Illustration, next page)

This highly complex computing would be bad for blockchains, it would be able to move coins from wallets, and would be able to make changes to the blockchain code itself. This is a real risk for blockchains, however, quantum computing is somewhat far off, and it is still being developed, but when it eventually is able to "hack" a blockchain, quantum resistant code can be incorporated into the blockchain code. This will end up being just another escalation in the blockchain arms race, each blockchain will need to run updates, and depending on the decentralization of the blockchain, this may happen fast or take time, and these updates, or improvement proposals will be covered later. The important takeaway here is that quantum computing is a very real possibility, but it is not the end of all blockchains, although some may be negatively affected, most will be able to adapt to this new type of attack and protect themselves with quantum resistant coding. However, once this level of computing is achieved just about all digital networks and information will be at risk, quantum computing is not just a risk for blockchains, it would be able to hack just about anything that involved a password, and could basically access any and all digital information. Unless that information is secured in a quantum resistant blockchain, this protection of digital information is what I believe to be the best use case for this technology, and we will go over more of these use cases for blockchain in detail later.

Conclusion:

These are just basic ideas that we will build on later, they may affect different blockchains in different ways, and we will expand on these ideas as we go over many of the individual aspects of a blockchain.

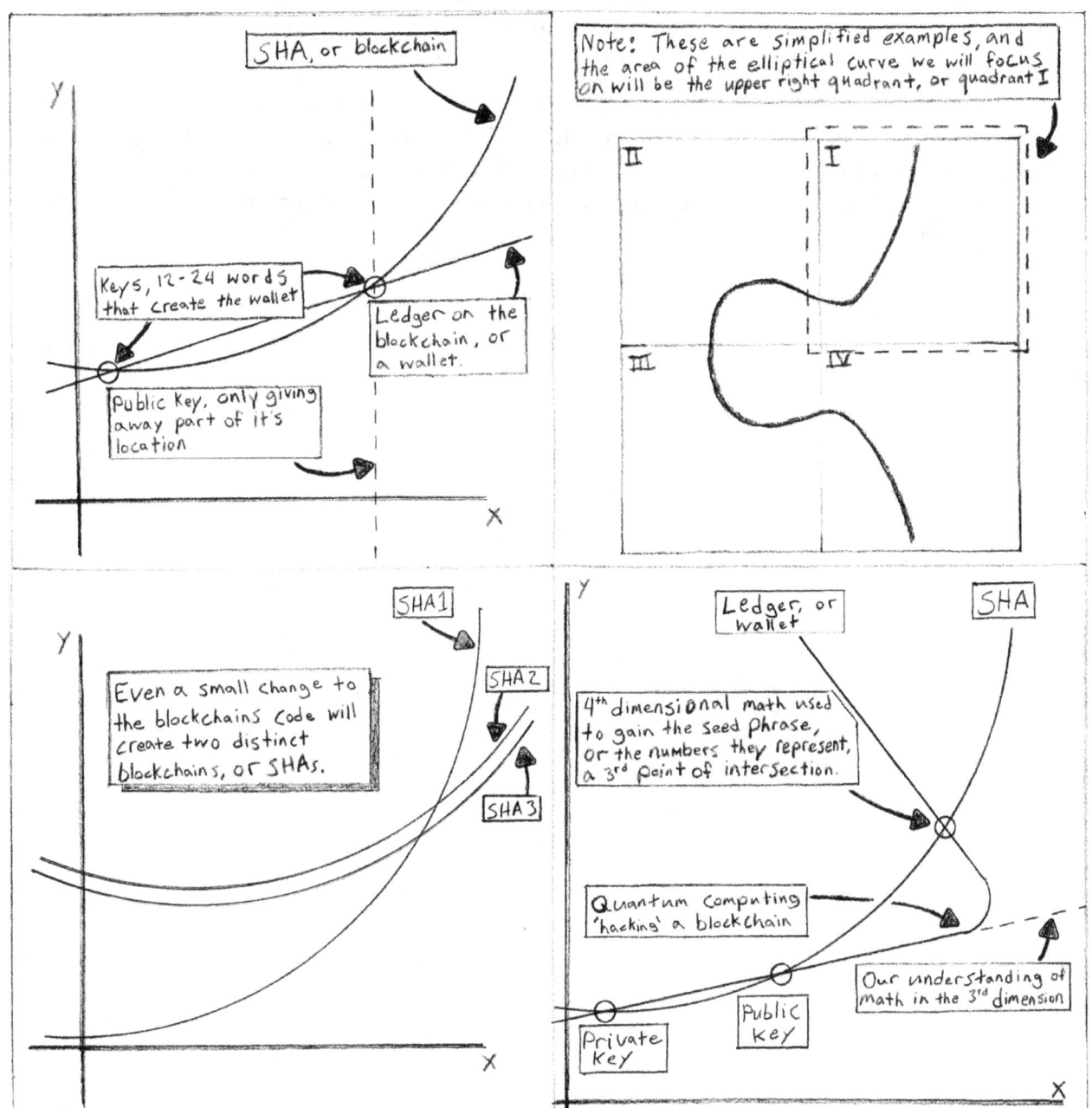

SHA, Curved and Liner Lines

The area of the SHA we are viewing is just one quadrant of the total elliptical curve, so these illustrations are not to scale or exact, but they do allow us to look at several aspects of blockchain technology in a simplified way. The sequence of numbers that represent the seed phrase create a wallet on the blockchain, represented as a liner line, the points of intersection can be thought of as the keys to the wallet, and knowing either location would be to know the full seed phrase, although the public key only gives away part of its location. There also might exist a third point of intersection, and finding this point is what quantum computing is trying to achieve, basically using a higher level of math to gain the sequence of numbers that created the wallet. This is technically not "hacking" a blockchain, it is only gaining the keys to a wallet, and transactions out of that wallet would be valid, since the hash of the transaction would include the correct sequence of numbers.

Pg. 6, upper left section: The liner line is the wallet, and the two points of intersection are the keys to the wallet. However, the public key does not give its exact location away, and this allows for information to be verified without knowing the exact point of intersection, basically this means transactions can be verified without knowing the entire seed phrase, which would give someone access to the contents of the wallet.

Pg. 17, bottom left section: Each blockchain can be thought of as a different curved line, even if they are almost identical, they are separate blockchains with separate units of account, and they would have a separate network of validators in their consensus method as well.

Pg. 32, upper left section: Voting coins or tokens are just units of account on a blockchain, and these units of account have voting power on the blockchain, but they are still held and accessed with the seed phrase of the wallet that holds the units of account, just like other units of account on the blockchain.

Pg. 35, bottom left section: Hard forks create two district blockchains, the original blockchain, and the "new" blockchain, their SHA's can be very similar, with few changes to the original blockchains code, or the SHA may be completely different, and this depends on the improvement proposal that created the hard fork of the blockchain.

Pg. 73, upper left section: Even though the whale wallet selling coins would negatively the value of those coins, this does not violate the blockchains code, and whoever had the keys to the wallet would be able to sell the coins if they choose to.

Pg. 77, upper left section: The seed phrase that creates the wallet on the blockchain is very important, it is what protects the wealth or information held in the wallet, and in order to reset a lost or forgotten seed phrase, there would need to be a 3rd party to that wallet, although, this is something some investors want.

Pg. 100, bottom left section: Bitcoin and Dogecoin can be thought of as very similar, there were few changes to Bitcoins original code when it was copied to create Dogecoin, and although there were only a few changes, these changes were to major aspects of the blockchain, such as its inflation rate, or block reward rate.

Most blockchains are just a ledger of wallet addresses and transactions between them, but depending on the blockchain there can be other factors involved, usually involving a use case on the blockchain, and we will go over blockchain use cases in more detail later. For now, let us look at the basics of consensus methods and the blockchains they help secure, so we can better understand how these transactions between wallets are added into blocks forming the blockchain.

Blockchain / Consensus Methods 101

More detail on how blockchains work, based off individual aspects, that may be common between many different blockchains*

- Basic Consensus Method
- Validator Locations
- Validators vs Nodes
- Majority Control of the Consensus Method
- 51% Attacks

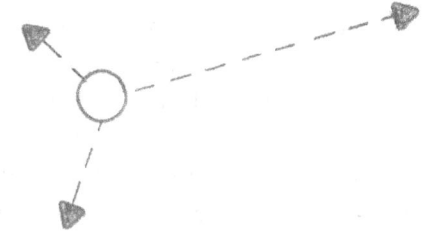

Basic Consensus Method:

We now understand how wallets and the updates in their ledger create transactions that can be traced back to the creation of a coin or token on a blockchain, and this is true for almost all blockchains, and exceptions like mixers will be covered later. These transactions take place all over the world, 24/7, running on the internet, all you need is an internet connection, and you have access to any blockchain, although some exchanges can limit the coins they offer on their platform, so some blockchain coins and tokens are harder to access for some people, and this is covered in more detail later. The validators for the blockchain can also be located anywhere on earth, all that is needed is an internet connection, this is covered more when we look at the two main consensus methods, POW and POS, for now let's focus on how a network of validators in a blockchains consensus method forms new blocks on the blockchain.

Validator Locations:

The area of the world a validator is in will be decided on by the miners or pools in a POW or POS blockchain, or the company that is setting up the equipment, and they will set up their equipment where energy is cheap and climates are cool to maximize efficiency, but they can be located anywhere they can get an internet connection. Although there are some consensus methods that allow for smaller hardware units that are designed to be spread out over major urban areas, providing faster transaction speed while remaining decentralized to an extent, an example of this is the Helium blockchain, and we will go over this type of consensus method a little more later. *(Reference page 50)* The location is important because, simply put, transactions are shared between validators, this takes time to spread from validator to validator around the world, and from our point of view blocks are agreed upon by validators for the Bitcoin blockchain every 10 minutes to an hour, this is usually around 10 minutes for the Bitcoin blockchain, and it can vary between blockchains. It is also important to remember, this is transaction finality, when the new block is created the coins, acting as a unit of account, move wealth from one wallet to another, there is no stopping this, there is no reversing this, unlike with most modern payment systems that can take days to finally settle a transaction, and can even be stopped or reversed. So even though settling transactions on the blockchain may take some time, it is their transaction finality that is far faster than payment systems we have today, and not all payments need to be settled on the layer 1 blockchain, side channels like the Lighting Network increase transaction speed, and we will go over the Lighting Network in more detail later. *(Reference page 123)*

All these transactions that are taking place all over the world, involve the hashing of information and the seed phrase that created the ledger holding an amount of wealth. Basically the keys of a wallet being hashed along with the transaction of coins to another wallet, either way these are transactions, and they need to be checked to make sure they are not an invalid transaction. What validators do is verify that this new transaction does not violate the consensus of the blockchain up until the last block, this could be something like, a wallet has 5 coins in the last block of the blockchain, and a new transaction attempting to be included in the next block says the wallet is sending 10 coins to another wallet, this violates the blockchain code, and it would be rejected by the validator network. The validator solves the hash function of the transaction, basically solving the equation of the hash, plus the information being sent (the unit of account, or coin), and the public keys of the wallet sending the coins. *(Reference page 2)* The validator computes the equation and if it violates the last consensus of the blockchain, meaning up until the last block in the chain, it will be rejected from being included in the next block. This process is done by all the validators, they will all compute every valid transaction, invalid transactions can be shared between validators, and this is explained more in a bit. But for now, just understand each validator is computing the same transactions, they keep doing this 24/7, and new blocks are formed at random according to the blockchains code. *(Reference page 5)* This is how new blocks are created and how the block rewards are distributed for most blockchains, none of the validators know when the next block will come out, so they must always have the most transactions computed as possible, and they do not want to include invalid transactions, or they will have less of a chance of receiving a block reward, and creating a new block. This prevents most validators from attempting to manipulate the blockchain, they will lose out on the chance of receiving block rewards, or the new coins that are created based on the inflation rate of that blockchain, and we will go over this more later.

Validators vs Nodes:

Nodes are similar to validators in a blockchain, in that they are also solving the hash functions of transactions, and we will go over nodes in more detail later, but the main difference between validators and nodes is that only validators receive block rewards. Nodes are a way for anyone to have their own "copy" of the blockchain, however they do not need to fully download the blockchain, meaning they are only tracing transactions as far back as they can with the amount of the blockchain they have downloaded, but they do compute all new transactions as they happen. They share this data with other nodes and validators on a blockchain, and when they need to verify a transaction from part of the blockchain they do not have stored, they will request this information from validators or nodes that have more of the blockchain downloaded. Most, if not all validators in a blockchains consensus method must have the entire blockchain downloaded, although some nodes can also have the entire blockchain downloaded, and this is why some nodes are referred to as a full node, or a partial node, basically meaning how much of the blockchain they have saved. We will go over use cases that involve nodes on a blockchain in more detail later, basically some nodes do not need to download the entire blockchain, while most validators of a blockchains consensus method need the entire blockchain downloaded, and this is why sometimes their version of transactions on a blockchain is trusted more than a nodes version.

Majority Control of the Consensus Method:

Whoever has the ability to create blocks and validate transactions on a blockchain has a great deal of control over that blockchain, and this will become more apparent as we continue to better understand how blockchains work. But from this basic understanding we can see how validators in a consensus method are responsible for verifying transactions, and invalid transactions can be added into a blockchain by mistake then reorged, this is why a decentralized consensus method is very important, and we will go over decentralization in detail later. We will also go deeper into two of the main types of consensus methods in a bit, the verification of transactions for both are about the same, however, who has control over the validation of new blocks is very different, and there are even some exceptions that exist like voting coins on a blockchain. This voting power is an ability only validators have in most POW blockchains, but these voting coins can exist in some blockchains, they deal more with updates to the blockchain, and we will go over voting coins more later when we look at the voting structures of several different blockchains. *(Reference page 66)* Even though the encryption of the information is very difficult if not impossible to decipher, bad actors can gain control over the consensus method and access or change the blockchain, validating invalid transactions and basically moving wealth from another wallet to their own, or any other type of malicious attack on the blockchain. This is why decentralization is very important, even with the security that a SHA provides, too much control in too few hands can still lead to manipulation of the information.

Not all of this is deliberate manipulation, orphan blocks are blocks added to a blockchain that invalid transactions were included in, this is possible but does not happen often, and it happens because of how the validators and nodes share their data, and we will go over this in more detail later. For now, a simplified example would be, in one area of the planet a few nodes and validators all agree that a transaction is valid, a wallet that had 10 coins in the last block of the blockchain is sending 5 coins to another wallet, and normally all validators are able to share this information before the next block is added to the blockchain, but not always. Sometimes this relay of information takes time, and this also has to do with what validators and nodes are pulling information from each other, for example an invalid transaction could be viewed as valid by some of the validators in a somewhat localized area, and we will go over geographic and digital validator locations in more detail later. For now just understand, it does not have to be a physical location where these validators are grouped, it just means many of the same validators and nodes are pulling information from each other, or from a common node with the wrong interpretation of the blockchain, and this usually happens because the node does not have the full blockchain downloaded. *(Reference page 50)* When one of these validators is randomly chosen by the blockchain code to receive the block reward for the newest block, it also means their version of the blockchain is the new consensus for the blockchain. Then the majority of the other validators and nodes pick up on this discrepancy, and this is what causes a reorg that creates the orphan block that was mentioned before. *(Reference page 5)* Although this can happen, it does not happen often, and these are either mistakes that are quickly fixed, or a coordinated attack on the blockchain by pushing these invalid transactions from one or several nodes to other validators. When this happens with a small percent of the total validators of a blockchain's consensus method it can be quickly fixed with a reorg, and this is a normal part of securing a blockchain. As long as the mistakes are corrected quickly there are no major negative effects to the blockchain, and most orphan blocks are short as mentioned earlier, this is because there are more validators that see it as an invalid transaction rather than a valid one. These are just one of the many types of constant attacks on a blockchain, most invalid transactions are rejected, some invalid transactions are rejected after a reorg, but decentralized blockchains have the ability to prevent these types of attacks, as long as the number of validators approving the invalid transaction is only a small percentage of the total number of validators for that blockchain.

51% Attacks:

When the majority of the validators all agree that an invalid transaction is valid on a blockchain, you get what's called a "51% attack," this means invalid transactions can be added to the blockchain, usually debiting wallets, and crediting wallets the hacker has the keys for, but these attacks can also be on updates to the blockchains code, and they can make changes and cause further damage to a blockchain. These types of coordinated attacks can happen, and the fewer validators a blockchain has the easier it is to gain control over 51% of them, and this threshold is not universal. Some blockchains can be manipulated with less than 51% of the validators, either way, the more validators there are, and the more decentralized the consensus method is, the more protected the blockchain is against these types of attacks. So now that we have a rough idea of how a consensus method uses validators to secure the blockchain and prevent invalid transactions, we can look at several different ways to set up a blockchain and its coin or token. There are many consensus methods types, and most blockchains differ in many ways including the type of consensus method they use, and although some of these consensus methods can appear similar, they vary slightly in how transactions are added to the blockchain and by whom. We will look at the two most commonly used consensus methods, POW and POS, in more detail next, and we will also briefly look at new types of consensus methods that are being developed later on.

Consensus Methods 202

Expanded information on prior concepts, bringing it together to go over consensus methods*

- **Proof of Work, POW**
- **Proof of Stake, POS**
- **Nodes**
- **Consensus Method Vulnerabilities**

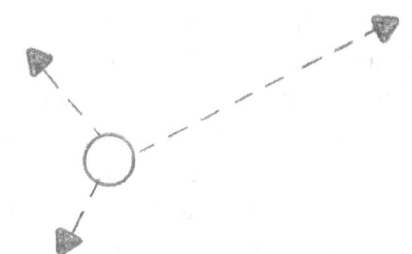
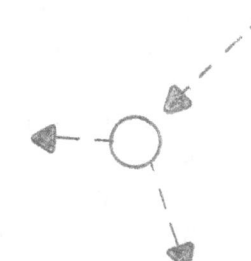

Proof of Work, POW:

First, we will look at proof of work, again each blockchain can be set up with slight differences, even two POW blockchains can vary in many ways, and we will look at universal similarities between this consensus method type before further explaining how Bitcoins POW blockchain is set up. For proof of work, it is all in the name, there is physical work that needs to be done along with digital computing, and the price a validator pays for trying to push invalid transactions on the blockchain, is the chance to earn a block reward, which the validator can then exchange for dollars to cover energy costs. This is the deterrent that stops most validators from wanting to include invalid transactions in their blocks, it is because they are spending their own wealth on equipment and energy costs. They are doing this to receive block rewards that they can monetize into dollars, this is basically a company that profits from the validation of blocks on a blockchain, and these are basically data centers, called a mining farm because the computers "mine" the block rewards. It is referred to as "mining" because of the time and energy required to hash the transactions, and this is similar to industries that mine valuable metals today, there is a great deal of energy and effort required to extract small amounts of metal. The same is true for mining block rewards, although the effort is hashing transactions, basically math, and not physical equipment removing metals from the earth. These computers are hardware, sometimes called ASICs, or miners, and some blockchains can be "mined" with gaming GPUs, there are many different types of validators for a POW blockchain, but they all have the common factor of hardware, and POS will be explained next, it is basically software, the basic difference between POW and POS is hardware vs software. *(Reference page 155)*

POW is Hardware:

These miners are the validators of a blockchain, so from now on when you hear, miner, ASIC, or GPU you can think of the validators that were discussed earlier. GPUs are usually used for gaming, but they can be used to earn block rewards on some POW blockchains, and ASIC stands for Application-Specific Integrated Circuit. Meaning the computer is built for mining a specific blockchain, and most do not even have a keyboard or screen, these computers use all their computing power on solving hash functions to validate new blocks. A miner is the term used to refer to any computer that hash's information on a blockchain in exchange for block rewards, so a miner could refer to a single ASIC unit, or to a GPU rig, and mining farms are simply several or many of these computers working together. Mining farms are basically a company that sets up the equipment, or miners, and attempts to earn block rewards, the company's goal is to have their energy costs lower than the block reward's value. We go over this more in a bit, but just understand these computers, or miners, require a lot of energy, and produce a lot of heat, they are hardware, and balancing out cooling systems becomes a major factor when mining farms are set up at scale. I cover this a little more later when I explain the process of setting up our Bitcoin mining farm, and building the cooling systems required for desert temperatures. The main takeaway here is, these computers are solving the complex hashing of all transactions on a blockchain, as discussed earlier this is very complex computing, and this requires energy and produces heat, along with block rewards from the blockchain's consensus method, these block rewards can then be exchanged for dollars and used to cover a mining farm's energy costs.

Anyone can mine a POW blockchain and earn block rewards, obviously they need equipment and knowledge, but most if not all, POW blockchains allow for anyone to download the blockchain and start hashing transactions. There are many factors to be considered like, does the equipment cost more than it will produce in block rewards, because if it does that mining farm will have to eventually shut down when they become unprofitable. We will discuss some of these factors later, but for now just understand that POW means anyone can join as a validator and begin solving hash functions, which strengthens the blockchain overall, and adds to its decentralization. These miners could try to manipulate the blockchain, they could try to approve invalid transactions, and pass them on to other nodes and validators trying to get them to agree with their violation of the blockchain code. But if they do, they would lose wealth, let's look at what it would cost a validator trying to push invalid transactions on a POW blockchain. The malicious validator would need to compute the invalid transaction going back many blocks, the shorter it is, the easier it would be for other validators and nodes to identify the transaction as invalid. This would require a lot of energy, but this is not the only cost the validator will have attempting to manipulate the blockchain, there is also the time spent setting up a mining farm, and the physical equipment that would be needed. This means manipulating, or attempting to manipulate, a POW blockchain is very costly and time-consuming, and this is very different from a POS blockchain, where a malicious validator would only be risking an amount of wealth. Basically, these miners require energy, whether that energy is used for hashing valid or invalid transactions does not matter, the mining farm will still have to pay the energy bill, and since invalid transactions are rejected from blocks, the mining farm would basically be paying a high energy bill with no block reward compensation. This plus the time and equipment needed to hash transactions on the blockchain, is what prevents most mining farms from doing anything to the blockchain other than solving blocks, and earning block rewards.

Mining Block Rewards:

There are many factors involved in setting up a profitable mining farm, let's start with at what rate do mining farms earn block rewards, remember, most blockchains vary in slight ways, but we can still look at the factors involved in calculating how many block rewards a mining farm receives. A mining farm's hash rate is basically its computing power, the higher the hash rate the more block rewards will be earned, the total hash rate goes up and down as new miners come online and offline globally, and the mining difficulty is what decides how many block rewards are compensated based on a mining farm's hash rate. Now before we go further, block rewards are distributed differently when many mining farms pool their hash power, and the mining difficulty is adjusted over set periods of time. We will go over both of these in a bit, but for now just understand that when a validator solves a block, they revive the block rewards directly. These block rewards are basically the inflation rate of the blockchain, this can be a continuing inflation or a reducing inflation until a max limit of coins is reached, and we will go over this in more detail later as well. Basically, block rewards can be measured by using these factors for each individual blockchain, usually referring to the number of new coins that are created with each block, for example, right now Bitcoins block reward is 6.25 coins per block added to the blockchain, and this is being reduced every 4 years.

Mining Farms:

As the blockchains overall hash rate increases, which is basically the number of miners and their computing power, it becomes harder and harder for smaller mining farms to earn block rewards, or solve a new block on the blockchain, and even larger mining farms can still decide to pool their hash rate rather than solo mining. Solo mining is where one ASIC, or a small group, mine a blockchain and earn block rewards, they are a validator in the blockchain's consensus method, but they have a very small hash rate, meaning even if blocks are added about every 10 minutes or so, it could take the miner months or even years before they are able to solve a block and earn a block reward. This is why most POW miners will pool their hash rates, it gives them a steady stream of block rewards on a constant basis, allowing them to exchange some of the new coins for dollars in order to pay the energy bill. Although, if they did not pool their hash power, they would be solo mining, basically paying the energy bill every month, and waiting months or years for a single block reward.

Mining pools have this name because they are pooling the blockchains hash rate, or computing power, and these are completely different from staking pools in a POS blockchain, where it is wealth that is being staked to the pool. A mining pool is basically many small and/or large mining farms, all sending their hash rates to the pool operator, and the mining pool is the validator that receives the block reward, which is then split between all the miners that are sending their hash rate to the pool. New blocks are solved often, and this keeps a steady supply of coins going to each miner, far less than solving a block individually, but it is a steady supply, and this flow of wealth is needed by most mining farms that have monthly power bills. Not all mining pools are set up the same, and fake pools can be set up as a scam, so it is important for a miner to understand how these pools make payouts, and what they think about the blockchain they are helping secure. This is because the pool is the one receiving the block rewards, basically acting as a 3rd party, and they have the voting rights for a miner's hash rate on the blockchain, and we will go over voting on improvement proposals in more detail later. Most pools charge a fee for their service, which is paid by taking a percent of a miner's block rewards, usually under 5%, and miners should look at what fees the pool has and their stance on changes to the blockchain code. If a mining farm does not like the way one pool is set up, they can send their hash power to another pool, and there are usually several mining pools for most large POW blockchains.

Mining a blockchain for block rewards can be done by a single ASIC unit, or at scale, which is just many ASICs working together, and most of the factors involved are digital, meaning mining farms can be easily scaled without adding additional costs, other than the larger energy costs and larger cooling systems required. For example, a GPU can be used to mine most POW blockchains, this can be one GPU on a home computer, or several thousand GPUs working together in a warehouse, however their computing power is low compared to most ASIC units, and even though they are able to run detailed graphics for computer games, hashing transactions on a blockchain is more complicated. This is why GPUs are used for smaller POW blockchains that have lower hash rates, this allows the miner to actually earn a decent amount of block rewards from the blockchain. For eample, Bitcoins hash rate is too high for GPUs, it would take a very long time to build up to the smallest payout in a Bitcoin mining pool, and this is why ASICs are the main type of miner used for Bitcoin mining. Application-Specific Integrated Circuits, are just computers that can only mine one blockchain, and as mentioned before, blockchains are just a secure hash algorithm, or SHA, an equation represented by a curved line on a graph. *(Reference page 9)* These ASICs are built to solve hash functions that run a specific SHA, they do not waste computing power on anything but verifying these transactions, they do not have screens or keyboards, and most have fans or some form of built-in cooling system. Some blockchains may run on the same SHA, but they have sight differences in their code making two distinct coins, and in some cases these computers can mine both blockchains, called dual mining. There are several examples of coins that can be dual mined, but this is not a normal part of most POW blockchains. ASICs can also be built for dual mining, it is easier to do with similar blockchains, but ultimately it comes down to what the hardware can compute, and there are new ASICs being developed each year.

Mining Farm Efficiency:

Now let us look at the major non-digital aspects to a mining farm, there are many physical things required such as, routers, Ethernet cables etc. but these are not recurring costs, and once set up they require little maintenance. Major recurring costs and maintenance are basically keeping the computers supplied with energy, and efficiently cooled to prevent overheating, finding this balance between block rewards, energy costs, and cooling costs, is the main issue a mining farm deals with. Energy costs vary depending on many factors, one would obviously be the local price for grid electricity, but another could be how much renewable energy is incorporated into the mining farm. We will go over many renewable energy sources that are used in Bitcoin mining later, and scaling up these mining farms to achieve a higher hash rate will obviously also increase the energy costs. Scaling up a mining farm will also increase its hash rate, and increase the amount of heat being generated, this is why mining farms prefer cooler climates, it allows them to use simple air-cooled systems that are much cheaper than other types of cooling systems, and we will go into more detail on several types of cooling systems later. What is important to know is, these miners produce a lot of heat and that heat needs to be efficiently dissipated, or the computers will overheat, and this affects their hash rate, either reducing it or going offline completely, and the cooler these computers are the more efficient they are. Overclocking an ASIC unit gives the miner more hash power, but it must be kept cool in order to do so, and I will go over the hash rates and cooling temperatures we were able to achieve on our Bitcoin miners later. But not all mining farms are set up the same, so these numbers may vary somewhat, and there are certain thresholds these computers cannot handle, so my numbers will be a ballpark average for the type of dielectric fluid cooling system that we used.

Another non-digital factor that is involved in a mining farm is its location, cooler climates allow for cheaper cooling systems as mentioned before, but location has another factor that does not deal with individual mining farms, but all of them as a whole. These mining farms are the validators that keep a blockchain going, if all of them were to go off at the same time the blockchain would stop and go offline, and no transactions could take place. This is covered more when we look at decentralization, but while we are looking at mining farms, it's important to realize that spreading out these mining farms helps prevent the blockchain from going offline, either from a natural disaster or a man-made disaster. If all the miners in a POW blockchain were in one location, then it is easier to attack the blockchain, either by cutting off power in the area, or directly turning off the ASICs. Natural disasters have the same effect, either cutting power or destroying equipment, and while this would be bad for the mining farm either way, they can recover and rebuild, but the blockchain would be offline and making transactions would be impossible until they are able to get the mining farm back up and running. This is why it's better, from the blockchains point of view, to have the miners spread out as much as possible, although when we go deeper into decentralization, we will see that mining farms can be in localized areas and still somewhat decentralized, by having their hash power sent to different mining pools. But this only protects the blockchains consensus method from digital centralization, these mining farms can still be damaged by physical natural disasters that can affect very large areas of the planet, and happen at random.

Conclusion:

These are just the basics for POW blockchains, and we will go over many individual aspects of a POW consensus method in more detail later. Blockchains can be set up in many different ways, these variables include the consensus method the blockchain uses, and even several blockchains that use a POW consensus method can be set up in slightly different ways. However, remember these mining farms in a POW blockchain are just the validators of the blockchain's consensus method as mentioned before, and other consensus methods do exist. We will go over several blockchains that use a POW consensus method in more detail later, including Bitcoins blockchain, but first let us look at the basics for blockchains that use a POS consensus method.

Proof of Stake, POS:

Now, we will look at proof of stake, again each blockchain can be set up with slight differences, even two POS blockchains can vary in many ways, and we will look at universal similarities for this consensus method type, POS can vary in more ways than POW, and not all of the topics explained are incorporated into all POS blockchains. For proof of stake, it is somewhat in the name, there is an amount of wealth that is staked to a pool, and the price a validator pays for trying to push invalid transactions on the blockchain is a portion, or all of that staked wealth. The hardware needed to set up most staking pools is minimal, hard disk space, good internet bandwidth, etc. nothing compared to a POW blockchain, especially one with a high hash rate like Bitcoin, where some mining farms can have 100s or 1000s of computers, or miners. This makes the energy consumption for a POS pool far less than any sized POW mining farm, and nodes also have similar low energy requirements, but as mentioned before nodes cannot receive block rewards like stake pools do.

Stake Pools:

Stake pools solve hash functions, or transactions on a blockchain, similarly to miners in a POW blockchain, they are the validators of transactions, and they are also similar to nodes, in that they require far less energy in order to hash transactions and solve blocks. However, they receive block rewards a little differently than miners do in a POW blockchain, basically the block rewards are based on how many coins are staked to the pool. The more coins staked, the more block rewards, and these rewards are sent to the stake pool operator and then distributed to individual wallets that are staking coins, referred to as stakeholders. These stakeholders are not required to do anything more than stake, and unstake coins when they want, and we will go over lock up periods in a bit. They may pay a fee, or portion of their block rewards to the pool operator, and this fee can vary between POS blockchains and individual pools on one blockchain. But stakeholders are not involved in the consensus method or the validation of transactions on the blockchain, all that is done by the pool operator, and they must keep the stake pool online in order to receive block rewards. This is somewhat like miners in a POW blockchain, turn them on and keep them running, little maintenance is needed after they are set up. For POS blockchains there are many different ways the validator network can be set up, but they all follow the same concept of stake pools, and locking up wealth as a way to secure the blockchain.

Some stake pools can be set up by anyone, other POS blockchains have limits on how many pools can be created and who operates them, either way most stake pools have the entire blockchain downloaded, and the stake pool operator is basically a validator on the blockchain. So, you can think of the staking pool itself as a validator, explained earlier, and they receive block rewards that are then distributed to their stakeholders. Some POS pools can be set up by anyone, they obviously need knowledge and a little hardware, but the blockchain code allows for basically an infinite number of pools, meaning anyone can set up a pool. While other POS blockchains will only allow for a certain number of pools to be created, and in order to set up a pool either way requires a number of coins locked in the stake pool. These coin requirements limit the number of people that are able to afford to set up a pool, this can be a few thousand coins or 10s of thousands of coins, for example, to create a pool in the new POS Ethereum requires 32 ETH. But this requirement is only to set up a pool, most POS blockchains allow for smaller amounts of wealth to be staked to pools by just about anyone. So, let's look at how staking works for pool operators and everyone else who stakes to the pool. First, we need to understand why and how these coins are staked, in a POW blockchain the validators generally do not attempt to manipulate transactions, if they do, they miss out on the chance of earning block rewards, and either way they have to pay the power bill. There needs to be the same loss of wealth to prevent stake pools from attempting to manipulate transactions as well, we will go over slashing next, but basically these coins are collateral, and they are locked in the stake pool. *(Reference page 23)* This means they are taken out of the circulating supply, and the pool operator's coins are not the only staked coins in the pool, the more people that stake to the pool the more block rewards the pool receives, but there are block reward limits for some POS blockchains, and we will go over this in more detail later. A simple way to think about staked coins is to compare them to the hash rate of a mining farm, the larger the hash rate the more block rewards, and the equipment required to increase the hash rate costs wealth. While with stake pools, coins are staked to the pool, and in order to receive more block rewards someone would have to stake more coins, which also requires more wealth. Either way it is wealth, or the fear of losing wealth, that deters validators from manipulating transactions on either a POW or POS blockchain.

Staking to a Pool:

These staked coins represent wealth, because they are bought by the stakeholder before staking, and this wealth is actually being held by the pool, unlike banks today that will take your wealth and lend it out to gain interest, so let's look at how this wealth is being securely held by the stake pool. There are many separate parties staking wealth to each pool, including the stake pool operator, all of these stakes of wealth are secured separately in a type of smart contract. We will go over use cases like smart contracts later, but they are basically two wallets jointly holding coins, and each wallet has some form of access or control over the wealth. When a stake pool operator sets up a pool, they are required to have a certain number of coins locked in the pool, this is like a smart contract between the pool operator and the blockchain code. The pool operator can move coins in and out of the pool, mainly moving block reward coins out of the pool to their individual wallet, but they must keep the required number of coins in the pool for it to continue operating as a validator on the blockchain. These coins cannot be lent out in any way by the pool operator or by the blockchain, with the exception of slashing which we will go over next, and this is because the sequence of numbers that represent the wallets have been hashed into the smart contract, this provides all the same encryption security that was discussed earlier for transactions from wallet to wallet. Simply put, the staked coins required to run a staking pool are locked up in an agreement between the pool operator and the blockchain code, if the validator attempts to manipulate the blockchain, their coins are slashed. And individual wallets staking coins to the pool are also locked up in a type of smart contract, this one being between them and the stake pool operator. The pool operator cannot move these staked coins, their access to them is pretty limited, but they have to have this proof in order to show the blockchain the coins are in the pool and deserve a block reward. The stakeholder also cannot move these coins or lend them out while they are being staked, and they do have the ability to move coins out of the pool, but once they do, they will no longer receive the block rewards. The ability to stake and unstake coins in a POS pool varies, it depends on several factors like lock up periods and epoch lengths, which we will go over later, the main thing to understand for now is, each stakeholder has coins locked in the pool. The more coins there are and the longer they are locked up for, the more block rewards the stakeholder will receive, and all the stakeholders have separate smart contracts with the pool, there is no mingling of funds in the traditional sense, and as said before, these coins cannot be lent out, they must remain in the pool in order to earn block rewards. This is how it works when directly staking coins from a hard wallet to a stake pool, but staking through a 3rd party wallet like an exchange is different, and we will go over this in more detail later.

Slashing:

Slashing is the penalty for a validator in a POS blockchain, just like in a POW blockchain if a validator includes invalid transactions, they will have less of a chance of earing block rewards, and the same is true in a POS blockchain, if the validator is attempting to manipulate the blockchain they will lose some or all of their staked coins. Some POS blockchains do not have slashing included in the blockchains code, ones that do usually have it set up to destroy, or "burn" the coins, meaning they are actually removed from the blockchain's ledger of accounts, or wallets. *(Reference page 23)* POS blockchains will sometimes not incorporate slashing, since most coins staked to a pool are usually the individual stakeholders coins. This would mean if a pool operator attempted to manipulate the blockchain, it would be the stakeholders that could be the ones getting their wealth destroyed, and this is not ideal, unless you know and trust the pool operator to not attempt this manipulation. Whether an investor knows or trusts the pool operator or not, they should be aware of slashing for every POS blockchain coin or token they are invested in, especially if they are staking wealth on the POS blockchain, and we will touch on slashing a little more later when we go deeper into the consensus methods of several individual blockchains.

Epochs:

An epoch is a certain number of blocks in a blockchain, they can vary in length and can be used for different things on a blockchain, and they are a part of the blockchain, basically they are just sections of the blockchain, used to measure passages of time that the blockchain needs to track. For example, Bitcoins halving happens every 210,000 blocks, this is how the blockchain code knows to reduce the block rewards, and the passage of a certain number of blocks can be used for many different things in a blockchain, one of them being lock up periods for POS pools. This passage of a certain number of blocks is basically what an epoch is, lock-up periods use these epochs as a way to measure when coins can be removed from a stake pool, and lock-up periods can vary between individual blockchains. For example, staked ETH coins were locked up for years until the recent upgrade that allowed for unstaking, and some POS blockchains do not even have lock-up periods for their staking pools.

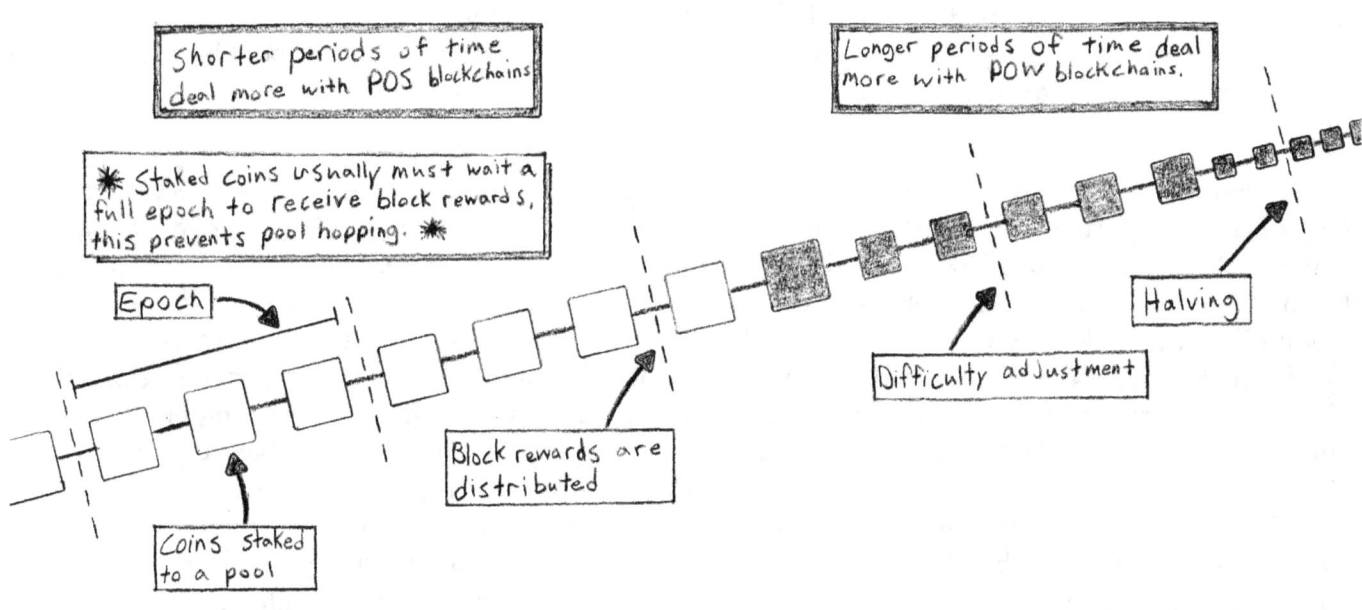

Block Height

Epochs can be used in different ways depending on how the blockchain is set up, POS blockchains use epochs to prevent pool hopping, and any blockchain can use the block height to measure time on the blockchain. This allows for Bitcoins halving event, as well as its difficulty adjustment which is more frequent, and it is not just the blockchain itself that can use a blockchains block height, it can be used by smart contracts and wallets as well, basically anything that requires measuring time on the blockchain.

Pg. 60, left section: Epochs are a set number of blocks used to prevent pool hopping, this means coins cannot exploit the block rewards, and earn more wealth then other stakeholders. Each POS blockchains consensus method can have the validator network set up in a slightly different way, and the lengths of epochs along with how block rewards are distributed can also vary.

Pg. 104, right section: Epochs are basically a set number of blocks that trigger an event on the blockchain, and they can be used to measure many things on a blockchain, such as the Bitcoin halving every 210,000 blocks, or the difficulty adjustment every 2,016 blocks.

Pg. 110, right section: The block height of the blockchain can be used to measure time on the blockchain, but these do not have to be repeating epochs, and the block height can be used for many different things on a blockchain, basically anything that would require a significant amount of time to pass before a transaction on the blockchain can take place.

Even though a POS blockchain might not have a lock-up period, the blockchain code still needs epochs, this is because coins could be moved between staking pools in a way that would give the coins more block rewards. A simple way to stop this is to have lock-up periods, but for blockchains that do not have these requirements the epoch still prevents coins from "pool hopping" by using the epoch to determine when block rewards start accumulating for the stakeholder. A simple example would be, a POS blockchain has an epoch length of 5 blocks, payouts, or block rewards are sent to stakeholders at the end of each epoch (every 5th block), meaning stakeholders could be using their wealth in other ways and then right before the payout, they could stake coins and earn block rewards. Having the coins locked for the duration of the epoch obliviously prevents this, but this example blockchain allows for anyone to stake and unstake coins whenever they want to, so let us look at how these stake pools could prevent pool hopping and the exploitation of block rewards.

(Illustration, previous page)

The simplest way to do this would be to have coins that are staked to a pool not start receiving block rewards until the current epoch was over, this means if coins were staked on the 3rd block into the epoch, they would not start earning block rewards for two blocks, and would not receive any block rewards until the end of the following epoch, 7 blocks after the coins were staked to the pool. There is a lot more going on with how these block rewards are calculated then in this simple example, but the important thing to understand is that these lock-up periods are usually to help prevent the block rewards from being exploited, and this is also true for any periods of time when an investor's coins might not be earning block rewards while staked to the pool. With some POS blockchains, pulling your coins out of a pool before an epoch ends will also result in the stakeholder losing a few blocks worth of block rewards, in the prior example this would be like removing your coins from the pool 3 blocks into the epoch, those coins should receive block rewards for those 3 blocks, but they do not because payouts are every 5th block, meaning they would lose out on those block rewards. This again is not that same for every blockchain, and the value of these lost block rewards are usually minimal (if the stakeholder has an extremely large amount of wealth staked to the pool, then this will obviously be higher), and fixed lock-up periods remove this risk altogether. So, it is important to understand how the POS blockchain is set up, how its validator network is set up, and how the stake pools are set up, as well as who runs them and how the compensation of block rewards are distributed to stakeholders. But there is another major factor that affects staking pools and the block rewards they receive, and this would be the number of coins that can receive block rewards per stake pool.

Block Reward Limits:

If these stake pools did not have limits on block rewards, then a large amount of wealth could be moved onto the blockchain, the coins representing that wealth could be staked to several or even one pool, and then receive a large portion or even all the block rewards created on the POS blockchain. This is because staked coins can be thought of as the hash rate in a POW mining farm as mentioned before, and a massive amount of wealth in one pool would be similar to one mining farm with most or all of the blockchains hash rate. This stake pool would receive the majority of the block rewards because the pool would be solving most of the new blocks added to the blockchain. This would cause several problems for a POS blockchain, the main one being most of the transactions and new blocks on the blockchain would be validated by one stake pool. This is a centralized point of control or failure, and could be used to approve invalid transactions, since the majority of the total validators for the blockchain would agree on these invalid transactions as explained earlier. This concentration of staked coins would also allow the stakeholder to earn the majority of the block rewards, this would deter others from staking small amounts of wealth that would receive next to nothing in block rewards, and these small amounts of staked wealth are what create decentralization, which we will go over in more detail later.

(Illustration, next page)

The balance that POS blockchains try to achieve is encouraging stakeholders to hold their wealth in a stake pool, but not so much wealth that they receive most or all of the block rewards. There are several ways

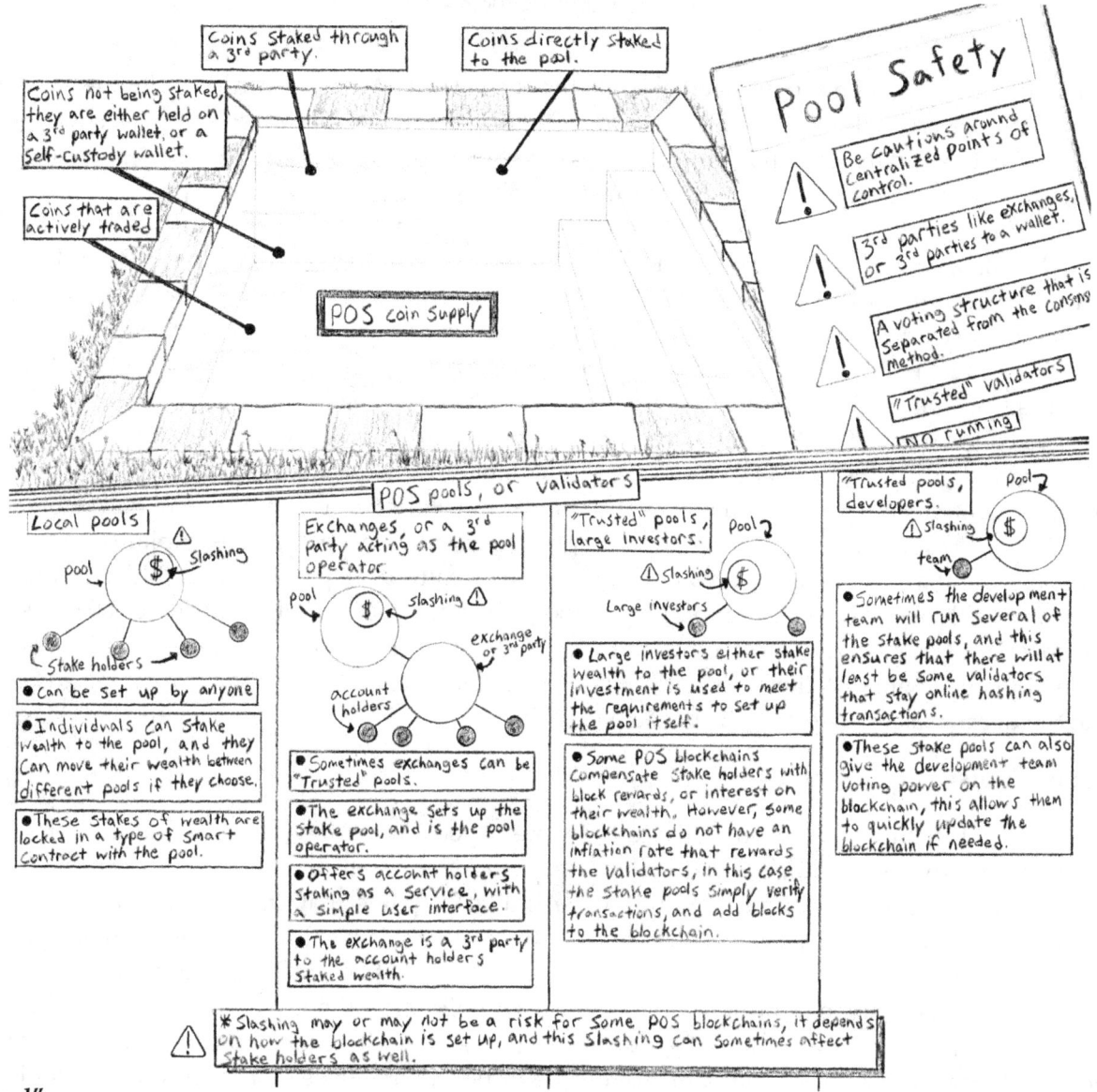

POS "Pool"

The pool shows the different states that coins can be in, basically how the coins are held on the blockchain, and this means a sizable portion of the total coins in existence can be locked in stake pools, this means they are not in the supply that is being bought and sold, and this can affect the coin or tokens dollar value. The pools that lock up this wealth can be set up by different types of pool operators, and the wealth staked to the pools can come from different types of investors as well. There can be centralized points of control in a POS blockchain, and even centralized points of control in how wealth is held in the blockchain, but these factors can be reduced by using self-custody wallets, and by having many individually controlled validators in the blockchain's consensus method.

Pg. 19, bottom section: The wealth staked to the pool by the pool operator could be destroyed if the blockchains consensus method included slashing, this collateral would be the loss of wealth the pool operator would incur if they attempted to manipulate the blockchain, and sometimes slashing can include a stakeholder's wealth as well.

Pg. 20, upper section: Slashing usually destroys the units of account in the stake pool, basically they are removed from the total supply of the coin or token, and this can vary depending on how the blockchains consensus method is set up.

Pg. 25, bottom section: Exchanges that offer staking as a service do not always have to add and remove coins from their pool. When account holders want to stake or unstake coins, their accounts are simply updated, while the actual wealth staked to the pool remains, although each exchange can be set up different, and this does not apply to wealth staked from a hard wallet directly to a stake pool.

Pg. 40, bottom section: Wealth locked in any type of stake pool is used to earn block rewards from the blockchain's consensus method, and this wealth is similar to the cost of equipment for POW blockchains, it is also the wealth that would be lost if the pool operator attempted to manipulate the blockchain's consensus method.

Pg. 52, bottom section: These stake pools are validators in the blockchain's consensus method, they are directly benefiting from the blockchain and would usually only vote on IPs that were good for the blockchain. However, when voting coins or tokens are used in the voting structure of the blockchain they lose this ability, and this is not necessarily a bad thing, since they still hash transactions and earn block rewards.

Pg. 55, bottom section: Staking through an exchange is similar to staking directly to a pool from a hard wallet, although there is a 3rd party involved, and this 3rd party allows account holders to easily stake and unstake wealth with the push of a button.

Pg. 58, bottom section: Staking wealth from a hard wallet to a stake pool is somewhat technical, many investors would like to earn block rewards, but they do not want to set up a self-custody wallet, and this is where exchanges can offer staking as a service to its account holders, taking care of the technical work and providing a simple user interface.

Pg. 63, bottom section: The Polkadot blockchain includes slashing, so if any of its validators attempt to push an invalid transaction, they will lose their staked wealth, which is a large amount when you look at what is required to become a "trusted" validator in Polkadot's consensus method.

Pg. 95, bottom section: When an exchange sets up a stake pool for one of the POS coins or tokens offered on the platform, they are usually only one validator in the consensus method, and although they could set up several pools depending on account holder demand, these stake pools usually do not come close to gaining the majority of the consensus method for that blockchain.

this is achieved, like limits on the number of coins that can receive block rewards, and allowing for many different pools to be created, which will then compete with each other for stakeholders. A simple example would be, a POS blockchain that allowed anyone to set up a pool, the required number of coins to do this is say 100, but each pool can receive block rewards for up to 600 coins, meaning the stake pool operator can have other stakeholders stake up to 500 coins and everyone will still receive their share of the block rewards. Additional coins can be staked to the pool, but they will not receive block rewards, although some blockchains like Cardano do not have hard limits where some staked coins receive block rewards, and some that do not, they instead have a sliding scale where the more coins there are in a pool the less block rewards that pool will receive. In our example this would be something like, 100 coins receives 100% of the possible block rewards (for that pool, not all the block rewards for the entire blockchain), the next 100 coins would receive 80%, and the next 100 coins would receive 60% etc. this incentivizes pool operators to create another pool rather than build up more staked coins in a single pool. This helps create decentralization for the POS blockchain, remember each pool is actually a validator for the blockchain, and the more validators there are the harder it is to manipulate the blockchain and approve invalid transactions, as explained earlier. These limits do not prevent an individual with a large amount of wealth from gaining more block rewards, it just prevents that wealth from being staked to a single pool, a wealthy individual could stake 500 coins to many different pools, and they would receive the full block reward amount for each pool, this is great for the stakeholder, but even better for the blockchain, since this would create the need for more pools to be created, adding to the decentralized aspect of the blockchain.

Number of Pools:

Not all POS blockchains allow for anyone to create a pool, some have a fixed number of pools that can exist, and the process for stakeholders staking to a blockchain with fewer pools is the same as staking to a blockchain with unlimited pools, although the limits for coins that can receive block rewards per pool is usually higher, allowing for many individuals to stake their wealth to a single pool. This reduces the decentralization of the blockchain, however these pools are not set up by just anyone, the blockchain developers usually have some kind of say or control over who runs these pools, and we will go into this more when we look at decentralization. The number of pools does affect the security of the blockchain, but from the stakeholders point of view the same factors are important regardless of the number of pools. Things like how the pool operator distributes block rewards, and if they take a cut of those rewards, is important to stakeholders. Other things like lock-up periods and slashing for the pool may be important to some investors, as well as the block reward rate, or the inflation rate, for that blockchain.

POS Pros and Cons:

POS blockchains are good because they allow anyone to earn block rewards and help secure the blockchain without having to set up expensive equipment like miners, in this way stakeholders could be thought of as the validators for a blockchain, however most stakeholders do not have access to the actual validator, which is the hardware that is set up by the pool operator. The pool operator would be the one with the ability to affect transactions on the blockchain, not stakeholders, but stakeholders are helping the pool which is validating transactions on the blockchain, so they are a part of the consensus method a little, more in name and not actual control though. POS blockchains are also good because they use very little energy, this is why most people think POS blockchains are "better" than POW blockchains, simply based on their energy consumption. However, it is important to realize why POS blockchains use less energy, as mentioned before it is wealth that secures a blockchain, or the fear of losing that wealth, but this only applies to stakeholders and pool operators that want to be a part of and profit from the blockchain's consensus method. For anyone looking to attack a blockchain for profit POS blockchains are easier to attack, this is because it is large amounts of wealth that can gain enough control over the consensus method to validate invalid transactions on the blockchain, unlike large amounts of energy that are needed to gain the same control in a POW blockchain. As mentioned before large stakeholders can earn the majority of the block rewards in a POS blockchain, but it is not just the block rewards they might be after, these block rewards come from new blocks added to the blockchain, and they are validating these new blocks, so if they wanted to approve invalid transactions they could. With POS blockchains, wealth can be quickly moved into pools, slashing may cause the malicious validator to lose some or all of their wealth, but this might not be a concern for them if their goal is to cause damage to the blockchain. Whereas with POW blockchains, a malicious validator would need to set up several large mining farms (depending on the blockchains total hash rate), and pay for large amounts of energy. Put simply, there is a lot more work that would need to be done to attack the blockchain, it would require more effort, not just a very large amount of wealth that the attacker might be willing to lose in order to negatively affect the blockchain. Now there are many more factors involved in the overall security of an individual blockchain, for instance, a POW blockchain with a low hash rate makes it easier for a large miner to set up and gain majority control of the consensus method. While a POS blockchain that allows for many individually operated pools, and has a block reward limit for those pools, would be more decentralized, and it would be harder for a single actor to negatively affect the blockchain with a large amount of wealth. Overall, there are pros and cons for POW and POS blockchains, and not all blockchains are set up the same, but at the most basic level the less energy required by POS blockchains is not a positive aspect of the consensus method, it requires less "work" and therefor is easier to manipulate.

3rd Party Staking:

We will go more in depth on exchanges later on, however it's important to make a distinction at this level of POS blockchains, everything we have just gone over refers to staking coins to a pool from a hard wallet directly. The stakeholder has the private keys to the wallet and there are only two parties involved, the stakeholder and the pool operator, or the pool operator and the blockchain code for coins required to set up the stake pool as a validator. Exchanges act as a 3rd party, which will be further explained later, but basically, on exchanges lock-up periods do not have to be the same as the lock-up periods for skate pools on a blockchain, and some POS blockchains that have lock-up periods, might not have a lock-up period when staking through an exchange. *(Reference page 23)* This is because you do not hold your coins on an exchange, you have an account at the exchange, and the exchange can move around or lend out your coins, much like banks and financial institutions do today. So, the exchange is staking coins to a pool on an account holders behalf, and they will often set up their own pools for coins they offer on their platform. Exchanges can take a cut of a stakeholders block rewards like pool operators do, and when an account on the exchange wants to unstake their coins, the exchange will simply credit the account with unstaked coins, not actually removing the coins from the stake pool. How exchanges can be set up will be explained in detail later, but for now let us look at how staked coins differ when staked through a 3rd party, and not from a hard wallet. First, an exchange is not the same as a hard wallet, it's more like a bank where you deposit wealth, and the bank promises to allow you access to that wealth through an account at the bank. This means any coins you have on an exchange are all held in one or several wallets that the exchange has the private keys for. The only time transactions happen on the blockchain is when coins move wallets, but wealth moving on an exchange is basically happening within one wallet. The only time transactions are settled on the blockchain is when an account holder requests to move their coins to their own self-custody wallet, and at this point the transaction actually happens on the ledger of accounts, which basically is the blockchain as discussed earlier. *(Reference page 80)*

A simple example would be, a POS blockchain that has roughly a one-week lock-up period, with a 4-6% block reward interest on staked coins, staking from a hard wallet would work as explained before, but let's look at how this staking process works for staked coins on an exchange. The exchange has many liquidity pools of coins, they have some of these coins unstaked, and most of them staked to one or several pools that they are the pool operator of. When a stakeholder sends their coins to the exchange, they are added to these liquidity pools, either staked or unstaked coins, and the investors account at the exchange is credited for the number of coins. The exchange could add these coins to a stake pool even if the account holder does not wish to stake their coins, in this case the exchange keeps all the block rewards for those staked coins. Or the account holder could choose to stake the coins through the exchange, they do this with the press of a button, and they can unstake coins at any time, there is no one-week lock-up period. The block rewards offered on the exchange can be thought of as interest on wealth that you do not have control over, this exchange offers 3% interest on staked coins, and the exchange keeps the 1-3% difference in block rewards as a fee. This access to easy interest on wealth benefits stakeholders that might not have the knowledge required to stake their coins from a hard wallet, or they just like the simple user interface. It is not complicated and it is easy to stake or unstake coins, account holders pay for this ability with some of their block rewards, and for some stakeholders this price is worth the convenience that the exchange offers. The pros and cons to exchanges will be covered in detail later, for now just realize if someone is staking through an exchange, there is a 3rd party between them and their wealth, this is not necessarily a bad thing, but it should be something an investor considers, and self-custody wallets, as discussed earlier, do not have this 3rd party access or control.

Nodes:

As mentioned before nodes verify transactions like validators do, but they do not receive block rewards or create new blocks on a blockchain, they also have low energy requirements like POS pools, and setting up a node is similar to a POS pool, requiring things like hard disk space, good internet bandwidth, etc. They can have some or all the blockchain downloaded, being either a full node or a partial node, this can be important when verifying some transactions on a blockchain, and each individual node is not exactly trusted by validators. Since their interpretation of the blockchain may be incomplete for some transactions, or the node could be purposely validating invalid transactions trying to pass them along to validators in hopes the transaction is included in the next block of the blockchain. This sharing of information between validators and nodes works both ways, nodes are verifying transactions and sending those transactions to other nodes and validators, to have them hash the transaction and verify it as well, and validators are also verifying transactions and sending them to other nodes and validators for verification. You can think of this like pushing and pulling data from a list of nodes and validators, all of them should have the same opinion about a transaction, but sometimes they do not. If a validator sends a node a transaction that means the validator believes the transaction to be valid, however the node will simply hash the transaction and let the validator know if the node thinks the transaction is valid or invalid. The validator does not need to agree with the node, and if the node does not think a transaction is valid, but the validator does think it is valid, then this has no effect on the validator's opinion of the transaction, and the validator might choose to remove that node from the list that it pushes and pulls data from. *(Reference page 50)*

Validators and nodes have a list of other validators and nodes that they share transactions with, this list can change and is decided on by the person running the validator or node, and if a malicious node is discovered, then that node is simply removed from the list. Usually somewhat local nodes and validators will be chosen by a node for their list, but they can pull information from anywhere on earth, and even choose validators or nodes that are more "trusted," meaning they rarely include invalid transactions. Validators also have a list that they send and receive transactions to and from, and nodes help move these transactions through the overall network of validators for the blockchain, not all nodes are good, but they offer a person the ability to have their own "copy" of the blockchain.

Copy of the Blockchain:

A node can be thought of as a copy of the blockchain, even if not fully downloaded, the node is verifying transactions as they happen, and it adds new blocks to its own copy of the blockchain as they are created by the majority of the validators in a blockchain's consensus method. This would be like someone's personal record of the ledger of accounts, which is basically a blockchain as discussed earlier. This allows the node operator to verify their own transactions, and this does not approve the transaction and add it to a block, it just gives the node operator peace of mind knowing the transaction they are about to make does not involve a malicious actor with "fake" coins for example. Although nodes can be set up by anyone with the knowledge and required equipment, most nodes are set up by people or companies with a large amount of wealth stored in the coin or token of the blockchain, or they are set up by community members that want to support the blockchain's consensus method.

Nodes create transparency for the node operator, and some node operators do not use the node for viewing this information, they simply set up the node and let it verify transactions and strengthen the overall blockchain, and for anyone with large amounts of wealth stored in the blockchain, a node serves two purposes. First, it allows the node operator to verify transactions, if large amounts of wealth are involved this gives the node operator some peace of mind. Second, if someone had a large amount of wealth stored in a blockchain, wouldn't they want to help make sure that blockchain is secure, since it is their own wealth that is being stored in the blockchain. Nodes require little energy and are not that expensive or complicated to set up, so for those storing large amounts of wealth in a blockchain nodes are a way to help secure the blockchain without setting up a validator on whatever consensus method the blockchain has, either a POS pool, or POW mining farm. This means nodes are valued by both the node operator, and the blockchain's consensus method, it helps both in different ways, but nodes are not required for some consensus methods, and some blockchains would still be able to function without nodes. Nodes can also be used as a way to interact with a blockchains use case, each blockchain can utilize nodes in different ways, and we will go over use cases involving nodes in more detail later. For now, just understand a node at its most basic level is just a running copy of the blockchain, and it is hashing the same transactions that validators are as mentioned before.

Oracles:

Nodes, simply put, relay information on a blockchain, they are not compensated for this, and overall, they help strengthen a blockchain by decentralizing the way this information is communicated to validators, and we will go over this more when we look at decentralization. Nodes are generally only verifying transactions on one blockchain, but information sometimes needs to be sent between blockchains, this is done by oracles, as they are commonly called, and sometimes they are referred to as nodes, or they have a name unique to the blockchains that it transfers information between. In general oracles can be thought of as nodes, however they are able to move information between blockchains, not just on one blockchain, and because this information is communicated between unique blockchains, most oracles are set up in different ways. They can be moving different types of information, some can have a community wallet controlled by a DAO, and some might even resemble a bridge between blockchains, where wealth can be moved between the different blockchains, and we will go over bridges and DAOs in more detail later. *(Reference page 155)*

There are many different types of oracles, but a simple way to think of it would be, oracles move information between blockchains in a trusted way, similarly to nodes that move information between validators on a single blockchain, and securely linking blockchains and allowing for this information exchange is complicated. There are many blockchain projects working on different types of interoperability, Chainlink is one example, and it is basically incentivizing a global network of computers to provide trusted information to the blockchain, this helps execute smart contracts on a blockchain, and we will go over use cases like smart contracts in more detail later. Nodes, validators, and oracles, are similar on at least a base level, they all verify information, some of this information is transactions on an individual blockchain, hashed by nodes or validators for that blockchain, and some information is relayed between blockchains, done by oracles. While some information does not even come from a blockchain, real-world data can also be sent onto a blockchain, things like weather reports and baseball game scores are needed to execute some smart contracts, Chainlink runs its oracle on the Ethereum blockchain, and provides the link between the blockchain and this real-world data.

(Illustration, next page)

We will go over nodes in more detail later when looking at decentralized blockchains, and we will go over oracles in more detail later when we look at use cases and layer 2 blockchains, for now just understand oracles can help a blockchain in several ways, but they are not incorporated in all blockchains. They only help blockchains that need to share information with other blockchains, or blockchains with use cases like smart contracts, in which case the blockchain may need real-world data outside its blockchain in order to execute some of these smart contracts.

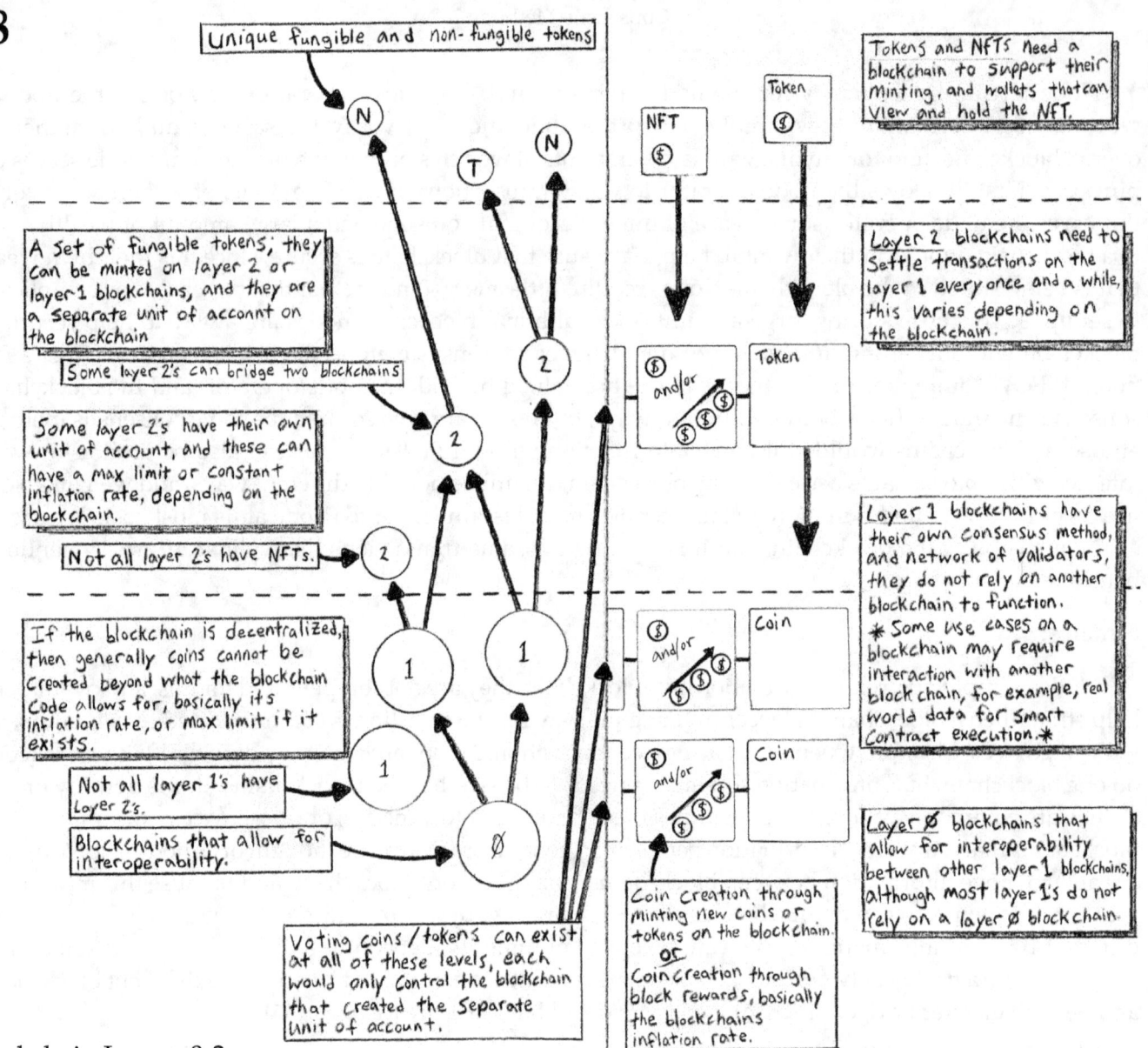

Blockchain Layers 0-2

Each layer relies on a lower layer for either transaction finality, or for security, layer 2 blockchains will settle on a layer 1 every so often, and some layer 1 blockchains rely on a layer zero for interoperability, or real-world data to execute smart contracts. Each blockchain layer has its own voting structure, and its own unit of account, along with either a max limit or inflation rate for that unit of account. Some blockchains even allow for the minting of tokens or NFTs, although this is not possible on all blockchains, and these unique units of account rely on the blockchain for transactions involving the token or NFT.

Pg. 3, upper section: These tokens and non-fungible tokens can be minted, or created, on a layer 1 or a layer 2 blockchain, these are separate units of account, and for NFTs there is unique information locked in the token, making it different from all other units of account on the blockchain.

Pg. 33, right section: Coins or tokens can be created in several ways depending on how the blockchains code is set up, layer 1 coins usually cannot create coins in excess of the inflation rate for the blockchain, unless an IP allowed for it, and mass token mints are possible, but again it depends on the validator network or voting structure of the blockchain.

Pg. 39, right section: Coin creation can be the set inflation rate of the blockchain, or it can be a rate of increase until a max limit is reached, and these are the most common ways coins are created on a blockchain, but there can also be a mass creation of coins, and these are not common for most blockchains, although they can happen if the blockchains code allows for it.

Pg. 39, upper section: Creating units of account through block rewards is not the same as creating fungible and non-fungible units of account on a blockchain, these tokens and NFTs are minted on a blockchain, they are usually involved in a use case on the blockchain, and they are not a part of the blockchains main unit of account.

Pg. 61, bottom section: Layer zero blockchains allow for interoperability between layer 1 blockchains, although not all layer 1 blockchains require a layer zero blockchain in order to function, and these layer zero blockchains are similar to bridges that may connect two layer 1 blockchains, but they are not exactly the same.

Pg. 67, bottom left section: Voting structures exist at each blockchain layer, layer zero and layer 1 blockchains usually have a set inflation rate, although layer 2 blockchains can be set up this way as well, and all layers could have a max limit for the number of units of account that can exist. These coins can be used in the voting structure of the blockchain, or a separate unit of account can be used, but it is important to understand that each blockchain will have some form of voting structure, and it is separate from other blockchain voting structures, even if they need to settle transactions on a lower level blockchain.

Pg. 83, right section: If the block reward rate for the blockchain is high, then validators will earn more block rewards, and they will likely sell some or all of the rewards at some point, this adds the coins or tokens into the circulating supply. This higher added supply will make it hard for the value of the coin or token to hold or increase in price over time, since there is a large, nearly constant sell pressure on the blockchains unit of account.

Pg. 119, upper section: NFTs minted on a blockchain are a separate unit of account on the blockchain, they are not similar to the main unit of account, and they are basically representations of the unique information locked in the NFT.

Consensus Method Vulnerabilities:

Validators and nodes in a blockchains consensus method can be used in a decentralized way, or a centralized way, and if the blockchain has centralized points of control in its consensus method, then that is a vulnerability for the blockchain overall. The control could be gained by a malicious actor, or could be controlled by developers and large investors, either way this centralized point of control could be used to negatively affect a blockchain, and decentralization it what prevents many types of attacks on a blockchain. We will go over decentralized POW and POS blockchains individually later, but for now just understand a blockchains consensus method can be a vulnerability for a blockchain if it is not decentralized enough. Although actually "hacking" a blockchain is possible with quantum computing, basically gaining the seed phrase which was explained earlier, it is not yet possible, but there are many other ways an attacker can try to manipulate and profit from a blockchain. One of these ways involves the consensus method of a blockchain, the hashing of transactions and approval of these transactions is the vulnerability. As mentioned before, a majority of validators can approve invalid transactions on a blockchain, basically, it is not the SHA (blockchain) that is being "hacked," it is the network of validators that secure the SHA's consensus method. Both POW and POS blockchains can have weak or centralized points that make it susceptible to attacks or exploitation, and this can be done several different ways. By either exploiting the consensus method's validator network, or its voting structure (through governance coins), or bridges between blockchains, and even physical centralized risks such as man-made or natural disasters that was mentioned earlier. We will go over several types of attacks for blockchains later while going over bridges and decentralization, but for now just understand a blockchain is only as secure as its weakest point, and for both POW and POS blockchains, gaining a majority control of the validators would allow someone or a group of people to more or less control the blockchain. This control could be something very noticeable such as, moving or creating coins, and preventing certain transactions from taking place, or it could be something most people would not notice or care about, like front running transactions that the validators know are about to take place. *(Reference page 2)* Either way blockchains can be manipulated in many ways, but it all comes back to whom the validators are and how decentralized they actually are. Also remember, it is not just validators that can be used to push invalid transactions, nodes can play a part too, and they are an easier avenue of attack for pushing invalid transactions since they are generally cheaper to set up than a validator. Although nodes do not have the same capabilities validators have, such as adding blocks to a blockchain that was explained earlier. *(Reference page 50)*

Everything mentioned before for POW and POS blockchains is what could allow them to be strong secure blockchains, where transactions are actually permissionless, and holding wealth in the coin of the blockchain would be relatively safe for investors. However, the way these blockchains are set up can also create a highly centralized and controlled blockchain, and these centralized points are what eventually will lead to the blockchains collapse or manipulation. Because as long as a vulnerability exists it will eventually be exploited, or it could lead to unintended outcomes that have the same effect as a planned or coordinated attack on a blockchain, and the consensus method for a blockchain is meant to be a way of preventing many of the types of attacks that exist. However, this technology is just a tool, it can be used in good ways and in bad ways just like any tool, and how the various aspects of a blockchains consensus method are set up is important. If done the wrong way, or a way with more vulnerabilities, then that blockchain is less safe as far as storing and securing wealth and data, but a decentralized network of validators would allow for the consensus method to work as designed, and would be a safe and secure way to store wealth and data. A shovel is designed to move earth, when used correctly it can plant gardens and dig wells, but it can also be used as a weapon, how a tool is used, not how it is designed is important, and how the consensus method of a blockchain is set up is also very important. It will either be used as intended, and decentralize the control, or it will be used as the form of control over the blockchain, and this is only one way a malicious actor can affect a blockchain, improvement proposals on a blockchain are another way, and we will look at how they work next.

Blockchain 202

How these blockchains work at basic generic levels, each blockchain is different, so these are still somewhat basic concepts that may or may not apply to all blockchain coins and tokens*

- Improvement Proposals, IPs
- Blockchain Users
- Blockchain Forks
- Coin Creation
- Consensus Methods and IPs
- Conclusion

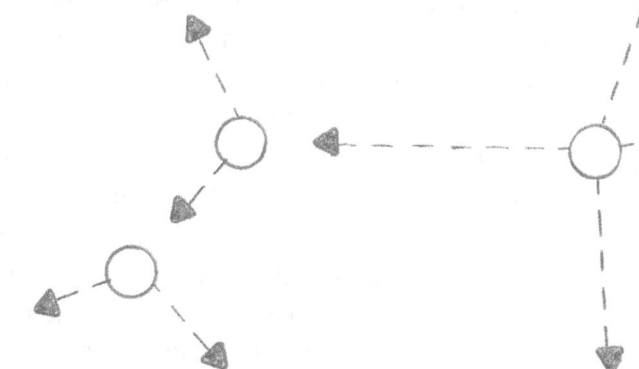

Improvement Proposals, IPs:

Improvement proposals are like updates to the blockchain code, they are part of building and maintaining a blockchain, and some blockchains allow for anyone to create and submit an improvement proposal on an individual blockchain. For Bitcoin, they are called BIPs, and for Ethereum they are called EIPs, once an improvement proposal, or IP, is created, it is voted on by those that have voting power on that blockchain, and we will go over this more next. But basically, if approved by the majority of the voters (some blockchain IPs have different thresholds for approval, like 70%, 80% etc.) then the update will be implemented on the blockchain. This allows for the users of a blockchain to be a part of its development, they can push for updates that add use cases to the blockchain, which we will go over in more detail later, and this ability for anyone to create an IP adds to the decentralized aspect of the blockchain overall.

POW IPs:

These updates and their voting structures vary between blockchains, and even the type of consensus method plays a part in how the IPs are voted on and implemented, validators that earn block rewards generally also have voting rights for POW blockchains, based on their hash power, or the percent of the total blockchains hash rate that they have. For POW blockchains, the validators are the miners and mining farms, they receive block rewards and can vote on IPs, they can vote for or against the IP, but they do not have to vote, and some blockchains require both a majority and a minimum number of votes to pass an IP. A simple example would be, a blockchain with 100 validators all with an equal vote, they vote on IPs for that blockchain, a simple majority approves the IP (51 validators), but what if only 30 validators vote, even if they all voted to pass the IP this would not be enough votes. The blockchain could require half of the votes that are cast to pass an IP, but then if only 30 validators voted it would only require 16 validators to pass an IP, not 51, this causes centralization and allows for an avenue of attack against the blockchain. We will go over this in more detail when explaining decentralization later, but for now just understand how IPs are passed on blockchains can vary in many ways, and each blockchain must take into account many variables when deciding where the thresholds for passing an IP should be set. Even how the validator is verifying transactions and creating blocks can affect the voting structure, for example in a POW blockchain, mining farms can pool their hash power, and this means the mining pool has the voting rights for the hash rate in the pool. This is because the pool receives and then distributes block rewards to individual mining farms, and this is why mining farms should look into the pool they send their hash power to. Making sure the pools opinions on what IPs should be passed and what ones should be rejected, are in line with the mining farms opinions, and if they are not, the mining farm can choose to send their hash power to another mining pool as described earlier.

POS IPs:

In a POS blockchain the voting structure would be the same, more or less, the stake pools are the validators for that blockchain, meaning the stake pool operator would be the one that can vote on IPs, however, because the staked coins are digital and not physical equipment like mining computers, these voting rights could be passed to individual stakeholders in some POS blockchains. This is where the validators of a blockchain start to lose voting rights and only receive block rewards as compensation, this is because voting can be done with tokens. Sometimes called governance coins, or voting coins/tokens, etc. and these coins or tokens can have value and be interchangeable with all other coins or tokens on the blockchain, or they can be unique coins that only allow the holder of the coin the ability to vote on IPs for that blockchain. *(Reference page 66)*

Remember coins are held on wallets, and wallets are accessed with keys or a unique sequence of numbers. This would essentially make the coins a secure voting system where it would be hard to gain control over these voting rights, and when voting coins are used in a blockchains IP voting structure they are usually held by the development team, this allows the team to quickly pass new updates that can affect the blockchain in many different ways. *(Reference page 9)* IPs can be just about anything, they can be bits of code that users don't notice, basically upgrades that are needed to maintain the blockchain, or they can be something more important like allowing for the unstaking of block rewards, an example would be the Ethereum blockchain and one of its EIPs. This allowed for some ETH coins to be withdrawn from pools that were previously locked until the upgrade took place, and these IPs can also be major changes to a blockchain. Such as the block reward payout to validators in a blockchain's consensus method, or even the switching of consensus methods, another example is the Ethereum blockchain moving from a POW to a POS consensus method. Developers are not the only ones that can hold these voting coins, they can also be given to large investors in a blockchain project, and can even be used for voting in a DAO, which we will go over in more detail later, and obviously a majority of these coins held by one or several people would create a centralized point of control. This is why some blockchains do not have a separate unit of account for their voting structures, they instead use the same coin or token that is traded on the blockchain, and we will go over the several types of voting coins and tokens in more detail later. *(Reference page 66)*

The more decentralized a blockchain is the better, as we have seen so far, centralization of validators in a blockchains consensus method can allow for these validators to gain the majority, or all, of the block rewards that are created when new blocks are added to the blockchain. This could also allow for the majority control of the voting structure of the blockchain, this would give the centralized validators the ability to change or update the blockchain code, and we will go over decentralization involving a blockchain's consensus method in more detail later. This centralization of validators in a consensus method would also allow the validators to ignore IPs from users of the blockchain, and this would allow the majority of the validators to pass IPs that users of the blockchain may not want, but ones that benefited the validators, or whoever operates them. These could be things like the inflation rate of the blockchain, basically the rate at which block rewards are issued, and these new coins are what validators receive for adding blocks to the blockchain as mentioned before. Increasing this rate would basically mean the validators of the consensus method would get paid more, something they would like, but not good for anyone else holding wealth in the coin or token of the blockchain. Each blockchain can be set up different as mentioned before, and we will go over IPs and the consensus method or voting structure that is used to approve them in more detail later as we go over several aspects of decentralization involving a blockchain's consensus method.

Blockchain Users:

There are several types of "users" of a blockchain, we will go over them in more detail later when we look at use cases, but simply put, there are people who actually use the blockchain, either minting NFTs, writing smart contracts, participating in DAOs, or creating IPs as mentioned before. But this also includes anyone holding wealth in the blockchain, or simply holding coins or tokens in a wallet on the blockchain. *(Reference page 96)* While some users want IPs that will allow them access to more use cases on the blockchain, others do not want the blockchain changed, and while most IPs are good for a blockchain, some updates could affect the holders of a coin or token. These users might not even interact with the blockchain in any way other than holding the coin of that blockchain in a wallet on that blockchain, such as a self-custody wallet, or even in a 3rd party wallet such as an exchange.

So how could IPs affect someone simply holding the coins of a blockchain, and sometimes not even in a self-custody wallet, they are not really "users" of the blockchain, in that they do not interact with the blockchain or its actual use cases, like smart contracts, etc. One way coin holders could be negatively affected by an IP would be something like, a centralized group of validators decides to increase the block rewards of the blockchain, this benefits the validators, but this is basically creating new coins at a faster rate, and this coin creation does not have to be in the form of block rewards, it could be the validators agreeing that thousands of coins suddenly exist in a wallet on the blockchain. *(Reference page 28)* Remember these coins represent a fraction of the blockchains total market cap, or the wealth stored in the blockchain, and creating these new coins (especially in large numbers) devalues all other coins, so even if all a person is doing is storing wealth in the blockchain they can still be affected by centralized validators that can vote on IPs. These centralized validators could move wealth from those holding coins on the blockchain to themselves, and they could do this several ways, either in the form of increasing block rewards, or in the form of mass token mints, and we will go over how this works in more detail later when we look at decentralization. This process is not that different from printing fiat and creating inflation, or the devaluing of the currency, and this is why keeping the consensus method decentralized is so important. However, coins cannot be simply created on some blockchains without creating what is called a hard fork of the blockchain, and we will go over the several types of forks that exist for blockchains next.

Blockchain Forks:

Improvement proposals create forks in a blockchains code, and they are just updates to the blockchain code, but there are two very different kinds of forks, a soft fork, and a hard fork, next let us look at what type of IPs create what type of blockchain forks. First, we will look at the more common type of fork, a soft fork, these are usually part of maintaining and developing a blockchain, and these types of updates might not affect users in any way, but they can also allow for new use cases on a blockchain. So not all soft forks are just background code updates, and soft forks are still voted on and implemented by those who have the majority voting control of the blockchain, and they are usually created by the development team to improve the blockchain in some way. A great analogy I heard from the MIT class can help us better understand the difference between soft and hard forks, think of the blockchain code as a circle, everything inside this circle is considered a valid transaction on the blockchain, when validators hash transactions on a blockchain if it is valid, it would be inside the circle, and if invalid it would be outside the circle.

(Illustration, next page)

Soft Fork:

A soft fork is creating a new circle within the existing circle, meaning everything within this new circle is valid for both blockchains, the "old" blockchain, and the "new" blockchain, which is the update implemented by the IP. Basically, the "rules" the blockchain follows have been updated in a way that does not break any existing rule, to do so would include an area outside the original circle. This is important because the validators of the blockchain all need to run the update in order to continue verifying transactions on the blockchain as explained earlier. Just like U-boats during WWII that needed to change the sequence of the rotors in their Enigma machine in order to decipher and send messages, but as mentioned before some validators set up their equipment and let it continue to run with little maintenance. A soft fork would allow for validators to continue verifying transactions even without the update, since most transactions would still be valid to a validator even without the update, however as discrepancies between validators occurred (more transactions involving the update) the validator without the update would begin to lose the chance to receive block rewards. This is because the majority of the validators would have run the update, and this is

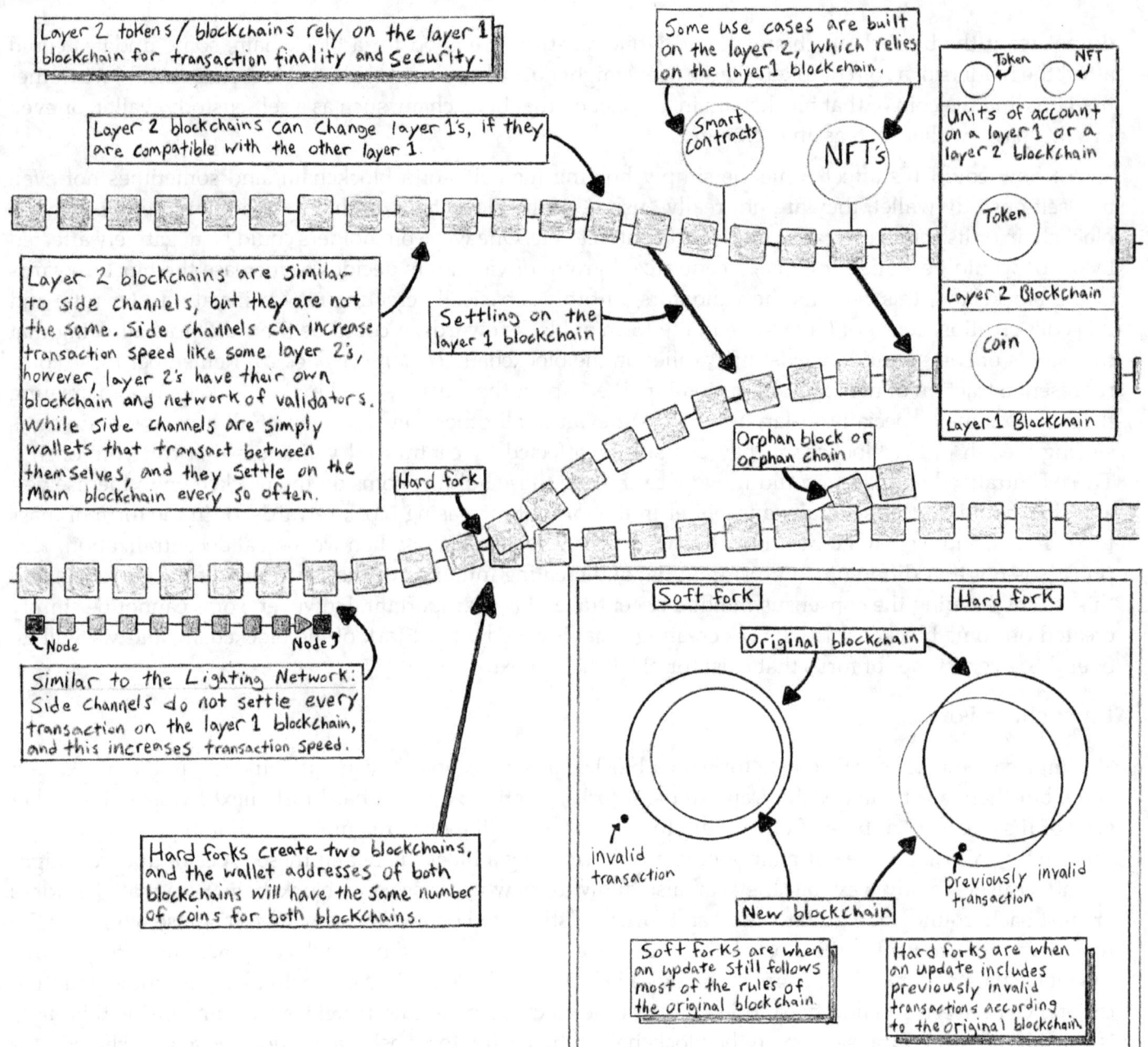

Circle Analogy, Hard / Soft Forks

Blockchain coins and tokens can be simply thought of as depicted, basically, layer 2 blockchains rely on a layer 1 blockchain for security or transaction finality, and other units of account such as NFTs or tokens can be created on some layer 2 blockchains. It is important to understand the difference between a layer 2 blockchain and a side channel, both might rely on a layer 1 blockchain, but layer 2 blockchains are a separate blockchain, with its own validators and unit of account, while side channels are basically a network of nodes within a blockchain's consensus method. These consensus methods can approve improvement proposals that split the blockchain, basically creating a hard fork, and although hard forks are not possible for all blockchains, they do involve the inclusion of previously invalid transactions. Basically, an area outside the original circle is now considered a valid transaction, this requires the validators of the blockchains consensus method to choose what version of the blockchain to support with its hash power, and this might affect the original blockchains consensus method depending on how many of its validators run the update.

Pg. 35, bottom section: When there is a hard fork of the blockchain, it means the creation of two distinct blockchains, basically the "new" circle crosses the original circle, and this includes previously invalid transactions, meaning validators for the blockchains consensus method must choose what blockchain they want to continue hashing transactions on.

Pg. 38, bottom right section: In this example, everything outside the original circle is an invalid transaction, including any transactions that involve a number of coins exceeding the 21 million max limit.

Pg. 100, bottom right section: The Bitcoin blockchain cannot have more than 21 million units of account, any BIP that included additional coins beyond the set inflation rate would create a separate blockchain, and Bitcoin mining farms would then choose what blockchain to continue hashing transactions for.

Pg. 101, bottom right section: If there is no numerical limit hard coded into the blockchain, then additional coins could be created with a soft fork, and this is because there is no violation of the blockchains code, or an area of the circle extending beyond the original circle.

Pg. 122, left section: Using nodes to increase transaction speed is similar to a layer 2 being used to increase transaction speed, but one is a separate blockchain, and the other is a network of nodes within the blockchain's consensus method.

what incentives a mining farm to run updates that are passed on a blockchain, however, it is something they must physically decide to do, or not do.

In this circle analogy, hard forks would be when the new circle crosses over the original circle, meaning, some transactions that would be thought of as invalid according to the original blockchain (outside the circle) would be considered valid in this "new" blockchain. This creates several problems for a blockchain's consensus method, especially a blockchain where the validators are somewhat decentralized, and might not run the update right away. One way developers can ensure validators of a blockchain run the update is to use something called a difficulty bomb, simply put, the "bomb" is a very complex equation, one that the validators will try to hash, or solve, but they will ultimately fail. This prevents the validators from continuing the "old" blockchain, or the blockchain without the updated code. By using a difficulty bomb developers can ensure the original blockchain is no longer being validated by mining farms or staking pools that may have forgotten to run the update, and in this scenario, after the hard fork there is still only one blockchain, and one coin or token acting as the unit of account for that blockchain.

Hard Fork:

Difficulty bombs are not used with all hard forks, and a hard fork is basically just an IP, which needs to be approved by the majority of the validators (or voters) of a blockchain. Hard forks used with a difficulty bomb usually are planned and approved by the development team, this would be similar to a soft fork in that after the update there is still only one blockchain and one coin or token acting as the unit of account for that blockchain. But most hard forks are associated with an update that "splits" the blockchain into two separate blockchains, each with its own coin or token acting as the unit of account for each blockchain. There are several ways this type of hard fork can happen, it usually involves a group of validators wanting to change or update the blockchain code in some way, but most of the other validators do not agree and do not vote to implement the update. These can be a significant percent of the total validators for a blockchain, or it could be just a few, either way validators of the blockchain are not in agreement, and some validators decide to approve the update anyway, this is what creates two distinct blockchains, and this is what difficulty bombs prevent from happening. However, this is not a majority of the validators for the blockchain, if the majority agreed then they would just approve the IP and include a difficulty bomb to prevent the second blockchain from being created. Usually this is a minority of the validators, but still a significant percent, and the fewer validators there are the easier it will be to attack the "new" blockchain.

For the "new" blockchain the same factors involved in a consensus method and having as many validators as possibly, applies to the new blockchain as well, if it has only a few validators it is more centralized and vulnerable to attack, even though the "original blockchain" would be able to prevent the same types of attacks. This is because they are now two completely different blockchains, as mentioned before a SHA is just a curved line on a graph, the IP changed the SHA, and it is now a slightly different curved line on a graph. *(Reference page 9)* This is because the "new" blockchain might consider a transaction outside the original circle a valid one, basically the "new" circle crosses over the original circle, and validators at this point must choose what blockchain they want to hash transactions on and earn block rewards from. *(Reference page 34)* The original blockchain (without the update) remains the same, it may lose 10%, 20%, etc. of its hash rate to the new blockchain, but other than that the original blockchain remains the same. While the new, or updated blockchain, is basically a copy of the original blockchain (not including whatever was updated), and its ledger of wallets and amount of coins or tokens in each is the same at first. But as buy and sell orders for both begin to be settled, and coins begin moving between wallets, the coin or token representing the two blockchains will start to be worth different amounts in dollar terms. Wallet holders of the original blockchain will now have the same number of coins for both blockchains, since the updated blockchain is just a copy of the original. They can then choose to hold or sell the new coins, basically presented with the same choice the validators had, choose what version of the blockchain you agree with, and sell the coins of the one you disagree with, although someone could hold both if they wanted to, or sell both, it comes down to what the wallet holder wanted to do. And remember this would only apply to self-custody wallets on the blockchain,

3rd party wallets would be the ones gaining these new coins on your behalf, and it would be up to them to allow you access to these new coins or not. Basically, hard forks would be bad for the value of both coins in the short term, since some people would buy or sell both of the coins, and this would add to price volatility for a while. However, it is possibly for both blockchains to develop and grow in dollar value over time, and a hard fork does not mean one of the blockchains will fail, but unless the new blockchain gains validators, its consensus method will be more vulnerable to attack.

Two Examples of Hard Forks:

There are two examples of hard forks where both blockchains continued but for very different reasons, and there are several types of hard forks, but let us look at these two hard forks in a little more detail, and understand why these hard forks happened and how both blockchains were able to continue and grow over time. The first hard fork we will look at is the Ethereum and Ethereum Classic hard fork that happened in July 2016, there was a lot happening behind the scenes and developers had several options, but they eventually decided on creating a hard fork of the blockchain. But it may not have been the best decision, and some people still disagree on exactly how and why the hard fork happened, but this is the version of the story I believe to be true, and I will keep it short and simple.

Ethereum and Ethereum Classic:

The Ethereum blockchain was exploited and a large number of coins were moved to the hacker's wallet, the vulnerability was fixed, but the coins were still in the hacker's wallet, and developers knew where the coins were (they could view the wallet on the Ethereum blockchain), but they had a decision to make as far as what to do next. They did not want to risk the chance of all the coins being sold at once, this would flood the circulating supply and cause the dollar value of the ETH coin to fall, and there were a few other reasons a decision had to be made, but either way there were really only 2 options for the Ethereum developers. Hard fork the blockchain with an update that basically said the "stolen" coins would no longer be accepted on the Ethereum blockchain, or use the majority of the validators (most were controlled by the development team in some way) to forcibly move the coins out of the hacker's wallet. Basically updating the ledger of accounts, crediting the coins back to the original wallet, and debiting the coins from the hacker's wallet, but this would be approving an invalid transaction on the blockchain. This was a tough decision for the Ethereum developers, obliviously a hard fork would be bad for the blockchain, some validators might stick with the original blockchain and not run the update that blocked the coins, and wallets suddenly having two different ETH coins would cause price volatility as many people sold the coins they did not want, adding sell pressure to both blockchains. However, the only alternative would be to use the majority of the consensus method to force these coins back to their original wallets, and this would let people know that the developers had this amount of control over the Ethereum blockchains consensus method. Whether or not the developers had this ability is debated, but they ended up choosing to go with a hard fork of the blockchain, and not everyone agreed with this new update, which was basically blocking these coins off from the rest of the blockchain.

Some ETH miners sided with the person who had exploited the Ethereum blockchain, this was back when Ethereum was still POW, and they decided to continue running the original blockchain without the update, this created Ethereum Classic (ETC), and the hacker set up more mining farms that would run this version of the blockchain. Basically, adding to the number of validators in its version of the consensus method, although perhaps not enough because over the years the Ethereum Classic blockchain has suffered several 51% attacks. Some people supported ETC because they believe in what is commonly called "code is law" or simply the exploit existed, and that means if someone is able to exploit the code, any wealth gained should be theirs to keep. People have many opinions about this hard fork, but at the end of the day, Ethereum did not lose many validators and was not impacted that much in the long run, it has continued to develop and grow far faster than ETC. While Ethereum Classic has had many problems, mostly from attacks and less development on this version of the blockchain, although the hacker setting up additional mining farms to keep this version of the blockchain going is probably why it is still around today, and ETC today is also developing and growing just at a slower rate than ETH, choosing to focus on immutability or "code is law."

Bitcoin and Bitcoin Cash:

The second hard fork we will look at is the Bitcoin and Bitcoin Cash hard fork that happened in August 2017, Bitcoin Classic was also trying to increase Bitcoins block size around this time, and sometimes this period is called the block size "battle." Bitcoin has a block size of 1MB, while Bitcoin Cash has a block size of 32MB, and these blocks are just grouped transactions that have been validated by the consensus method for the blockchain as mentioned before. The larger block size allows for more transactions per block, meaning faster transaction speed, and some of the Bitcoin community believed Bitcoin needed to become the "electronic cash system" that was mentioned in the Bitcoin white paper, and this means increasing the block size to allow for the faster transaction speed, which other blockchains are able to achieve. However, this increased block size meant nodes would not be so inexpensive to set up, basically the additional hardware and energy required to set up and run a node would be greater with a block size of 32MB. This means there would be fewer nodes set up, since nodes cannot receive block rewards as compensation for their energy and equipment costs. As mentioned before, nodes play a part in the consensus method of a blockchain, they are pushing and pulling transactions to and from other nodes and actual validators of the consensus method. This adds to the decentralized aspect of the blockchain, and we will look at how nodes add to this decentralization later, but for now just understand there were many somewhat small changes to Bitcoins original code, and several communities supported their own side or version of the original Bitcoin blockchain.

There were many that supported this idea, and Bitcoin Cash has a development team and a community that supports it, most of the original Bitcoin code remains the same, for example Bitcoin Cash has a max limit of 21 million coins like Bitcoin, with about 2 million coins left to be mined, and it has a halving similar to Bitcoins halving schedule which we will go over later. With the code being so similar why did BCH lose value compared to BTC over the years, some miners moved to Bitcoin Cash early on, and many still mine it today, they go back and forth between BCH and BTC, and we'll look at why they do this in a bit. The simplified reason is the majority of the Bitcoin community have a very hard line when it comes to hard forking the original Bitcoin code, these supporters sold the "new" Bitcoin Cash coins they had, and held onto the Bitcoin, this along with the crypto bear market is what caused both Bitcoin and Bitcoin Cash to drop in dollar value, although Bitcoin Cash hasn't recovered like Bitcoin has so far.

This is a perfect example of what gives a blockchain coin or token its value, the code is almost the same, there is even the same limit on the number of coins that can exist, and they have the same halving schedule. Yet Bitcoin is trading in the 10s of thousands of dollars while Bitcoin Cash is trading in the hundreds of dollars, and during the last bull run, when Bitcoin was topping out around 70k, Bitcoin Cash was topping out around 1k. This is simply because there are more people holding their wealth in Bitcoin, the market cap is much higher, and even though Bitcoin Cash made it to about 5k dollars during the hard fork, the added sell pressure on Bitcoin Cash, along with a lack of buy pressure, caused the coins dollar value to collapse and never really run up to the values that Bitcoin has over the last crypto bull cycle in 2021.

Overall, Bitcoin was not really affected by this hard fork in the long term, in the short term the price did fall as the crypto bear market started, but it would eventually recover to new all-time highs. Bitcoin Cash however, has not reached its prior highs, and its hash power is about 1/10 of Bitcoins (as mentioned before, fewer validators in a blockchains consensus method increases the chances of a 51% attack), its trading volume and coin pairs are also lower than Bitcoins, and we will go over how these can affect a coin or tokens value later. For now, just understand Bitcoin Cash has lower usage and adoption, in both mining farms, basically those who are willing to mine BCH, and traders or holders, basically individuals who are willing to buy and hold BCH, put simply, there are just more people who stuck with Bitcoins original blockchain.

Although, this does not mean Bitcoin is better than Bitcoin Cash, or vice versa, these are now separate blockchains, and run independently of each other, this means both can grow and develop at different rates or in different directions. Although most Bitcoin miners originally stuck with BTC, and continued using their hash power to secure Bitcoin's consensus method, over time some small mining farms started moving their hash rate between the two when difficulty adjustments made mining Bitcoin Cash more profitable in dollar terms, and we will go into difficulty adjustments for the Bitcoin blockchain later. There are many more factors involved with hard forks, and each one is different depending on the blockchain and what update is being implemented, some hard forks will see both blockchains continue for one reason or another, and hard forks implemented with a difficulty bomb will prevent the old version of the blockchain from continuing at all.

Simple Hard Fork Examples:

Hard forks can be thought of as a way to prevent the devaluing of a coin or token by creating additional coins or tokens for the blockchain, so let's look at an overly simplified blockchain and see how coin creations can happen on different blockchains, and why hard forks prevent this from happening on some blockchains. Imagine the first blockchain has a limit of coins that can exist on the blockchain, for this example we will use a limit of 21 million coins, and this is hard coded into the blockchain, going back to the circle analogy this would mean the existence of even one additional coin would be thought of as outside the circle, violating the blockchain code, and viewed as an invalid transaction on the blockchain. *(Reference page 34)* In order to increase the number of coins that can exist on the blockchain an IP would have to be approved, it would have to be a hard fork since the new circle would cross the original circle including previously invalid transactions. In this case, the number of coins that exceeded the original limit, and unless a difficulty bomb prevented the original blockchain from being run by validators, this would create two blockchains and two unique coins. As we saw with the two prior hard fork examples, this is not necessarily a bad thing for the original coin, and these additional coins would only exist on the updated blockchain, the original blockchain would not see inflationary pressures based on the new coin limit.

Another example blockchain does not have a max limit of coins hard coded into its blockchain, invalid transactions attempting to create "new" coins could still be rejected by the consensus method for the blockchain, and this is because the coins can be traced back to their creation. The SHA is still very secure and not susceptible to manipulation (if decentralized enough), however, this means new coins could be added to the ledger of accounts as long as the majority of the validators agree to the update, in this case the coin creation. Now if the validators of the blockchains consensus method do not agree on this update, then there could still be a hard fork that creates two blockchains. But if the validators do agree, then the coins can be created, and this would be considered a soft fork, because there was no limit for coins included in the blockchain code, or circle, and this update adding coins would not violate any existing rules, or include areas outside of the circle. This is how some blockchains create and destroy coins, stablecoins have this ability, and we will go over them later, but other blockchains with coins not fixed to a set price could also have this ability. And as coins are added to the circulating supply the value of each coin becomes less, because the market cap, more or less remains the same, while the supply of coins representing that market cap is increased.

Now imagine the same scenario, no max limit for coins is coded into the blockchain, and there is an IP that creates additional coins or tokens, but these coins are not immediately sold into the circulating supply, they are held on one or several wallets on the blockchain, and we'll go into how circulating supply can affect the dollar value of a coin or token later. But for now, just understand that coins can be created and not affect the dollar value of the coin, but this is because those coins are held in a hard wallet on that blockchain, they are not in the many exchanges being bought and sold, or basically the circulating supply. This is not how coins are usually created though, they do not sit in a hard wallet and never move into circulating supply. They are either given to development teams and early investors as compensation or payment, and when these coins are sold by the developers or early investors the coins are added into the circulating supply, lowering the value of the coin, unless there is added demand for the coin. There are several methods to get coins into circulating supply, air drops are another way, and we will go over air drops more later. But no matter what way these coins are added into circulation, the purpose is to set up a market of both buyers and sellers, and coins held outside this market would be basically removed from the supply and demand ratio. This is basically a balancing act, new coins can be added to the circulating supply when there is higher demand, and this won't cause the value of the coin to fall. But there are many additional factors involved in the value of a coin or token that should be taken into account, and we will go over several of them in more detail later.

Coin Creation:

Being able to create additional units of wealth is not a good trait to have for a currency, fiat or blockchain, and the ability to create additional coins on a blockchain, or the ability to add units of account to the ledger of accounts that is the blockchain, will end up devaluing the coin or token, and this is because the market cap is the same, but the number of coins that get a share of that market cap has increased. If demand also increased, then we might not see a drop in the coin's value, and this is why mainstream adoption helps a blockchain grow, there is added demand for both use cases on the blockchain, and for the unit of account of the blockchain. Another way to increase the value of the coin or token is to reduce the supply, or at least the supply that is available to be bought and sold, and this would be similar to staking pools in a POS blockchain. Basically, the coins are locked in the pool and cannot be lent out or borrowed against in any way as detailed before, they are simply removed from the circulating supply, and with demand being constant the value of the coin would increase. This is basic supply and demand, however there are many variables at play here, for instance stakeholders in a POS blockchain can remove their coins from the pool and realize any wealth gain, but this would be adding those coins back into circulating supply. The same is true for long-term "hodlers," they may not move coins out of a wallet for years, but once the value of the coins has grown to a certain level, a person may decide to sell and realize this increase in wealth, and this would also be adding the coins back into the circulating supply. "HODL" comes from the misspelling of the word hold, a social media post with the misspelling became popular, and it became an acronym for, Hold On for Dear Life, referring to Bitcoins early price volatility.

Basically, the creation of additional coins or tokens on a blockchain will result in the value of the coin or token dropping, unless demand for the coin is increased, or if many coins are removed and held outside the circulating supply. This is similar to a POS blockchain and its staking pools, or anyone that holds coins for long periods of time on a self-custody wallet, and this type of coin creation only applies to IPs that may or may not happen. While the inflation rate for a blockchain is a set rate at which coins can be created, these are block rewards as mentioned before, and we will go over how a fixed inflation rate for a blockchain is not necessarily a bad thing later on.

New coins created on a blockchain usually come from the set limit, or set inflation rate, of coins and tokens that represent the unit of account for that blockchain, and simply creating coins or tokens as mentioned before is not a part of this limit or rate of increase. *(Reference page 28)* The inflation rate of the blockchain would be decided on by the developers at first, but it could be changed later by the majority of the validators, or whoever has majority voting power on the blockchain. This could be the development team depending on how the blockchains voting structure is set up, however if malicious actors were able to gain this majority control of the consensus method, they could use this control to exploit the blockchain, and we go over this in more detail when we look at decentralization. It is important to note, these coin creations are not the same as minting NFTs on a blockchain, or even minting unique tokens on a blockchain, this type of coin creation would be adding to the unit of account for the blockchain itself, not a use case built on the blockchain, and we will look at NFTs and layer 2 tokens in more detail later. *(Reference page 28)* For now, just understand how coins are created on a blockchain is important, earlier we looked at coins being created in the form of block rewards, now we know coins can also be created through an improvement proposal, and these types of coin creations are on one blockchain, or SHA. Basically the layer 1 blockchain, and NFT or token mints are a separate and distinct unit of account on the blockchain, although their transactions are still usually settled on the layer 1 blockchain, and we will go over separate units of account like NFTs and tokens in more detail later. *(Reference page 120)* As mentioned before, blockchains can be set up in many different ways, creating additional coins on some blockchains is not possible, for other blockchains it is possible, it depends on many factors like the blockchain's consensus method, and so far, we have gone over POW and POS, but next we will briefly look at several other types of consensus methods.

Consensus Methods and IPs:

As we have seen, improvement proposals are voted on and implemented by either the consensus method of the blockchain, or by whatever voting structure the blockchain has like voting coins, tokens, etc. These IPs can be background updates that do not affect users of the blockchain or the value of the unit of account for that blockchain, or they can be major updates that can affect many aspects of the blockchain, and these IPs are what create soft and hard forks of the blockchain as mentioned before. Soft forks are basically updates implemented by the developers of the blockchain, while hard forks can create two distinct blockchains, but not when implemented with a difficulty bomb. Hard forks that do create two blockchains can happen several ways, and they can be good or bad for both blockchains, depending on the update and many other factors. As mentioned before the Ethereum Classic blockchain was able to survive and grow because more miners, or validators, were brought online, while Bitcoin Cash was also able to grow because it had a community of supporters, and it also saw some hash power move from BTC to BCH. Although both of these forks had far lower hash rates compared to their original blockchain, this lower number of validators for the consensus method allows for an avenue of attack against the blockchain, and it is important to remember this type of attack is not "hacking" the SHA, it is exploiting the weakened consensus method and its few validators. This can be done by either pushing invalid transactions, or approving IPs and changing the blockchain code in a way that would benefit the malicious actors. This is why the way a blockchains consensus method is set up is so important, it is one of several ways to attack the blockchain and negatively affect it, as mentioned before there are two main consensus method types, POW and POS, but there are more consensus methods being developed, and we will briefly look at a few other examples next.

Other Consensus Methods:

There are many consensus method types, this is because a consensus method is just an agreement between validators or nodes that are verifying transactions on a blockchain as mentioned before. They can come to this agreement in many ways, and there are checks and balances in each type of consensus method that protect the blockchain from invalid transactions. By either rewaring "good" validators, usually through block rewards, while "bad" validators will be punished by causing them to lose wealth, or the chance to earn block rewards as compensation for their expenses. In POW this is pretty clear, mining farms that do not include invalid transactions are given block rewards to compensate them for the equipment and energy costs required to hash transactions on the POW blockchain. While with POS, the staking pools hold wealth in a pool and receive block rewards as compensation, but if the pool attempts to include invalid transactions, then slashing will destroy some or all of the wealth in the pool as mentioned before. *(Reference page 23)* This balance of rewarding good actors with block rewards, and punishing bad actors by causing them to lose wealth in one way or another, is what each type of consensus method tries to achieve, and this balance can be done many ways. The Helium blockchain is trying to achieve this balance in a unique way, not like POW or POS, so let us look at how the Helium blockchain works in a little more detail.

Helium Blockchain:

The first thing we will look at is the hardware that secures the Helium blockchain, the information is open-source, so anyone can build a Helium miner if they have the knowledge to do so, but there are several companies that build Helium miners that anyone can buy. These miners are not like most POW miners, they do not require large amounts of energy, they produce little heat, and they cannot be grouped together into a mining farm to increase their hash power. Helium miners resemble routers, they are pretty small and designed to be set up by many people in densely populated areas, and this type of consensus method is sometimes called proof of coverage. The idea is to have many individually controlled Helium miners spread out over major cities, these miners are pushing and pulling data from each other much like validators and nodes do, and they receive block rewards in the form of the HNT coin. This allows for data to move fast and for low cost in areas where many of the Helium miners are set up, and the end game is to eventually have these miners set up across all urban areas, and around the world, this would allow companies to use the network to move data faster, cheaper, and more securely than they do today. *(Reference page 50)*

Companies or individuals that want to access or send data through this network do so by buying data credits, and in order to buy these data credits HNT coins must be burned, basically destroying them and reducing the supply of coins that exist. This means that companies must first buy the HNT coin, adding to demand for the coin, and then use the HNT to create the data credits, destroying the HNT coin and reducing its supply in the process. This destruction of the HNT coin is good because it offsets the new coins that are being created by all the Helium miners, and they only receive about 1/3 of all block rewards for the Helium blockchain. There are also large investors who receive about 1/3 of the block rewards as well, this is basically like staking wealth to a POS pool and earning block rewards, however the Helium developers did not sell these coins to early investors, they instead sold them security tokens that represent the block rewards and wealth that is locked up. This is a little redundant because they could have just sold the actual HNT coins and had them locked up in a staking pool, this is less complicated than issuing a security token, that at the end of the day just represents other coins and their block rewards. However, they did this because rules and regulations around blockchain coins and tokens have not been defined yet, and the security tokens allowed the developers to let investors invest wealth in the blockchain project without getting randomly sued by the SEC, like several other blockchain projects have been over the last few years.

We will go into the "token-omics" for a blockchain coin or token later, for now let's look at several of these factors for the Helium blockchain, basically token-omics is taking in many of the factors unique to a certain blockchain coin or token, and seeing how these separate factors interact and affect the blockchain overall. For the Helium blockchain, there is a max limit of coins that can exist, 223 million HNT coins, and block rewards are distributed between the Helium miners, large investors who own security tokens, and validators that ensure the Helium miners are not approving invalid transactions on the blockchain. These block rewards are split into about thirds between these parties, and their rewards are reduced by 50% every two years by the halving schedule, which will see the last block reward issued in about 50 years. There is also a fee structure for data usage, this involves the data credits mentioned earlier, and the governance structure for approving improvement proposals is governance tokens controlled by the development team and the community, with hopes that in the future the Helium network will be completely controlled by the community, or holders of the HNT coin.

This is a simple and brief overview of the Helium blockchain, but it is an example of a consensus method that is not POW or POS, although it is still being developed the concept seems to work, and more Helium miners are being set up across many cities, allowing for others to use the network to move data faster and cheaper. However, there are some obstacles that need to be navigated, burning HNT coins for data credits could outgrow the rate at which new coins are issued as block rewards, and this would make the HNT coin deflationary. This would be good for investors and holders of the HNT coin, but it would make the data credits harder to get and more expensive, and this might affect usage and adoption of the Helium network. This has led to some of the community wanting to increase the block reward limit and issuance to some validators, this could further offset the coin burning, and it might be able to find a balance, but that will only happen with further development of the blockchain. While Amazon has a similar idea called the Amazon Sidewalk Initiative, so even if the Helium blockchain cannot achieve its goals of moving data faster and cheaper at scale in a decentralized way, then others in the industry will likely create something similar to the Helium blockchain, although maybe in a more centralized and controlled way.

This is just one example, and I would suggest further research for anyone looking to better under the Helium blockchain. But there are many more consensus methods being developed and tested, some are being used by blockchains today, and some are still just ideas or concepts that will be developed in the years to come. Although there is no guarantee that these new consensus methods will work and be able to secure a blockchain and prevent invalid transactions on that blockchain. Next, let us briefly look at a few other consensus method types that are being developed.

Proof of Time:

Proof of space and time (sometimes called proof of capacity) is basically rewarding data storage providers and charging for data storage services, this is basically how Filecoin works, FIL, anyone who has data storage space can participate, and they are paid for securely storing data that they cannot manipulate in any way. If they do, they will lose out on the chance to earn block rewards in the form of the FIL coin, and this creates a very secure way to store data, which is starting to create demand for this type of data storage. The blockchains unit of account is the FIL coin, storage providers are paid in FIL, and people that want to store data on this blockchain need to pay in FIL. This creates a market of buyers and sellers for the coin, and this along with demand for the coin, or its use case (in this case data storage) is what will cause the coin to hold its value, or even grow in value, and this is common for most consensus method types, there needs to be a balance between those receiving coins and eventually selling them, and those buying coins for whatever use case the coins have on the blockchain.

Proof of Authority:

Proof of authority (sometimes called proof of reputation) is very similar to a POS blockchain, however with POS anyone can become a validator for the blockchain by setting up their own stake pool, but with proof of authority, only known and "trusted nodes" can verify transactions on the blockchain. There can be many nodes (or validators in my opinion, since they create blocks on the blockchain), but these nodes are operated and controlled by these trusted and selected parties, which are often the development team or early investors. This type of consensus method is more centralized, however this allows for faster transaction speed, which some use cases on a blockchain require, there are many pros and cons to more centralized consensus methods, and we will go over this more when we look at the "blockchain trilemma" later on. *(Reference page 88)*

Unique Node List:

Another consensus method is called a unique node list, Ripple, XRP, uses this consensus method, and it is basically using nodes that do not receive block reward compensation to verify transactions for the blockchain. Validators have many nodes on their list of nodes, basically the nodes simply hash transactions and respond with whether it thinks the transaction is valid or not, and validators send the same transaction to many different nodes. If a transaction has only a few or none of the nodes verify it, then the validator can assume the transaction is invalid and remove it from the next block of the blockchain, or add it to the block if most or all the nodes think it is a valid transaction. This is obviously an over simplified explanation of how the XRP blockchain works, and XRP holders have been affected by the SEC's lawsuit against Ripple since late 2020, so the development of the blockchain has slowed since then, and I would encourage further research for anyone looking to better understand how the XRP blockchain uses nodes and validators in its consensus method.

Vulnerabilities exist for all consensus methods, and how the blockchain comes to this consensus can be done many ways, some are more decentralized and some are more centralized, but as long as the validators in the consensus method are able to prevent attacks on the blockchain (such as an invalid transaction) then the consensus method is strong. Although this only applies if there are "good" validators, and ensuring there are enough good validators to counter possible bad validators will be explained later when we go deeper into decentralization. For now, just understand that not only does the consensus method need to be able to prevent invalid transactions, but it must also be able to protect itself from its own validators that may try to push invalid transactions into blocks deliberately. This basically means a consensus method needs to be developed and tested before it can be accepted as "safe," and this does not mean that all new types of consensus methods are bad. But there are many variables at play in each blockchain, and even a good and proven consensus method such as POW or POS can be set up with too few validators and be more susceptible to manipulation. However, new consensus methods will allow for new use cases on a blockchain, and some of these consensus methods will require validators that receive block rewards. This will create new opportunities for people and companies to make a profit off securing a blockchain by validating transactions on that blockchain. This makes a consensus method one of many aspects to blockchain technology that will continue to develop and grow in the years to come, with new ideas being tested and developed over time.

Conclusion:

Everything we have covered so far may or may not apply to all blockchain coins and tokens, it would depend on how the blockchain and its consensus method is set up, much of what we have covered is just the basics, and we will build on these concepts when going into more detail on several individual aspects of decentralization next. For now, just understand the encryption of information on a blockchain involves the seed phrase, or the numbers it represents, and the transaction taking place on the blockchain, both are hashed together at least once. This makes the SHA very hard to hack, and this is why blockchains are usually exploited by attacking another part of the blockchain, by either exploiting the validator network or voting structure for example, and this is why decentralization is so important, it is what protects aspects of the blockchain like the consensus method. These consensus methods are made up of validators and nodes, and they can vary in many ways, the validators could be physical hardware hashing transactions, or the validators could be software, basically stake pools hashing transactions based on the number of coins staked to the pool. However, these are not the only two consensus methods, and validators can be used in many different ways depending on how the blockchains consensus method is set up, there can even be aspects from both that are incorporated into one blockchain, and we will look at a few examples later.

There can be disagreements between validators or even the community that supports a blockchain, this could cause a hard fork of the blockchain, and while a hard fork that creates two distinct blockchains is not necessarily a bad thing, it is not ideal and causes volatility in both blockchains network of validators, and the value of their units of account. However, the ability for validators to decide what version of the blockchain they support is important, if the blockchain did not allow for individual validators then there would be a centralized form of control, in that there are some restrictions on who can become a validator for that blockchain, and this control is usually held by the development team if it exists. *(Reference page 88)* We will go over this in detail when looking at the many aspects of decentralization for a blockchain next, what we have gone over so far can be thought of as basic addition and subtraction when it comes to blockchain technology, and understanding decentralization or other use cases on a blockchain would be like learning multiplication and division. *(Reference page 96)* We will keep the "high school" level theme when going over decentralization and Bitcoins blockchain, and I encourage further research for anyone looking to understand certain aspects of blockchain technology in more detail. For now, we will look at identifying points of control involved in many aspects of a blockchain, and how they are used to determine if the blockchain is decentralized or not.

Decentralization

The many different aspects of decentralization for blockchain technology*
- Introduction
- Decentralized Consensus Method
- Decentralized Voting Structure
- Other Aspects of Decentralization
- Decentralized External Factors
- Decentralization is Not Exact
- Advantages of Decentralized Blockchains
- Decentralization Conclusion

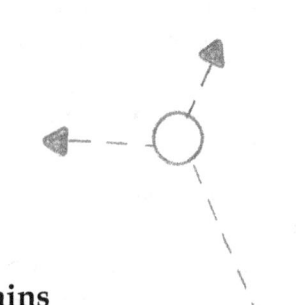
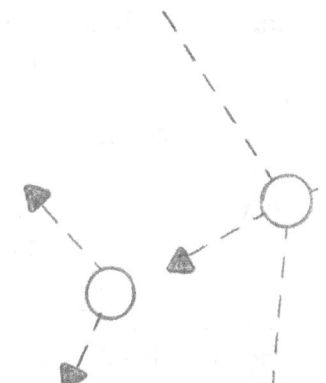

Introduction:

Decentralization for blockchain technology basically means, what centralized points of "control or failure" exist on that blockchain, these can be many different things, and they can involve just about any aspect of the blockchain. Many times, these points are unknown or not understood by the blockchain developers at first, this is what leads to a blockchain being exploited or "hacked," but they can also be something like too much transaction volume on the blockchain, causing transaction fees to increase, or even causing the blockchain to go offline, stopping all transactions. Both of these outcomes negatively affect the blockchain, but one is a bad actor exploiting the blockchain, while the other is not deliberate, and as a blockchain grows and develops it will continue to find and solve these problems that may develop over time, from added users, to added transaction volume, etc. and these can be thought of as the "failure" side in the point of control or failure. The "control" side would be points where the development team know the possibility of the vulnerability exists, this is what leads them to controlling this aspect themselves, and this is usually a good thing because it would prevent bad actors from exploiting the centralized point. However, this does not stop the point of control from existing, developers come and go, just because someone has this control, and they are not using it in a negative way today, it does not mean that the control will not be used in a negative way tomorrow, and if bad actors are able to gain this control, then they can obviously use it to exploit the blockchain in whatever way they can with the type of control they have.

So, decentralization can be thought of as having the fewest centralized points of control or failure, the fewer the better, but not all centralized points of control directly threaten the blockchain itself, just certain aspects of the blockchain, which we will go over next. There is decentralization/centralization in almost all areas of a blockchain, each blockchain is set up different as mentioned before, and even blockchains with the same type of consensus method can have different levels of centralization. The majority of blockchain coins and tokens today are not very decentralized, and we will go over Bitcoin and its decentralization later, but in general most coins and tokens that claim to be decentralized are only decentralized in name, that is they just claim to be decentralized. Most blockchains have centralized points of control or failure, in one or many areas of the blockchain, and a centralized point might not affect the voting structure or transaction validation of a blockchain, but it could allow for manipulation of a certain aspect of the blockchain, and this makes some centralized points more important, or less important, to developers and users of the blockchain. This is because some centralized points can affect major aspects of a blockchain, such as validators in its consensus method, and this could affect block rewards, transaction approvals, even the dollar value of the coin or token. While other centralized points might only give developers the control over what coins and tokens can be listed on a DeFi exchange, and we will look at Uniswap as an example in more detail later. For now, just understand some centralized points of control are not necessarily a bad thing for a blockchain, and they don't really affect the blockchain enough to cause the value of the coin to increase or decrease, but they do have some form of control, and what that control is may or may not be important for some users of the blockchain.

Some use cases on a blockchain may require more centralization, that is they require the development team or large investors to maintain some form of control over some aspect of the blockchain, but this is not always the case, and the fewer centralized points of control or failure there are for a blockchain, the better it is, and the more decentralized it is. This is my rough definition of "decentralization" it is not just measuring one or two aspects of a blockchain, but it takes into account many factors, and weighs their importance on how much they "could" affect the blockchain, if used in a negative way, either deliberately or unintentionally. I believe the bulk of what I will go over is the most important parts of decentralization for a blockchain, there are many smaller areas that could be included as well, but I think these are the main areas to focus on, and they are what I built the Arizona Blockchain Standards around. It is basically accounting for a blockchains level of decentralization, and using that to disclose risk to investors in that blockchains coin or token, and I will go over this in more detail later. It is important to know that the definition of decentralization for blockchain is still being decided on by many in the industry today, basically, what coins and tokens are "decentralized" is still being argued, since this label is what somewhat protects a blockchain project from being sued by the SEC. Many blockchain projects will call themselves decentralized to both attract investors, and to avoid security laws, and we will look at this a little more later when we look at interpreting the Howey test for blockchain coins and tokens. It is also important to remember some of these centralized points can exist for a long time before they are exploited, an example would be the voting structure of a blockchain, the control would be approving IPs on the blockchain, but the blockchain will not be affected until the majority holder of the voting power actually implemented a change or update to the blockchain code. Meaning some centralized points of control can exist and not affect the blockchain in a negative way, until this control is used. Basically, the blockchain will work (or be unaffected by this control) until it doesn't (or until it is negatively affected by this control).

Decentralized Consensus Method:

The consensus method of a blockchain must be as decentralized as possible, as mentioned before a 51% attack is when more than half of the validators all agree that an invalid transaction is valid on a blockchain, and the percentage of validators required can vary, being lower than 51%, such as 40% or 30% depending on the blockchain and its consensus method. Gaining enough validators to break this threshold would allow the bad actor, or actors, to approve invalid transactions and violate the blockchain code in some way as mentioned before, or it could allow for the approval of IPs on the blockchain, by affecting the blockchains voting structure. We will look at POW and POS individually next, but there are other consensus methods that exist, and who controls the validators, or the voting power they have, is important and will affect how secure or vulnerable the blockchain is overall. As mentioned before, new consensus methods are being developed, and how decentralized the validators are will be a factor in the success or failure of the new type of consensus method.

Decentralized POW Blockchain:

For a POW blockchain, validators are the mining farms, both large groups of ASICs and smaller farms with lower hash rates, and these farms can be run by anyone with the wealth and knowledge required to set up the hardware and equipment that was mentioned before. If these farms are large enough, they will not need to send their hash rate to a mining pool, although they can if they want to, and obliviously smaller mining farms must pool their hash rate if they want a consistent block reward payout in order to pay for their energy costs. For a POW blockchain, centralization exists around how many individual miners there are, but also how many mining pools exist and how much of the total hash rate for the blockchain they have in their pool. Meaning even if a POW blockchain has many small individually controlled GPU mining farms, it can still have major centralized points such as 1 or 2 mining pools with the majority of the total hash rate for the blockchain. These small mining farms can still decide to move their hash power to another mining pool, or even to a completely different blockchain if they want, so there is still some decentralization in that these miners could choose to leave the pool if it tried to manipulate the blockchain, or voted on an IP that most of the miners did not agree with. This is a decentralized check to the pool having a majority of the total hash rate, but obviously the mining pool would still have this control, and it would continue to have this control as long as many mining farms continued to send their hash rate to the mining pool. So having many or several mining pools for a POW blockchain helps keep it less centralized and susceptible to manipulation, however this only applies to miners sending their hash rate to a mining pool, smaller solo miners and larger mining farms would not need to send their hash rate to a pool, and they would basically be individual validators for the blockchain's consensus method, adding to the total number of validators and further decentralizing the consensus method.

Simple Example:

This seems complicated, but let's look at an overly simplified example to understand how mining pools can affect the consensus method, making it more centralized, or more decentralized, based on the number of validators and mining pools there are for the blockchain. First imagine a blockchain with a POW consensus method, there are 100 validators approving transactions on the blockchain, and there is one mining pool for that blockchain. For these examples each validator has the same hash rate and voting power that comes with it, but note in reality each validator varies in their hash power, and it's based on the size of the mining farm. Let us say about 40 of the validators are hashing transactions on the blockchain itself, not pooling their hash power in a mining pool (these would be larger mining farms, but for this example we are counting all validators as equal), the other 60 validators are sending their hash power to the pool, and as blocks are solved by the mining pool the block rewards are distributed to the 60 individual mining farms, or validators. The mining pool charges a fee for their services, and without the choice to send their hash power to another pool, the smaller mining farms must give a percent of their block rewards to the mining pool. It is their only option if they want to hash transactions on this blockchain and earn steady block rewards, and they could try solo mining as mentioned before, but depending on their power bill this may not be an option. This scenario basically gives the mining pool 60% of the validators and their hash power/ voting power on the blockchain, and if the mining pool wanted to approve an improvement proposal that none of the validators wanted it could. While 40 of the validators could all vote no on the IP, the mining pool controls the other 60 of them, this would give the mining pool the majority vote, and this obviously only applies to POW blockchains that have their voting structure based on the hash power of a mining farm.

Now let us imagine another blockchain with a POW consensus method, there are still 100 validators approving transactions on the blockchain, but there are 3 mining pools for this blockchain, and just as before 40 of the validators are large enough to not need to send their hash power to a mining pool. This leaves 60 validators that can choose what mining pool they want to send their hash rate to, and this creates competition between mining pools. They will lower fees in order to attract more mining farms that will send their hash power to the mining pool, and should the mining pool ever support an IP that most validators disagree with, then the mining farms could switch the mining pool they send their hash rate to. This allows small mining farms to still have somewhat of a say in the direction the blockchain is developed, and this adds to the decentralization of the consensus method. Several or many mining pools prevent a centralized point from being created, in this case a single mining pool with no check to its voting power, or to what it can charge a mining farm that is sending its hash rate to the pool. This is obviously a simple example, and does not take into account many additional factors that play a part in the consensus method of a blockchain, but it shows how even 100 unique validators can have a centralized point that gives the mining pool operator control over new updates for the blockchain or transactions added to the blockchain. Having many mining pool options for a blockchain allows for small mining farms to decide which one they will send their hash rate to, they can make this decision based on fees for the mining pool, or based on who runs the mining pool and what direction they want the blockchain to go in. Making the hash rate sent by a small mining farm similar to a vote for elected officials, as long as the mining pool is doing things the small farms agree with, then the pool can act on behalf of the small mining farms (as far as voting on IPs go), but that vote of support can be withdrawn at any time, by moving their hash power to another mining pool.

Large Mining Farms:

A somewhat straight forward example of a centralized point would be a single mining farm that has the majority of the total hash rate for a blockchain, and this can be a single large farm, or several large mining farms that are owned and controlled by the same person or company. This gives the mining farm similar capabilities to a 51% attack, but they don't need to "attack" the blockchain because they have over half of the validators already, and this might be common for new blockchains as the developers update and grow different aspects of the blockchain. Basically, sometimes the developers will run most of the validators for the blockchain, this helps them implement updates faster, and ensures there will at least be some miners securing the blockchain that they are working on. Although this means they would be getting the majority of the block rewards as well, if they stacked these rewards and did not sell them into circulating supply, then the coin or tokens dollar value might increase and not have this inflationary pressure on it. But it would also mean fewer coins being sold into the circulating supply, and this might reduce the market of buyers and sellers that most blockchains need to see the coins value increase over time, and we will go over this in more detail later.

This is why large investors will sometimes control the majority of a new project's validators, the block rewards are compensation for investing in the blockchain project, and those block rewards will be sold when the investor wants to take profits, adding the coins into the market of buyers and sellers. Even if others are able to set up miners and start hashing transactions on the blockchain, they will not come close to gaining the majority of the validators and the hash power that the large investors have. This type of centralized point is only really possibly with blockchains that have low hash rates, or new projects that are being set up, and this does not mean this type of centralized point is always bad. New projects may need this added control to build and develop the blockchain before it starts handling mainstream adoption and the high transaction volume that comes with it, and these types of blockchain projects should not and in many cases cannot comply with existing securities rules and regulations. They need time to develop and should not be subject to the same rules and regulations that other larger blockchain projects should have to comply with, and I detail this more in the Arizona Blockchain Standards, which I will explain later. However, it's important to remember that the centralized point of control exists, and if the blockchain project grows and becomes more decentralized, than it will be harder to manipulate or attack the blockchain. But if it does not, then this control will remain with the developers and/or large investors, both of which may want to change an aspect of the blockchain over time for their own benefit, such as the block reward rate as mentioned before. This type of centralized point can be both good and bad, this control over updates to the blockchain and compensation for investors is good if used to develop and grow the blockchain to fulfil a specific use case. Basically meaning, if they are good actors honestly trying to provide users with something they want, then this centralized point of control is ok, but only at first. If this control is needed to maintain the blockchain indefinitely then this would be a major centralized point of control that investors should consider before investing wealth in the blockchain. This is because trust has shifted from trusting the decentralized blockchain, to trusting these parties that have the majority control over the consensus method, and/or majority control of the voting structure.

Mining Farm Locations:

The location of mining farms can affect the POW consensus method in several ways, as mentioned before natural disasters can affect large areas of the planet, and miners that either lose power or are damaged could be offline for a while depending on the natural disaster. The same is true for man-made disasters or attacks, large numbers of validators could be affected and go offline, either from physical damage or loss of power to the mining farm for one reason or another. If there are miners located all around the world, it would be hard, if not impossible, to knock all the mining farms offline at once and cause the blockchain to stop processing transactions. However, it might be possible to attack many large mining farms and of the ones that remain there might be a majority of them that are controlled by a single person, or company, or country. This means spreading out the mining farms geography helps prevent the blockchain from going completely offline due to natural or man-made disasters. But a large number of miners going offline could give the remaining majority control over the consensus method to a single actor, giving them more block rewards and more voting power, and this would not cause the blockchain to go offline, but it would affect the decentralization of the blockchain's consensus method.

Validators can avoid physically grouping in only one area of the planet, but there is another way they can decentralize themselves and prevent a large group of validators from all being affected by a single event, as mentioned before validators and nodes push and pull data to and from each other, and they can choose what connections to make with other validators and nodes. *(Reference page 123)* This is a way to add decentralization to the validators in a blockchain's consensus method, the first obvious reason this is a good thing is that nodes or validators trying to push invalid transactions can be removed from the list that a validator receives information from, and this is an ongoing process because new nodes may be set up specifically to try and push these invalid transactions as mentioned before. *(Reference page 50)* Another reason this adds to decentralization is that validators can pull data, or transactions, from other validators that may be far away geographically, as well as local connections that are able to push and pull data slightly faster based on their closer location. Basically, this means the validator's interpretation of the current state of the blockchain is always as up to date as possible, this is because it is pulling transaction data from around the world. Closer connections may be a little faster, but others further away may be more "trusted," and as mentioned before most validators do not want to include invalid transactions in their blocks, because they might lose out on the chance to earn block rewards. So, validators that only pull transactions from their local area, or only from a few other validators and nodes, might miss some transactions, and this would affect their ability to earn block rewards by solving the next block in the blockchain. Simply put, it is hard to be the first to solve a puzzle if you are missing a few pieces. These longer or more trusted connections ensure the validator is getting a chance to hash each transaction on the blockchain, this helps prevent the spreading of invalid transactions, and prevents isolated pockets of validators from only pushing and pulling data between themselves. These isolated pockets can happen, and when one of the validators in them gets chosen to receive the next block reward their version of the blockchain is the new consensus of that blockchain. However, when the rest of the validators realize the new block is wrong there is a reorg of the blockchain, and this is what creates an orphan block that was mentioned before. *(Reference page 5)*

(Illustration, next page)

This means the location of validators in a POW blockchain can be decentralized geographically and decentralized in the way transaction data is shared between validators, and this can be thought of as the physical location and digital location for the validators. Just like grouping mining farms in a physical location adds centralized risks, collecting information from a centralized group of validators and nodes also adds risks. The more interconnected the network of nodes and validators, the more decentralized the consensus method, and nodes play a significant part in this decentralization even though they do not receive block rewards for verifying transactions on the blockchain. This is because they allow validators more options on where they push and pull data to and from, although nodes are not always pushing valid transactions as mentioned before. Nodes are usually set up by someone who wants a low-cost way to help secure the blockchain, and they can also be used to push invalid transactions to validators in hopes that the transaction will be included in the next block, but unless it is done with a large number of nodes there is little chance of this happening. Meaning overall, individually controlled nodes help a blockchain more than they might hurt it, and they add to the decentralization of transaction data that is sent between validators in a POW consensus method.

Barrier to Entry:

In a POW blockchain there is hardware required, this means mining computers and cooling systems need to be set up as mentioned before, and it requires knowledge and an investment of time and wealth to set up

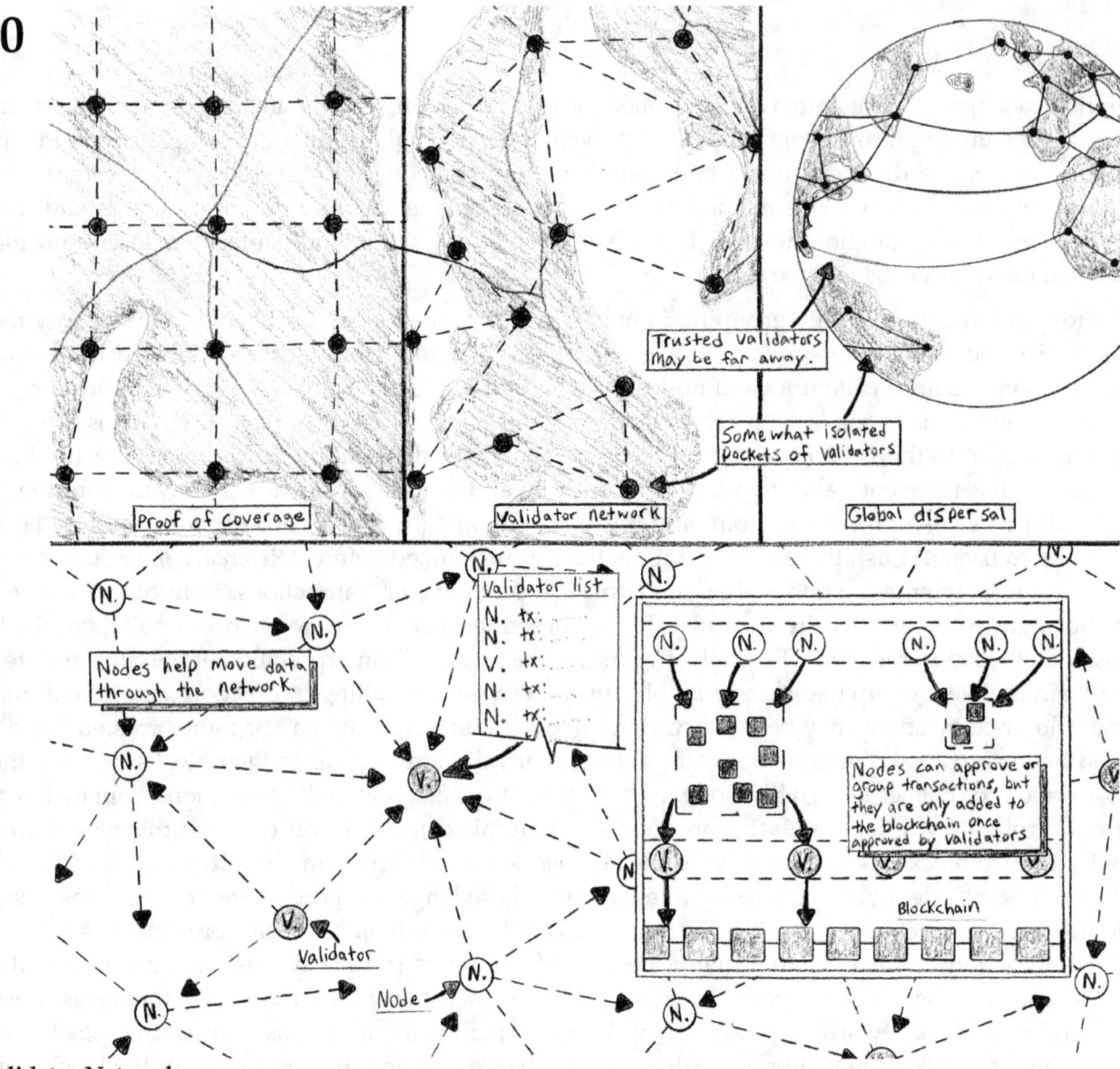

Validator Network

Validators can be located anywhere globally, and they can affect the consensus method of a blockchain to an extent, depending on how many there are, and where they are located. Spreading out the validator network prevents isolated pockets of validators, and it helps keep the blockchain online during large natural or man-made disasters. Although the illustration only depicts geographical validator locations, the concept is the same for digital validator locations as well, and it is important to remember nodes can be involved in some consensus methods to an extent, but they are not adding transactions to the blockchain like validators are.

Pg. 7, upper right section: Isolated areas in a network of validators can cause them to have a slightly different interpretation of the next block in the blockchain, and when the consensus method chooses one of these validators to receive the next block reward, it is their version of the next block that is added to the blockchain. The other validators in the network pick up on the discrepancy and reorg the block, basically removing any invalid transactions, and creating an orphan block in the process.

Pg. 11, upper left section: The location of validators is important because it ensures transactions are quickly spread throughout the network of validators, giving each of them a chance to hash the transaction, and this proof of coverage consensus method has pros and cons since there are other validators in the process of creating blocks and earning block rewards.

Pg. 13, upper right section: Geographic validator locations can be spread out, or grouped into isolated pockets, and this is true for the digital location of the validators as well. Basically, even validators located in the same building can send their hash power to different mining pools, and they can choose what nodes and validators are on the list they receive transactions from.

Pg. 26, bottom section: Each validator and node have a list of connections that they send and receive transactions to and from, this list can be changed at anytime by the validator, and this is how malicious nodes pushing invalid transactions can be ignored.

Pg. 29, bottom right section: Nodes are usually cheaper to set up than a validator, this means they might be more likely to push an invalid transaction through the validator network, however, it is important to remember nodes do not add transactions to the blockchain. Although some blockchains allow nodes to batch or group transactions, they are not actually approving the transaction and adding it to the blockchain, this is only done by validators in the blockchain's consensus method.

Pg. 41, upper left section: The Helium blockchain uses proof of coverage in its consensus method, this allows data to move fast and for low cost in areas where many Helium miners have been set up, and these miners require less energy and produce less heat than ASIC miners.

Pg. 49, bottom section: Validators can remove a malicious node from their list, and each validator and node can change their connections at any time, this is an ongoing process that will continue to change as validators and nodes in the consensus method come online and go offline globally.

Pg. 70, upper right section: Although data can move very fast around the world, when those connections are far apart it might make more sense to connect to closer nodes or validators, and these closer sources of data would not be the only source the validator is pulling from, it just adds to the number of transactions the validator is able to hash, giving it the best chance to earn a block reward.

Pg. 109, upper right section: Bitcoins blockchain allows nodes to interact with validators in the consensus method, and this helps prevent isolated pockets in the validator network, basically these nodes simply allow for more connections between validators, but nodes on the Bitcoin blockchain can be involved in use cases on the blockchain as well.

a mining farm, both larger ASIC mining farms, or smaller GPU mining farms. A somewhat less important point of control for a POW blockchain is the cost of the equipment being a barrier to entry for many smaller mining farms, even a small Bitcoin mining farm requires 10s of thousands of dollars for the ASICs, cooling systems, and warehousing of the equipment. This means the mining farm would be less likely to attempt to manipulate the blockchain in any way, as mentioned before many farms are set up and just left running 24/7, this is more of a business for them, basically balancing hash power and energy costs for block rewards at a profit. These smaller or medium-sized mining farms have tight margins, if the equipment required to set up a mining farm was more expensive than they might not have the ability to hash transactions and earn block rewards on that blockchain. However, larger investors would still be able to set up large mining farms, and depending on the total hash rate of the blockchain, they might have a majority of the hash power if fewer small mining farms are set up. This majority of the hash power creates a centralized point of control as mentioned before, also wealthy investors might be more likely to have other reasons for setting up a mining farm, major ones like pushing an invalid transaction, or minor unseen ones like front running transactions, and both of these are not good for users and investors in the blockchain. *(Reference page 2)*

Small and medium-sized mining farms are less likely to attempt to manipulate the blockchain they are earning block rewards on, and this makes them the "better" type of mining farm from the consensus methods point of view. While larger mining farms and their investors might have ulterior motives, but with a high barrier to entry as far as equipment costs go, it is the smaller somewhat more trustworthy mining farms that are prevented from participating in the consensus method for that blockchain. This is why the cost to participate in the consensus method matters a little, in a POW blockchain if the ASIC costs are too high fewer people can hash transactions on the blockchain and add to its decentralization. But the costs must be somewhat significant, otherwise margins would not be as tight on these mining farms, and they might be more open to exploiting the blockchain, if they could make a large profit. GPU mining allows for smaller mining farms to move between the many new blockchains that are being developed using a POW consensus method, GPU costs are somewhat cheap, so most new POW blockchains probably have a low entry level cost. As mentioned before, the Helium blockchain has very cheap miners that use little energy and could even be built by someone if they had the knowledge to do so. They have a very low entry level cost, but they only receive 1/3 of the total block rewards, and other validators receive 1/3 of the block rewards for basically checking on the home miners and making sure they have not manipulated transactions on the blockchain in any way, which they might try since the cost of the hardware is relatively cheap. So, the cost to participate in the consensus method matters a little, it should be inexpensive and easy to set up, but not too cheap or there will need to be added checks to transaction authenticity, like the additional validators in the Helium blockchain, and this is only true for POW blockchains. In a POS blockchain there is no large investment for hardware and equipment, this is why wealth must be staked to pools, it is the cost to participate in the consensus method, and we will look at the POS consensus method in more detail next.

Decentralized POS Blockchain:

For a POS blockchain, validators are the stake pools, and there can be a set number of pools for the blockchain or unlimited pools. Some blockchains allow for the creation of any number of stake pools, and anyone with the wealth and knowledge to set up the minimal hardware can create their own stake pool and be a part of the consensus method for that blockchain. While other POS blockchains only allow for a certain number of validators, these stake pools could be set up and maintained by developers, large investors, or other "trusted" parties. The voting structure varies depending on the number of stake pools, or if tokens are used in the voting structure of the blockchain, which we will go over in more detail later. *(Reference page 66)* Either way there is a cost to participate in the consensus method, although these costs can be substantial there is not much physical work required to set up and run these stake pools, and this is why some people believe a POW consensus method is more secure, wealth cannot be simply transferred into the blockchain to gain majority control of the consensus method and/or the voting structure. Either way stakeholders, or those staking wealth to a pool (sometimes called a delegated stake) will receive block rewards whether the stake pools have voting power for the blockchain or not, and these block reward rates can vary between different POS blockchains as mentioned before.

Stake pools require a little hardware and knowledge to set up, but they also require a certain number of coins to be locked in the stake pool in order for it to receive block rewards for verifying transactions on the blockchain, and this amount varies between blockchains, it can be any amount. Typically, POS consensus methods with more validators will have a lower required number of coins to set up a pool, while consensus methods with fewer more "trusted" validators have a larger number of coins required to set up a pool. This serves several purposes, one is to limit the number of people that are able to afford to set up a pool, or to incentivize more people to set up a pool if the coin requirement is lower. This basically means the more "trusted" pools would be required to lockup say 10s of thousands of dollars compared to other POS blockchains that allow anyone to set up a pool for say a few hundred dollars, not including the hardware required. This cost to set up a pool is meant to be similar to the investment of wealth required to set up a POW mining farm, it is the cost to participate in the consensus method, and if the validator attempts to manipulate the blockchain, it is this wealth that would be lost by the bad actor/ stake pool operator. In a POW blockchain this wealth is a power bill that needs to be paid even if the mining farm does not receive any block rewards, it is also the cost of the equipment and cooling systems mentioned before. But for a POS blockchain, this loss of wealth would come from slashing the coins locked in the stake pool, and we will go over this more next. The main thing to understand is that the coins required to set up a stake pool are what creates "trust," and the more wealth the pool operator must lock in the stake pool, the less likely they would be to attempt to manipulate transactions on the blockchain. This higher coin requirement also allows for the development team to have a say in whom these "trusted" stake pool operators are, they are usually large investors who want to see the blockchain project succeed, but this does not mean they will not try to manipulate the blockchain and make a profit in some way. For example, they could profit from front running transactions, and this would not directly affect or hurt the blockchain necessarily. *(Reference page 2)* This is why blockchains that allow for many stake pools to be created in their consensus method are considered more decentralized, simply put, there are more validators and this creates more decentralization. Even if "trusted" validators do not manipulate the blockchain, they are still more centralized in that there are fewer pools involved in creating new blocks on the blockchain.

So far, we have looked at POS blockchains that have a consensus method that allows the validators to vote on IPs as well as verifying transactions on the blockchain, these can be a few "trusted" pools, or many individually controlled stake pools, and stakeholders can lock up coins in either type of POS consensus method and earn block rewards as compensation. However, some POS blockchains can be set up with voting coins/ tokens, and the stake pools will still verify transactions and earn block rewards that will be distributed to stakeholders as mentioned before. But IPs will not be voted on by these validators in the consensus method, and this is where coins/ tokens can be used as the voting structure for a blockchain. *(Reference page 66)* It is important to understand what these voting coins/ tokens do and how it affects the blockchain, when validators have voting power in the consensus method this means they are profiting from the block rewards, and their coins locked in the pool is the wealth they might lose if they try to manipulate the blockchain, they can also vote on IPs, and this is good because they would usually only vote on IPs that benefit the blockchain. *(Reference page 23)* They are profiting from the blockchain, so they would want to see that continue, and not much changes for these validators if voting coins are used, they still validate transactions, create blocks, and earn block rewards from the blockchain. How the voting structure is set up can vary depending on how the coins/ tokens are used, and we will go over this in more detail later, but for now just understand if there is a separate voting structure that the validators are not a part of, then the blockchain would have an additional area that could be subject to centralization risks. Such as, a decentralized network of individually controlled stake pools, which is good, but with all voting power for the blockchain being controlled by one person, which is bad, and this would not mean all voting structures that use coins/ tokens are bad, it simply means there is additional information to consider when determining if the blockchain is actually decentralized or not.

Cost to Become a Validator:

The cost to participate in a POS consensus method is the coins required to set up a stake pool, these coins can be destroyed, or slashed, if the stake pool operator attempts to manipulate the blockchain, and this is similar to a POW mining farm's loss of wealth if it attempts to manipulate the blockchain, which is a power bill that needs to be paid. Slashing is not a part of all POS blockchains, it can be incorporated by developers or not, but it is the loss of wealth that would prevent a stake pool from attempting to manipulate the blockchain, basically it is what keeps the stake pools honest. This slashing can be done to just the stake pool operators coins held in the pool, basically a smart contract with the blockchain as mentioned before, or it could include the wealth staked to the pool by stakeholders, basically all coins staked to the pool. This is not common for most POS blockchains, however, it is something investors should be aware of since it is their wealth that may be at risk, and they have no control over what the stake pool operator does, so they would be punished for something someone else did. Most developers are turning away from punishing stakeholders for a stake pool operator's actions, but the idea that the stakeholders are participating in the consensus method by staking wealth to the pool is somewhat true, it is that wealth that earns block rewards, and those are determined based on how much wealth is staked to the pool.

These block rewards come from verifying transactions and creating new blocks for the blockchain as mentioned before, however a stakeholder is only agreeing to lock up wealth in the pool and receive block rewards. They do not have any control over the stake pool, this is all done by the stake pool operator, and I detail this more in the Howey test interpretation for blockchain coins and tokens. Simply put, staking wealth to a stake pool does not count as work or effort on the part of the stakeholder, any wealth gained comes from the efforts of the stake pool operator and the inflation rate of the blockchain, or the block rewards. It is likely most POS blockchains will eventually not include slashing on individual stakeholders, this is unfair since the stakeholder has no ability to cause the manipulation that would result in their wealth being destroyed. However, slashing is what prevents pool operators from manipulating transactions on the blockchain, so if there is no slashing for a POS blockchain then there is no possible loss of wealth for stake pools that attempt to manipulate the blockchain. Basically, slashing is good, it is what prevents validators from attempting to manipulate the blockchain, it would stop individually controlled pools and larger "trusted" pools from attempting this. But it should not include a stakeholder's wealth, and there are many other factors to consider that are involved with slashing, this is why some POS blockchains include slashing and others do not. Either way, anyone investing wealth in a stake pool should be aware of slashing, and how the blockchain's consensus method that they are investing in is set up.

Stake Pool Types:

Validators in a POS consensus method that have voting power on the blockchain can vary in how decentralized they are, and we will look at how stakeholders play a part in this decentralization even though they are not directly voting on IPs. How the stake pools are set up, and how many there are play a part in how decentralized the consensus method is, but this only applies to POS blockchains that allow the validators to vote on IPs, there are additional factors involved when coins/ tokens are used as the voting structure for the blockchain, and we will go over this in more detail later. For now, let's just look at how the wealth staked to pools in a POS blockchain can vary and affect the decentralization of the blockchain, and where centralized points of control may exist, depending on the number of "trusted" and "local" stake pools for that blockchain's consensus method.

"Trusted" pools: As mentioned before some POS blockchains can have several "trusted" stake pools, these pools would be most likely set up and run by large investors in the blockchain project, and wealth staked on the blockchain would fall into one of these several pools. They usually all offer the same block reward rate and do not vary that much between pools, and from the stakeholders' point of view there is no noticeable difference, they earn a set block reward rate based on how much wealth they stake to the blockchain, so investors are happy. However, when it comes to voting on IPs for the blockchain, stakeholders do not really have a voice, the large investor and developers will decide what updates to implement, and the only thing stakeholders could do to show disapproval would be to remove their wealth from the stake pool, basically removing their wealth from the blockchain completely. This is somewhat oversimplified, since blockchain projects will work with the communities and take into account their opinions as far as what direction the blockchain should be developed in, since it is this community that will utilize the use case that the blockchain creates. However, when it comes to who actually has the final say, or vote, on these updates, it would be only the large investors and developers. This creates a centralized point of control, but it does not mean the investors or developers will abuse this control to implement updates that would negatively affect the blockchain, it only means they have the ability to if they ever choose to. *(Reference page 88)*

Local pools: Also, as mentioned before some POS blockchains can have many stake pools, these can be thought of as "Local" pools, meaning they can be set up by anyone with enough coins and the knowledge to set up the minimal hardware. If a blockchains consensus method allows for many stake pools to be created, then those pools will have limits on how many coins can earn block rewards in the pool, and we will look at how this balance works in more detail later, for now just understand these smaller local pools cannot grow to be the majority of the consensus method. These local pools can vary in the amount of fees they charge stakeholders, and how they vote on IPs, this creates competition between stake pools, and they will try to attract more stakeholders to their pool, so they can maximize the amount of block rewards they are able to receive. This creates a way for stakeholders to show their support for IPs on the blockchain, by moving their wealth from one stake pool to another on the same POS blockchain, the stake pool's block reward rate would be affected, and the voting power that comes with it. This is similar to mining pools that small mining farms send their hash rate to, with more mining pool options, small mining farms can move their support to the pool that aligns with the direction they want to see the blockchain developed in, and the same is true for local stake pools who have voting power on a blockchain. Basically, the staked wealth would be similar to the hash rate in a POW blockchain, allowing for stakeholders to choose the stake pool operator they want to represent their vote on the blockchain, and as these pools fill to their max limit of coins that can receive block rewards, a stake pool operator can create additional stake pools by setting up the hardware and locking up the required number of coins in the additional pool.

Stakeholders:

This ability to move wealth between stake pools allow the stakeholders to support pool operators who they agree with, as far as voting on IPs go, and this adds to the decentralized aspect of this type of POS consensus method. Basically, people are voting with where they store their wealth, and although Bitcoin has a POW consensus method, what happened between Bitcoin and Bitcoin Cash is a good example of voting, or showing support, with where you store your wealth. As mentioned before, the Bitcoin and Bitcoin Cash hard fork left wallets with the same amount of Bitcoin and Bitcoin Cash, wallet holders sold the coins they did not want and likely used it to buy more of the coin they did want. This affected the market cap of both blockchains, and it caused price volatility for both coins, but years later we can clearly see where most people chose to store their wealth, Bitcoins price in dollars has far exceeded Bitcoins Cashes price, and this is also apparent with the hash rate for both blockchains. As mentioned before many miners do switch in between hashing transactions on both blockchains, based on several factors, but the majority of the hash rate chose to stick with Bitcoins original blockchain. Because hash power is measured by the size of the mining farm, and the investment that is required to set one up, the more hash power a blockchain has can be thought of as support for that blockchain, or the amount of wealth backing that high hash rate and the computing power required to achieve it. This is similar to staked coins in a POS blockchain, except this wealth is not represented by costly equipment, it is represented by the coin of the blockchain and the amount of wealth required to buy the coins.

Basically, stakeholders that have the ability to choose the pool operator that represents their wealth, will have more of a say in the direction the blockchain is developed, even if it results in a hard fork of the blockchain. While POS blockchains that only have a few "trusted" pools would not give stakeholders the option to move to a different pool that may vote a different way on an IP, and this would mean the stakeholder could either remove their wealth from the blockchain completely, or accept whatever updates are implemented on the blockchain. This all assumes the stakeholder actually cares about updates to the blockchain, there are many that do not follow the development of the blockchain they are invested in, and for them other factors will determine what stake pool they decide to store their wealth in, if there is an option at all.

For some people, how the blockchain is developed over time is not a factor in choosing where to store their wealth, both in the POS coin they invest in, and what stake pool in the POS blockchain they choose to stake their wealth to. These stakeholders would care more about things like fees for local pools, the inflation rate of the blockchain or what the block reward rate is, and how easy it is to stake coins and earn block rewards from the blockchain. POS blockchains that have few "trusted" pools would not always have fees, and if they do, they are usually the same, but they would all offer the same block reward rate based on the number of coins staked to the blockchain. This is thought of as interest on an investor's wealth by many people, so higher block reward rates would attract more stakeholders to that POS blockchain. However, it's important to remember block rewards are not interest, they are the inflation rate for that blockchain, and if this inflation rate is too high then it will affect the value of the coin of that blockchain over time. For POS blockchains with more local pools the fees can vary between stake pools, what the fee will be is decided on by the stake pool operator, and this creates competition between stake pools for stakeholders looking for the lowest fees possible. These concepts are easy to understand, stakeholders want as many block rewards as possible, and they want to share those block rewards with the stake pool as little as possible, this maximizes the amount of wealth they can gain by staking to the blockchain.

However, one of the biggest deciding factors for some stakeholders is, how easy is it to stake and unstake wealth to the blockchain, as mentioned before coins can be staked from a hard wallet to the stake pool, and this requires some knowledge and a little work from the stakeholder, but there are 3rd party wallets that can also offer staking services. *(Reference page 23)* Sometimes called, staking as a service, these can be centralized 3rd party exchanges, or DeFi exchanges, and we will go over the differences between exchanges later, but for now just understand that these exchanges allow for stakeholders to earn block rewards on the exchange. The exchange does this by setting up a stake pool on the POS blockchain, or by sending coins to a stake pool, but with the large number of coins on the exchange it usually makes more sense for the exchange to run their own stake pool. There are many pros and cons to holding wealth in a 3rd party wallet, but one of the pros would be the ability to stake wealth to a POS blockchain and earn block rewards with just the push of a button. On some exchanges there would be no lock-up period, even if the POS blockchain has lock-up periods, this is because the account holder's coins on an exchange might not even move when they stake or unstake coins, there is just a credit or debit to the account, and we will go over this more later. Basically, stakeholders have an easier time staking and unstaking wealth, they pay for this convenience with some of their block rewards, because many of these exchanges will take a cut of the block rewards just as local pools do. For some investors this convenience is worth the price and risks that come with 3rd party wallets, simply because staking and earning block rewards can be done with the push of a button.

Fewer Stake Pools:

POS blockchains that have fewer "trusted" stake pools have many pros and cons, centralized points of control are in the hands of developers and/or large investors, and each POS blockchain should be judged individually, some can be set up in a way that balances this control, while other blockchains might be more susceptible to exploitation. These "trusted" stake pools are usually operated and controlled by those that want the blockchain project to succeed, and they are invested in the project, with either the wealth required to set up and fund the stake pool, or they are investing their time developing the blockchain. This means if they are honest actors, they would not try to manipulate the blockchain or negatively affect it in any way, and some use cases for the blockchain may require this added control, so putting this control in these "trusted" hands may benefit the blockchain. However, this is not always the case, many POS blockchains have been able to set up a balanced and somewhat decentralized consensus method, and we will look at Polkadot, DOT, as an example a little more later. For now, just understand it is always better to lean more to the decentralized side, rather than to the centralized side, especially when transaction validation and voting on IPs are involved.

Some blockchains need time to develop and grow, this means the developers need more control over certain aspects of the blockchain like the ability to implement IPs quickly, without this ability the new blockchain may be susceptible to attacks, and this growth and development is what prevents rushed blockchain projects with concepts that may not have been fully tested. However, this control over the validation of transactions and implementation of IPs on the blockchain is a major-centralized point of control. If the blockchain developers need this control to exist for the blockchain to function indefinitely, then these risks need to be disclosed to investors that hold wealth in the blockchain, both for stakeholders, and for those that just hold the coin of the blockchain. We will go over this in more detail later when we look at the Arizona Blockchain Standards, simply put, not all blockchain projects can be regulated by the same rules, and this is why the standards break coins and tokens into different categories of risk, as well as passing disclosures of these risks on to investors. If new blockchain projects were required to meet the same standards as larger or more developed blockchains, then this would prevent growth in the industry, and this is what the blockchain standards are trying to prevent, blanket regulations that would move the industry away from regions with these restrictive regulations. So, for POS blockchains that have "trusted" validators, they must be set up in a way that breaks up that control as much as possible, and blockchains that are able to do this would be considered more decentralized. However, as mentioned before each blockchain can be set up differently and these "trusted" pools must not be able to totally control the voting structure or the validation of transactions on the blockchain, if they can then these are major centralized risks that need to be disclosed to investors in the blockchain. This control can be temporary if the blockchain is still being developed, so these "trusted" pools should not always be thought of as a bad thing, as long as that control is dispersed away from individual companies and developers over time.

Individually Controlled Validators:

POS consensus methods are similar to POW consensus methods in that the more individually controlled validators there are, the more decentralized the consensus method is, and this idea is simple but true. For a POW blockchain, wealth is used to buy mining equipment and cooling systems, the hash rate the mining farm is able to achieve with this wealth and equipment is what gives the mining farm block rewards and a vote on how the blockchain will be developed, and this is important to a mining farm since they are investing wealth into the equipment that will secure the blockchain. This is a somewhat similar concept to POS blockchains and their stake pools, wealth is used to support the blockchain by validating transactions, and stakeholders receive block rewards in compensation, but the number of stake pools and how the voting structure is set up for the POS blockchain can affect how decentralized the blockchain is. Simply put, for both a POW and a POS consensus method, the more individually controlled validators there are, the more decentralized the blockchain is. This is because the individual mining farms or individual stake pool operators are making a profit from the block rewards, and this along with voting power for updates of the blockchain ensures these validators would be less likely to try to manipulate the blockchain, since they are directly profiting from it. Staking to a stake pool also allows smaller amounts of wealth to participate in the consensus method, but it is important to remember limiting who is able to set up a stake pool on the blockchain also limits the voice of stakeholders, since they are not able to move wealth between stake pools and affect the voting power of those individual stake pool operators, and this affects an aspect of the decentralization of the blockchain overall.

These "trusted" validators in a POS blockchain are sometimes referred to as having a proof of authority consensus method rather than a POS consensus method, but basically it is a POS blockchain, just with a limited number of validators, or stake pools, and this limit on the number of pools prevents one of the pools from growing to be the majority of the consensus method. *(Reference page 88)* This is because the number of pools is known and usually fixed, transactions are verified by all the validators, and block rewards are equally distributed between the stake pools, who then distribute the block rewards to individual stakeholders. However, POS blockchains that allow anyone to set up a stake pool on the blockchain have additional factors to take into account, if most wealth staked to the blockchain was in a single stake pool then that pool operator would have the majority of the voting power for the blockchain, and most of the block rewards. So, let's look at some of the unique factors involved in a POS blockchain that allows anyone to set up a stake pool, and directly take part in the consensus method and transaction validation of the blockchain.

Block Reward Limits:

A POS consensus method that allows for anyone to become a validator needs to be balanced in several areas, if it is not then the blockchain may be more susceptible to exploitation, and because we know blockchains can be set up in different ways, each POS blockchain and how its consensus method is set up should be individually judged when deciding how decentralized the blockchain is. We will go over several factors that are important for POS blockchains that allow for local pools to be set up, things like block reward rates for stake pools, and how the staked coins can affect the dollar value of the blockchains coin. Although there are many other factors involved, these are ones that could form centralized points of control, and they are important in understanding the balance needed for these blockchains to be considered decentralized.

Local pools have limits on the number of coins that can receive block rewards, this is hard coded into the blockchain, and additional coins can be staked to the stake pool exceeding the limit that are able to earn block rewards, but this does not affect the voting power of the stake pool, since only wealth that receives block rewards is given voting power in this consensus method. This prevents any single stake pool from growing to a size that would make it a large percent of the consensus method, each stake pool would be capped at a certain threshold, although nothing would prevent the stake pool operator from setting up additional stake pools as mentioned before. This would mean stake pool operators would only set up additional pools if they had enough demand, and we will look at who stake pool operators are in a bit. For now, just understand these local pools can be set up by anyone, but it does not mean their stake pool will fill up with a stakeholders coins, and this means stake pool operators will only set up additional pools if they have enough stakeholders willing to stake their wealth to the pool.

This wealth locked in the stake pool is achieved by using the unit of account for the blockchain, or the coin of the blockchain, and stakeholders that just want to stake their coins and leave them in the pool to earn continuous block rewards can do so, however this would mean those coins are removed from the circulating supply. Stakeholders may sell the block rewards they receive in order to realize the wealth gain, but they would not be selling the coins locked in the stake pool, so there is not much sell pressure added to the coin, but the supply of coins available would be reduced, and this reduced supply generally increases price if the demand for the coin remains constant or increases. This is true for all POS blockchains, the coins locked in the stake pools reduce the number of coins in circulation, and as long as there is demand for the coin, then this reduced supply will add upward price pressure to the coin's dollar value. However, there are many factors at play here, so there is no guarantee the coin will increase in dollar value, and this is because the staked coins can be removed from the stake pool and sold whenever the stakeholders want. As long as it is in accordance with any lock-up periods that may exist on the blockchain as mentioned before, and as the price of the coin increases more stakeholders may choose to remove their wealth from the stake pool and sell the coins to realize the wealth gain.

This sell pressure would then cause the coin's value to fall, and this would be a large drop in price when large amounts of wealth are sold, or when many stakeholders all sell around the same time, this is just a basic explanation, and each stakeholder and their decision to sell or hold coins in the stake pool is only one small factor that affects the coins value. But for coins that remain in a stake pool, when the majority of stakeholders are removing wealth and selling their coins, they will now receive more block rewards, since there are now fewer stakeholders for the same amount of block rewards. This is the balance that POS blockchains need to achieve, they need a lot of the coins in existence to be locked in stake pools, this keeps the value of the coin high since there is limited supply. But these coins can be sold at any time, so there must be demand for the blockchains use case to absorb this possible sell pressure when stakeholders decide to realize their wealth gain. This is just one small factor to consider, and there are many other factors that could upset this balance, such as a high inflation rate of the blockchain, since these block rewards would usually be sold into the circulating supply, adding constant sell pressure to the coin. Also too low of a block reward rate for stakeholders would mean fewer individuals lock their wealth in stake pools, meaning there are more coins in circulation making it harder for the coin to increase in value, and hold that value over time.

Stake Pool Operators:

As mentioned before, stakeholders do not always have a vote on the blockchain, it is the stake pool operator that has voting power for IPs on the blockchain, and stakeholders can decide what stake pool operator they want to represent their vote, although some stakeholders will care more about the fees a stake pool charges rather than how they vote on IPs as mentioned before. So, let's look at whom these stake pool operators can be, how they attract stakeholders to choose their stake pool over other stake pools, and how much of a part they play in the consensus method of the blockchain. Some stake pool operators are supporters of the blockchain project, they are members of the community that follows the development of the blockchain, and they may interact with the blockchain and its use cases, although they do not have to, at the very least they are participating in the consensus method of the blockchain.

All stake pools are listed for the blockchain, they can display fees that the stake pool charges, or the pools vote on upcoming IPs, and many times fees will be competitive between pools, so a stakeholder could pick any stake pool and receive a similar block reward rate based on the amount of wealth being staked. This is where promoters will encourage stakeholders to send their wealth to a certain pool, it is usually a YouTube channel or other type of content creator urging followers to support the channel by staking to their own stake pool. And fake stake pools can exist, so stakeholders should do research on the stake pool they choose to hold their wealth with. This benefits both the stake pool operator and the stakeholders, the pool operator will have more wealth staked to the pool, earning the pool as a whole more block rewards, and this means they get more in fees. While the stakeholder is able to earn block rewards from the wealth they stake to the pool, they might feel a little more comfortable knowing the pool operator, and could even ask about how the pool will vote on upcoming IPs, and they can voice their opinion. Stakeholders would also have less concern if the blockchain had slashing, since they "know" the pool operator, there is obviously still risk the pool operator may attempt to manipulate the blockchain and cause a stakeholders wealth to be destroyed. But if a stakeholder does their due diligence, they would be able to find these local stake pools set up by members of the community that follow and use the blockchain without attempting to manipulate it.

Staking as a Service:

Other stake pools may be set up by companies, or even exchanges as mentioned before, these stake pools would not always need to compete with the low fees offered by other local stake pools, this is because the stake pool operator already has large amounts of wealth looking to gain an "interest" on that wealth, and most of these stake pools would fall under the staking as a service category. This basically means the stake pool operator is providing the service to a new area of investors, for exchanges this is simply offering staking services on their platform, since some account holders at the exchange may not want to set up a hard wallet, and directly stake to a stake pool. *(Reference page 23)* But they would now have the ability to stake wealth and earn block rewards from the blockchain, and they are usually ok with a slightly higher fee because of the convenience. Other stake pools may be set up for large investors, especially if the limit for coins that can receive block rewards is somewhat low, these would be wealthy investors looking to invest large amounts of wealth, and they would want to directly know the pool operator that is running the stake pool that holds their wealth. They might be ok with higher fees for this sense of security, although, they would still be staking from a hard wallet, so it is not like the stake pool operator can run off with the investor's wealth. Basically, these large investors would want to make sure their wealth was not at risk from slashing, and they would want to make sure they maximize their block rewards, because if the stake pool operator does not keep the pool running, then the investor would lose out on the chance to earn block rewards.

This loss of possible block rewards is very important for investors who are staking very large amounts of wealth to the stake pool, or several stake pools if the investor's wealth exceeds the limit for block rewards of an individual stake pool. With blocks being created say every 10 minutes, a stake pool that is offline for even an hour could see a loss of block rewards worth a lot in dollar terms for the large investor. But this is true for smaller investors that stake wealth to local pools as well, or use staking as a service through an exchange. YouTube channels would promote that they will do everything possible to keep the stake pool online and earning its stakeholders, or followers, their block rewards on that staked wealth. While exchanges would see the stake pool as just another expense to running their platform, they would want to keep the pools online, and would have more resources to ensure this is done, giving account holders more confidence that their staked wealth is gaining as many block rewards as possible.

Decentralization for "Trusted" and Local Stake Pools:

A POS consensus method can be affected by many things, the number of stake pools that can exist, whether the stake pools have voting power on IPs, and if there is a limited number of validators for the blockchain, then who is in control of these "trusted" stake pools. As we have seen, the more individually controlled validators there are for the blockchain, the better, and although "trusted" validators are not necessarily bad, they do have certain centralization risks. This can be balanced by breaking up the control over the voting structure, and separating it from the transaction validation process, basically using voting coins/ tokens. This separates the voting structure of the blockchain from the consensus method of the blockchain, and this adds to the factors involved in determining if a POS blockchain is decentralized or not. *(Reference page 66)* We will go over this more in depth when we look at several ways that voting coins/ tokens can be used, for now just understand this voting power is moving away from the validators of the blockchain, or the stake pools in this case. These stake pools with voting power are perhaps the only ones who are actually incentivized to want to see the blockchain continue and grow, since they are directly profiting from the blockchain's consensus method, and having a separate voting structure would mean they are no longer in control of the direction the blockchain is developed in. It would be in the hands of the separate voting structure, for now let's look POS validators that are local pools with voting power for the blockchain.

Local Stake Pools:

"Trusted" pools are pretty straight forward as far as who controls them and how block rewards are distributed, there are few players involved, and the block rewards are split between these validators at rates decided on by the development team. Simply put there are no new validators that can come online and affect the block reward ratio for the stake pools, unless the developers decided to include additional pools. But they would be in control of deciding the new block reward distribution rate through an IP, so there would still be some control over this possibility. For local pools, there are additional variables involved in the block reward distribution to stake pools, this is because additional stake pools can be set up by anyone and come online at any time. This also means stake pools can go offline at any time, and this is similar to mining farms in a POW blockchain, they can be turned off or on by the mining farm at any time, although the goal is to have the mining computers running 24/7. A POS blockchain that allows for anyone to set up a stake pool, maintains the block reward distribution between stake pools in a complex way. Let's look at an overly simplified POS blockchain, and see how max limits on the number of coins that can revive block rewards encourages more stake pools to be set up, and thus creating more individual validators for the blockchain's consensus method. This is a very simplified example, it is similar to the Cardano, ADA, blockchain, and to understand how it works I would encourage further research on how Cardano's stake pool structure is set up, for now let's look at how these block reward limits can be used to encourage stake pool operators to set up additional validators for the blockchain's consensus method.

Local stake pools receive block rewards based on the number of coins staked to the stake pool, the more wealth locked in the pool, the more block rewards the pool operator will receive, and these block rewards will be distributed between the pool operator and individual stakeholders. As mentioned before, these block rewards are the inflation rate for the blockchain, and these rates come to an average over time, sometimes giving a percent range such as 4-6% "interest" on wealth staked to the blockchain. This means sometimes stake pools may receive 4% on staked wealth, and other times it may be closer to 6%, but over time the block rewards average out, and for this example we will imagine a fixed 5% as the block reward rate for staked wealth. Keep in mind the individual stake pool operators are similar to mining farms in a POW blockchain in that, the block rewards can be affected by many factors, and for mining farms it is a higher hash rate that gives the mining farm more block rewards, while for stake pools it is a larger amount of wealth that gives the stake pool more block rewards. This means each local stake pool will receive a different amount of block rewards, based on, how many coins they have in the stake pool, how often these coins are added to and removed from the pool, and as mentioned before, epochs prevent pool hopping, ensuring stakeholders must lock up their wealth for a period of time in order to receive block rewards. *(Reference page 21)* All of this ensures stakeholders receive a steady block reward interest on their wealth, stake pool operators receive steady fees from the many stakeholders in their pool, and the blockchain has a validator that is verifying transactions and creating new blocks on the blockchain, now let's see how block reward limits can incentivize the creation of more validators for this example blockchain.

Local Pool Example:

For this POS blockchain stake pools can be set up by anyone with the knowledge and 1000 units of account for that blockchain, these 1000 coins will be staked to the blockchain by the stake pool operator, and it would be these 1000 coins that are destroyed if the blockchain has slashing, and if the pool operator attempted to manipulate the blockchain as mentioned before. This blockchain would allow for coins in the stake pool to receive block rewards up to 10k coins, and there can be more than 10k coins staked to the pool, however it is only the first 10k coins that will receive block rewards, all other coins will just sit in the pool, not increasing in number. These block rewards could also be scaled to zero, basically the first 5k coins get 100% of the possible block rewards (5% on staked wealth in the pool), while the next 2.5k coins in the stake pool get 60% of possible block rewards, and the next 2.5k get 30% of the block rewards, leaving any number of coins over 10k receiving 0% block rewards. This max limit of coins that can receive block rewards affects how many local pools will be set up, and if this block reward rate is reducing, then as stake pools start to reach the max limit it actually becomes more profitable for a stake pool operator to set up an additional stake pool to maximize their profits in block rewards. This would mean stake pools set up by supporters of the blockchain, or members of the community, could use social media platforms to attract more stakeholders to their pool, and set up additional pools as their following grew. It is similar for stake pools set up by an exchange, as more account holders deposit the coin in the exchange, the more stake pools the exchange would be able to set up. All stake pool operator types would eventually reach this threshold for block rewards, and they would see the ability to increase the fees/ block rewards they can receive by simply creating a new stake pool, and this is only profitable if there is demand for additional pools.

For this example, the stake pool operator has locked 1000 coins in the stake pool, and for the next 4k coins staked to the pool, the pool operator will receive 100% of fees on staked coins, however when the stake pool reaches 7.5k coins the stake pool operator would be losing 40% of the possible block rewards on 2.5k of the staked coins. When the stake pool reaches 10k coins the stake pool operator would be losing 70% of possible block rewards on the last 2.5k coins in the pool, but at this point the stake pool operator has 5k coins that could be earning more block rewards, and if they set up a new stake pool, that would mean 4k of those coins would be at 100% block rewards, and only 1k earning 60%. The stake pool operator would have to stake another 1000 coins to the new stake pool, and they would have to set up the hardware for the second pool as well, so there are added costs for them if they do this. However, if they know they have enough stakeholders willing to stake their wealth with the pool, then it would be more profitable for them if they set up an additional pool. This benefits the blockchain's consensus method because it is basically adding an individual validator, even though they have the same pool operator the stake pool itself is a unique validator hashing transactions and rejecting invalid transactions on the blockchain, and this adds to the decentralization of the blockchain overall.

There are many more factors at play in a POS blockchain with local pools, and this is an overly simplified example, however we can see that as long as there is demand for additional stake pools (basically stakeholders willing to stake wealth to the blockchain), then stake pool operators would be incentivized to set up the additional pools, and this benefits the blockchain's consensus method. Many other factors affect when stake pool operators would bring additional pools online, and stakeholders could remove their wealth from the pool at any time, depending on if the blockchain has lock-up periods or not. This could cause stake pool operators to either shut down a stake pool, or set up additional pools if more stakeholders were coming to the blockchain. This type of POS consensus method allows for an individual stakeholder to have more of a say in the direction the blockchain is developed, but it also brings the uncertainty of what stake pools will stay online hashing transactions, and what stake pools may be shut down by these individual stake pool operators. This is why some POS blockchains have a few "trusted" validators for the blockchain's consensus method, these stake pools are controlled by those invested in the blockchain, and they will do everything possible to keep the stake pool online and earning block rewards, and we will go over these "trusted" stake pools in more detail next. *(Reference page 88)*

"Trusted" Stake Pool:

As mentioned before each blockchain can be set up in a different way, for example POS blockchains can vary in how their stake pool structure is set up, and the Polkadot, DOT, blockchain is a great example of this. We will briefly look at how the Polkadot blockchain works and how its consensus method uses "trusted" stake pools, and something that can be thought of as local pools. The blockchain also adjusts the block reward distribution rates between these stake pools, and it can change the required number of coins to set up a validator on the blockchain as well. Before we look at the validators of the blockchain, it's important to know the Polkadot blockchain has two settlement layers, the relay chain, and the many parachains that settle transactions separate from the relay chain. However, they must eventually settle on this relay chain, sometimes called layer zero, in reference to layer 1 and layer 2 blockchains, and this is a layer zero chain that other blockchains can settle transactions on, allowing for interoperability between different blockchains. *(Reference page 28)*

(Illustration, next page)

Parachains are a separate blockchain built on the relay chain, there can be up to 100 different parachains that settle on this relay chain, and these parachains can be set up several ways. Some are new blockchain projects, they are looking to develop and test the new blockchain, and they rely on the relay chain for security and transaction finality. Other parachains can be large institutions, they bid on the parachains and use/control them for several months or years at a time, and there can only be so many parachains that can be bought by the highest bidder. The community can also vote on what parachains will be used as bridges to other existing blockchains, and all the parachains are leased with the DOT coin, creating demand for the coin. However, these coins are just locked in the parachain for a set amount of time (the lease length of the parachain), this can vary in length up to 2 years, and after that the locked DOT coins are returned to the investors/ supporters of the parachain. This allows investors to support the parachain projects by locking up their own wealth, and these new projects may reward these supporters with coins of the new blockchain. But the important thing to understand is that the DOT coin is required to show this support for the new parachain blockchain project. However, the DOT coin is not required for transactions on the individual parachains, they are only needed on the relay chain to represent the wealth needed to gain access to one of the parachains, either through bidding by large institutions, or community support, which also uses the DOT coin to show support for a new project or new bridge to an existing blockchain. This can be thought of as an ICO (initial coin offering) which is similar to an IPO (initial public offering), and there is no guarantee

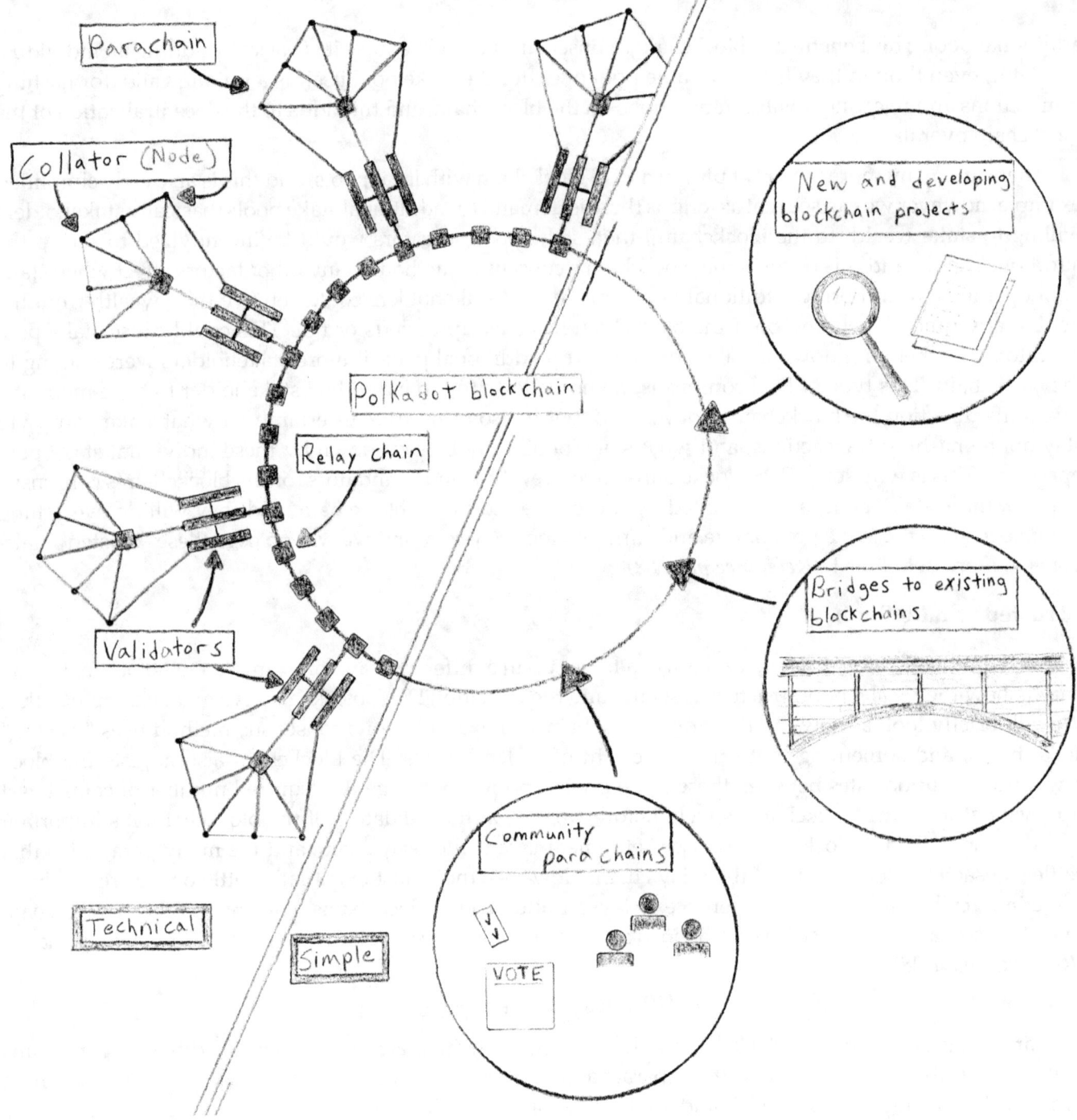

Polkadot Blockchain

On the left, parachains are drawn as they are commonly depicted, with their nodes and validators that are connected to the relay chain, and these can be simply thought of as use cases, which are represented on the right. It is important to understand that many blockchains are involved in the Polkadot ecosystem, and the DOT coin is not involved in all of them, it is mainly needed on the relay chain, interacting with the many parachains.

the new blockchain will be successful, but either way supporters would be rewarded with coins of the new blockchain, usually at discounted values, and if the new blockchain project grows then the value of the new coins or tokens may increase as well. This is a simplified description of Polkadot, and there are many more factors to consider in how the Polkadot blockchain achieves interoperability between blockchains, and I encourage further research for those looking to better understand the Polkadot blockchain overall. For now, we are just going to focus on how the stake pool structure is set up, what is required to be a "trusted" stake pool on the blockchain, and what is required to be a nominator on the blockchain.

The Polkadot blockchain has two types of validators, "nominators" can be thought of as local stake pools, and "validators" can be thought of as "trusted" stake pools. The nominators must link up with several of the "trusted" validators on the blockchain, and they receive block rewards from these validators, so they are not the same type of validator that directly receives block rewards from the creation of new blocks on the blockchain. Nominators are basically a way to allow for small amounts of wealth to earn block rewards on the blockchain, nominator pools are where individuals can pool their DOT coins to reach the required threshold to set up a nominator on the Polkadot blockchain. This is a simple explanation, and I would encourage further research to understand how Polkadot's consensus method utilizes validators and nominators in the transaction validation process. Basically, stakeholders can lock small amounts of wealth in nominator pools, and these can be set up by anyone with the required number of DOT coins, this would be the local pool operator, and stakeholders would be able to choose what nominator pool holds their wealth. However, to be a validator on the blockchain requires a very large number of DOT coins, these are locked-up to create a stake pool and earn block rewards from the blockchain, and the Polkadot blockchain includes slashing, so if these validators attempt to manipulate transactions on the blockchain they could lose this wealth locked in the stake pool.

There can be up to 1000 validators on the Polkadot blockchain, this can increase as the blockchain is developed, but there are currently about 300 validators, and this can vary as new investors lock-up wealth and create validators, or as investors remove wealth and remove the validator from the consensus method. The required number of DOT coins to create a validator, or "trusted" pool, changes over time, around 1.8 million DOT coins is the current requirement (DOT at $5 would mean it costs 9 million dollars to set up a validator), and this only makes the wealth eligible, the development team still has some say in who becomes an actual validator on the blockchain. This wealth can come from a single investor, or it can come from several investors and nominators who are linked to the validator, basically using the DOT in the nominator pool to show support for the validator. But either way this is a very high threshold of required coins, and this wealth is also susceptible to slashing, adding risk for large investors. *(Reference page 23)* While the required number of DOT coins to set up a nominator is around 128, it can also vary over time, but there is a clear gap in the amount of wealth required to set up a validator vs a nominator, and these nominator pool operators do not need to come up with the full 128 coins, other stakeholders can pool their DOT coins to reach the required number. This obviously affects the amount of block rewards the nominator pools receive compared to what the validators would receive, since block rewards are based off the amount of wealth staked to the pool, and the Polkadot blockchain has a block reward rate of 14-15% for staked wealth on the blockchain.

The Polkadot blockchain has a 28-day lock-up period for staked wealth, on some of the parachains the lock-up period can be less, although the coins locked-up are not always DOT coins, and they can be the coin of the blockchain running on the parachain. This lock-up period only applies to DOT coins locked-up with the validators, the nominators, and the stakeholders in the nominator pools, and this only applies to DOT coins being staked directly to the blockchain. Some exchanges offered staking services for the DOT coin, allowing for account holders to stake and unstake DOT coins whenever they wanted, and this is because exchanges would not always need to remove wealth from the stake pool when an account holder wanted to remove their wealth from the staking service. They would only update the account holder with a credit of wealth, and we will go over this more in depth later. Also know that several exchanges in the U.S. have removed the option to stake the DOT coin, and this has to do with unclear securities laws around blockchain coins and tokens.

The Polkadot blockchain is far more complex than this simple explanation, and how the blockchain creates interoperability between other blockchains involves far more than just the validators and nominators for the blockchain, but we can now see the clear wealth gap between the required number of DOT coins to be a validator vs a nominator. This large amount of wealth required to be a validator on the Polkadot blockchain is what makes it a "trusted" stake pool. The pool receives block rewards for validating transactions on the blockchain as mentioned before, and this is profitable for the "trusted" stake pool, so there would be less chance of the validator attempting to manipulate the blockchain. There is also slashing on the blockchain, so that large amount of wealth could be destroyed if the validator attempts to manipulate the blockchain, and this means there would be even less of a chance the stake pool operator would attempt this, since it would be their wealth that would be destroyed. However, these validators have the ability to push invalid transactions on the blockchain as mentioned before, it would not be wise since they would lose wealth, and there would be no guarantee the invalid transaction would be added into a new block on the blockchain. This is because there are several hundred other validators, and 10s of thousands of nominators on the blockchain, all of which are hashing the same transactions and rejecting invalid transactions as mentioned before. But even if it is unlikely, the reason these are considered "trusted" stake pools is because we must trust that the validator, or validators will not manipulate the blockchain, something they most likely will not do, but something they have the ability to do if they control a large percent, or the majority of, the consensus method for the blockchain.

If the validators had voting power on the blockchain based on how much wealth was locked in the stake pool, then they would clearly have the majority voting power when compared to nominators and their wealth. However, the Polkadot blockchain has a complex voting structure, one that does not give the majority voting power to these large "trusted" stake pools. We will look at the different ways to use voting coins/ tokens next, for now just understand even though these "trusted" stake pools lock-up far more wealth than the nominator pools, they do not have the ability to pass IPs for the blockchain. There is a separate voting structure for the blockchain that does not involve the validators of the blockchain, and this is different from everything we have gone over up until now, where validators for both POW and POS blockchains have had a vote in how the blockchain is developed over time. This separate voting structure prevents a centralized point of control over the implantation of IPs, and the nominator pools allow for individual stakeholders to participate and earn block rewards from these validators as well. This also adds to the decentralized aspect of the blockchain since they can choose the nominator and validators that their wealth supports (although that support would not be for IPs on the blockchain, it would only be for the operator of the nominator pool and/ or the validators linked to the nominator pool). It is also important to remember that this locked wealth is represented by the coin of the blockchain, the more wealth staked the fewer coins there are in circulation, and with demand being constant this should increase the dollar value of the coin over time, we will go over this in more detail later, but for now let's look at several ways voting coins/ tokens can be used on a blockchain.

Decentralized Voting Structure, Voting on a POS Blockchain:

If there is a separate voting structure for the blockchain that does not involve the validators (and nodes if they are allowed to vote on the blockchain) of the blockchain's consensus method, then IPs would not be voted on by these validators, however, other aspects of a validator that were mentioned before remains the same. These validators without voting power still hash transactions on the blockchain, they still reject invalid transactions and are rewarded with block rewards when new blocks are solved on the blockchain, and the SHA is still a very secure way to store and send information as mentioned before. The only real change is that the voting power has shifted away from the validators (and sometimes nodes) of the consensus method, this voting power controls the direction of development for the blockchain, and we will look at several ways a separate voting structure can be set up and who can gain this voting power on the blockchain. *(Reference page 66)* As mentioned before, blockchains can be set up in different ways, their voting structures can also vary in how the voting coins/ tokens are used, and who has control over the separate voting structure can also vary. This is why there are more factors to consider when determining if a blockchain that uses voting coins/ tokens is decentralized or not.

There are basically 3 ways coins or tokens could be used as the voting structure for a blockchain, and we will look at each of these next, but first understand these coins can be held by different types of people or groups, and how the voting structure is set up might be far more complex than these 3 examples. This is because voting coins are different from voting tokens, and who holds these coins/ tokens can also affect how the voting structure is set up, simply put there are many variables involved in a blockchain voting structure. This voting power can be held by the community of the blockchain, or by developers, or investors (both institutional and retail), or even in a DAO, which is a decentralized autonomous organization, and we will go over DAOs in more detail later. For now, just understand who holds the voting power for the blockchain, and whether the voting structure uses coins or tokens, affects how IPs are passed on the blockchain, and can affect how decentralized the blockchain is overall. The voting structure can be used for more than just implementing IPs, and we will go over this more later, but for now let's just look at 3 simple ways coins and tokens can be used to vote on a blockchain.

(Illustration, next page)

Voting Coins:

The coin of the blockchain can be used as a way to vote on the blockchain, and if the blockchain is a layer 2, then the token can be used as a way to vote on the blockchain, both of these basically mean it is the unit of account for that blockchain that has voting power. It is the same unit of account that is represented as the coin or token for that blockchain that has the ability to vote on IPs, this is the same coin that is traded on exchanges, and the same coin that is created as new blocks are added to the blockchain. Basically, the coin has tradable value, it can be bought, sold, or held, by anyone with a wallet address for that blockchain, and with the wealth required to buy the coins on any exchanges that offer the coin of that blockchain. The more coins a wallet has, the larger the vote they would have on the blockchain, and this is a simplified example because many times the coins must be locked up or used in some way on the blockchain in order for the coins to cast a vote. However, the concept remains the same, the more coins someone had the larger their vote could be, and this is why blockchains will sometimes require these coins be locked on the blockchain for periods of time, it limits the amount of wealth that may move in and out of the blockchain trying to manipulate the voting structure.

The way the voting structure accounts for votes on the blockchain can vary, but they all would have in common one thing, the unit of account for that blockchain is involved in the voting process, and this is the same coin that is traded on exchanges, and created in the form of block rewards on the blockchain. Locking up coins for periods of time is how voting on the Polkadot blockchain works, for both parachains and the relay chain, and this is different from locking up coins in a stake pool, or in Polkadots case a nominator pool. As mentioned before Polkadot's voting structure is complex, and I would suggest further research to better understand how it is set up, but it is a good example of a blockchain that uses its coin in its voting structure. Not all of the coins in existence on the blockchain must vote, and many coin holders will not take the additional time and effort to use their coins to vote on upcoming IPs for the blockchain. It is usually not hard to vote on a blockchain, but many holders of the coin are usually just investors, they are only invested in hopes that the value of the coin will increase, or they are staking the coin to gain block rewards, also increasing their overall wealth. This is why the voting structure for these blockchains can vary, there is no guarantee all coins will vote, and blockchain projects must set up the voting structure in a way that prevents a large amount of wealth from moving into the blockchain, buying the coin, and gaining a large part or the majority of the voting power for that blockchain. Although as mentioned before, majority control of the voting structure does not mean the blockchain will be exploited or negatively affected, it just means the individual or group in control of that majority vote could update and change the blockchain if they wanted to, and in some cases this could be done with a soft fork, rather than a hard fork, since there is a majority in control of implementing IPs on the blockchain.

If the unit of account for the blockchain is used in the voting structure of the blockchain, then this can be thought of as a voting "coin." Although some layer 2 tokens may use this type of voting structure as well, so

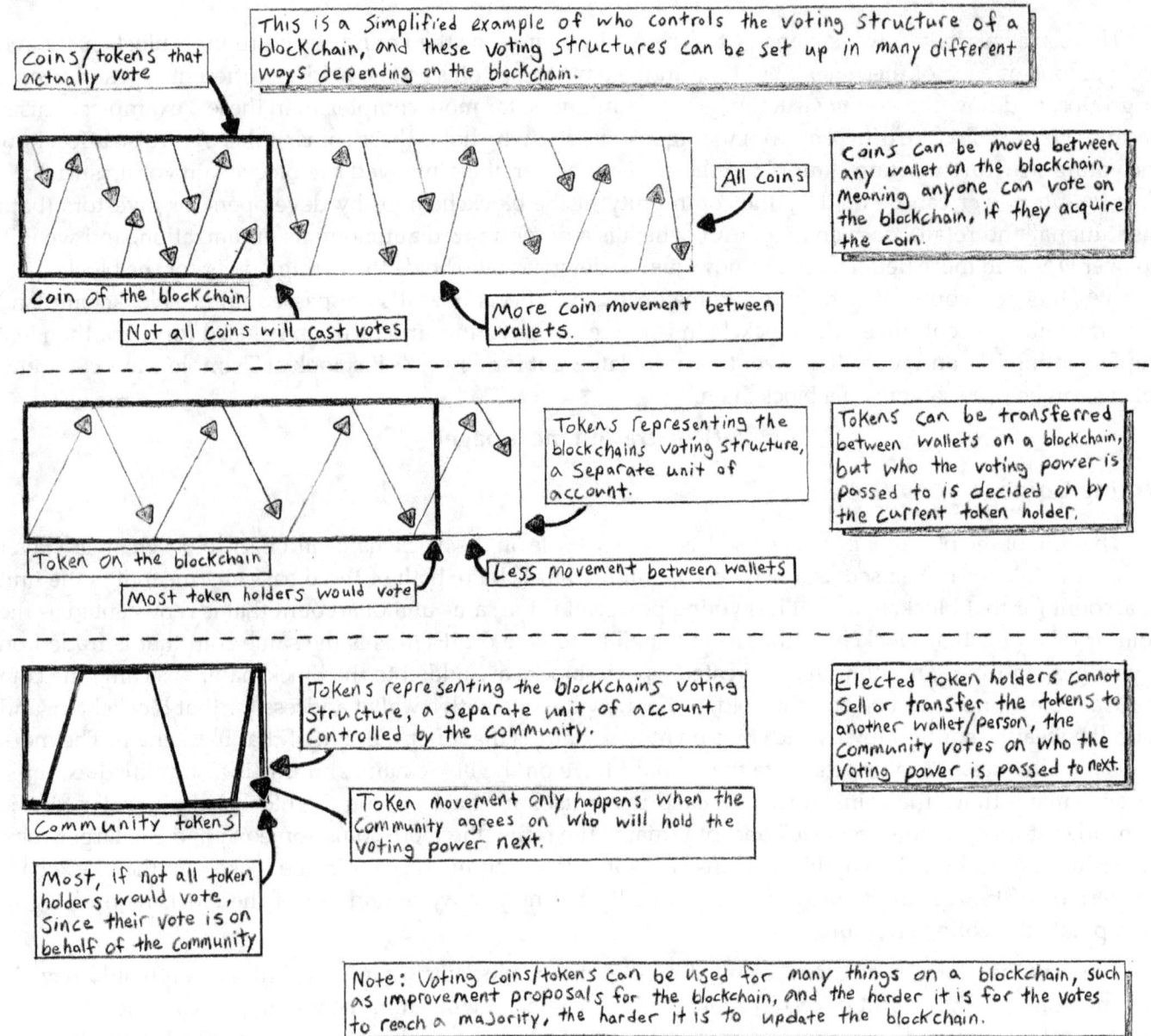

Voting Coins / Tokens

Voting structures can widely vary, they are usually unique to the blockchain that uses them, and all the coins or tokens do not necessarily need to vote on each IP for the blockchain. These can be voting "coins" being the unit of account for the blockchain, or they can be voting "tokens" basically a separate unit of account on the blockchain, and these voting tokens can either be held by anyone, or only by individuals elected by the community.

Pg. 12, middle section: The voting power for a blockchain is not always held by validators in the consensus method, this voting power can be represented by a separate unit of account on the blockchain, or by using the actual unit of account for the blockchain, and this is what separates voting coins from voting tokens.

Pg. 32, middle section: When the validators in a blockchains consensus method lose the ability to vote on IPs for the blockchain, some other type of governance structure must be created, and this can involve the unit of account for the blockchain, or a separate unit of account.

Pg. 32, upper section: When the main unit of account is used in the voting structure of the blockchain, it means anyone can vote on the blockchain, all they need to do is buy the coin or token, and these voting structures can vary between blockchains, each one can be set up differently.

Pg. 51, bottom section: When "trusted" validators are a part of the consensus method of a blockchain, they usually do not have voting power on the blockchain, and this means the separate voting structure is in the hands of developers, or the community.

Pg. 52, bottom section: Validators in a POS blockchain can still hash transactions and earn block rewards based on how many coins are staked to the pool, even without voting power on the blockchain, and either a separate unit of account can be created for the voting structure, or the unit of account for the POS blockchain can be used in the voting structure.

Pg. 59, middle section: When the validators have voting power on the blockchain, decentralization can be determined by looking at the network of validators, however, when voting power on the blockchain is separated from the validator network, it creates more factors involved in determining the overall decentralization of the blockchain.

Pg. 64, right section: Each type of voting coin or token can be held by different types of individuals, the coin of a blockchain can be bought by anyone, while some tokens can only be held by individuals appointed by the development team or community, and who is able to hold this voting power can affect the blockchains overall decentralization.

Pg. 67, middle section: Voting tokens that can be transferred to anyone allow for the possibility of an individual eventually gaining the majority of the tokens, and this is why development teams will sometimes hold on to this voting power, until it can be passed on to the community in some way.

Pg. 69, bottom section: Community tokens are similar to other voting tokens in that, they are a separate unit of account on the blockchain, but they are not held by just anyone, and the community votes on who will hold the voting power for the blockchain next.

it's best not to think of this as a voting structure that only layer 1 coins can incorporate into the blockchain code. It just means there is no separate unit of account on the blockchain for the voting structure, it is the unit of account that is traded on the blockchain, and the unit of account that is created as a block reward on the blockchain that can vote. These types of voting structures would need to involve the coin being used in some way on the blockchain, simply put, there would need to be a transaction of some kind on the blockchain to record the vote. This could be anything from locking up the coin for a day or a week, or any other action that the coin holder could take with the coins that represent their wealth on the blockchain. These would be coins that they hold in their own wallet on the blockchain, and wealth held on exchanges may not be able to participate in the voting process, and we will go over exchanges in more detail later. However, the fact that not all the coins would vote on the blockchain presents developers with a problem, how do they ensure one large coin holder does not out vote other coin holders on the blockchain. Remember these coins are the unit of account for the blockchain, so anyone could buy more coins from exchanges and increase their potential vote on the blockchain. Again, this possibility is reduced when the voting structure requires coins to be locked up or used in some way on the blockchain, but it does not always remove the risk of a large amount of wealth moving onto the blockchain and gaining the majority of the voting power.

This is why some blockchains incorporate a voting structure with a separate unit of account for voting on the blockchain, and we will look at these other 2 types next, but for now just understand using the coin of the blockchain in the voting process has pros and cons. By using the unit of account for the blockchain in the blockchains voting structure, developers are giving anyone the ability to buy the coin and use it to vote on IPs for the blockchain, this is good and adds to the decentralization of the blockchain. However, it also means that those with more wealth would be able to buy more coins and pass or reject IPs for that blockchain, and this reduces the decentralization of the blockchain. Simply put, blockchains must find a balance between these pros and cons if the voting structure involves the unit of account for the blockchain, either the coin of the layer 1 blockchain, or the token of the layer 2 blockchain, and this is why some blockchain developers will create a separate unit of account for the voting structure of the blockchain. *(Reference page 28)*

Voting Tokens:

Another way the voting structure can be set up, is by using a separate unit of account for voting on the blockchain, this can be thought of as using tokens for the voting structure of a blockchain, and it is important to understand this is a separate unit of account on the blockchain, these tokens are not the coins that are traded on exchanges, and they are not issued as block rewards for the blockchain. However, these tokens can still have value, they can be sold or traded by the owner of the tokens, or whoever controls the wallet that holds the tokens, and this does not have to take place on an exchange. These tokens often just move between wallets, and they represent a portion the voting power for the blockchain. Who controls the wallet that holds the voting tokens is important, this is because those tokens that represent the voting power for the blockchain can be given to anyone, either sold to someone looking to control the development of the blockchain, or simply transferred to another wallet. *(Reference page 66)* This means the voting power can be given to anyone, there are no restrictions on who can hold the tokens, however, it is ultimately up to the current holder of the tokens to decide who to give this voting power to next. The ability to decide who is transferred the voting power for the blockchain is the main difference between the two types of voting tokens. For this type of token, wallet holders could be developers or large investors, and this would be a way to give developers the control they need to further develop the blockchain through IPs. This would also be a way to compensate large investors, since these tokens would basically represent the ownership of the blockchain since they controlled its development, and this ownership would have value, so the large investors could sell the voting tokens if they ever wanted to regain their investment. Some blockchains will eventually disperse this voting power to the community, and we will look at this more next, but for now it is important to understand even if these tokens have no dollar value on exchanges, they are still valued, and holders of the tokens would be compensated when the blockchain is developed and the voting power is dispersed.

The type of voting structure that uses tokens can be thought of as owning a part of a company, or stock in a company, the control can be sold to anyone the owner chooses, this makes these tokens valuable for those looking to invest in, or develop a blockchain project, and this would be considered somewhat centralized if there are only a few players investing in the blockchain and holding the voting tokens. As mentioned before, sometimes blockchain projects require this greater control over the implementation of IPs since it allows developers to quickly update the blockchain if needed, but this should only be needed for a period of time, and the blockchain should grow and develop into a more decentralized voting structure over time. Otherwise, this would be a major centralized point of control or failure, the voting power could be transferred over time to those that might negatively affect the blockchain by approving updates that users of the blockchain did not like, or even ones that would cause the dollar value of the coin or token to fall. If this type of centralized control over the voting structure of the blockchain is required for the blockchain to run indefinitely, then these centralized points would need to be disclosed to investors in the blockchain. Even if the blockchains roadmap is to eventually disperse this control, investors need disclosures of who actually controls the voting structure of the blockchain at that point in time. This does not mean developers or investors who have a large percent of the voting power for a blockchain will abuse this power, both developers and investors have a reason to want to see the blockchain project succeed. Some investors may only be interested in the short term, but if they are long-term investors, then they would want to see the blockchain develop and grow its use cases over time, creating demand for the coin or token of the blockchain, and thus increasing its value and increasing the investor's investment in the blockchain.

If these tokens are spread out between wallet holders than there is still some decentralization in that it is not just a few individuals that control the implementation of IPs on the blockchain, but these tokens could eventually be accumulated by one or several large investors, and this would be a centralized point of control for the blockchain, one that could be achieved with a large amount of wealth. This makes these tokens ok, but not great for decentralization in the voting structure of a blockchain, although new and developing blockchains may use voting tokens in the early development stages as mentioned before. But the goal of this development should be to eventually reach a voting structure that is decentralized, and control over updates to the blockchain is handed off to the community and users of the blockchain, and we will look more at how tokens can be used in this way next.

Community Voting Tokens:

Another way tokens could be used in the voting structure of a blockchain is similar to the previous way tokens could be used, in that there is a separate unit of account created on the blockchain for voting, and the voting tokens themselves are not really different, it is who holds the tokens that make this type of voting structure different. This voting power is held by the community, either through DAOs or some other governance structure built on the blockchain, the voting power would remain in the community's control, and individuals would be appointed or elected to control this voting power for a period of time. How the community controls this voting power can vary between blockchains, each one can have slight or major differences in how the tokens are held. Basically who controls the keys or seed phrase to the wallet holding the voting tokens, and this is important because it means the elected or appointed individual would not have complete control over the tokens. They would not be able to send the tokens to another wallet and decide who controls the voting power after them, it is the community that would vote on who would hold this voting power next, and this adds to the decentralization of the blockchain overall. Some blockchain voting structures could allow for the community to vote on who has this voting power and for how long, while other blockchains could see the development team appoint individuals to have this voting power for a period of time at first, and this lets the developers have more control over the early development of the blockchain through the implementation of IPs.

This type of voting structure would allow the community that follows a blockchain more of a say in how the blockchain is developed, this adds to the decentralization of the blockchain, but it also removes the ability for the tokens to be sold or given to just anyone, and although anyone can be appointed or elected to hold this voting power, they do not have complete control over the tokens. *(Reference page 66)* This further adds to the decentralization of the blockchain, since the tokens and the voting power they have on the blockchain cannot be transferred to another individual without the approval of the community or development team, and development teams may appoint individuals to hold this voting power at first. But this would be how they eventually disperse the voting power, allowing the community to vote on who holds the voting power next. It is also important to understand this voting power does not have to be given to a single individual, there can be several people that hold a percent of the voting power for the blockchain, and we will go over this more later when we look at how DAOs work. It is also important to understand that because these tokens do not move between wallets often, and because even the holders of the tokens do not have complete control over the tokens. These tokens do not really have value in dollar terms, their value comes from the ability to vote on the blockchain, and they are not traded on exchanges like voting coins, or traded between wallets like some voting tokens.

One thing all voting coins/ tokens have in common is that they need to be used in a way that creates a transaction on the blockchain, this is how the blockchain is able to verify the votes, and only valid transactions are included in the blockchain, so malicious actors attempting to push invalid transactions on the blockchain would be rejected as mentioned before. These transactions can be anything, usually requiring the coin or token holder to lock up the wealth for a period of time, or anything that would create a transaction on the blockchain, and this is to prove the vote comes from someone who has a unit of account that is allowed to cast a vote on that blockchain.

Other Aspects of Decentralization, Nodes:

Nodes were mentioned before, but now let us look at how nodes can play a part in the decentralization of a blockchain. Nodes are like validators in that they hash transactions on the blockchain, sometimes nodes can have voting power on the blockchain as well, and they pass on valid transactions, while rejecting invalid transactions on the blockchain. This allows the validators of the blockchain's consensus method more options when it comes to where they push and pull data to and from as mentioned before. Nodes allow validators to receive new transactions to hash from more than just the other validators of the blockchain, and for blockchains with fewer validators this would help reduce the centralized point of control that would be only a few validators hashing transactions on the blockchain.*(Reference page 123)* However, nodes are not incorporated in every consensus method, some blockchains would not allow validators to receive new transactions from nodes, and this would not prevent a node from simply storing a copy of the blockchain, this would be possible and could be updated as new blocks are agreed upon by validators. However, these nodes would not be pushing and pulling data to and from other nodes and validators, they would only be a copy of the blockchain, and this would not add to the blockchain's decentralization overall. Decentralization comes from nodes that are hashing transactions on the blockchain, they send and receive these transactions to and from other nodes and validators, and even though they do not receive block rewards for doing this, they are interacting with the validators of the blockchain's consensus method, and this can affect the decentralization of the blockchain overall. This is because there are more individually controlled nodes hashing transactions on the blockchain, remember each validator and node are hashing the same transactions, they should all agree, but discrepancies can happen, and when they do, the more individually controlled transaction validators there are (including nodes), the better it is for the blockchain's consensus method.

There is no guarantee that a node will be set up by a good actor, as mentioned before some nodes could attempt to include invalid transactions in the next block of the blockchain, but nodes still require some investment of time and wealth to set up. So, bad actors would be limited in the number of nodes they could set up, and the wealth they could gain by exploiting the blockchain might be minimal depending on the type of invalid transaction the node is pushing. This means most nodes would be set up and run by supporters of the blockchain, as long as the node is cheap and somewhat easy to set up than this would be a great way for investors to have a copy of the blockchain, and these nodes help all parties even though they do not receive block rewards for their efforts. The blockchain gains a node that is validating transactions and passing them on to validators of the blockchain, and the node operator gets a running copy of the blockchain that is as up-to-date as possible, along with voting power in some blockchains. They set up a node because they are a supporter of the blockchain and want to help its consensus method, or they are a large investor in the blockchain, basically meaning they hold a lot of wealth in the coin or token of the blockchain, and they want to have an up-to-date copy of the blockchain to further protect this wealth.

Nodes also reduce centralization risks, they can reduce centralized points like physical locations and digital locations that were mentioned before, and this is because the node is both located in a physical location, and offers an additional digital location to other nodes and validators of the blockchain's consensus method. Nodes may be set up in a physical location that is closer to a validator than other validators in the blockchain's consensus method, they would provide a relay of this information between validators, and nodes could give the somewhat isolated validator a closer and slightly faster source to push and pull data to and from. *(Reference page 50)* The node is also added to the list of possible sources a validator can push or pull data to and from, this adds to the number of connections possible between nodes and validators, and validators can remove a malicious node from their list, so additional nodes would give the validator plenty of alternatives to replace the malicious node with. Basically, the more possible connections between validators and nodes there are, the more the blockchains consensus method is decentralized, and more connections are possible as more nodes are set up on the blockchain. Blockchains that do not allow for nodes to interact with validators are not all bad, as mentioned before nodes can also be used as a way to attack the blockchain with invalid transactions, so some blockchains would rather just remove this possibility altogether, and the blockchain may be a little less decentralized overall, but it would not have to worry about nodes pushing invalid transactions on the blockchain. However, when nodes are a part of the transaction validation process (basically the consensus method, although they are not adding blocks and earning block rewards) it allows for any individual to be a part of that process, and this adds to the decentralization of the blockchain's consensus method overall.

Overall, nodes are good for a blockchain's consensus method, as long as they are cheap and somewhat east to set up, then more individuals would be able to set up a node on the blockchain, and this allows them to be a part of validating transactions and pushing this data throughout the blockchain's validator network. Although nodes interact with the validators of the blockchain's consensus method, they do not benefit from the block rewards, the only benefit to setting up a node is that the node operator has a running copy of the blockchain, and sometimes voting power on the blockchain. But running a node does require some time and knowledge to set up, so not everyone will run a node. Later we will cover use cases on a blockchain, and nodes are often involved in these use cases, each blockchain can be set up differently as mentioned before, so nodes can be much more than just a running copy of the blockchain. Depending on the blockchain, nodes could be used specifically for use cases involving the blockchain, they would still be hashing transactions and rejecting invalid ones as mentioned before, but they would also be involved with the transactions of a use case on the blockchain. An example would be the Lighting Network, these nodes allow for a faster transaction speed than settling the transaction on the blockchain through the validators, and ordinals can only be identified using a wallet set up on a partial node, both of these are use cases for the Bitcoin blockchain, and we will go over each of them in more detail later. *(Reference page 120)* For now, just understand nodes at a basic level are just running copies of a blockchain, but nodes can be used for many different use cases on a blockchain, and some blockchains have unique names for the nodes on their blockchain. These nodes are able to interact with the blockchains use case because they have a portion of the blockchains code downloaded, and some use cases many require the entire blockchain to be downloaded, either way most nodes are simply hashing transactions on the blockchain, either transactions involving the network of validators, or transactions involving a use case on the blockchain.

Think of a blockchain as a cake, there are many ingredients that all come together to make the cake, and nodes would be like the eggs, they help add structure to the cake. Some cakes do not need to use eggs, and they can be substituted with other ingredients, but for recipes that require the use of eggs, the taste of eggs is lost in the making of the cake. People do not take a bite of cake and say they can really taste the eggs, but there is a taste difference if the eggs are not added, and they might not even know what ingredient is missing, but clearly the cake would not taste right if no eggs were used. This is kind of like nodes in a blockchain's consensus method, they play a part in validating transactions, and push that data to validators of the blockchain. But they are not always needed and there are alternatives, and even when they are included in a blockchain's consensus method, they do not form blocks or earn block rewards, so their taste if you will, is lost or overshadowed by the other ingredients in the cake. This makes nodes an important part of a blockchain's consensus method overall, they are not always required, but when they are included in a blockchains code they are in the background, and sometimes their importance is forgotten, like eating cake and not tasting the eggs that were used to make it.

Improvement Proposals:

As mentioned before who can vote on IPs for a blockchain is important, this can affect the decentralization of the blockchain, and these voting structures can vary, either allowing validators or nodes of the consensus method to vote, or allowing coins/ tokens to represent votes on the blockchain. The ability to create IPs for the blockchain is also important, and how IPs are voted on and created must be balanced, to understand this let's look at a simple example. The first blockchain allows for anyone to create and submit IPs on the blockchain, however the voting power for that blockchain is held by the developers and large investors, and this means they could ignore any IPs they did not like, for one reason or another. The second blockchain would allow for anyone to create and submit IPs on the blockchain as well, but voting power for this blockchain is not centralized into the hands of a few, and this can be a decentralized network of validators (POW or POS), or a separate unit of account for voting on the blockchain, like voting coins or tokens as mentioned before. For the first blockchain IPs would basically be suggestions, they could be completely ignored even if the community supported the IP, and the second blockchain would allow for new ideas to be considered, and if the community supported the IP than it would be implemented.

If the voting structure of the blockchain involves voting coins/ tokens, then it must be set up in a way that does not allow for an individual or group to acquire the majority of the voting power for the blockchain, basically buying up large numbers of coins or tokens. If it is possible to gain this majority voting power for the blockchain, then even if anyone can create an IP, that majority holder of the voting power could simply ignore IPs they did not like, and obviously they could pass IPs they did support. This is one way malicious actors could try to attack the blockchain, if they were able to gain the majority of the voting power for the blockchain they could pass IPs that make the blockchain easier to exploit, or even change things like the block reward rate. This would give validators more block rewards, but it would also increase the inflation rate of that blockchain, which would negatively affect the dollar value of the coin over time. The voting structure for the blockchain matters, this is because if it is exploited than IPs could be used as a way to attack the blockchain, but most IPs are carefully considered, and they usually do not negatively affect the blockchain.

The ability for anyone to create and submit an IP for a blockchain adds to the overall decentralization of the blockchain, this is because more people and more ideas could be involved in the development of the blockchain over time, and these new ideas would still need to be voted on, not all new ideas are good ideas. However, this allows for the community of a blockchain project to have more of a say in how the blockchain is developed, either through voting or through creating IPs, and they would be able to have an active role in new use cases for the blockchain. This is important because the community of the blockchain are usually users of the blockchain, and they are the demand for the use case. Giving them more of a say in how the blockchain is developed would mean there would be actual demand for the use case that is being developed, and this would cause increased transaction volume on the blockchain, and over time increase the dollar value of the coin or token for the blockchain.

These added use cases for the blockchain create demand for the coin or token, we will go over this later when we look at use cases in more detail, for now just understand that adding use cases to a blockchain that the community of that blockchain actually want is good for the blockchain overall, and it is what creates demand for the coin or token involved in the use case. This is good for investors that hold their wealth in the blockchain, even if they do not care about new IPs and use cases for the blockchain, they would benefit from the higher demand, and the value increase of the coins they hold. Developers would also benefit from this growth and development of the blockchain, both because they would be working on a popular and growing blockchain project. But also because they are usually compensated in the coin or token of the blockchain, so they would also see their wealth grow, just as investors would. Users of the blockchain would also be happy, since it would be their demand that is driving these factors, if they did not like the use case then there would not be as much demand for the coin or token and its value would not increase as much or at all.

Simply put, the ability for anyone to create an IP on the blockchain is good, but these IPs are basically a suggestion box if the voting structure for IPs is controlled by only a few validators of the consensus method (POW or POS). Or if the voting power is held by the developers and large investors holding voting coins/tokens, and these types of voting structures are not necessarily bad, they can be decentralized in other ways. By allowing users of the blockchain and its community to both vote on and create IPs for the blockchain is what adds to the decentralization of the blockchain overall, however this does create more avenues of attack against the blockchain. For example, a voting structure that is separate from the consensus method of the blockchain has more factors involved and more centralized points that can exist, and as mentioned before this does not mean blockchains that use this separate voting structure are bad, it only means there are more factors to consider when determining if the blockchain is decentralized or not.

Not all investors will care about voting on the blockchain, or about the direction the blockchain is developed in. They could be short-term investors, ones that do not care about long-term growth, or they could be long-term investors that think the blockchain will grow over time, but ones that don't follow or care about how the blockchain is actually developed. Their investment would still grow as the blockchain grows, and there will be many investors like this, it is not necessarily a bad thing. For whatever reason the investor has chosen to invest in the blockchain, and whether they participate in the voting structure of the blockchain or not, the creation and implementation of IPs on a blockchain is a factor to consider when determining if a blockchain is decentralized or not. IPs are a part of the blockchain's code, and they are a factor in how decentralized the blockchain is, however, not all aspects of a blockchain's decentralization have to do with the blockchains code, and next we will look at other factors that may create centralized points that can affect a blockchain, but might not involve the blockchain code itself.

Decentralized External Factors:

Most of the factors involved in a blockchain's decentralization are a part of the blockchains code, in one way or another the blockchains code, or how it is set up, play a part in either its centralized or decentralized aspects. However, there are other factors that could affect the blockchain that might not involve the blockchains code, these can be thought of as factors outside the blockchains code, and although some of these might involve the blockchains code to an extent, overall, they can be thought of as an external factor. One of these external factors would be the development team, so far we have seen how the development team can control and affect the blockchain as it is developed through IPs. The development team can also have voting power on the blockchain, and they can even control large numbers of coins that exist on the blockchain. These coins can be used to pay for the development of the blockchain, or they can represent the blockchains voting structure that was mentioned before. The main thing to understand is that this control over the coins or tokens exists because of the blockchains code, and this means the coins or tokens can only be used in accordance with the blockchains code. However, some blockchains allow for developers or large investors to have control over aspects of the blockchain that might not affect the blockchain code itself, and these centralized points might not have the ability to attack or negatively affect the blockchain, but they can affect how the blockchain is used, or how users interact with the blockchain. The Uniswap blockchain is an example of this, even though its blockchain code could be considered decentralized, the development team has the ability to add or remove trading pairs on the exchange, and we will go over Uniswap in more detail later, for now just understand development teams can have centralized control over some aspects of the blockchain, even if that control does not directly involve or affect the blockchains code itself.

External Factors, Development Team:

The development team of a blockchain would also have control over areas like advertising, working with exchanges to list the coin of the blockchain, and working with regulatory bodies by providing required information or disclosures. Although advertising for a specific coin or token can be done by anyone, the development team would use advertising as a way to get more investors to hold their wealth in the coin or token of the blockchain, and this type of promotion would affect the blockchain's usage, drawing in more investors and increasing the dollar value of the coin or token. This is a centralized point of control; however, it does not control the blockchain code, it only affects the number of possible investors in the blockchains coin or token, and this type of advertising should be required to disclose the risks associated with the blockchain. This could be achieved by disclosing the risk level of the coin or token according to the blockchain standards, it could be as simple as a disclaimer at the end of the promotion, something similar to alcohol or medication warnings, and we will go over this in more detail later when we look at the Arizona Blockchain Standards.

The development team would also work with exchanges to list the coin or token on the exchange, although they do not have to, if account holders at the exchange want to be able to invest in a particular coin, then the exchange would be incentivized to list the coin. As more exchanges offer the coin or token, more investors would have the ability to invest and hold their wealth in the blockchain, adding to the demand for the coin or token. Development teams can also work with regulators providing them with required information regarding the blockchain, this approval from regulators would allow more investors to invest in the blockchain, and currently the lack of approval from regulators is holding many investors back from storing their wealth in a particular coin or token. As a blockchain gains more support from regulators, the more investors, particularly large investors, are willing to invest in the coin or token of the blockchain. This gives the development team some control over how the blockchain grows and is adopted overall, it would be their efforts, or lack of efforts, that allow more investors to hold their wealth in the blockchain, and this will add to the coin or tokens value if factors like the block reward rate and circulating supply are balanced as mentioned before. Even if control over advertising does not directly affect the blockchains code, it could affect the dollar value of the coin or token for better or worse, and this would affect the wealth that an investor holds in the blockchain, so who controls these factors are important to an investor and users of the blockchain. Although these factors would not be as important as who controls the validators of the consensus method, or who controls the voting structure of the blockchain, these are far more important when determining if the blockchain is decentralized or not. But investors should still consider external factors such as the development team, since their actions, or lack of actions, could affect the dollar value of their investment.

External Factors, Whale Wallets:

Some external factors might involve the blockchains code to an extent, an example would be large wallet addresses, or whale wallets, these wallet addresses are just ledgers on the blockchain as mentioned before, and these wallets do not negatively affect the blockchain by violating the blockchains code, but they can affect the dollar value of the coin or token. They could do this by selling a large number of coins all at once, this does not violate the blockchains code, unless the large wallet has a vesting schedule, and this would prevent the wallet from causing this large sell pressure for the blockchains coin or token. However, if there was no vesting schedule, the blockchain would have no control over the possibility of the large wallet holder selling all their coins, and this sell pressure would cause the dollar value of the blockchains coin or token to fall. Whale wallets could be considered a centralized point for a blockchain because they would allow for the possibility of the coin's value to collapse, the blockchain code itself has no control over this, only the individual who has the keys to the wallet has control over this possibility. *(Reference page 9)* This is a good example of an external factor that involves the blockchains code, in this case the wallet address, but the blockchain has no control over the possibility of that wallet selling all the coins at once, creating a centralized risk for the blockchain.

This sell pressure would cause the coin's value to collapse if enough coins were sold at once, although it does not necessarily negatively affect the blockchain overall, it only affects the coin or tokens dollar value, and the blockchain might still be able to validate transactions and create new blocks, although smaller blockchains with lower market caps would be affected more by a large wallet selling all at once. Making whale wallets more of a centralized point of failure rather than a point of control, this is because the control over the blockchain is deliberately used to negatively affect the coin's value. At least this would be the case for unknown whale wallets that sell to crash the price of a coin or token, while other large wallets with vesting schedules can be trusted to not sell all at once since it would violate the blockchains code. This external factor is more of a risk for new and developing blockchains, ones with low market caps would be greatly affected by a large amount of sell pressure, while blockchains with a higher market cap, and ones with more buyers and sellers, might be able to absorb this added sell pressure with the higher demand for its coin or token. This makes external factors like whale wallets important for some blockchains, and less important for other blockchains (obviously depending on the total number of coins that exist on the blockchain, and how many are held in a single wallet). Each blockchain can be set up different as mentioned before, and large wallets holders on a blockchain should be judged based on their size, as well as several other factors, especially if those wallets are known wallets and have vesting schedules, since this removes the risk of the coins being all sold at once. *(Reference page 103)*

External Factors, Front Running:

Validators in a blockchains consensus method have the ability to decide what transactions they include in their version of the next block in the blockchain, meaning they could ignore certain transactions, even if these transactions are valid and do not violate the blockchains code. However, if they did this and other validators in the consensus method included the transaction, then the validator attempting to exclude the transaction would be less likely to receive block rewards, and the transaction would be added to the blockchain anyway by another validator. Although their block rewards would only be affected if they were excluding a large number of transactions, not just one or two. While transactions that are ignored by most, if not all the validators of the blockchain's consensus method, could be prevented from being added to the next block in the blockchain. This basically means the ledger of accounts for the blockchain is not updated to include this transaction, preventing the movement of coins or tokens on the blockchain, or any other type of transaction on the blockchain. This can be just a delay of adding the transaction, or completely preventing the transaction, and front running might not even involve preventing transactions. This would only be adding in transactions prior to other transactions, and all of this can be done by the validators of the blockchain's consensus method, whether the individual validator's version of the next block is added to the blockchain or not. It's important to understand that these transactions are valid transactions, they do not violate the blockchains code, it is only the order of transactions as they are settled on the blockchain that is changed, and this is not like validators attempting to manipulate the blockchain with invalid transactions as mentioned before, all validators would view these transactions as valid, the difference being the order in which they are settled and added to the blockchain. *(Reference page 2)*

This is why front running blockchain transactions is usually only possible for blockchains that have "trusted" validators, these validators have a large percent of the blockchain's consensus method, and they could also push their version of the blockchain to other nodes or validators that may rely on the "trusted" validator for transaction data. This would sometimes have to be several "trusted" validators, depending on how much of the blockchain's consensus method they controlled. As mentioned before, blockchains can have "trusted" validators in their consensus method, and these can be sent up in many different ways to prevent centralized points of control over the blockchain, and these "trusted" validators are not always bad. *(Reference page 88)* If the blockchains code included slashing then the validator would lose wealth if it attempted to manipulate the blockchain, but front running transactions does not always violate the blockchains code, and if this manipulation does not violate the blockchains code, then these "trusted" validators would be able to change the order of transactions and/or front run the transactions. These "trusted" validators are usually set up and controlled by large investors or developers of the blockchain, as mentioned before these investors and developers are usually good actors who only want to help the blockchain develop and grow, however some of the investors, or even developers, may want to use this control to increase their own wealth. This type of front running is possible with any type of exchange that is settling buy and sell orders, so in this aspect things like the stock market and how it settles transactions is similar to how a blockchain settles transactions. The control would come from either clearing houses and stockbrokers, or validators in the blockchain's consensus method, they both have the same control, and we must trust them to not abuse this control for their own befit. This is why "trusted" validators, or "trusted" stake pools are not as decentralized as local pools, or any consensus method that allows for anyone to set up a validator and earn block rewards, be it POS pools, or POW mining farms. This is because the ability to decide the order of transactions cannot be controlled when the validator network is made up of many different individuals who care more about earning block rewards than they care about the order of transactions as they are added to the blockchain. An exception would be fees or tips that can be added to transactions and given to the validator as compensation for prioritizing that particular transaction, and we will go over this in more detail later.

Front running transactions is different for exchanges, the exchange would have the ability to see buy and sell orders on its own platform, however it would not have access to or control over all transactions that take place on the blockchain of each coin and token they offer on their platform. This is because account holders on an exchange are not always settling their transactions on the blockchain of the coin or token they are buying or selling. Their accounts would either be credited or debited, and we will go over exchanges in more depth later, for now just understand front running can exist in several ways for blockchain coins and tokens. But when the validators of a blockchains consensus method have the ability to decide the order of transactions, and even prevent certain transactions, then there exists a centralized point of control based on external factors for that blockchain, even if other aspects of the blockchain are considered decentralized.

Controlling the order of transactions does not negatively affect the blockchain, depending on the transaction volume for the blockchain sometimes transactions take longer to be added to the next block of the blockchain, and this is where transaction fees could be used to pay the validators to prioritize the transaction. For now, just understand the point of control is the validator's ability to pick and choose the order of transactions as they are added to the blockchain, or even prevent a transaction from being added to the blockchain, and this control only exists if the "trusted" validator, or validators, have a large percent of the blockchain's consensus method. Again, this does not negatively affect the blockchains code, most transactions are still added to blocks, and these blocks are added to the blockchain earning the validators block rewards, and as long as transactions eventually settle on the blockchain, then there is no violation of the blockchains code. This is a good example of an external factor that could lead to a centralized point of control for the blockchain, but one that does not affect the blockchains code, only the order of transactions as they are added to the blockchain. This delay is normal for blockchains when transaction volume is high, simply put it may take longer for all the transactions to be added to the blockchain. However, even though the blockchains code might not be violated, these transactions would affect the individuals making the transactions, since usually it is their wealth that is moving in the transaction on the blockchain.

This type of front running can be used on many types of transactions that take place on the blockchain, and can even be used on exchanges or other platforms that settle buy or sell orders which we will go over later, but when front running takes place on the blockchain itself, it is because of the validators in the blockchain's consensus method. This shows the importance of having a validator network that is not controlled by an individual, or small group of individuals, and although many of these "trusted" validators would not abuse the order of transactions as they are added to the blockchain, for some blockchains they would have the ability to do this. Having this ability to pick and choose transactions based on the goal of front running those transactions, or preventing the transaction completely, is a centralized point of control for that blockchain. One that might not necessarily be bad for the blockchain or violate the blockchains code, but it would be a point of control that could be used to gain a profit, and this profit is not from exploiting the blockchain code, such as changing the block reward rate that was mentioned before. This profit would come from front running transactions, meaning the wealth being gained comes from knowing the buy and sell orders of the blockchains coin or token, basically the wealth is being extracted from users or investors in the blockchain, not from the blockchain itself. Making this an external factor that should be considered when deciding how decentralized a blockchain is overall, and a factor that investors in the blockchain should consider as well, since it would be their transactions that could be exploited.

These example external factors are not major factors in accounting for how decentralized a blockchain is overall, these are just centralized points of control that can exist with some blockchains, and how much these points of control affect a blockchain can vary, and some of these external factors do not exist for some blockchains. There are many smaller examples like the ones mentioned before, but even these smaller centralized points of control can be disclosed to investors, much like disclosures of a blockchain's consensus method or voting structure, which are far more important in determining the decentralization of a blockchain. These external factors are sometimes hard to account for, this is because they do not always involve the blockchains code, while all other centralized points of control or failure involve the blockchains code in some way, but this does not mean disclosing these risks to investors is impossible. For example, in the Arizona Blockchain Standards the risks that might be associated with whale wallets, both known and unknown wallets, are disclosed to investors in sub category disclosure information numbers, 6, 8, 12, 13, and 19. This means even these smaller risks to a blockchain can be accounted for by investors, and this helps investors with risk management when considering what blockchain coin or token to invest their wealth in. However, as mentioned before these are only smaller centralization risks for a blockchain when considering all other factors, this is because the centralized control does not affect the blockchain to the same extent that manipulation of the validator network or voting structure would, and this makes them less important when it comes to the overall decentralization of a blockchain. But these external factors could still be something that investors want to know before investing their wealth in the blockchains coin or token.

External Factors, Exchanges and Wallets:

Exchanges and how they hold an account holder's wealth will be explained later, but these wallets are just like other wallets that can be created on a certain blockchain, and this would include self-custody wallets, since all wallets are simply ledgers on a blockchain that was explained before. Centralization risks around wallets can vary in several ways which we will go over next, but these risks do not affect the blockchain code, they only affect the wealth that an investor is storing in the wallet set up on the blockchain. How these wallets are controlled is important for investors, even if it does not affect the overall decentralization of a certain blockchain coin or token, it would affect an investor's investment and access to their wealth on that blockchain. We will go over DeFi exchanges in more detail later, but for now just understand that wallets interacting with DeFi exchanges, or ones on DeFi exchanges, would be similar to a self-custody wallet, in that the exchange does not have access to the keys of that wallet. Whereas other exchanges could have access to the wallet's keys, or hold an account holder's wealth in an exchange wallet that they have the keys for. How an investor's wealth is held on a blockchain depends in part on what type of wallet holds their wealth, and as mentioned before the keys to the wallet allow access to this wealth. So, who has access to the keys of a wallet is important to investors, and there are many ways these wallets can be set up, there is not just two extremes, but many shades of gray between them. Let's look at several ways wallets can be set up, who is allowed access to the keys of the wallet, and separate the many types of wallets into a few defined groups, or shades of gray. *(Reference page 80)*

Access to the keys of a wallet can be thought of as a 3rd party to that wallet, basically allowing an exchange or other 3rd party some form of access to the keys of the wallet, or even storing an investor's wealth in a centralized wallet, usually an exchange wallet. Exchanges can hold an investor's wealth in several ways, they can also have access to or use an account holder's wealth in several ways. Depending on the exchange they can, lend out wealth to gain interest on the loan, or they could use that wealth to buy other assets in hopes their value will increase, and they could comingle account holders wealth in one or several exchange wallets, and we will go over this in more detail later. Some exchanges clearly disclose to account holders how their wealth is stored and if it is used by the exchange in any other way, although there are limited rules and regulations requiring exchanges to do so. This has allowed some exchanges to take more risks with an account holder's wealth, and the FTX exchange would be an example of this. DeFi exchanges can offer similar services that centralized exchanges offer, they can offer interest on an investor's wealth, and they offer many coins and tokens for investors to buy and sell, but they do not always have access to or control over this wealth. This is because the exchange does not have the keys to wallets interacting with it, and any form or interest or yield that can be earned is locked in a type of smart contract. We will look at the many types of smart contracts later, for now just understand most DeFi platforms do not have the same control over wealth that many other exchanges have, although they can offer similar services to investors.

Not all centralized exchanges are bad and use an account holder's wealth in risky ways, just like not all DeFi platforms are actually decentralized, and some might have access to, or control over wealth being traded and/or stored on the DeFi platform, this is why each exchange or wallet must be judged individually. However, the less control a 3rd party has over an investor's wealth the better, this generally makes DeFi exchanges safer than centralized exchanges, but self-custody wallets that only the investor has the keys for would be the safest, and this only applies for wallets that do not allow for any type of access to the wallet's keys. Some exchanges can offer hard wallets to account holders, they might be wallets with hardware (a hard wallet), or what is sometimes called a soft wallet (no hardware, just software), and we will go over the differences later, for now just understand the "hard" wallet that some exchanges offer would mean they do not have access to the wallet's keys. This would be a separate unique wallet from other wallets that an exchange might have, and it would only hold the investor's wealth. Whereas some exchanges will hold all account holder's wealth in one or several wallets and just update the account when an investor buys or sells a coin or token, and we will go over this in more detail later. For now, just understand exchanges can be set up in many ways and hold an investor's wealth in several ways, and even though they could help an investor set up a self-custody wallet, they could also offer password resets for that wallet, and this may be important for some investors that are afraid of forgetting or losing their seed phrase. This is because the 12 or 24 words representing the 48 or 96 numbers are the only way to access the wallet and move the wealth it holds, losing this sequence of numbers would mean the wealth would be "lost" or locked in the wallet with no ability to retrieve it.

Large investors or anyone that worries about losing access to their wealth would like the idea of being able to reset the password to their wallet, this is why some exchanges will offer this form of self-custody to its account holders, and this is also why some hard wallets have offered this password reset option as well. This password reset ability has several pros and cons, but this type of wallet would basically be a wallet that is on the blockchain of the coins and tokens held in the wallet. It is not an account at an exchange, where the coins might be moved by the exchange itself without the permission of the account holder, meaning this wallet is a separate wallet were only the investor has the ability to move the coins and tokens. One pro for this type of wallet would be that it is not directly controlled by a 3rd party, however one con for this type of wallet would be that the exchange or company would have access to the keys. They need to have this ability if they are going to be able to offer password reset capabilities, but this also means they could access the keys for other reasons as well. *(Reference page 9)* There are many people on both sides to this argument, some people want the ability to reset passwords for fear they might lose or forget the seed phrase, and this would be a concern for many types of people, both old and young, investing a small or large amount of wealth. But this idea at its simplest form is basically what we have in the banking industry today, there is a 3rd party that has the ability to control an individual's wealth, and this is why decentralized blockchains were created, to remove this 3rd party control. So many people see the idea of password resets as going backwards, as opposed to embracing true self-custody and financial freedom. This is definitely a shade of gray as far as wallets and centralized 3rd party control goes, there are groups of people that will only store their wealth in a wallet if they can reset their password with the help of a trusted party, while there are other groups that will only store their wealth in a wallet if there is no 3rd party access to or control over the wallet. However, both these groups make up a large number of people, and if there is enough demand for a service then eventually it will be provided, Ledger is an example of this, and we will look at Ledger's password reset capabilities next. *(Reference page 94)*

In 2023 the Ledger wallet offered the ability to reset lost or forgotten seed phrases, this was possible with a software update to the hard wallet, and wallet holders would have to opt in if they wanted these services for a small monthly fee. We will go over the Ledger wallet in more detail later, for now let's just look at how the keys to the wallet are stored and recovered if needed, and what other access this service could allow for. Basically, this hard wallet is like other hard wallets, there is a seed phrase that gives the wallet holder control over coins and tokens moving out of the wallet. These wallets are on the blockchain of the coins and tokens that the wallet has the ability to hold, and Ledger has no direct control over transactions moving in or out of the wallet since these transactions are settled on the blockchain of the individual coin or token. In order to prevent these transactions, they would need to manipulate the blockchain code, or control the majority of the validators in the blockchain's consensus method as mentioned before, and this is not always easy depending on how the blockchain code is set up. Ledger only has the ability to retrieve the seed phrase, and it does this by taking the 48 or 96 numbers and breaking them into 3 parts, each section of the seed phrase is stored with a different trusted data storage provider. Meaning if any of them have a data breach the entire seed phrase would not be at risk, and this is a simplified example of how the keys to the wallet are stored in order to recover them later if needed. The main issue critics have, is that Ledger has the ability to access the seed phrase and store it with these other companies, but another reason this would be considered a risk for investors is that the keys can be recovered at any time by Ledger. Either at the request of a wallet holder who lost their seed phrase, or at the request of say the government, who may want to prevent the wallet from making transactions. This again is why decentralized blockchains like Bitcoin were created, to prevent a centralized group or government from having the ability to control wealth and transfers of that wealth. However, the Ledger password recovery has a monthly fee and users must opt in for this ability, so it would not necessarily affect all Ledger wallets, especially ones that did not run the update that includes the password reset capability. A true self-custody wallet would be one that does not even have the ability to reset the seed phrase, making password resets a shade of gray when it comes to centralized control over the wealth held in the wallet, and this may or may not be something investors want for the wallet that holds their wealth. *(Reference page 96)*

External Factors, Hard Wallets:

Another external factor would be hard wallets (or soft wallets) that may have 3rd party access to the wallets seed phrase, and this would not negatively affect the blockchain, but it could negatively affect the investor holding wealth in the wallet. True self-custody wallets are when you and you alone hold the keys to your wallet, this means the wealth in the wallet cannot be accessed or used by any other party without permission from the wallet holder, and this can be thought of as one of the extremes on either side of the many shades of gray. *(Reference page 80)* Let's look at a few examples, so we can get a better idea of the types of wallets that can exist, what access they have to an investor's wealth, and if this access would be considered a pro or a con for investors storing their wealth in the wallet or exchange wallet. The first extreme would be a wallet where only the investor knows the seed phrase, there is a risk of losing or forgetting the keys to the wallet, but this ensures no other 3rd party would have this access to the wallets keys either, and some hard wallets can be created where no one knows the seed phrase to the wallet. An example would be the Tangem wallet, basically a card with an NFC chip in it, and the keys to the wallet are generated when the user activates the card, but these keys are held in the chip and even the user does not know the seed phrase. This is a very simplified description of the Tangem wallet, I would encourage further research to understand how the cards/ wallets work, basically there are back up cards in case one of the cards is lost or damaged, and this is because the card itself is the keys to the hard wallet, not even the investor has access to the seed phrase stored in the chip.

The other extreme could be considered an exchange wallet that lends out an investor's wealth, the wallet or wallets holding this wealth would be controlled by the exchange, they have the keys to the wallet and the ability to transfer its wealth, and this all happens behind the scenes if you will, investors will still be shown their account at the exchange through the app or user interface. However, even if an investors account at the exchange shows their wealth, or the number of coins and tokens representing that wealth, the exchange could still be using the wealth in other ways. This is because the investor is simply shown their account at the exchange, and their actual wealth may be lent out or invested by the exchange. This is how the banking industry works today, banks are not required to keep all of an account holder's wealth, they lend out or invest a portion of that wealth, this is called fractional reserve banking, and it is similar to exchanges that use an account holder's wealth to grow that wealth through investing or lending. The investor might not care if the exchange does this, exchanges usually split any interest or wealth growth with the investor, giving them a steady interest on wealth that they have in the exchange. But this does not mean there is no risk for the investor, and if the exchange makes bad investments or issues loans that are not repaid, then the investor's wealth will be lost. These two extremes for investors are either total control over the wallet and the wealth it holds, or little to no control over their wealth, although investors would be able to increase their wealth through the interest offered by an exchange, so there would be different pros and cons for different types of investors, and many shades of gray in between. *(Reference page 94)*

Decentralization is Not Exact:

Defining decentralization is not exact, as we have seen there are many different aspects to decentralization, and each one can effect a blockchain or not affect a blockchain, depending on how the blockchain is set up. As mentioned before, there are many shades of gray when it comes to wallets and who has access to the seed phrase, and the same is true for other aspects of decentralization. There are pros and cons for everything from the consensus method of a blockchain, to its development team and community of supporters, and this is why each blockchain should be looked at individually when determining if the blockchain is decentralized or not. A simple example would be POW blockchains, just because they are POW does not mean they have a large number of validators and nodes hashing transactions and securing the blockchain, and this creates many shades of gray when it comes to the individual aspects of decentralization, they must be taken into account along with many other factors in order to be accurate. We will go over these shades of gray for wallets in more detail next, and we will also look at why it is hard for decentralization to be exact when rules and regulations around the technology do not exist, and where they do exist, they are over restrictive and fail to accurately account for the technology and many of its aspects.

(Illustration, next page)

Hard Wallets, Shades of Gray:

Hard wallets that allow for password resets would be one step down from a true self-custody wallet, this is because the keys to the wallet can be recovered, and this would require a 3rd party to have access to the wallets keys in order to do this. Password recovery would give a wallet holder a little more peace of mind, and this would only allow 3rd party access to the keys of the wallet, they would not be investing or using the wealth in the wallet in any other way, but they could move the wealth out of the wallet if they ever wanted to, and this is why it is one shade of gray away from a true self-custody wallet. On the other extreme, a centralized exchange could offer soft wallets to its account holders, this would be a soft wallet that holds an investor's wealth separate from other wallets at the exchange, and the exchange may or may not offer password reset abilities for these wallets. If they did not, then the wallet would be a self-custody wallet that only the investor had access to, if they did offer password resets, then there would still be a 3rd party to the wallet, however wealth in these wallets would not be lent out or invested like wealth in an account at the exchange might be. This makes soft wallets offered by an exchange, with password reset abilities, one shade of gray away from simply an account at an exchange, this is because the exchange would still have access to the keys of the wallet, but it would not use the wealth in the wallet like it might with other wealth held in the centralized exchange wallets. How wealth is held and used will vary between investors, pros and cons will be different depending on the investor and their individual risk tolerances, creating many shades of gray as far as who has access to the keys of a wallet and therefore access to the wealth held in the wallet. *(Reference page 96)*

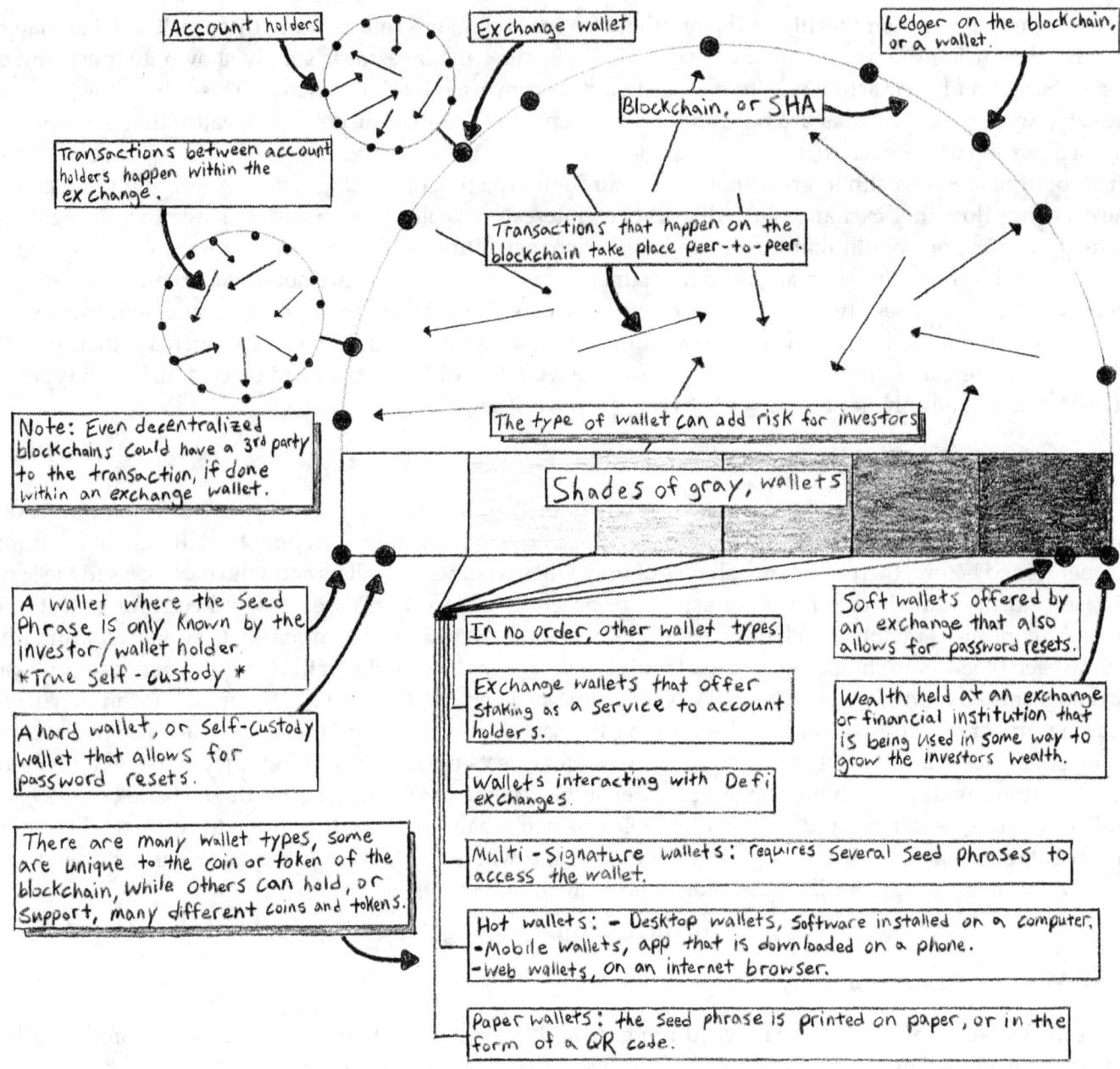

Wallets, Shades of Gray

Shades of gray for wallets can be any level of 3rd party access to, or control over, wealth in a wallet, this can be complete control such as wealth held at an exchange, or no control, such as a self-custody wallet, and many shades of gray between the two. The amount of control the 3rd party has over the wealth can affect the ability for that wealth to transact peer-to-peer, basically there is someone that could restrict or stop transfer of that wealth. Although this would not mean the blockchain does not allow for peer-to-peer transactions, it just means the way an individual holds their wealth in the blockchain allows for a form of control that could restrict transactions of that wealth.

Pg. 6, upper left section: Trades of an individual coin or token on an exchange do not need to be settled on the blockchain, basically these trades take place within the exchange, and accounts at the exchange are updated, but the coins remain in the exchange wallet.

Pg. 25, upper section: Wallets on a blockchain are basically all the same, a wallet can be the seed phrase that holds an individual's wealth, or it can be the seed phase that holds the wealth of many account holders at an exchange, and transactions only take place on the blockchain when wealth is moving from one wallet to another.

Pg. 76, bottom section: The many shades of gray for wallets can be simply thought of as 3rd party access to or control over wealth in the wallet, and these wallets can be self-custody wallets, or exchange wallets, which is basically just wealth held in an exchange.

Pg. 78, bottom section: A true self-custody wallet, is a wallet where you, and you alone know the seed phrase to the wallet, and there is no password reset ability, or access to the seed phrase in any form.

Pg. 81, upper section: A decentralized blockchain allows for peer-to-peer transactions between wallets, these transactions can be restricted if the wealth is held at an exchange, but other 3rd party access can prevent peer-to-peer transactions as well. This would be like a hard wallet with password resets, the 3rd party could access the seed phase at any time, and this would allow them to access wealth in the wallet as well.

Pg. 95, upper left section: Although exchanges can set up a stake pool and offer staking as a service to its account holders, this does not mean the exchange controls the majority of that validator network, and this means exchanges only control transactions of wealth within the exchange, not all transactions taking place on the blockchain that they set up a stake pool for.

These many shades of gray are basically how wealth is held on a blockchain, and who has control over certain aspects of the wallet and the wealth it holds, and investors will vary in how much 3rd party access they want involved with securing their wealth. The best option is obviously a self-custody wallet that you and you alone have the keys for, but other options will appeal to some investors, and if they are looking to earn interest on their wealth, then they can take on more risk for more rewards. They can earn block rewards from POS blockchains, either from a hard wallet or on an exchange that has set up a stake pool for the blockchain, or investors could let the exchange invest or lend out their wealth in exchange for an interest on that wealth. There are many additional options for investors looking for interest or yield on their wealth, but who has access to that wealth during this process is important, and investors should fully trust any 3rd party with access to their wealth, otherwise investors should remove their wealth from the 3rd party wallet or exchange. Ultimately this trust would involve the company offering the password reset services, either the company behind the hard wallet, or the exchange offering the soft wallet. This is because they would have access to the keys of the wallet, and decentralized exchanges might reduce some risks when it comes to accessing the keys of an investor's wallet, however DeFi investors should still be aware of how their wealth is being used on these platforms, they are not all risk-free.

The centralized control that is involved with wallets and access to the keys for that wallet is only a risk for investors, this centralized control does not affect the blockchains of the coins and tokens held in the many different wallet types, and this is because the wallets are just ledgers on the blockchain as mentioned before, they do not affect the blockchain code other than being a ledger on that blockchain. There are some exceptions such as wallets that hold the majority of coins or tokens that exist on a blockchain, these would be whale wallets, and the risk to the blockchain would be the massive amount of sell pressure that was mentioned before. Also, exchanges that set up a large number of stake pools for a POS blockchain could control the majority of the blockchain's consensus method as mentioned before. But these risks can be accounted for by understanding the blockchain's consensus method, not by accounting for wallet addresses staking large numbers of coins, either from a hard wallet or through an exchange. In most case's wallet addresses, even large wallet addresses, on a blockchain do not affect the decentralization of the blockchain overall. But an investor holding wealth in the wallet could be negatively affected by 3rd party access to the wallet, and this makes centralized control over access to the keys of a wallet more of a centralized risk for investors rather than the blockchain itself. DeFi exchanges reduce some of these risks for investors, but they do not completely remove risk for investors, and the use of DeFi exchanges generally does not negatively affect the blockchains of the coins and tokens that interact with the DeFi platform.

Exchanges and DeFi exchanges will be covered in more detail later, for now it is important to understand the centralized points of control around the wallets that hold an investor's wealth, and there needs to be a distinction between 3rd party wallets and true self-custody wallets, because 3rd parties are centralized points of control, even if the points of control do not affect a blockchains code. There are many ways wealth can be held on a blockchain, this is what creates the many shades of gray as far as how wallets secure that wealth. But the ability to move wealth peer-to-peer is what makes a blockchain decentralized, and access to a wallets keys would be a risk for peer-to-peer transfers, since there is a 3rd party involved in storing and moving wealth in the wallet. *(Reference page 80)* This centralized point of control comes from the need to trust a 3rd party, be it an exchange or other, and these 3rd parties have the ability to break that trust if they choose to, or are forced to, and this includes hard wallets that have access to the wallets keys through the ability to reset the seed phrase of that wallet. *(Reference page 94)* As mentioned before this centralized point of control does not affect a blockchain overall, it only affects an investor's wealth and access to that wealth, the blockchain code would only be involved in this point of control to the extent that coins or tokens could only move from the wallet if the transaction was hashed with the seed phrase, and this would make it a valid transaction on the blockchain, regardless of who was moving the wealth. *(Reference page 2)*

Howey Test Definitions:

Defining decentralization for blockchain coins and tokens is important, it is a core issue for rules and regulations around blockchain technology, and these rules and regulations are being written by governments around the world, as of April 2023 the EU leads the way with its Markets in Crypto Assets regulation (MiCA). How decentralized or centralized a blockchain is can be used by regulators to better define each individual blockchain, some existing regulations would not be able to account for this new technology, while others like the Howey test could be adapted to include blockchain coins and tokens, and this would allow regulators to break the 10s of thousands of coins and tokens into several groups. We will go over the Howey test interpretation in more detail later, for now let's just look at how blockchain coins and tokens could be split into 3 groups based on the decentralization or centralization of the individual blockchain, and these groups would be, digital securities, digital commodities, and digital assets.

Digital commodities are decentralized blockchains, this is because there is no individual or small group that controls the blockchain, and this would include all aspects of the blockchain, such as the validator network of the consensus method, or the voting structure of the blockchain as mentioned before. The Howey test does not account for commodities, and the CFTC would be better suited for regulating digital commodities, since these blockchains would not have centralized points of control, making them similar to traditional commodities. Blockchains with some centralized points of control would be defined as digital securities, they could fall under the SEC and its regulations, and this makes defining decentralization important for blockchain projects and those that invest in the blockchain. This is investor protection since these centralized points of control could negatively affect the blockchain and the value of its coin or token, which would affect the value of an investor's investment. But these risks need to be clearly defined and disclosed to investors, so they can make the decision as to where their wealth is stored. Blanket regulations and restricting investors from holding their wealth in certain blockchains would not be investor protection, it would prevent growth in the industry and cause blockchain projects to relocate to friendlier regions. In order to clearly define digital commodities, a separate standard would be needed, one under the CFTC, but one common factor for blockchains that are considered digital commodities would be that they are actually decentralized, and for blockchains that are not fully decentralized the Howey test can be used to define them as digital securities.

Digital Securities:

Digital securities would mean the blockchain has centralized points of control, there could exist one or several centralized points of control, and these could be used to affect the blockchain, for better or worse. Some of these centralized points of control would be in the hands of developers and large investors, some investors would be ok with this if they trusted the individuals who controlled that certain aspect of the blockchain, such as developers adding updates to improve the blockchain or its use case. As mentioned before, some of these points of control are not always bad, since the developers and large investors would want the blockchain to develop and grow, growing their investments. However, many of these points of control can also be used to negatively affect or exploit the blockchain, so investors should consider what centralized control exists and who controls it, since it could affect their investment. External risks could also be considered centralized points of control to some regulators, these would be risks that do not affect the blockchains code, but could affect other aspects of the blockchain such as the value of its coin or token as mentioned before. A blockchain standard would allow for regulators to create these thresholds between what centralized points of control are important, and what ones are less important. This would allow the regulators to focus on the actual points of control and who has that control, this would protect investors simply by disclosing these risks, but regulators would also be able to create rules around these centralized points of control, and regulations in these areas would be beneficial to investors.

These centralized points of control for a blockchain allow for that aspect of the blockchain to be manipulated or exploited, and as mentioned before some centralized points of control can exist and not be used to negatively affect the blockchain, but this does not mean that the control will not be used forever, and it is still considered a risk for the blockchain. These centralized points of control can be anything from the consensus method of the blockchain, to the development team advertising or promoting the blockchains coin or token, and/or the use case. But the common factor between these blockchains would be that there is an individual, group of individuals, or enterprise behind the blockchain and the wealth it holds. This means the actions of this enterprise could affect an investors wealth held in the coin or token of the blockchain, this is why these blockchains would be more likely considered a security, since the control can be used to affect an investor's wealth for better or worse. A blockchain standard would disclose these centralized risks to investors, both retail and institutional investors, these investors would be able to better manage their risk when deciding what blockchains to store their wealth in, and we will go over this in more detail later when we look at the Arizona Blockchain Standards and its category requirements and sub category disclosure information.

(Illustration, next page)

A blockchain with a lack of centralized points of control would mean there is no enterprise that is liable when an investor loses wealth held in the blockchain, this can be broken down further with the second prong of the Howey test, where common enterprises are grouped into 3 types, horizontal approach, vertical approach, and broad vertical approach. In the Howey test interpretation for blockchain coins and tokens decentralized blockchains would fall under the horizontal approach, while both vertical approaches more refer to blockchains with centralized points of control. This would be the distinction between digital commodities and digital securities, and the Howey test is able to do this by using the blockchain standards risk category levels. We will go over both of these more later, for now just understand these blockchains that are considered decentralized enough, would simply be a market of buyers and sellers, obviously this market would be affected by the demand for the blockchains coin or token, but other than that there is no individual to blame if an investor loses wealth. This is similar to traditional commodities in that there is no CEO of gold or bananas, the price is only affected by what the market of buyers and sellers are willing to pay, and this is also true for most blockchain coins and tokens that are decentralized enough. However, this does not mean decentralized blockchains do not have risks, digital commodities could be at risk from whale wallets that might crash the dollar value of the blockchains coin or token, and even low transaction volume on the blockchain might affect the value of the coin or token. This is because transactions for the most part represent a use case for the blockchain, basically the demand for the coin or token. If this demand falls then so will the value of the blockchains coin or token, and this is just one of many factors that can affect the value of a coin or token over time. This makes the blockchains use cases a driving factor in the value of its coin or token, and the ability to hold that value and increase in value over time. Some blockchains will prevent this long-term increase in value with a high inflation rate created through block rewards to miners or stake pools as mentioned before, or any other type of coin creation for the blockchains unit of account. *(Reference page 28)* While other blockchains will be more balanced, they would allow for the increase of the coin or tokens value over time without diluting its supply, even if that blockchain has a small inflation rate for the coin or token. There are many use cases for blockchains that can affect the demand for that blockchains coin or token, and we will go over many examples later, but for now just understand that higher demand for a coin or token will affect its value in a market of buyers and sellers.

Defining decentralization for blockchain coins and tokens is important for regulators, by doing so some existing rules and regulations like the Howey test can break the many coins and tokens into groups, and bring clarity to the industry. This clarity comes from defining decentralization, and as we have seen defining decentralization is more like identifying centralized points of control for the blockchain, and these points of control can exist around many aspects of the blockchain as mentioned before. This clarity would allow the industry to develop and grow, while providing disclosures to investors, and blockchain projects would be able to provide required disclosures to regulators as well, all of this is possible with a blockchain standard. Clear requirements for the risk category levels in a blockchain standard would allow existing rules and regulations to create lines between the different groups of coins and tokens, these lines are defined in the Howey test interpretation, and they separate digital securities from digital commodities, as well as creating

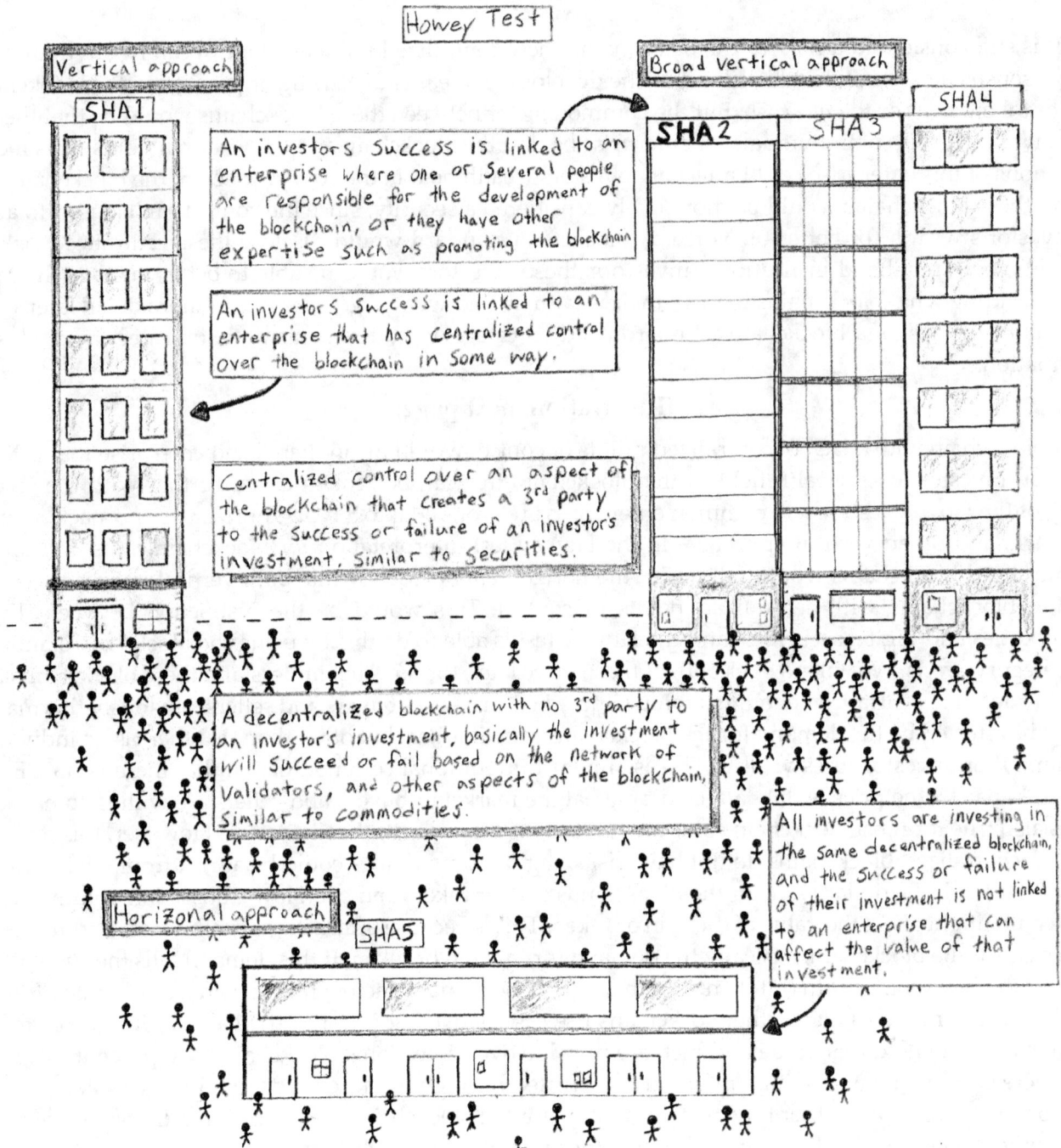

Howey Test

The Howey test can be simply thought of as, who is the enterprise that is being invested in, and what type of control over the value of the investment does the enterprise have. Some points of centralization in a blockchain would give a company or a group of individuals control over an aspect of the blockchain, and these can be thought of as all investors investing in that company or group of people. This can be thought of as investing in a traditional company, or enterprise, and this vertical approach is then further broken down to individuals who have control over an aspect of the blockchain, either as developers, or as promoters. Both of these approaches mean the investor's investment is linked to the success or failure of these parties, represented as a large amount of space, such as a tall building, and the entry points are limited, basically all investors are invested in the common enterprise. While towards the bottom of the illustration there is also a large amount of space, however, access to this building is not concentrated around one enterprise, or around one individual, and access to this building would be similar to an investment in a commodity, in that there is no company or individual that can affect the value of the investment. The Howey test would use the risk levels in a blockchain standard to make the distinctions between digital securities and digital commodities, and we will cover the Howey test interpretation and the Arizona Blockchain Standards in the second part of this book.

a 3rd group of digital assets. Basically, digital assets are new and developing blockchains, they are higher risk level coins and tokens, because of the added risk for investors, and we will go over how these lines are created using the risk level of a coin or token later. For now, just understand that clearly defining what a decentralized blockchain is, would allow existing rules and regulations to be able to account for these new blockchain assets. Most of the disclosure information that allows for this clarity comes from the Arizona Blockchain Standards, which uses much of the information that we have covered so far, and this information can then be used by regulators to create clear rules around blockchain coins and tokens. But there are many additional factors that regulators could include that we have not covered, and these disclosures when all combined would at least be some evidence proving the blockchain is actually decentralized, instead of just calling a blockchain decentralized, which we will go over next.

"Decentralized":

The word "decentralized" is used a lot when referring to blockchain coins and tokens, some blockchain projects will promote their coin or token as decentralized, even if one or several aspects of the blockchain are controlled by an individual or small group, and this is because all other aspects of the blockchain might actually be decentralized. As mentioned before centralized points of control vary in how they can affect the blockchain, so some centralized points of control might not be a concern for some investors, it depends on what aspect of the blockchain the control has, but these centralized points of control should still be disclosed to investors. This is because many investors do not fully understand what decentralized means, they simply think that it is a zero-sum game, either a blockchain is decentralized or not, and they need to be made aware of all the risks involved with holding wealth in a certain blockchain coin or token. These disclosures of risk ultimately benefit the investor and help them better manage their risk when investing, it would be the guidance that investors are looking for, and the guidance that most regulators have failed to provide up until today. *(Reference page 96)*

This makes the word decentralized more like slang or hype, something that is used to promote the blockchain while not actually proving anything, and this became more widespread around 2017 when many large investors started moving into the space. Making the hype around "decentralized blockchains" similar to the dotcom hype in 2000, and this is because although websites are good, back then users could not interact with websites as we do today. They could only display words or images, and prices for goods were not always shown since prices could vary between regions. During this time, companies spent a lot of money setting up what would be considered a very basic website today, and there was no demand for what the websites offered back then. This is similar to "decentralized blockchains" today, many get funding even if they are not actually decentralized, some might not even have a use case there is a demand for, and these blockchains will fail in the long term. Even good use cases there is a demand for, need a safe blockchain and a good development team, this is because even good ideas that are poorly executed are bad ideas, and the hype that saw so many new blockchains created will lead to a washout of poorly developed blockchains, or ones with little to no use case. This means many blockchain coins and tokens will likely fail in a similar way to early websites, only those with use cases there is a demand for will have an opportunity to grow in the future. However, this does not guarantee other blockchains with good use cases will succeed, there are many factors involved in the long-term development and adoption of each blockchain. Many of these factors we have already gone over, they play a part in a strong and secure blockchain, and if they have a use case there is a demand for, then they may continue to grow, but other blockchains with no use case might grow in value as well. This is because as long as individuals are willing to store their wealth in the blockchain, then the blockchains coin or token will have value, represented as its market cap. It takes time for blockchains to develop, gain supporters, and gain users, over this time centralized points of control or failure may negatively affect the blockchain, and how much the blockchain is affected will depend on the aspect of the blockchain that was exploited. If these centralized points of control were disclosed to investors, then at least the investors were aware of the possibility, while investors that thought they were investing in a "decentralized blockchain" would be surprised to hear the blockchain was exploited through a centralized point of control.

The hype behind calling a blockchain decentralized is somewhat still around today, some blockchain projects will claim to be "decentralized" when most of the main aspects of the blockchain are actually decentralized. They just retain centralized control over certain aspects of the blockchain, and this is not always bad, as mentioned before some developing blockchains need more control over things like IPs to update and develop the blockchain. However, any centralized control over a blockchain needs to be disclosed to investors, since it would be their wealth that could be lost if the blockchain was negatively affected through manipulation or exploitation, and these disclosures are what a blockchain standard would provide to regulators and investors. This hype was far more widespread in the early 2010s, the fact that a consensus method could actually be run by a decentralized network of validators was a new idea, and this led to just about all blockchain projects calling themselves a "decentralized" blockchain coin or token, including the central banks. When the idea of central banks creating a blockchain coin or token started it was called, central bank decentralized currency, CBDC today stands for central bank digital currency, and they changed it after they realized the "central" part was obviously in contrast to decentralization. This example just shows how much the word decentralized can be thrown around, something centralized by design such as a CBDC is almost the exact opposite of a decentralized blockchain, and we will go over how CBDCs could be set up later. For now, just understand every blockchain can claim to be decentralized, but very few actually are, most have some form of centralized control over at least one aspect of the blockchain. This is another reason why defining decentralization is so important, until these terms are decided on and the limits for them defined, just about any blockchain project could claim to be decentralized, and this would put investors that hold their wealth in the blockchain at risk of losing some or all their investment should the blockchain ever fail.

Investors should be able to manage their own risk when it comes to investing in blockchain coins and tokens, in order to do this, they need disclosures about important aspects of the blockchain they are investing in, and a blockchain standard would be able to provide these disclosures to investors, and we will go over this in more detail later. For now, just understand that allowing investors to manage their own risk is better than the alternative where the regulators would tell investors what coins and tokens they can or cannot invest in, and this would not only restrict investors, but it would push many blockchain projects to regions where there are more friendly regulations around the industry. Regulators need a way to define and account for this new technology, and as mentioned before, creating a standard that can separate all coins and tokens into digital securities, digital commodities, and digital assets, would need to be able to define what a decentralized blockchain is, and there are many factors involved in determining if a blockchain is decentralized or not. Simply put, the idea of a decentralized blockchain is one where 3rd parties have been removed from the blockchain, this must be verified with the blockchains code and proven, simply saying a blockchain is decentralized is in no way a guarantee, and many blockchain projects will continue to use the word "decentralized" until it is properly defined by regulators.

Advantages of Decentralized Blockchains:

Some aspects of decentralization not only protect the blockchain from invalid transactions or attacks, but they also create advantages for the blockchain, and we have gone over several of these advantages already, but next let's look at a few that do not necessarily have to do with the blockchain itself. Allowing for anyone to become a validator for a blockchain adds to the blockchain's decentralization, and it is also good for individuals because they can earn a profit from block rewards as mentioned before. But it also creates another advantage for the blockchain, minute man validators that can come online when they are needed the most. We will also go over several other advantages and disadvantages for a blockchain, basically how much do certain aspects of centralized control affect the blockchain overall, and how do some aspects create more of an advantage for the blockchain overall. Some advantages come from individuals interacting with the blockchain, and this can help the blockchain in several ways, by either participating in the blockchain's consensus method, or by simply interacting with a use case on the blockchain. The main takeaway here is that some of these advantages for the blockchain come from individuals, and these advantages are not part of the blockchains code like a balanced consensus method and governance structure for example, instead the advantages come from many individuals interacting with different aspects of the blockchain, either for profit, or for one of the blockchains use cases.

Minute Man Validators:

Allowing anyone to set up a validator in a blockchains consensus method has several benefits for the blockchain, it adds to the overall decentralization of the blockchain, and it also helps the blockchain recover from large drops in its total hash rate. This would not be like a large company repairing a damaged data center, there is no coordinated effort, just many individuals being incentivized with more block rewards. Each blockchain can be set up different as mentioned before, and the number of validators and nodes in the blockchains consensus method can vary as well. So, some blockchains would not benefit as much as other blockchains would, but simply having this ability is an advantage for the blockchain, and it is something more centralized networks do not have the ability to benefit from. "Good" blockchains that have many mining pools, mining farms around the world, and use renewable energy sources, could still benefit from allowing anyone to become a validator, and this is because even if the blockchain is able to balance many of its aspects, it is still vulnerable to a rapid drop in its hash rate. This is caused by mining farms going offline, basically the consensus method is losing validators, and if it loses a large part of the validator network it becomes more vulnerable to attack or exploitation, but individuals stepping up when they are needed most helps the consensus method recover its total hash power, and we will look at this a little more next.

(Illustration, next page)

As mentioned before there can be centralized aspects of a blockchain's consensus method, and these points of control can be reduced in many ways. For example, small mining farms hashing transactions on a POW blockchain must pool their individual hash power together into mining pools, and if there is only one or two pool options for small mining farms, then this could be a centralized point of control over the validator network of the consensus method for that blockchain. So, the number of mining pools for a POW blockchain can affect the blockchains overall decentralization, since the mining farms are pooling their hash power into what is basically a single validator on the blockchain. The more mining pools there are, the more validators there would be for the blockchain, and other mining farms that do not need to pool their hash power would be individual validators for the blockchain's consensus method as mentioned before. These individual validators could be further decentralized by powering the mining computers with different energy sources, as mentioned before spreading out validators around the world adds to decentralization by preventing man-made or natural disasters from knocking the blockchain offline, and different energy sources would allow for some mining farms to stay online when others lose power. If validators are running on both grid power and renewable energy sources, then even if a region of the world experienced a grid failure, some of the validators would be able to remain online, and this does not only benefit the blockchain, it also reduces the mining farms energy costs adding to the profitability of the mining farm. For a POW blockchain mining farm, their main goal is to earn block rewards, they do this by staying online 24/7, but when a large natural disaster or man-made disaster knocks most of the blockchains validators offline the remaining mining farms will receive more block rewards, since there are fewer validators but the same amount of block rewards each time a new block is added to the blockchain.

Many validators going offline would cause the blockchains hash rate to fall, this would mean validators that do remain online would receive more block rewards, and this would incentivize smaller mining farms to start hashing transactions on the blockchain. It may have been unprofitable to run these smaller mining farms when the hash rate was high and block rewards did not cover their energy costs, but with a lower hash rate many smaller mining farms may become profitable again, and this increased profit would be determined by how much the total hash rate dropped. The lower the hash rate drops the more block rewards would be available to any validator that was still verifying transactions and solving blocks as mentioned before, basically this means as validators go offline the block reward rate increases. This incentivizes more validators to come online, which will increase the hash rate of the blockchain, and this balance is ongoing

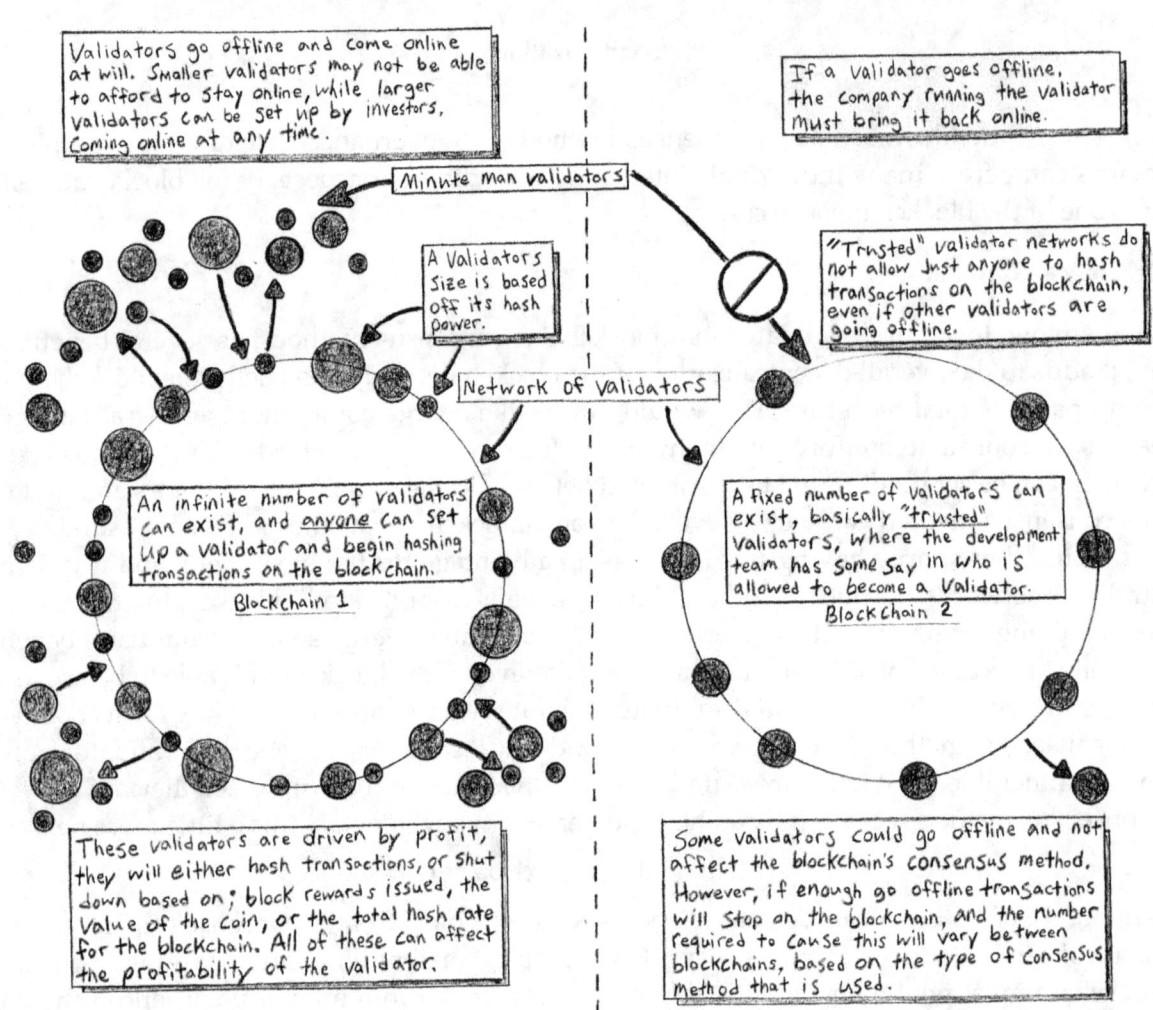

Minute Man Validators

A blockchain's consensus method that allows for anyone to become a validator, will have validators coming online, and going offline at random, these can be POW mining farms, or POS stake pools, and these validators can be different sizes, their size is basically their hash power, based on the computing power of the ASICs, or the number of coins locked in a stake pool. These independent validators are usually driven by profit, in the form of block rewards from the blockchain's consensus method, and the value of these block rewards will determine whether the validator is able to remain online hashing transactions at a profit or not. In order to ensure the validators of a blockchains consensus method stay online, some blockchains will only allow for some form of "trusted" validator in its consensus method, and this can help with transaction speed on the blockchain, as well as other use cases on the blockchain. But it is important to remember if these "trusted" validators go offline, there is no way other validators can step up to keep the blockchain going, it would be up to the company or individual running the validator to get it back online, and sometimes this is not done right away, causing the blockchain to go down for a period of time.

Pg. 42, right section: A consensus method with "trusted" validators sometimes allow for faster transaction speed, this is required for some use cases on a blockchain, and this is not necessarily a bad thing, since most "trusted" validators work with developers in some way. But it is important to remember these are the validators of the blockchain's consensus method, and this gives whoever controls them a form of control over transactions on the blockchain, especially if they control a large percent of the total validator network.

Pg. 43, right section: If there are limitations on who can become a validator, then the blockchains consensus method is slightly centralized to an extent, and this is because it is not possible for anyone to become a validator that hashes transactions on the blockchain. These "trusted" validators are not always bad, depending on how the blockchain is set up, and the centralized point of control is usually in the hands of developers.

Pg. 54, right section: Stakeholders staking wealth to a pool do not have a vote on IPs for the blockchain, this is because the pool operator would be voting on behalf of the stakeholders, and when the pool operators are large investors and developers of the blockchain, these "trusted" validators can update the blockchain in whatever direction they want.

Pg. 56, right section: "Trusted" validators usually cannot increase their percent of the total consensus method, unlike mining farms in a POW consensus method, and this is what prevents a single "trusted" validator from controlling the consensus method. But it also means there is a limit on the number of validators that can exist, and this limit can come in the form of the amount of wealth required to set up a stake pool, or the limit could be requiring approval from developers before becoming a validator.

Pg. 61, right section: "Trusted" validators are not always bad, they allow the blockchain to remain up and running by ensuring the validators do not go offline for any reason, and these validators are usually controlled by those invested in the blockchain, or by those developing the blockchain, so they have an incentive to keep the blockchain online.

Pg. 74, right section: Front running transactions on a blockchain is easier when the consensus method has "trusted" validators, this is because there is a limited number of validators, and these validators usually all have a common link, such as the development team that allows the validator to be set up on the blockchain. This does not mean these validators will manipulate the order of transactions on a blockchain, but it would be possible if enough of them worked together.

Pg. 89, right section: There is no way for individually controlled validators to begin hashing transactions on the blockchain, even if they wanted to, and once enough "trusted" validators go offline the blockchain will stop.

Pg. 104, left section: Bitcoins consensus method allows anyone to become a validator, hash transactions, and earn block rewards, and this means the blockchain can recover from a large drop in its hash rate. When this happens more miners come online, and the hash rate for the blockchain increases, but this is not possible for consensus methods with only "trusted" validators.

Pg. 147, left section: When a data center goes offline it is up to the company operating the hardware to get it back online, until they do transactions on the network may stop, and there is no way for the company to pay other data centers to keep the network running. While Bitcoin mining farms are compensated for their efforts from the consensus method in the form of block rewards, and when validators start to go offline these rewards increase, incentivizing other mining farms to being hashing transactions, keeping the blockchain online.

for POW blockchains, since miners can come online and go offline at will. Usually, validators do not go offline on mass, it would only happen if there was a large power outage that affected a large number of validators for a particular blockchain. This makes some POW blockchains very hard to stop, because as the blockchain's consensus method losses validators, other validators are ready and willing to start hashing transactions and earning a higher block reward rate for the same energy costs, and this would apply more to larger blockchains with higher hash rates. Since there are generally more mining farms with equipment that is able to hash transactions on that blockchain, while blockchains with lower hash rates would have fewer individuals with the equipment needed to hash transactions on that particular blockchain. GPU mining farms could switch to hashing transactions on smaller blockchains, but ultimately it would be the larger more popular blockchains that would have the most individuals willing to begin hashing transactions on the blockchain when the consensus method needs it most. Bitcoins blockchain has experienced a massive drop in its hash rate before, around mid-2021 China cracked down on crypto trading and mining, and we will go over this in more detail later when we look at Bitcoins blockchain, but for now just understand that many mining farms in China went offline causing a drop in Bitcoins hash rate. *(Reference page 106)* These mining farms moved from China to, Northern Asia, Europe, and North America on mass, and during this time mining farms that remained online saw more block rewards than normal, my companies mining computers were some of these miners, and we will go over the block rewards and hash rates we were able to achieve during this time later. For now, just understand ever since that drop in hash power Bitcoin has recovered and increased its hash rate, and more and more mining farms are coming online, which continues to grow the consensus method and make the blockchain harder to attack or exploit.

In the event of Bitcoins hash rate falling again, I am an example of what could be thought of as a "minute man" for the Bitcoin blockchain, my mining farm is ready and able to be turned on within a few hours, and I would do this in order to earn more Bitcoin block rewards. This is not unique to Bitcoins blockchain, any large POW blockchain with a somewhat high hash rate would see mining farms switch to hashing transactions on the blockchain if it ever became more profitable for them to do so, and this can be done easily with most GPUs as mentioned before. POS blockchains could also see more stake pools set up on the blockchain if their block rewards ever increased, this could be caused by many other stake pools going offline, and this would only apply if the POS blockchain allowed for local pools to be set up by anyone. If there were only "trusted" validators for the blockchain, and if they all went offline, then the entire blockchain would stop, and no transactions could take place. *(Reference page 88)* I would become this minute man for Bitcoins blockchain for the same reason others would, people like wealth, humans are always looking for ways to gain more wealth for the same amount of work or even less work, this is basically what innovation is, and when an opportunity like more block rewards for the same energy cost arises, individuals will set up the equipment needed to hash transactions on the blockchain.

This increase in block rewards for validators, as the total number of validators for the consensus method decreases, does not apply to all blockchains, it depends on whom the blockchain allows to become a validator, or who is allowed to verify transactions and actually add blocks to the blockchain. As we have seen, consensus method types for blockchains can be very different, stake pools can be set up far faster than a mining farm and its cooling systems can be, and some POS consensus methods do not allow for local pools, meaning individuals could not set up a stake pool to take advantage of a higher block reward rate even if they wanted to. This makes some POW blockchains, more decentralized than some POS blockchains, this is because they have the ability to incentivize validators to come online. While other blockchains do not allow for individuals to become validators of their consensus method, and this adds a centralized risk for the blockchain should some or all of the "trusted" validators ever go offline.

Advantages and Disadvantages:

Decentralization involves many aspects of a blockchain, many of the factors mentioned before play a part in determining if a specific blockchain is decentralized or not, and this is done by identifying centralized points of control or failure that could exist on the blockchain. Overall, decentralization can simply be thought of as advantages for the blockchain, while centralized points of control could be thought of as disadvantages for the blockchain, and each blockchain will vary in how many advantages and disadvantages are a part of that blockchains code. In life survival is the goal, it is better to have more advantages and fewer disadvantages, this makes survival easier, and the same is true for blockchains, the more decentralized the blockchain is, the less likely the blockchain code will be exploited or negatively affected over time.

There are many decentralized advantages for a blockchain, several examples would be, there would be certainty in the rules for that blockchain, basically meaning the blockchains code cannot be changed without implementing an IP as mentioned before. For decentralized blockchains these updates take time, this is because the IP must gain enough votes before it is added to the blockchains code, and because there is no one person with a majority of the voting power, it may take time for a majority to come to an agreement. This is good because changes do not happen fast, and investors see this as a good thing, but this is also good for the blockchain since decentralized voting structures include the community of the blockchain, and that community is made up of the users of the blockchain, who ultimately will only want change if it improves the blockchain. A decentralized voting structure might mean IPs are passed at a very slow pace, but at least the decision is being carefully considered by many individuals who are a part of the blockchains use case. In contrast, a small group of individuals with the majority control of a blockchains voting structure could make changes to the blockchains code whenever they wanted, and most investors do not like this type of uncertainty because of the added risks involved. As mentioned before, sometimes developers will control certain aspects of the blockchain to improve the blockchain, such as controlling the approval of IPs for the blockchain, and this allows the developers to quickly address problems that may arise involving the blockchains code. If this control is eventually dispersed to the community, then this could be thought of as an advantage for the blockchain, however it's important to remember that the control exists, and the blockchain should not need to rely on this centralized point of control indefinitely, otherwise this control might not be temporary, and this would not be considered an advantage for the blockchain.

There are many centralized disadvantages for a blockchain, one example would be 3rd parties that control an aspect of the blockchain, such as the validator network, and these could be large "trusted" validators that were mentioned before. This is because the 3rd party could obviously use whatever control they had in a negative way, for this example, the "trusted" validators could manipulate transactions or even front run the transactions as mentioned before, but if they are good actors not negatively affecting the blockchain in any way, they could still be a centralized risk for that blockchain. If the 3rd party were to fail, or itself be exploited by a bad actor, then the blockchain would be negatively affected. In this example it would be something like the "trusted" validator going offline and all transactions on the blockchain stop, or the 3rd party could be hacked and access to the transaction data the validator is hashing could be used by the malicious actor. If the "trusted" validator also had majority voting power for the blockchain, then the malicious actor would also have control over the implementation of IPs for the blockchain. Both of these are possibilities even if the centralized control is in the hands of a good actor, basically even if that control is held by developers or large investors there is still a risk for the blockchain, and this is why it is better to have no centralized points of control, although there are tradeoffs as mentioned before, and many shades of gray when it comes to decentralization.

Self-custody wallets could also be thought of as an advantage for a blockchain, even if most of the blockchain's coins are traded on a centralized exchange, and this is because individuals have the ability to self-custody their wealth, even if they choose not to. Wealth that can be held in a blockchain on a self-custody wallet, where only the wallet holder has access to the seed phrase, is an advantage for the investor more so then for the blockchains code, but it is still an important decentralized aspect of the blockchain, and it is the removal of a possibly 3rd party to the wallet. Other decentralized advantages can exist, ones that are not only an advantage for the blockchain, but for investors and users of the blockchain as well. Open-source code would be an advantage that allowed users of the blockchain to ensure the blockchain is what it claims to be. This would allow for the verification of information, and this is where the phrase "don't trust, verify" comes from. Some advantages will only be considered an advantage to some individuals, as mentioned before there are many groups or types of investors, and some will want to hold their wealth on a hard wallet with no 3rd party access to the seed phrase. While other investors will only be comfortable holding wealth in a hard wallet that has password reset capabilities, they would consider the ability to reset a lost or forgotten seed phrase as an advantage for the hard wallet, and this decision should be theirs to make, since it is their own wealth being held in the wallet. Advantages for investors or users of the blockchain can be anything that helps them protect their investments, and as we have seen there are many factors that can affect an investor's wealth, but reducing 3rd parties and centralized points of control would be a common factor between the advantages for investors holding their wealth in the coin of a blockchain.

Hope:

Centralized points of control, ones that are known, and not points of failure which can be unknown, require an investors hope, that is to say people must hope the control is never used in a negative way against the blockchain, or used against their own trading of wealth on the blockchain. People have hope that everything will be ok because there is someone in control, either a company behind a blockchain project, or skilled developers creating exciting new use cases for blockchain coins and tokens. There is even hope in new types of blockchains, with new consensus methods and voting structures that claim to be "decentralized," and all of these centralized points of control would require hope or faith in who has the centralized control over an aspect of the blockchain. This would include aspects like centralized exchanges where account holders do not have direct control over their wealth, and account holders must hope the exchange is not taking excessive risk with their wealth, however some investors are ok with this added control because they find setting up and using a self-custody wallet to be difficult. Even staking wealth to a POS blockchain from a hard wallet is not as easy as staking and unstaking wealth on an exchange, as mentioned before. Basically, hope could be considered bliss and ignorance, more control over an investor's wealth means the investor has a less complicated experience, and as mentioned before exchanges can offer account holders many options as far as gaining an interest on their wealth, either through lending or block rewards from a POS blockchain. However, simply having hope in something does mean it will happen or not happen, hope is meant to motivate a person to be a part of making that hope a reality, and this means hope is either used as an excuse to live in bliss and ignorance, or it is used to motivate a person. Hope, in centralized blockchains, or centralized exchanges, or 3rd party access to a wallets seed phrase, could be thought of as faith in the company or blockchain project in control of an aspect of the blockchain, or access to a wallets seed phrase, and this is not that different from other traditional assets likes stocks, or storing wealth at a bank or brokerage account, because investors ultimately must trust the 3rd party to their investments and wealth.

For blockchain, hope can be used to motivate a person to be a part of making that hope a reality, this is decentralization for individual blockchains, and this could include aspects of the blockchain that would be considered a decentralized advantage for investors more so than for the blockchain itself. This is because that hope, or decentralization, is participated in by the investor and users of the blockchain, and they can participate in many areas of decentralization, from using self-custody wallets, to helping protect the blockchain that holds an investor's wealth. Investors that hold wealth in a certain blockchain would be able to help protect that blockchain, as mentioned before many blockchains vary in how they are set up, but investors could set up a node on the blockchain that holds their wealth, and this would help the consensus method validate transactions and create new blocks for the blockchain. The same is true for investors that set up a mining farm or stake pool for either a POW or POS blockchain that holds the investor's wealth. They would be participating in the blockchain's consensus method, and they would receive block rewards for doing this unlike nodes, making this a more expensive option as far as helping the blockchain, but one that could create a profit for the investor as well. Even voting on IPs for a blockchain is helping the blockchain overall, and would require less work than setting up a node, stake pool, or mining farm, but it would still add to the blockchains overall decentralization, in this case adding to the decentralization of the blockchains voting structure. Basically, hope must be put in yourself, not in 3rd parties, your future is in your own hands, and passing that responsibility on to someone else is not what self-custody and peer-to-peer transactions were created for, although as we have seen there are many shades of gray when it comes to some decentralized aspects of a blockchain. Seed phrases could be lost or forgotten, to err is human, and this is where some investors might welcome some 3rd party access that allows for password resets or even interest on wealth held at an exchange. But deciding how and where an investor's wealth will be held should always be made by the investor, and as long as there are self-custody options, then people have the ability to remove their wealth from the system of control. Ultimately it should be up to them where they store their wealth, and investors will have different thresholds for risk when it comes to how they want to protect their own wealth. *(Reference page 94)*

Decentralization Conclusion:

Decentralization can be measured by identifying centralized points of control and failure for a blockchain, as we have seen there are many different aspects of a blockchain that are involved in defining a certain blockchain as decentralized or not. This includes major centralized points of control such as the validator network of the blockchain, or external factors such as advertising or promoting for the blockchain. While some centralized aspects of the blockchain are not as important to the blockchain, and they might not affect the blockchain code itself. But they are important to investors or users of the blockchain, and these would be things like how an investor's wealth is held on the blockchain and who else has access to or control over that wealth. Development teams may hold control over small aspects of the blockchain as well, most of these would be considered external factors for the blockchain as mentioned before, and although these aspects of the blockchain might not affect the blockchain code itself, it is still important to identify the centralized point of control, since it is likely these would be the areas of blockchain technology where rules and regulations would be beneficial to the industry.

There are many more aspects to a blockchain that might create centralized points of control or failure, most of them would be external factors that are limited in how much they could negatively affect the blockchain, although regulators would still consider some of these centralized points of control important for investor protection. These points of control would be the areas where realistic rules and regulations could help the industry, rather than blanket regulations that would prevent growth in the industry, and we will go over this in more detail later when we look at the Arizona Blockchain Standards and the Howey test interpretation. For now, just understand the areas of decentralization that were covered are what I believe to be the most important aspects of decentralization. Although I do note there are many more that could be added, and the concept behind how these centralized points of control could affect a blockchain would be the same for other centralized points of control not mentioned before. Any individual or small group, basically any 3rd party, that has the ability to manipulate or negatively affect a blockchain, would be considered a centralized point of control for that blockchain, and it along with many other aspects of the blockchain would determine the overall decentralization of the blockchain.

Defining decentralization for blockchain technology is very important, we will look at how regulators could do this later when we go over the Howey test interpretation, but we have seen how creating lines between digital securities, digital commodities, and digital assets, could help regulators better account for and define the many blockchain coins and tokens that exist. These lines can be adjusted by regulators as they see fit, but there must be a balance if investors are to retain their financial freedom in this new asset class. Basic freedoms like self-custody and the ability to hold your wealth in whatever blockchain you want must be a part of the rules and regulations for this industry. This becomes even more important when we start to see the transition to a tokenized economy, basically when real world assets start to be represented by blockchain coins and tokens, and we will go over this more later when we look at the use cases for blockchains. But for now, just understand, up until now we have only gone over coins and tokens that are nothing more than units of account for a blockchain. Once these coins and tokens represent ownership of real world assets, any form of control over an investor's wealth would no longer be control over just their liquid wealth. Deeds and titles to real estate will be tokenized, stocks will be tokenized, vehicle title and registration will be tokenized, and if the blockchain these tokenized assets run on is centralized, then ownership of these assets could be manipulated, or transactions involving these assets could be limited or prevented. This is why investors should understand how decentralized the blockchain is that holds their wealth, this wealth will soon be real world assets too, and if companies or governments have control over centralized points of that blockchain, then they could have control over the tokenized assets on the blockchain, and even the transaction of these assets between individuals.

Creation of a Cage:

There is a cage being created around us, although blockchain technology can be used in a truly decentralized way, centralized points of control are being adopted instead, and as the blockchain industry grows, coins and tokens will start to be used in many other traditional industries as well. Lack of action by investors during this transition would be like sitting and watching a cage be built around you, and this cage would be 3rd party access to or control over your wealth, this is why protecting self-custody is so important. Even if most investors still use centralized exchanges and want hard wallet seed phrase resets, they must have the option to store their wealth without a 3rd party of any kind to that wealth. This can be thought of as building a window in the cage being built around you, there is no stopping the cage from being built, and there are many good use cases for blockchain coins and tokens, so a tokenized economy is an inevitability. However, if investors have a window, then they can remove their wealth from the system of control that is being created around them, and it's important to understand this would be a choice for investors, many would still prefer to have a 3rd party to their wealth in a limited capacity. This would be like an individual holding their wealth at a traditional bank, but they would keep some of their wealth in the form of gold bars in their own safe at their house, while they must keep the wealth safe from theft, there is no one else that has control over this wealth. If their bank restricted their accounts or had a failure and lost that wealth, then at least the person would have some wealth that was safe and outside the system of control. This is likely how most people would want to use and interact with blockchain technology, some 3rd party control would be welcomed, like password resets for hard wallets, or even centralized exchanges that offer interest or block rewards on wealth held at the exchange, even though there is added risk from the 3rd party access to, or control over that wealth. However, many people would want to have some "gold under the mattress" so to speak, something that holds wealth that the person could use as payment for goods or services should their wealth in centralized exchanges or 3rd party wallets be lost, or if it becomes inaccessible due to transaction restrictions by the 3rd party.

(Illustration, next page)

Basically, this means some investors will not want to be in the cage at all, they will self-custody their wealth and only store it in blockchains that are actually decentralized, and they would put in the extra work or effort in order to achieve this. While other investors would be ok with some centralized control for some of their wealth, and they would also hold some of it outside the cage, so to speak. Holding wealth in the cage would not be forced if there was a window to escape from, but many would still hold their wealth in the cage because of the benefits it offers, not because they are forced. They can simply stake and unstake wealth through an exchange, and gain interest on wealth through lending and investing, this is something investors want, and there is a demand for it. But this idea of the cage being an "ok" place for an investor to hold their wealth is only possibly if there is a window, there must be a way for investors to hold their wealth outside the system of control, and yet still interact with it for payments. If all wealth and assets are to be held in a system that does not allow you to remove that wealth from the system, then you and your wealth are completely controlled, you are in a cage without a window, for better or worse.

Decentralization at its simplest form, in my opinion, is being able to truly self-custody your own wealth, and transfer that wealth peer-to-peer. There are many layers to decentralization, but these would be the foundation of decentralization, and other layers like 3rd party wallets or exchanges could allow investors to buy, hold, and sell, many coins and tokens, and some of these could be the units of account for a decentralized blockchain. However, because the coins and tokens are held with a 3rd party they can be controlled, and this could involve the exchange using an account holder's wealth, or even restricting transactions of that wealth.

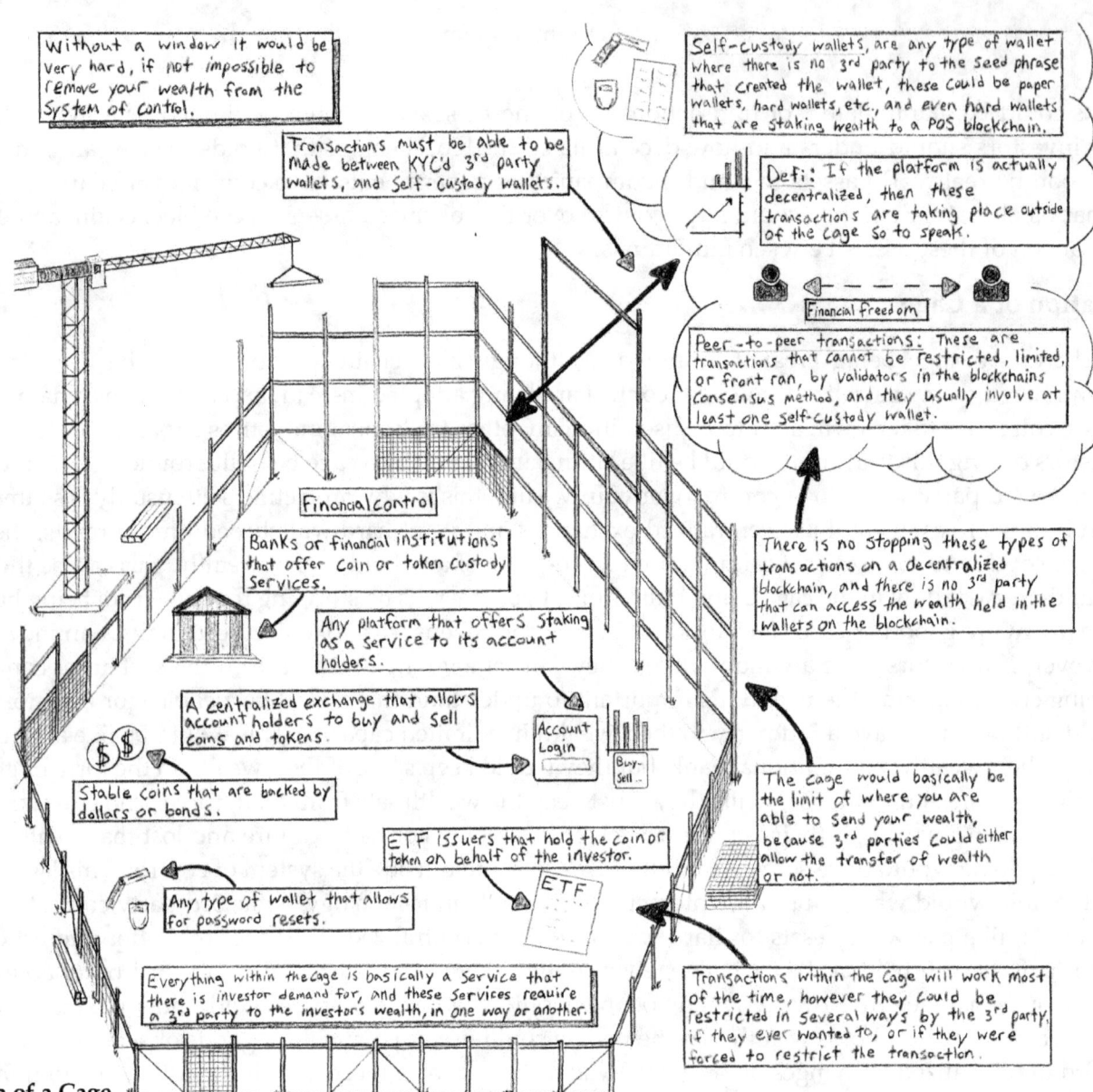

Creation of a Cage

Wealth held in the cage is not necessarily a bad thing, it would depend on the investor and what risks they are comfortable with when it comes to 3rd parties to their wealth, basically many of the services or use cases in the cage are something some investors want, and they are ok with the added risk. While other investors will not be comfortable with the risks, they will self-custody their wealth, and many investors will likely do both. Basically, holding some or most of their wealth in ways that allow them to increase their wealth with the help of a 3rd party, but also holding some of their wealth outside the cage, and a similar concept would be something like storing gold bars at your home. The important part of the illustration is the window that allows wallets of all types to move wealth between each other, if the window did not exist, then wealth inside the cage would have no way out, and wealth outside the cage may not be able to interact with platforms within the cage. There are pros and cons for all the ways wealth can be held on a blockchain, but the only way those investors have financial freedom is if they have the option to leave the cage, if no such option exists then the investor's wealth will always have some form of a 3rd party to it, for better or worse.

Pg. 77, lower left section: If there is enough demand for a service then eventually it will be provided, even if this service involves a 3rd party to the wealth or information, and this can be thought of as inside the cage, although many of these services are something investors want, so they are not forced to be in the cage so to speak.

Pg. 79, lower left section: How wealth is held in a wallet on a blockchain, and who has access to or control over that wealth is what determines if an investors wealth is in the cage or not. But investors have the choice to hold their wealth in whatever type of wallet they want, so there is still financial freedom, even if many investors end up holding their wealth in the cage so to speak.

Pg. 81, lower left section: Hard wallets with password resets of the seed phrase, would be considered in the cage to an extent, this is because there is a 3rd party that has access to the seed phrase of the wallet, and even though they should only access the seed phrase at the request of the wallet holder, the company offering the reset ability could access it at any time.

Pg. 92, upper right section: As long as investors have the option to self-custody their wealth, then they have financial freedom, even if they choose to have a 3rd party to their wealth, and this is because there is a window in the cage, so investors that want to self-custody some or all of their wealth, have the ability to do so.

Pg. 95, lower left section: Any wealth held within the cage "could" be affected by the 3rd party, but this does not mean it will be, most exchanges would not want to do anything that would scare away account holders, and the same is true for other services offered within the cage, any manipulation would only drive users away from the platform. However, these services are often provided by companies or centralized enterprises that must comply with laws and regulations, and this means they would have to comply with a government order to freeze or restrict an account holder's wealth.

Pg. 150, lower left section: Wealth held in a Bitcoin ETF would be considered in the cage so to speak, this is because there is a 3rd party to that wealth, the ETF issuer, and this wealth cannot be sent to another wallet without the ETF issuer allowing for the transaction of that wealth.

Pg. 156, lower left section: Even decentralized blockchains like Bitcoin can have 3rd parties involved in how wealth is held on the blockchain, a simple example is BTC held on a self-custody wallet vs BTC in an ETF, while transactions cannot be restricted from the self-custody wallet, they could be restricted by the ETF issuer for one reason or another.

(Reference page 94) The same is true for hard wallets, while the ledger on the decentralized blockchain does not allow for wealth in that wallet to be used or accessed by a 3rd party, if that hard wallet offered seed phrase resets, then there would be a 3rd party, although it would not be the same as an exchange investing an account holder's wealth without their knowledge. The many levels of decentralization exist because there is demand for that service, it could be interest on wealth at an exchange that invests that wealth on an account holder's behalf. Or it could be earning block rewards on staked wealth through an exchange, and many wealthy individuals and companies like the idea of being able to reset a hard wallets keys, rather than being locked out of that wealth forever if the seed phase is ever lost or forgotten. There are many pros and cons for certain centralized points of control, they vary in how much control the 3rd party has, and these pros and cons themselves will vary between investors as well, each investor will have different thresholds for the amount of risk they are willing to take with their own wealth.

(Illustration, next page)

Must Have the Option:

The demand for 3rd party access to or control over an individual's wealth, in whatever form that takes, should be something investors want, and this is why it would be considered demand, because if there were no other options, then it would be called force. Basically, this 3rd party control must be something an investor wants, if they do not want it then they have the option to self-custody, and this option is the only difference there is between an economy with financial freedom, and one where there is financial control. This control can exist on many levels as we have seen so far, the control could be at the blockchain level where individual transactions can be affected, or the blockchain may actually be decentralized, and the control comes from the centralized exchanges that have access to an account holder's wealth, and could restrict movement of that wealth. Although, it is important to remember the difference between the two, control over the blockchain code itself would affect all wallets or ledgers for that blockchain, both individual hard wallets, and exchange wallets that list the coin or token of the blockchain. While control over transactions on an exchange would not affect other wallets on an individual blockchain, it would only affect transactions taking place on the exchange, and could prevent some wealth from entering the exchange, but we will go over this in more detail later when we look at how exchanges work. Basically, exchanges can really only affect transactions of wealth that take place in the exchange, although they could also set up stake pools for POS blockchains that they offer staking services for. And this would be playing a part in the blockchain's consensus method, where the exchange could be a "trusted" validator that has control over validating transactions for the entire blockchain. *(Reference page 23)* This would give the exchange control over transactions that take place in the exchange, and transactions for the blockchain that they have the majority control over, although generally exchanges only have control over transactions coming to the exchange, leaving the exchange, and ones taking place between accounts at the exchange. *(Reference page 80)*

Hard wallets also allow for additional levels of control, as detailed before the seed phrase of a hard wallet can be stored with a 3rd party in case of the need for a password reset, and although this does not give the 3rd party direct control over wealth in the hard wallet, they would have this ability. This is something some investors want, and other investors do not want, and this is why some services can be both seen as a pro and as a con depending on the investor, but there must exist options for investors when it comes to where they hold their wealth and who has access to it. The ability to truly self-custody your own wealth, and transact peer-to-peer with that wealth, must be a part of the blockchains code if it is to be considered decentralized, even if other centralized points of control exist for other investors holding wealth in the blockchain. For blockchains that do not even allow for self-custody of your own wealth, or for ones that require a 3rd party for transactions of that wealth, the blockchain is not decentralized, and this is because the control that exists does not even give investors an option to remove wealth from the system of control. Basically, the control exists all the way to the core of what decentralization is, there are many ways to hold and transfer wealth on a decentralized blockchain, some may involve 3rd parties or some type of centralized control, but at its core, individual investors should have the option to control their own wealth and transact with others. If this basic

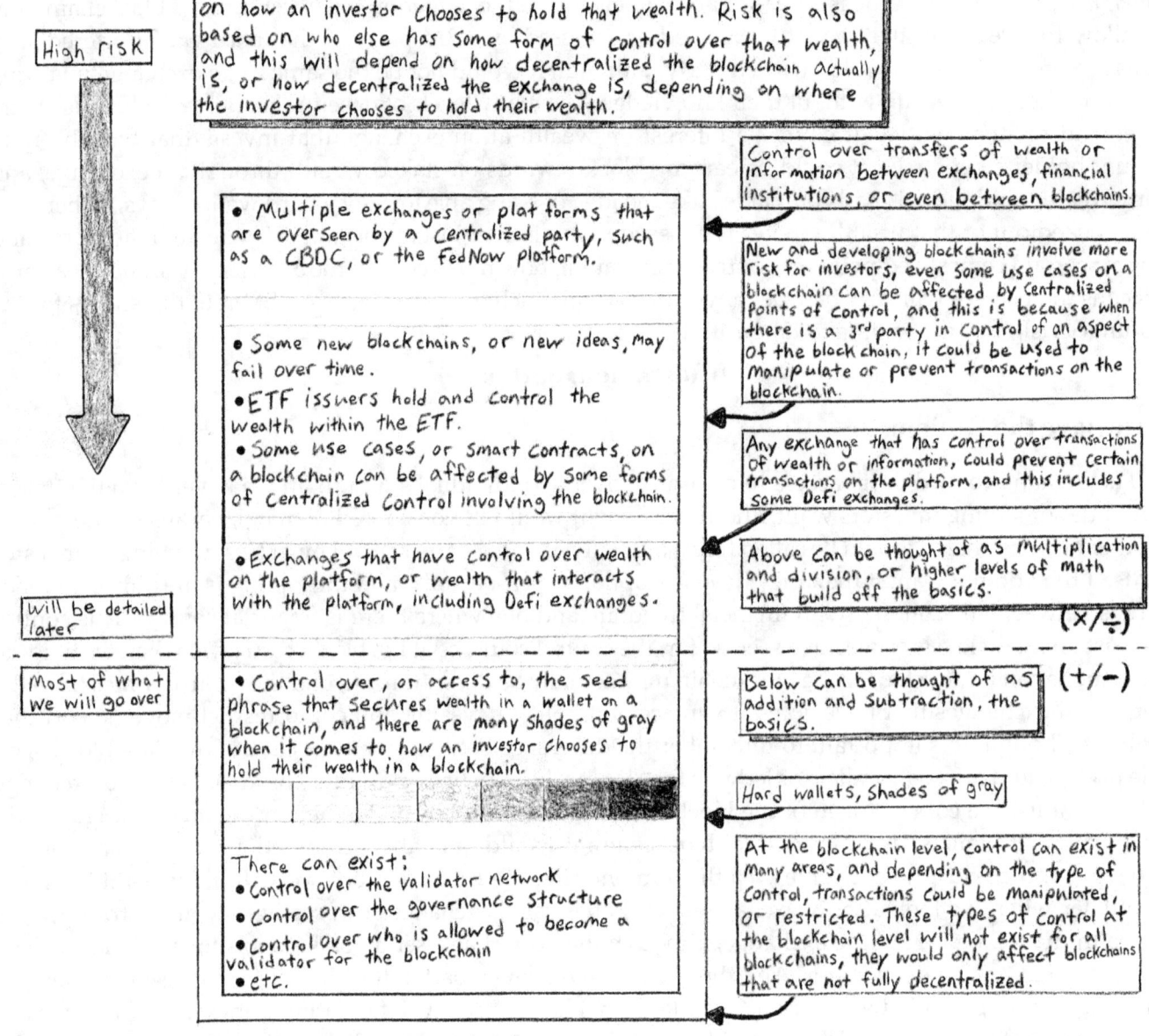

Risk Levels for Blockchain Technology

Most of the upper section will be detailed in the second part of this book, there are many different types of risk, and they can exist at different levels, depending on how the blockchain is set up, but not all these risks are bad for all investors. Some investors will want more rewards, and they will be ok with the additional risks involved, and they should have this option, just as other investors should have the option to self-custody their wealth. Basically, without options investors would be told where they can and cannot hold their wealth, and if all options involve some form of 3rd party access to, or control over that wealth, then investors would have lost the ability to truly self-custody and transact peer-to-peer.

    Pg. 32, bottom section: Individuals can interact with a blockchain in many ways, even simply holding the coin or token on a self-custody wallet is interacting with the blockchain and its unit of account, although this is the most basic level of interacting with a blockchain, and other interactions with a blockchain or its use cases might involve more risk.

    Pg. 43, right section: Most of what we are covering would be considered the basics as far as blockchain technology, but there are many more use cases for blockchain technology, some are more technical, and some use cases have added risk for users.

    Pg. 78, bottom section: There are many shades of gray when it comes to how wealth is held in a blockchain, basically there are many different types of wallets, and who has control over, or access to, the wealth is important to investors, this is because it either adds risk, or reduces risk for the investor and their wealth.

    Pg. 79, upper section: How an investor's wealth interacts with a blockchain, and how it is held on a blockchain can vary, different investors will be comfortable with different levels of risk, and this is because there is a greater reward possible. Either in the form of interest on an account holder's wealth at an exchange, or a simple and easy to use app, or user interface, may be something that some investors are looking for, and they are ok with the added risk that it may come with.

    Pg. 85, upper section: Even good use cases there is demand for can be risky for investors if the blockchain involved in the use case has centralized points of control, this means transactions involving the use case might be susceptible to manipulation, and this is why clearly defining decentralization is so important. It would allow for blockchains and their use cases to be grouped into several levels of risk, and this would allow investors the ability to better manage their risk when investing in blockchain coins and tokens.

    Pg. 156, upper section: Many Alt-coins have use cases that users and investors are looking for, but not all Alt-coins are decentralized, and centralized points of control could affect users interacting with the blockchain, or investors holding wealth in the blockchain. Basically, there are many aspects of decentralization for a blockchain, and the type of control a centralized point has can vary depending on what aspect of the blockchain it controls, adding risk for investors.

ability is not possible for someone holding wealth in a blockchain, then it might be very hard to remove their wealth from the blockchain, and this would include removing wealth from any platform that has the ability to prevent transactions as well. Including exchanges and CBDC type platforms, that themselves might not be a blockchain, but the control they would have would be the same, and we will go over CBDCs in more detail later.

Bitcoin Blockchain

The many decentralized aspects to Bitcoins blockchain, and how they play a part in securing the blockchain overall*

- Blockchain Basics, Bitcoin
- Centralization Risks
- Bitcoins History
- Bitcoins Future
- Bitcoin Validators
- Renewable Energy Sources Being used Today
- Our Mining Farm
- Bitcoin Conclusion

Blockchain Basics, Bitcoin:

There are many detailed resources on Bitcoin's blockchain, this will be a brief summary of the many aspects that make Bitcoin decentralized, and we will go over how all these aspects play a part in securing the Bitcoin blockchain. I would suggest further research for anyone looking to understand Bitcoin on a deeper level, for now we will just take what we have gone over so far, and see how the Bitcoin blockchain works overall. We will look at the validators for the Bitcoin blockchain, as well as nodes, its consensus method and voting structure, as well as major events in Bitcoins past over the last decade, and new developments that may grow in the years to come. There is a balance that decentralized blockchains need to achieve, there is no single right way to do this, and we will look at ways Bitcoins blockchain could one day create centralized points of control, and why this would not be likely, but nonetheless it could be possible. It is important to understand the risks for Bitcoins blockchain as well as its strengths, and these strengths come together to form a secure blockchain that has slow steady progress, one that is not easy to pass IPs for, and a blockchain that allows for price discovery by creating a supply shock every 4 years, although this may become less of a factor as institutional adoption of Bitcoin continues.

SHA-256:

As mentioned before, secure hash algorithms are the constant that transactions on the blockchain are hashed together with, along with the keys or seed phrase, and this type of encryption is very complex and hard to decipher without the sequence of numbers that were scrambled up with the transaction. SHA-256 is the algorithm Bitcoin runs on, but there are many other SHAs as mentioned before, and they can differ in almost every way, or in very few ways, this is what allows for some mining farms to dual mine different blockchains. Basically, as long as the SHA of both blockchains is similar enough, then certain ASIC units would be able to hash transactions and earn block rewards on both blockchains, and this not possible for all blockchains, but there are many that can be dual mined. This is because some SHAs today are just copies of Bitcoins original code, they were copied and altered to fit whatever use case developers wanted to create, and this led to many of the larger blockchains today. Including Dogecoin, which is almost an exact copy of Bitcoin, and very little was changed from Bitcoins original code, although Dogecoin does use a diffrent scrypt. We will go over the inflation rate difference between Bitcoin and Dogecoin later when we look at Alt-coins, for now just understand Bitcoins original code is open-source, and this lets anyone simply copy past Bitcoins code. With any changes the developers wanted to include, in the case of Dogecoin, there were few changes, other than the block reward rate to miners. Even with two very similar SHAs they are two distinct blockchains, and this makes the coins of each blockchain different from one another, this is easier to understand if we think of the SHA as a curved line on a graph as mentioned before. Even adding one small change to the algorithm would create a new curved line, very close to each other and similar in shape, but they are not the same, and this is what creates the distinction between blockchains like Bitcoin and Dogecoin. *(Reference page 9)*

There is really nothing that makes Bitcoins SHA better or worse than other SHAs, simply put it is just the algorithm that is hashed with all transactions on the blockchain, and these transactions are just updates to the blockchain's ledger of wallet addresses as mentioned before. The way a SHA and private keys interact to encrypt transactions on the blockchain is very secure, malicious actors usually try to exploit other aspects of the blockchain rather than actually trying to hack the SHA itself, and this would be something like gaining the majority control of the validator network, or governance structure of the blockchain which was mentioned before. Basically, this means most SHAs are secure, however the term blockchain includes the SHA, and many other aspects like the consensus method and voting structure set up by developers, and usually blockchains are "hacked" by exploiting these aspects that control the SHA, not by directly deciphering transactions and hacking the SHA itself. This is why blockchains can be set up almost identically, and still vary in how secure the blockchain is, it depends on the number of validators in the consensus method, how IPs are voted on and implemented, etc. all of this plays a part in preventing exploits of the blockchains code, and we will look at all these aspects for Bitcoin individually next, we will start with how coins are created on the Bitcoin blockchain.

Coin Creation:

Bitcoin has a POW consensus method, block rewards are distributed to the miners that are hashing transactions on the blockchain, there is a cap of 21 million coins that can exist, and we will go over the reducing block reward rate next. *(Reference page 103)* This limit is hard coded into Bitcoin's blockchain, meaning if additional coins were ever allowed to exist on Bitcoin's blockchain, there would have to be a hard fork of the blockchain, and we will look at Bitcoins many hard forks later. For now, just understand there is no way a soft fork or IP could allow for additional block rewards in excess of the current block reward rate. Think of the circle that represents the blockchain as mentioned before, soft forks are smaller circles within the original circle, for Bitcoin there can only ever be 21 million coins, and any update to Bitcoins code that included additional coins would be a new circle that crosses the original circle, creating a hard fork and two separate blockchains. *(Reference page 34)* This would not stop Bitcoins blockchain, but it could split users and validators into supporting either blockchain, this was mentioned before with the Bitcoin and Bitcoin Cash hard fork, and we will look at a few other Bitcoin hard forks later. For now, just understand a hard fork of the Bitcoin blockchain does not mean Bitcoin will end, or be changed, it has happened many times before and will likely happen again in the future.

It is important to stress that this 21 million cap for the number of coins that can exist is hard coded into Bitcoins blockchain, that means there would be a hard fork of the blockchain if there was an attempt to change this limit, and this needs to be verified in order to be trusted, which you can do by looking at Bitcoins code. However, other blockchains could say there is a max limit of coins that can exist just like Bitcoin, but unless the limit is hard coded into the blockchain, a soft fork, or IP, could allow for additional coins to be created. These other blockchains could still have code that prevents additional coins from being created as new blocks are added to the blockchain, but the devil is in the details. Let us look at a simplified example to understand the difference between having a limit of coins that can exist, and having that limit hard coded into the blockchain, like with Bitcoin, or other blockchains that actually hard code this limit into their blockchain, this is not necessarily unique to Bitcoin, but it must be verified. The consensus method of this example blockchain would have "trusted" validators, but the example would still be somewhat true if anyone could become a validator for the blockchain, and these validators would control the implementation of IPs for the blockchain. There is a limit of coins that can exist, say 1 million coins, the SHA still secures the transactions of wallet holders, and there is no inflation rate for the blockchain, all 1 million coins are in circulation. As blocks are created, the code makes sure the sum of all transactions and wallet addresses equal 1 million total coins, and if a block contains the sum of 1 million and 1 coins, the validator that created the block will be rejected by the consensus of the rest of the validators. This is because all the validators run the same version of the blockchain that says 1 million coins exist, there cannot be more, and invalid transactions that attempt to create more coins are rejected by validators and nodes hashing transactions on the blockchain. In this example, there is code that says there is a limit of 1 million coins, but this limit is used each time a new block is added to the blockchain. Basically, this code says the last block had a total of 1 million coins, so the next block needs to also have a total of 1 million coins, either coins being transferred or coins held in wallets, as mentioned before this would be a sum of all coins that exist. This example blockchain would be secure, and no new coins could be created with invalid transactions, however, additional coins could be created if all the validators agreed to it.

For Bitcoins blockchain this would technically be the same, if all validators agreed to an IP than it would be implemented. However, if the BIP allowed for say 22 million coins than it would create a hard fork of the blockchain, and Bitcoins original code would continue as long as some validators did not update their version of the blockchain to the new version, they would simply continue to run the original version of Bitcoin. This has happened many times before, and these changes to Bitcoins blockchain do not always involve increasing the max limit of coins, but it does create a hard fork and two separate blockchains after, allowing the original version of Bitcoin to continue. However, for our example blockchain the limit is not hard coded into the blockchain, there is just code making sure each time a block is added to the blockchain it does not include more than 1 million coins in total, basically, the blockchain has hard coded into it that new blocks must contain the same number of coins as the prior block. This means there is no numerical value hard coded into the blockchain, and if all the validators agreed to an IP that, say added 1 million coins into existence, then the blockchain code would now ensure that each new block contained a total of 2 million coins. This would not violate the blockchains code if all the "trusted" validators agreed to this update, it would be a soft fork since it did not violate the original limit hard coded into the blockchain, which is not a numerical limit, so there is no violation of the code, or a part of the circle extending beyond the original circle as mentioned before. *(Reference page 34)* Because this would be a soft fork there would not be two separate blockchains created, simply put the blockchain would now have a limit of 2 million coins instead of 1 million, and because the "trusted" validators all agreed to the update, the old version of the blockchain would no longer exist. With this example we can see that even blockchains with "limits" on the number of coins that can exist, can under certain circumstances create additional coins, and this would not have to be done all at once, it could simply be increasing the block reward rate until the new limit is reached. This is why any blockchain that claims there is a max limit for the number of coins that can exist on its blockchain, must hard code this number into the blockchain and make that code viewable for anyone to verify, and if this limit is not hard coded into the blockchain then the limit could be changed with a soft fork. This example would be true for "trusted" validators and for blockchains that allow anyone to become a validator, the main difference would be, if the soft fork was approved by the majority of validators, and anyone could be a validator, then there might be some that would choose to continue the old version of the blockchain. This is why it is important that Bitcoin allows anyone to hash transactions and earn block rewards, it ensures there is an option for those that do not agree with a hard fork or soft fork of the Bitcoin blockchain, an option that does not exist for blockchains if all the validators of the blockchain are "trusted" validators.

Bitcoin Block Rewards:

Bitcoins block reward rate is reducing every 4 years, we will look at this more when we go over the Bitcoin halving, but this simply means fewer and fewer Bitcoin are created until the 21 million cap is reached. When Bitcoin started, each block added to the blockchain gave 50 Bitcoin to the miner that was randomly chosen by the consensus method. Basically the miner solved the block, and in these early days of Bitcoin the coins did not have actual value, meaning they could not be exchanged for dollars, they were simply the unit of account for the Bitcoin blockchain. About every 4 years there is a 50% reduction in block rewards for miners that are hashing transactions on the blockchain, in 2012 the block reward rate was reduced to 25 Bitcoin per new block, in 2016 it was reduced to 12.5, in 2020 it was reduced to 6.25, and sometime around April 2024 the block reward rate will drop to 3.125 Bitcoin per new block added to the blockchain. This reduction will continue until about 2140, when the last sat, or the smallest unit of account for Bitcoin, is created as a block reward for miners, and we will look at this in more detail later when we go over the Bitcoin halving and the difficulty adjustments for Bitcoins hash rate. For now, just understand the block reward rate will slowly reduce over the next 100 plus years, and this will make mining Bitcoin profitable for mining farms that are able to reduce their energy costs for many years to come.

(Illustration, next page)

After the last block reward is created, some larger mining farms will be able to continue hashing transactions and earning transaction fees, also by this point there will be many additional Bitcoin nodes hashing transactions on the blockchain, and the end of block rewards will not mean the end of Bitcoin. This slow distribution of coins over long periods of time can be thought of as a fair launch, simply put a market of buyers and sellers is created for the coin, these coins are evenly distributed over time, and this allows for price discovery as long as there is a demand for the coin. We will go over fair launches later when we look at Alt-coins and their circulating supply, for now just understand many new blockchains will give some of their coins away in order to create a market of buyers and sellers. Either through an air drop or some other way to disperse the coins, and what they are doing is trying to create what Bitcoin and other older blockchains have achieved over long periods of time, except they are trying to speed up that process. It is also important to understand that Bitcoin is only created in the form of block rewards to validators, or miners that are hashing transactions on the blockchain, and this is the only way to earn Bitcoin. Any exchange or platform offering interest on Bitcoin held by an account holder would not be gaining block rewards. This is possible if the blockchain is POS and the exchange is operating a stake pool for the blockchain, but this is not possible for the Bitcoin blockchain, and any interest earned on Bitcoin would come from that wealth being lent out or invested by the exchange. We will go over this in more detail later when we look at exchanges, for now just understand new Bitcoin is only distributed to mining farms, and this supply of coins is then sold into circulating supply, either sold on exchanges, or sold directly to the exchange, or buyer through an over-the-counter transaction.

Bitcoin Distribution:

Bitcoin wallets can be viewed on the blockchain, just like other blockchains that are open-source, this allows anyone to see how the coins are distributed, and large wallets, or whale wallets, can be somewhat identified. Some large wallets can be linked to exchange wallets, but not all of them are identifiable, the wallets are pseudo anonymous. Basically, the wallet and the coins are viewable to anyone, but there is no identity linked to the wallet, and this is changing as blockchain tracing companies like Chainalysis continue to develop the ability to trace transactions and link identities to wallets. For now, let's go over the coin distribution for the Bitcoin blockchain, there are many old wallet addresses that have not sent or received coins in many years, some over a decade, and this can be for several reasons. Such as the wallet holder lost or forgot the seed phrase to the wallet, and this means they can no longer access the wallet. However, old wallets that have not moved coins in years are continuing to become active again, so although some of these large wallets could be lost due to forgotten seed phrases, there is no real way to know this for sure, and the wallet holder could have access but just chooses to hold long term. Some of these large wallets were created back when the block reward rate was much higher, while most early investors would buy and sell Bitcoin, some people would mine Bitcoin and sell some or all of the block rewards, and some of these wallets have been able to hold onto the large amounts of Bitcoin over the years, and their value has increased over this time. Most of these larger older wallets are from mining Bitcoin, and the largest wallet holder is believed to be Bitcoins creator, Satoshi Nakamoto, and we will go over who could have created Bitcoin later. For now, just understand these wallets were able to accumulate large amounts of Bitcoin because they were mining Bitcoin back when block rewards were higher. In the case of the Satoshi wallets, there were several early Bitcoin miners sending their block rewards to several wallets, and these block rewards were issued when there were not many people mining Bitcoin. This basically means these Bitcoin miners were getting 50

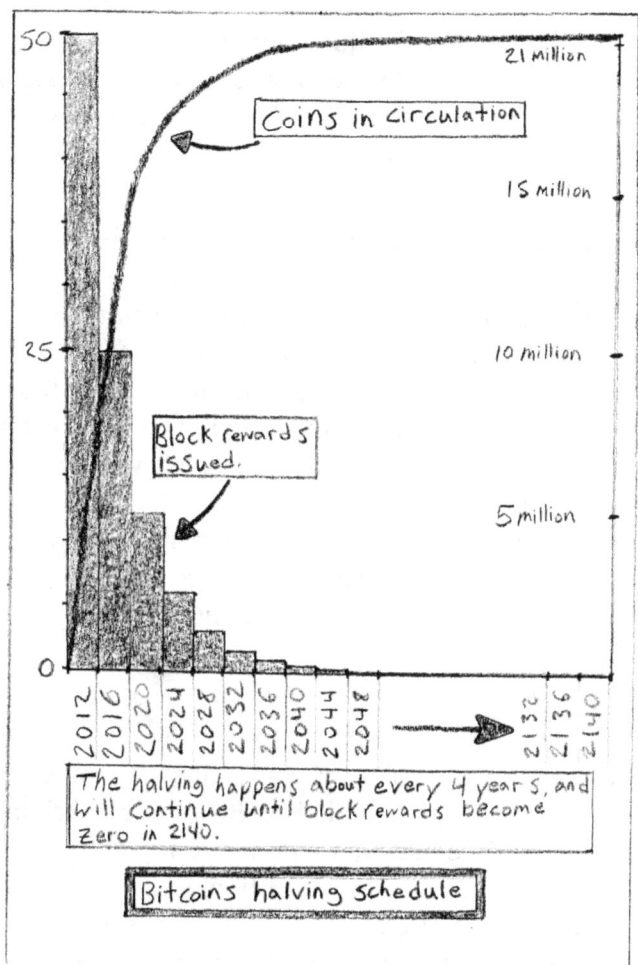
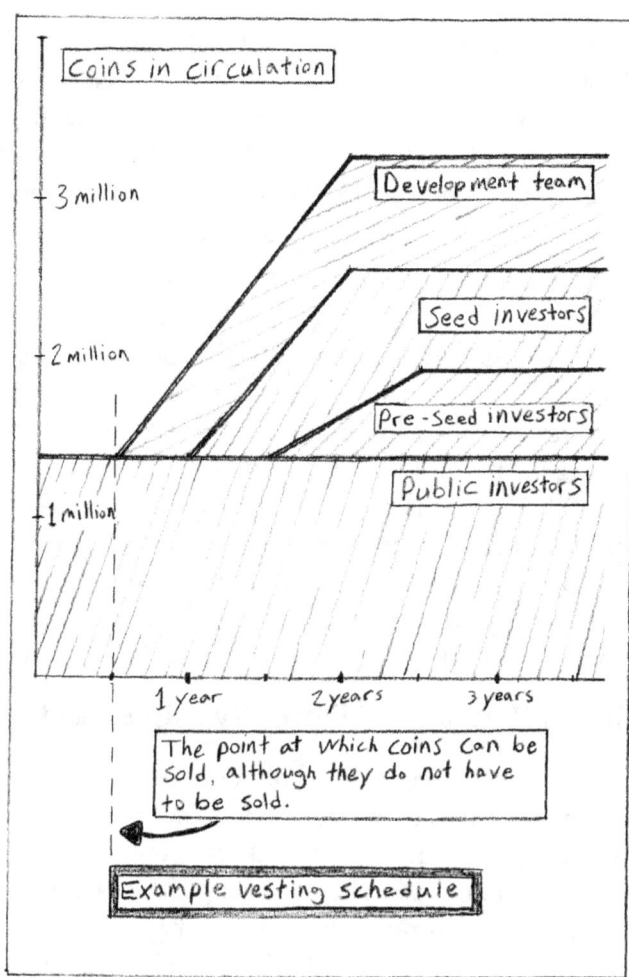

Bitcoin Halving

Bitcoins halving event has allowed for the dispersal of BTC over time, some of these block rewards are sold by miners to cover energy costs, while some BTC holders will hold for long periods of time before selling. There is over 1 million BTC left to be created as a block reward over the next 100 plus years, and this means most of the 21 million BTC that will ever exist are in circulation now, with most of the BTC being dispersed between many wallet holders. Other blockchains will distribute their coins to large investors or developers as compensation, and these large wallets will have vesting schedules, this prevents a large number of coins from being sold into circulating supply all at once. These wallets with vesting schedules can be trusted to not sell their coins before a certain point, this is because the transfer of coins from these wallets before a certain point would violate the blockchains code, and this does not apply to all large wallet holders, for example, whale wallets do not usually have vesting schedules.

Pg. 4, left section: If block rewards only came from transaction fees for the Bitcoin blockchain, then blocks without transactions would not credit the miner with block rewards, and this would affect their ability to stay online hashing transactions. This is why Bitcoin has a reducing inflation rate, basically the creation of new coins until the max limit of 21 million coins is reached, and these block rewards are reduced by 50% about every 4 years.

Pg. 74, right section: Whale wallets are basically any large wallet holder that has a significant percent of the total number of coins or tokens that exist on the blockchain, and some of these large wallets have restrictions on when they are allowed to sell their coins. These are wallets with vesting schedules, and the rate at which the wallet is able to sell its coins can vary, these rates are locked in the blockchains code, so there is no way to move the coins until the vesting schedule allows for it.

Pg. 100, left section: Bitcoins block rewards are being cut in half every 4 years, currently block rewards are 6.25 per block added to the blockchain, and in about a decade there will be less than 1 BTC issued per block added to the blockchain. Basically, this means fewer and fewer Bitcoin are being created, and this will continue until the year 2140, when the last sat is issued as a block reward, and the 21 million coin limit is reached.

Pg. 107, left section: The Bitcoin halving creates a supply shock, this is because large buyers of Bitcoin, such as exchanges, get accustomed to the steady supply of Bitcoin being sold by mining farms to cover their energy costs, and when the number of Bitcoin being created drops below 1 BTC, exchanges will have to find other sellers to meet their higher demand.

Pg. 119, left section: Bitcoins block reward rate is important, and it affects the value of Bitcoin over time, simply put Bitcoin has scarcity, and even though large numbers of Bitcoin were created at first, this has been reduced over time. As Bitcoins value increases, earning block rewards will continue to remain profitable for some mining farms, and this will lead to many mining farms being weeded out overtime, however for those that are able to continue hashing transactions, the blockchains code ensures they will be compensated in an amount of BTC.

Pg. 125, left section: Bitcoins 3.125 block reward cycle will last from April 2024, to sometime in 2028.

Pg. 148, left section: The new supply of Bitcoin is being reduced at a rapid rate, and this is happening as demand is growing globally.

Bitcoin every 10 minutes as new blocks were created, this would be about 1.5 million dollars at a Bitcoin price of 30k. But back when these Bitcoin were issued as a block reward they had very little to no value, so many miners simply stacked Bitcoin in these early wallets. This is what allowed the early Satoshi wallets to stack up about 1 million Bitcoin, they have not moved since being issued as a block reward over a decade ago, and these wallets together are the largest holder of Bitcoin.

There are about 1.5 million Bitcoin that have yet to be issued as a block reward, and these will be created over the next 100 plus years, following the block reward distribution rate in Bitcoins code, and these block rewards will continue to get smaller and smaller. This is because each Bitcoin is divisible to 8 decimal places as mentioned before, and these sats, sometimes called "Satoshis", will increase in dollar terms as the market cap increases over time. *(Reference page 120)* So even as fewer block rewards are issued, the value of those block rewards in dollar terms might still be worth it for some miners, and this is what both weeds out some mining farms, and rewards mining farms that have been able to reduce their energy costs. We will go over how Bitcoin weeds out inefficient mining farms in more detail later when we look at how Bitcoin mining will develop the renewable energy sector. For now, just understand the supply of Bitcoin being added into circulating supply is being reduced as time goes by, and Bitcoin is able to adjust the block reward rate with the difficulty adjustment that happens every 2 weeks, this is in addition to the 50% reduction every 4 years, and we will look at Bitcoins halving and difficulty adjustment next.

Bitcoin Halving and Difficulty Adjustment:

The Bitcoin halving is only one of several factors that affect Bitcoins block reward rate, as mentioned before the halving happens about every 4 years, or every 210,000 blocks added to Bitcoins blockchain, and because blocks are created on average every 10 minutes, the time between halving's can vary a little. *(Reference page 106)* This reduces the block rewards by 50%, however there are additional adjustments to the block reward rate over the 4-year period as well, these adjustments are based on the number of miners hashing transactions for the Bitcoin blockchain, and as the hash rate increases block rewards are slightly reduced for miners. This difficulty adjustment does not actually reduce the quantity of Bitcoin distributed to Bitcoin miners, it just makes it harder to solve the next block of the blockchain, meaning it will take miners longer to earn the same amount of block rewards, and these difficulty adjustments happen about every two weeks, or every 2,016 blocks added to the blockchain. Basically, what's happening is, as more miners come online and start hashing transactions, Bitcoins total hash rate increases, this affects how fast blocks are added to the blockchain, and this adjustment will either make it harder for miners to earn block rewards, or easier for them to earn block rewards. The difficulty adjustment takes into account the total hash rate for Bitcoin, and adjusts the difficulty so that blocks are added about every 10 minutes, if there are many new miners coming online then it will be harder to earn block rewards, but if the hash rate falls, then it will become easier for miners to earn block rewards. This was mentioned before when we went over Bitcoin and Bitcoin Cash miners, they will switch to hashing transactions on one blockchain when it becomes more profitable to mine than the other blockchain, and this is possible for any mining farm that has the ability to hash transactions on both blockchains. But it is not unique to Bitcoin, and many GPU miners regularly switch between POW blockchains that are profitable for them to mine. It's important to note that the blockchains block height is what creates these events, both the halving, every 210,000 blocks, and the difficulty adjustment, every 2,016 blocks, and using a blockchains block height as a measurement of time is not unique to Bitcoin, it is used in some POS blockchains to create epochs as a way to prevent pool hopping as mentioned before. *(Reference page 21)*

To understand how the difficulty adjustment works, and what information it takes into account, I would suggest further research, put simply, the difficulty adjustment is one of many ways Bitcoin creates a balance, and this balance would be one where, as more miners come online it is harder to mine Bitcoin, and as miners go offline, mining becomes more profitable. This ability to recover from a large drop in hash power is not easy for most blockchains, and some blockchains do not even have this ability if their consensus method only has "trusted" validators. *(Reference page 88)* This is an ongoing process for Bitcoin, although Bitcoins hash rate has continued to reach new all-time highs over the years, so overall it is constantly becoming harder to mine Bitcoin, not easier. This process is another area where Bitcoin has created a balance so to speak, as Bitcoins price reaches new highs more miners are able to hash transactions and earn block rewards at a profit, this brings many new miners into the space, and these miners will be weeded out over the 4-year cycle. Either miners will shut down their equipment and wait for an opportunity where Bitcoins difficulty drops to a level where they are profitable again, similar to myself being a minute man for Bitcoins blockchain as mentioned before. Or miners have to increase their hash power by adding ASIC units and their cooling systems, and they would do all of this only to see their block rewards cut by 50% during the next halving. This is how mining farms are weeded out, only miners that are able to reduce their energy costs and increase their hash power over long periods of time will be able to continue to earn block rewards at a profit. Some small mining farms are able to do this, but not all of them, while most large mining farms are able to upgrade their equipment regularly, since they usually have more capital to throw at improved equipment over time.

Each Bitcoin halving has a price rally and correction, which we will briefly go over next, for now just understand these price rallies bring in many new Bitcoin miners, this causes the difficulty to increase, which is good for Bitcoins blockchain since this added hash power is what further protects the blockchain from invalid transactions and other attacks. However, this increase will make it harder for all Bitcoin miners, and they will have to increase their hash power or energy efficiency if they want to continue mining Bitcoin at a profit. Many mining farms will rotate their equipment and try to recover some of their costs by selling older ASIC units to new miners just starting out, or existing mining farms growing out their facilities, and we will look at this a little more later. For now, just understand there are a lot of factors at play for Bitcoin miners, and only ones that are constantly adapting will be able to mine Bitcoin long term. This mining farm cycle is just one of many created by the Bitcoin halving event, and these cycles do not always line up with the exact halving date and block reward reduction, another cycle would be the Bitcoin price cycle during the 4-year period, which we will look at next.

(Illustration, next page)

Bitcoin Price Cycle:

The Bitcoin halving effects the supply of Bitcoin being created and added into the circulating supply, this creates a supply shock, and this leads to a spike in price, although it does not happen right away. During Bitcoins first few years its units of account did not have value since they could not be converted to dollars. Once early exchanges were created Bitcoins price spiked to around $20 in 2011, and crashed to just a few dollars later that year, then over 2012 it slowly rose back to around $10. In late 2012 Bitcoin had its first halving, and during 2013 Bitcoin would spike to over $1000, only to drop back down to about $250 during 2014 and 2015, and by mid-2016 Bitcoin had recovered to about $500 and the second Bitcoin halving took place. By late 2017 Bitcoin was near $20,000, and by early 2019 it had dropped to under $4000, however by the 3rd halving in mid-2020 Bitcoin had recovered to about $9000, and after this halving Bitcoin rose to above $60,000 twice in 2021. During 2022 Bitcoin fell to around $15,000, and as of mid-2023 Bitcoin has recovered to around $30,000, with the 4th halving taking place in less than a year. This is not financial advice, we are just looking at Bitcoins value over the last 3 halving's, but there is a clear upward pressure in price, and this price cycle does not follow the exact halving date. These cycles are usually measured from price top to bottom, they also last about 4 years, and they vary in when the top is reached during the 4-year cycle, taking place about 1-2 years after the halving date. The blow off top is usually followed by a large correction that takes place over the next few years of the halving cycle, and this price bottom will recover a little over the remainder of the halving cycle, not necessarily to new all-time highs, but usually significantly higher than the bottom. The reduction in block rewards by such a drastic amount causes this price spike and crash, and we will go over why next, but for now just understand with each halving Bitcoin tends to jump orders of magnitude, only to have a large crash in price afterward, and as soon as a price balance is reached, the next halving event occurs and starts the process over.

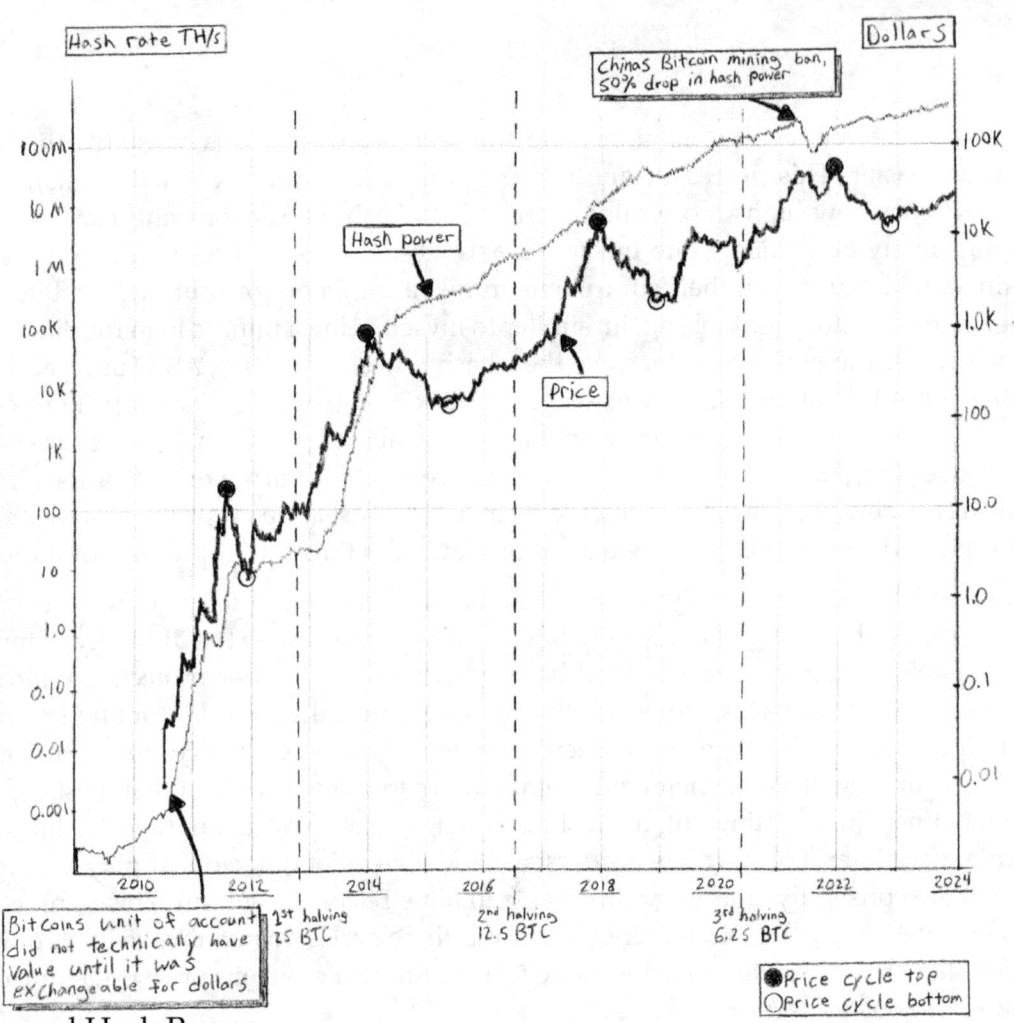

Bitcoin Price and Hash Power

Bitcoins total hash rate seems unaffected by the halving event, and although some mining farms will eventually shut down, many more are brought online each year, and existing mining farms can rotate their ASICs, basically maintaining a high hash rate that will earn them more block rewards. These halving events are predictable, happening about every 4 years, and it affects the block rewards of every mining farm that is hashing transactions on the Bitcoin blockchain. The halving event also creates Bitcoins price cycle over the 4-year period, these cycles have a price top and bottom, and they tend to increase orders of magnitude with each price spike, which is then followed by a long correction to the price bottom for the cycle. Over the last 3 halving cycles we can clearly see the price pressure to the upside, with the price bottom of a cycle usually ending up around the last price cycle top, and these cycles may become less extreme as more institutional investors enter the space.

Bitcoin ETFs have accumulated 100s of thousands of Bitcoin as of early 2024, this lead to Bitcoins price reaching a new all-time high before the halving in April, and this increased demand from larger investors will continue to keep Bitcoins price pressure to the upside in the long term. The Bitcoin halving has a similar effect on Bitcoins long-term price, however instead of increasing the demand side, the Bitcoin halving affects the supply side, and this will create a supply shock that leads to a price spike. This will continue until Bitcoins block rewards are reduced to a point where they no longer affect the market of buyers and sellers in a significant way, and this would likely not happen until block rewards were well under 1 BTC per block added to the blockchain. Simply put, Bitcoin has scarcity, and any large increase in demand for Bitcoin, such as approval of a spot Bitcoin ETF, will cause the value of Bitcoins unit of account to increase.*

Pg. 89, upper section: During China's mining ban Bitcoins hash rate dropped by about 50% for a period of time, although it recovered somewhat fast as mining farms moved to other locations around the world, and this event did not have a long-term effect on Bitcoins price or hash rate, as both have recovered since then.

Pg. 104, bottom section: Bitcoins halving happens about every 4 years, with the first halving taking place in 2012, the second taking place in 2016, the third taking place in 2020, and the next halving will be around April 2024.

Pg. 116, left section: Bitcoins hash rate really started to increase at an exponential rate after exchanges were set up, these allowed BTC to be exchanged for dollars, and this is what created many mining farms that were set up specifically to earn block rewards. They would sell some of the block rewards to cover the power bill, and the rest would be their profit, this is what led to mining farms becoming more of a business, and this idea has rapidly grown since 2011.

Pg. 117, upper section: This 50% drop in Bitcoins hash rate was caused by many mining farms going offline all at once as they moved to areas of the planet with cheap abundant energy sources, and friendlier regulations around Bitcoin mining.

Pg. 128, bottom section: Each Bitcoin halving cycle has a price top followed by a correction and price bottom, these are created by the supply shock that comes from the block rewards being cut in half, and mining farms will try to hold their block rewards until the price reaches a level the mining farm is comfortable selling at, sometimes only happening once or twice each 4-year period.

Pg. 139, upper section: During the drop in Bitcoins hash rate following China's mining ban, payout periods for mining farms became shorter, basically meaning the mining farms were earning more block rewards each month, and this only lasted for a short period of time, by late 2022 the hash rate was reaching new all-time highs again.

Pg. 148, bottom section: Bitcoins halving event creates cycles for the Bitcoin blockchain, and Bitcoins price cycle tends to top some time after the actual halving date. While Bitcoins hash rate seems unaffected by the halving over the long term, with small pullbacks every so often, only followed by new all-time highs that happen almost every year.

Pg. 151, right section: Each Bitcoin halving has a price top and bottom over the 4-year period, some investors will try to time these price tops, with the goal of selling the top and buying the bottom, increasing the number of Bitcoin they own, and this is easier said than done since the price top varies each halving cycle, unlike the halving event which is predictable.

Pg. 153, left section: Bitcoins hash rate will continue to increase over time as more mining farms are set up globally, and although some mining farms will be weeded out over time, the overall hash rate will continue to increase as the computing power of ASICs increases in the future.

This price spike is caused by Bitcoins supply and demand, simply put, trades that take place on exchanges are usually buy and sell orders, and this is the reason the exchange exists, to match up buyers and sellers at a certain price. The exchanges can acquire Bitcoin in several ways, usually they are buying Bitcoin through over-the-counter transactions that do not affect Bitcoins price, these purchases are usually large quantities of Bitcoin, and these large holders are either long-term holders, or Bitcoin miners. Large whale wallets can only sell their Bitcoin once, and as soon as their coins are transferred to an exchange, they would need to buy Bitcoin in order to refill their large wallet, while large Bitcoin mining farms have a somewhat steady supply of Bitcoin, and they can sell these coins to exchanges on a somewhat consistent basis, or sell them regularly in order to cover energy costs. Either way, Bitcoin miners have the only new supply of Bitcoin being added into circulation, they sell their block rewards when they want to, or when they have to cover their energy costs, and this new supply of Bitcoin will usually end up in an exchange wallet. This supply of Bitcoin is somewhat constant, since a portion of a mining farm's block rewards need to be sold to cover operating costs such as the power bill, and although miners usually save their Bitcoin until the price spikes, this is not the case for every Bitcoin mining farm, and some must sell on a regular basis to keep the power on. The exchanges get used to this supply of Bitcoin over the 4-year cycle, and as block rewards are reduced during the halving some miners shut down. Others that are still able to mine at a profit do not have the same quantities of Bitcoin as they had before the halving, and in order for them to earn the same amount of block rewards they would need to increase their hash power by about 50%, not easy for a mining farm, especially a large farm that already has a high hash rate.

Exchanges then need to find Bitcoin from other sources, and sometimes they pay a premium to acquire large amounts of Bitcoin, this is in part why older Bitcoin wallets may suddenly become active again and send their coins to an exchange wallet, however there are only so many of these large wallet holders, and as times goes by there will be fewer and fewer options for exchanges. One option an exchange has to acquire more Bitcoin is to price Bitcoin higher than other exchanges, or higher than what the market thinks fair value is. This would allow arbitrage traders to make a profit from buying Bitcoin on one exchange for a lower price, and selling the Bitcoin on the exchange offering a higher price than what the trader paid for the Bitcoin. This allows the arbitrage trader to gain a profit, the exchange has more Bitcoin, and this does not happen all at once because of huge price differences between the exchanges, it takes place over time and the price variations are usually small. The exchange would have more Bitcoin moving into its exchange wallets, but this would push Bitcoins price higher, and this adds to the many other factors that push Bitcoins price up over time, simply put Bitcoin has scarcity, much like Real Estate, and commodities like gold. We will go over exchanges in more detail later, for now just understand there are many additional factors to take into account, and exchanges are able to acquire enough Bitcoin for trades taking place on their platform for now, but as time goes by this will become more difficult for exchanges, unless large institutional investors begin holding Bitcoin on their balance sheets.

As more institutional investors move into the blockchain space many of them will hold large amounts of Bitcoin as an investment, and these large holders would be able to supply exchanges with a steady supply of Bitcoin if an exchange needed it, although they would likely pay a premium. This means even as the block reward rate drops, exchanges will still be able to acquire Bitcoin, however as Bitcoins block reward rate falls below 1 BTC per block added to the blockchain, exchanges will become less and less dependent on miners for their supply of Bitcoin. This will not happen overnight, in 2032 the block reward rate will drop from 1.5625 per block, to 0.78125 Bitcoin per block, and larger mining farms still might earn enough block rewards to meet the needs of an exchange, but most miners will be earning very small amounts of Bitcoin by this point. **(Reference page 103)** If Bitcoins price keeps increasing, then these block rewards could still be worth a lot in dollar terms, this could cover the mining farm's energy bill, and this would allow the mining farm to continue hashing transactions and earning block rewards at a profit. However, the quantity of Bitcoin being created would not be enough to keep up with the demand from exchanges, this is where institutional holders of Bitcoin could step in to provide the exchanges with the Bitcoin they need, and we will look at why exchanges will have a constant need for Bitcoin and other coins that there is a demand for on their platform next.

Bitcoin Demand:

This pressure on exchanges to acquire Bitcoin comes from account holders at the exchange, and this is not unique to Bitcoin, exchanges will offer trading pairs for coins and tokens that there is a demand for from account holders at the exchange, and we will go over exchanges in more detail later. For now, just understand these account holders will buy and sell Bitcoin on the exchange, and new account holders will add to this demand, creating the need for the exchange to acquire more Bitcoin. Another reason exchanges must acquire more Bitcoin on a regular basis is that many account holders will buy Bitcoin on the exchange and transfer that Bitcoin to a self-custody wallet, either all of it or just a portion, and this would be a constant drain of Bitcoin from the exchange wallet, although this would be a slow process. Basically, as more account holders come to the exchange, a small number of them will remove some of their Bitcoin to self-custody wallets, and there is a balance to this since as Bitcoins price rises, self-custody wallets will start selling Bitcoin on the exchange in order to realize the wealth gain. This is normal for most markets, but the slow drain of Bitcoin would come from long-term Bitcoin holders that do not buy and sell shorter term price swings. As long as there is demand from investors to hold their wealth in Bitcoin, then Bitcoins price will continue to have price pressure to the upside, this is because Bitcoins new supply is being drastically reduced every 4 years, and this is happening as demand is growing globally.

Adoption of Bitcoin and other blockchain coins and tokens is still happening, even though Bitcoin has been around for over a decade, there is still only a few people and companies that hold their wealth in Bitcoin, and as more people are able to invest in Bitcoin, some will choose to hold long term. There are obviously many factors at play involving Bitcoins price in dollars, but a simple way to think of it is, many people have a goal of holding 1 BTC for the next several decades, or the rest of their lives, eventually passing that wealth on to their family. This will continue to slowly drain the exchanges of Bitcoin, and basically reduces the circulating supply of Bitcoin, causing the price to increase over time if demand is somewhat constant or increasing. This demand would come from over 360 million Americans, and of the 8 billion people on earth about half have access to the internet, which is all you need to access Bitcoin, and there will only ever be 21 million Bitcoin, so you can see how holding even 1 BTC in the years to come will be less and less common. This is because as Bitcoins price continues to rise, fewer people will be able to afford 1 BTC, but as mentioned before Bitcoin is divisible to 8 decimal places, this allows for very small dollar amounts of Bitcoin to be transacted, and this is true for many blockchains that are also divisible to very small units of account. At its simplest, Bitcoin is accessible to every person on the planet that has access to the internet, although not every person will hold their wealth in Bitcoin. But with a limit of 21 million coins there would not be enough for everyone to hold 1 BTC, and those that are able to accumulate one whole Bitcoin would hold it until the value increased enough for them to want to realize the wealth gain, but this may take many years, and during this time the Bitcoin would not be in circulating supply, further adding price pressure to the upside for Bitcoin.

Bitcoin Nodes:

The Bitcoin blockchain allows for its validators to push and pull data to and from other validators, as well as nodes, these nodes are fairly simple to set up for anyone with the knowledge, and the minimal hardware needed, they require an internet connection and use little energy. Some nodes can be bought prebuilt, this makes it easy for anyone to run a node, and they are fairly inexpensive, espically compared to the hardware required for a mining farm. Bitcoin nodes can be a full node or partial node as mentioned before, basically meaning how much of the Bitcoin blockchain the node has downloaded, and these nodes will all hash transactions on the Bitcoin blockchain, although partial nodes will not be able to verify transactions involving blocks they do not have downloaded. Partial nodes would need to request information about the transaction from either a Bitcoin validator or a full node, depending on the node operator this is not necessarily a bad thing, and partial nodes still provide the node operator with a running copy of the Bitcoin blockchain, which is updated as new blocks are added to the blockchain. Having this copy of the blockchain can be important to a node operator for several reasons, and this is not unique to Bitcoins blockchain, other blockchains that incorporate nodes can allow the node operators many use cases on the blockchain, but at its simplest a node is just a running copy of the blockchain. Other blockchains could allow nodes to play more or less of a role in the consensus method of the blockchain, and use cases involving nodes usually also include interacting with the blockchain. This might be things like smart contracts on the blockchain, or transferring wealth on the blockchain, but for Bitcoins blockchain nodes basically hash transactions and push and pull that data to and from other nodes and validators of the Bitcoin blockchain. They also have voting power on the blockchain, and they can vote on some of Bitcoins improvment proposals, but they are usually BIPs that are more of a backround code up date, not actual changes to Bitcoins blockchain. Nodes will be used for many new use cases on the Bitcoin blockchain in the future, and this will happen as Bitcoin continues its development, but right now most Bitcoin nodes simply hash transactions and provide the node operator with a running copy of Bitcoins blockchain. However some nodes are already involved in use cases on the Bitcoin blockchain, such as the Lighting Network, and ordinals, both of which we will go over in more detail later. *(Reference page 123)*

Nodes are how anyone can participate in Bitcoins blockchain with minimal costs, nodes are far cheaper than even the cheapest Bitcoin ASIC, and they do not require a lot of hardware, cooling systems, or energy, unlike Bitcoin mining farms, however they are not validators for the Bitcoin blockchain, nor do they receive block rewards for hashing transactions as mentioned before. This participation in Bitcoins blockchain basically means, the node operator runs the node, they do not manipulate transactions or try to push invalid transactions on the blockchain, and they have some voting power on the blockchain as well. Although these may seem like small aspects of Bitcoins blockchain, when more and more nodes are set up by good actors it makes it harder for malicious actors to negatively affect Bitcoins blockchain by setting up a node and trying to push invalid transactions. This was mentioned before when we looked at how nodes and validators work together in a blockchain's consensus method, basically, having more nodes allows for more possible connections between nodes and validators. This interconnection can help reduce orphan blocks, or simply allow validators more options on where they push and pull their data to and from, meaning malicious nodes can be ignored, and the validator still has plenty of transactions to hash from other nodes. *(Reference page 50)* Nodes can be set up by anyone, so obviously some nodes will be set up by bad actors looking to attack the Bitcoin blockchain in some way. They do this by pushing invalid transactions to other nodes and validators as mentioned before, and although a single node is unlikely to get its invalid transaction added to the blockchain, if enough nodes are able to push this invalid transaction to one or several validators then it could form an orphan chain or block. *(Reference page 5)* This was detailed before, and it is not a common occurrence, but it can happen, and when it does, there is a reorg of the blockchain by the consensus method. Not all blockchains incorporate nodes in its consensus method, but many do, and developers that decide to include nodes that hash transactions and interact with the validators of the blockchain's consensus method, create a stronger blockchain. This is because if invalid transactions are possible, then the blockchains consensus method must be able to constantly overcome and prevent these invalid transactions, ultimately making the blockchain more secure.

The importance of nodes in a blockchains consensus method was detailed before, and although they are not required for a consensus method to operate, they do have many benefits for a blockchain, and they allow anyone to participate in the blockchain's consensus method to an extent. Blockchains that do not allow for nodes are basically preventing what could be bad for the blockchain, but blockchains should allow for both the good and the bad aspects that nodes offer. By restricting the bad there is centralization to a small extent, this is because decentralization is when anyone is allowed to participate in the blockchain. So, it is good that Bitcoin's blockchain allows anyone to set up a node and hash transactions on the blockchain, even if some of those nodes try to negatively affect Bitcoins blockchain. Ultimately these nodes will help further secure Bitcoin's consensus method, and the number of nodes will continue grow as more large investors start to hold large amounts of their wealth in the Bitcoin blockchain, and as new use cases involving nodes are developed and implemented on the Bitcoin blockchain.

Centralization Risks, Bitcoins Creator:

The creator of Bitcoin is unknown at this time, there are many theories, but there was some communication from Bitcoins creator at first, and they were able to accumulate the 1 million Bitcoin held in the Satoshi wallets. Satoshi Nakamoto was the pseudonym used by Bitcoin's creator, we will look at what control "Satoshi" had, and might still have, over the Bitcoin blockchain, and we will focus more on what can be done with the Satoshi wallets rather than trying to connect an identity to them. This is because it does not really matter who created Bitcoin, there are some risks that we will go over, but overall Bitcoin's creator does not have any control over the Bitcoin blockchain, and this adds to Bitcoins overall decentralization. Whoever created Bitcoin had some control over the blockchain at the beginning, Satoshi set up several Bitcoin validators that earned the block rewards held in the Satoshi wallets today, and becoming a validator back in 2009 could be done on a home computer. The computing power required to hash transactions on the Bitcoin blockchain was far lower than it is today, there were also fewer people mining Bitcoin back then. Meaning fewer validators for the Bitcoin blockchain, and back then Satoshi could have tried to manipulate the consensus method, but as more and more validators started hashing transactions on the blockchain Satoshi would lose this ability. Over the last decade Bitcoin has continued to add validators and increase its hash rate, as mentioned before this helps secure the blockchain and prevent invalid transactions, so even if Satoshi had some control at the beginning, that control has been dispersed over time. However, the 1 million Bitcoin held in the Satoshi wallets remain, and some people believe these wallets are no longer accessible, either from a lost or forgotten seed phrase, and we will look at why this could be the case, but it is not the only possibility.

The reason some people believe Satoshi does not have access to the wallets anymore is because of how much the Bitcoin in them has increased in dollar value over the years, during the price spike in 2011 the Satoshi wallets were worth 20 million dollars. During the spike in 2013 they were worth 1 billion dollars, during the spike in 2017 they were worth 20 billion dollars, and during the last price spike in 2021 they were worth about 70 billion dollars. Many believe that if Satoshi is still alive and was still able to access the wallets they would have done so already, or at least sold some of the Bitcoin, but so far none of the Bitcoin has moved. However, there is another reason the BTC may not have moved in such a long time, and although the Bitcoin in the Satoshi wallets could be lost due to a forgotten seed phrase, it would be a mistake to think this is the most logical explanation. This is because the seed phrase is just a sequence of 48 or 96 numbers as mentioned before, and this sequence is hashed with transaction data to encrypt the transaction. Meaning only the wallet holder has the ability to access and transfer the coins in the wallet, and any other transactions not involving the seed phrase would be considered an invalid transaction and rejected by validators and nodes hashing transactions on the blockchain as detailed before. However, the seed phase could have additional information required in order to access and transfer wealth from a wallet, and there would be no way to know if a wallets keys required additional information, only the wallet holder would know this. So, there is no way to prove the keys to the Satoshi wallets require this information, but it is possible with blockchain technology, and this is not unique to Bitcoins blockchain, technically any wallet on a blockchain could be set up like this.

The additional information could be anything that can be verified on the blockchain, the one mentioned in the MIT class I watched detailed using the block height of a blockchain, but any information could be used since the data would be numerical and simply added to the hash of the transaction and seed phrase. This means if the additional required information cannot be verified on the blockchain, then the wallets keys would not be able to transfer coins out of the wallet, they can try, but the transaction would be rejected as an invalid transaction by Bitcoins validators and nodes. Let's look at a simple example to understand how this works using the block height of the blockchain as the additional information required along with the seed phrase, and as mentioned before a blockchains block height can be used for many things on a blockchain. *(Reference page 21)* It is basically how to measure time on the blockchain, and this is the same thing used for epochs in POS blockchains, and it is used to trigger the Bitcoin halving and difficulty adjustment as mentioned before. For this example, a wallet is created on the Bitcoin blockchain, this wallet is just like other Bitcoin wallets, it has a public key and private key, however in order for the private keys to be complete

Bitcoin's blockchain must have a block height greater than say, 900,000 blocks. The wallet holder would know the seed phrase, and they could even know the required block height, but they would not be able to transfer Bitcoin out of the wallet. They could not just type in 900,000 in addition to the seed phrase, this information would need to be verified on the blockchain, but it is still a wallet, and could receive Bitcoin with its public key. In order to be a valid transaction on the Bitcoin blockchain the transaction would have to be hashed with the keys and the current block height of the Bitcoin blockchain. This means the wallet holder would have to keep the seed phrase private, and wait until Bitcoins block height reached 900,000, after that their seed phrase would be able to transfer the Bitcoin held in the wallet. *(Reference page 2)* If they tried to transfer Bitcoin out of the wallet at Bitcoins next halving in April 2024 the transaction would be rejected, this is because Bitcoins next halving is at a block height of 840,000, and validators would continue to reject any transaction from the wallet until the 900,000 block height is reached. This could be the reason we have not seen the Satoshi wallets move Bitcoin in over a decade, and there is no way to know if this is correct, or what the required block height is for the wallets. But it is a possibility, and could be the reason the Bitcoin was never transferred even as they started being worth 10s of billions of dollars in recent years. We will go over what happens if the Satoshi wallets ever become active again in a bit, for now we will look at the risk of large mining farms growing to a size that might create centralization in Bitcoins consensus method, this would be similar to the control Satoshi had at the beginning of Bitcoin, and even though this risk is possible, it is unlikely given how Bitcoin and its halving are set up.

Large Bitcoin Mining Farms:

One risk for the Bitcoin blockchain is its consensus method and network of validators, although the hash rate and number of validators has continued to increase, if large mining farms ever grew to a size where one or a small group of mining farms controlled the majority of the hash rate, then these mining farms could manipulate Bitcoins blockchain, and this would not be something like increasing the number of Bitcoin that can exist, that would require a hard fork as mentioned before. However, if a small group controlled the majority of Bitcoin's consensus method, then they could use this centralized control to prevent certain transactions on the blockchain, front run transactions, implement BIPs, and obviously they would receive the majority of block rewards issued on the Bitcoin blockchain. This is similar to how the Satoshi wallets were able to accumulate 1 million Bitcoin, although earning these large numbers of Bitcoin is no longer possible because of the halving that has taken place every 4 years since Bitcoins beginning. Because anyone can become a validator for the Bitcoin blockchain this centralized control is very unlikely, but this control over the consensus method can happen several ways, and does not require one or several large mining farms. Mining pools for Bitcoins blockchain could also gain this centralized control, if one or several mining pools ever controlled enough of the total hash rate for Bitcoin, then they would gain the same control as a large mining farm would, and this was detailed before when we looked at small mining farms and why they pool their hash rate. These mining pools help Bitcoin miners earn consistent block rewards, so as long as Bitcoin mining pools somewhat evenly split Bitcoins total hash rate, then there is not a risk of centralization, and allowing small Bitcoin mining farms the ability to earn block rewards is what plays a part in preventing large mining farms from growing to gain the majority of Bitcoins total hash rate.

These new miners will compete for block rewards and increase Bitcoins total hash rate, forcing all Bitcoin miners to improve their energy efficiency and increase their hash rate as well, and this is part of the mining cycle that takes place during the halving. Bitcoin miners need to be constantly improving if they want to earn block rewards long term as mentioned before, and this takes place over the 4-year period, it is not a daily goal of improving these systems. This is another aspect to Bitcoins blockchain where there is a balance that is achieved, simply put, new miners are incentivized to hash transactions on Bitcoin's blockchain, not all these new miners will mine Bitcoin long term, but some will as they increase their efficiency, and this could be achieved with cheaper power sources. Later we will go over how Bitcoin mining will drive development in the renewable energy industry, things like nuclear power would provide large amounts of near free energy, and Bitcoin mining farms that have access to energy sources such as this would be able to remove the largest reoccurring cost for a Bitcoin mining farm. Although, they would still need to develop and improve cooling systems and the computing power of its ASICs over time. These large power sources would eventually create larger and larger mining farms, this is where the concern of one or several mining farms gaining control over Bitcoin's consensus method comes from, and taking into account all the factors involved this would not be very likely. But it is possible, and it is important to remember that as these mining farms get larger so does Bitcoins hash rate, further securing the Bitcoin blockchain. So, although this is a centralized risk that could happen, it is kept in check by the reducing block reward rate, and many other factors involving the cycles that are created by the Bitcoin halving, and this growth in the hash rate is ultimately beneficial for Bitcoins blockchain, making it stronger and harder to exploit.

Satoshi:

Satoshi could be an individual person, or they could be a group of people, these people could all work for a company or government, and all communication with Satoshi was digital, so there is no solid proof that Satoshi was one person or several. Although it does appear that he was an individual, he communicated through email and other digital platforms, he worked with many early Bitcoin developers improving Bitcoins code, and the last public communication from Satoshi was in December 2010. These early Bitcoin developers would continue to work on the Bitcoin blockchain for years to come, and developers are still working on improvements for the Bitcoin blockchain today. Some individuals have come forward over the years claiming to be Satoshi, however none of them were able to prove they were him, and again it is important to stress even if one of them was actually Satoshi, they would not have any control over the Bitcoin blockchain. There are now Bitcoin miners hashing transactions around the world, and there are far more validators for Bitcoins blockchain than there was in the first few years of Bitcoin. The only thing Satoshi would have control over would be the Bitcoin in the Satoshi wallets, and we will go over this next, but for now just understand knowing who Satoshi is does not mean they have any control over Bitcoins code, and if the public knew who created Bitcoin the media would use this as a way to attack Bitcoin. This is a common tactic when trying to discredit a certain cause or company, attack the CEO, if the general public thinks the creator is "bad" then so is what they are involved in or what they have control over. The media could say Satoshi is a criminal, or has a questionable personal life, and the general public would associate those actions with Bitcoin, even though who Satoshi is does not affect Bitcoins blockchain in any way. Basically, the mystery behind who created Bitcoin is a good thing, it is not something to be taken as shady behavior by Bitcoin's creator, it is something that prevents an avenue of attack on Bitcoin, and this means Bitcoin must be judged on its own. Critics will have to address Bitcoins code, not a person who no longer has any control over that code, and this includes companies or governments that could be behind the creation of Bitcoin, they no longer have control over Bitcoin's blockchain, they would only have the 1 million Bitcoin in the Satoshi wallets, and we will look at the risks involved with these wallets next.

The creator of Bitcoin has lost the ability to control the blockchain through the validator network, but the Satoshi wallets still pose a risk to the value of Bitcoin, and we will look at what these risks are and how much they could affect Bitcoin overall. If the 1 million Bitcoin were sold into circulating supply this would cause the dollar value of Bitcoin to fall in the short term, this is because over the short term demand would not change much, while there would be a large increase in the supply of Bitcoin being bought and sold, this constant demand with added supply is what would cause Bitcoins value to fall. However, in the long term Bitcoins price would recover, basically this additional supply would be absorbed by demand over time, whether that demand is investors buying Bitcoin on exchanges and moving that Bitcoin to self-custody wallets, or if the demand is from the exchanges buying up Bitcoin to offer to their account holders. Either way Bitcoins limit of 21 million coins still stands, and this sell pressure would not last, over time the dollar value of Bitcoin would continue to increase, as will its use cases and overall demand. Remember this is a one-time event, either the 1 million coins are all sold at once or they are slowly sold over a period of time, once these large wallets begin selling, they obviously no longer have the Bitcoin they sold, and in order to create the same sell pressure a second time, these wallets would need to buy large amounts of Bitcoin. This buying pressure would increase Bitcoins dollar value, and even if the large number of coins were then sold, this buying and selling of the same asset would somewhat counter each other out, and this second large selling of Bitcoin would not affect Bitcoins price as much as selling the Bitcoin in the Satoshi wallets. This is obviously an over simplified example, and there are many other factors that affect the price of an asset in a market of buyers and sellers, and these same risks exist for other markets as well. This is not just a risk that Bitcoin faces, let's look at a commodity like gold to understand what this large sell pressure could do to the dollar value of an asset.

Gold is a physical metal, and fiat currencies are what used to represent gold in order to allow for a lighter form of payment, and one that could be divided into small units of wealth to be used for everyday goods and services. Gold is the metal that has value, anything used to represent gold does not have actual value, although a market of buyers and sellers could still give it value since there is always someone willing to buy if the price is right. This is how paper gold was created, these are things like gold ETFs or any paper or digital representation of gold, and some of these can be backed by actual gold and allow for investors to take physical delivery of the actual gold. Although some gold ETFs do not hold gold or offer investors the option to take physical delivery of gold, they are backed by bonds or any other asset that allows investors the dollar equivalent of the "gold" they own. The size of the paper gold market is disputed, this basically means for every 1oz of gold that actually exists, how many paper ounces of gold exist, or how many investors think they have a claim on an individual ounce of gold, and this ratio varies from a few hundred paper ounces per 1 actual ounce of gold, to 10s of thousands of paper ounces per 1 actual ounce of gold. Either way, this allows for the dollar value of gold to be suppressed, this is because there can be large amounts of selling pressure on golds price, without needing to buy actual gold in order to achieve this sell pressure. A simplified way to think of this is, dollars can be used to buy paper gold, this does not require the actual gold, just a gold ETF, these dollars can be created from thin air by the Federal Reserve, and these dollars can be turned into sell pressure for gold if done in a large amount, or at a steady pace over time. However, we will not focus on the risks that may or may not exist in the gold markets, instead we will just look at the concept of using wealth to buy one asset, and then selling that asset to affect the price of another asset. This can be used to artificially keep the asset's dollar value low by not actually buying the physical asset itself, and if you want the full "orange pill" experience, do further research and better understand how the traditional markets actually work.

This price suppression can be done with any asset where paper or digital versions of the asset exist, this is because things like paper gold can be "created" by backing something like a gold ETF with dollars, and this basically creates more units of account for the asset than actually exist, keeping its value suppressed. The Satoshi wallets, if sold on mass, would create the same kind of price suppression for Bitcoin, but as mentioned before this would be a one-time event, and in order to do it again someone would need to buy large amounts of Bitcoin, causing Bitcoins value to increase. Bitcoin ETFs have been allowed in several countries, and they will be coming to the U.S. stock market in the coming years, these spot ETFs mean Bitcoin will need to be held by the ETF, causing more demand for Bitcoin, so not all ETFs are bad, as long as they are required to hold the actual asset. The main takeaway here is, the Satoshi wallets could be used to lower the dollar value of Bitcoin by a significant amount, but this is not a reoccurring risk, and once the Bitcoin is sold the only new supply of Bitcoin would come from Bitcoin miners. Which have a supply shock every 4 years, allowing for price discovery and price pressure to the upside over time. This means the Satoshi wallets have a short-term risk, but not really a long-term risk for Bitcoins value, and this is only a risk if the 1 million Bitcoin were sold on mass, or at a steady rate over time, but this is not the only option for whoever has access to the Satoshi wallets, it might not make sense to sell the Bitcoin, and we will look at this possibility next.

Satoshi Wallets:

It is impossible to know if the Satoshi wallets will ever become active, but if they did, the wallets might not sell the 1 million Bitcoin, it would be more profitable for the Bitcoin to be used as collateral, and we will look at how this could work. It is possible to borrow dollars against Bitcoin, and we will look at this later when we go over use cases for blockchain coins and tokens, but for now just understand these loans exist today, and there are collateral requirements when Bitcoins price falls, so there is risk in doing this. A simple example is borrowing dollars against Bitcoin to buy an investment property, the Bitcoin is locked in a type of smart contract, and payments plus interest are paid to the lender. This allows the borrower to still have control over the Bitcoin in the smart contract as long as payments are made to the lender, and the lender would have access to the Bitcoin if payments from the borrower ever stopped. We will go over the differences between a debt-based economy and an asset-based economy later, for now just understand if payments on the loan stop, or collateral requests are not met by the borrower, then the smart contract will execute, and sell the Bitcoin in order to recover the lenders original loan. This is done almost instantly, reducing the lenders risk, and it does not involve foreclosures on a property that would have added costs for the lender, it would also not require any kind of repossession on the lenders part, their loan would be covered by the sale of the Bitcoin. In the example of borrowing against Bitcoin in order to buy an investment property, the lender would not be involved in the property itself, the borrower would put up enough Bitcoin to cover the loan in excess, and this amount would be agreed upon by the borrower and lender. As long as the borrower was able to rent out the property, the rent could cover payments on the loan, and once the loan was repaid with interest, the borrow would own the investment property and get the Bitcoin back from the smart contract with the lender. However, if the borrower for whatever reason could not make the payment, or could not meet a collateral request from the lender, then the Bitcoin in the smart contract would be sold, and the borrower would still own the investment property, but they would lose the Bitcoin that is worth far more than the investment property. So, there are still risks for the borrower, but collateral requests can be done with Bitcoin, so the Satoshi wallets would have no trouble coming up with the additional Bitcoin needed, and these Bitcoin would still be theirs after the loan was repaid and the smart contract ended.

The Satoshi wallets might use some of the Bitcoin as collateral, and some could be sold, but they would gain more wealth by borrowing against the Bitcoin rather than just selling it, and the reason they might sell some Bitcoin is that they would be selling it at a premium. Exchanges or other platforms that require large amounts of BTC for their account holders usually get it from whale wallets or Bitcoin miners, but they could buy some Bitcoin from the Satoshi wallets if the price was right. Either way most of the Bitcoin in the Satoshi wallets probably would not flood the circulating supply, and not negatively affect Bitcoins price. If the Satoshi wallets choose to use the Bitcoin as collateral, then we would see a very small amount of Bitcoin enter the circulating supply, some may be sold to exchanges, but most of the 1 million coins would remain in the wallets, or locked in a type of smart contract with a lender. Overall, the risks involved with the Satoshi wallets exist, but in the long term they are not that bad for Bitcoins value in dollars, and whoever Satoshi is, they do not have any control over Bitcoin's blockchain, so they could not negatively affect Bitcoins code, leaving the mystery behind who created Bitcoin left unanswered. Ultimately this is a good thing for Bitcoin, the Satoshi wallets only pose a limited risk for Bitcoins long-term price, and critics of Bitcoin will have to address Bitcoins code directly when trying to find flaws, since there is no individual to directly attack.

Bitcoins History:

Bitcoins history started before the first block was created in Bitcoins blockchain, in August 2008 the domain Bitcoin.org was registered, and in October 2008 a paper titled, Bitcoin: A Peer-to-Peer Electronic Cash System, was posted to a mailing list. This shows that Bitcoin was being developed before January 3, 2009, when the genesis block for the Bitcoin blockchain was created, basically the first block in the blockchain. As mentioned before block headers are a way for blocks and transactions to point back to their prior transaction on the blockchain. For genesis blocks or new coins being created through block rewards, there is no prior transaction to point back to, and this is why the block header is blank, allowing the miner that earned the block reward to put any information they want into the block header. We will go over what information the first block header of Bitcoin contained next, for now just understand the next block added to Bitcoins blockchain did not happen for 6 days, and this is far longer than the average of block time of about 10 minutes. But the Bitcoin blockchain had begun, with the first client on the blockchain happening on the 9th, and the first transaction of 10 Bitcoin taking place on January 12th 2009 between Satoshi and one of the early Bitcoin developers. Bitcoin would continue to be developed over the years to come, and many more validators were created as people begin to hash transactions and earn block rewards from the Bitcoin blockchain.

The block header of Bitcoins genesis block reads, "The Times 03/Jan/2009 Chancellor on brink of second bailout for banks" this referenced the headline of a London newspaper published on January 3rd, this is important because it is believed Bitcoin was created to replace the fractional reserve banking and fiat systems that were breaking in 2008-2009. Bitcoin and its limit of 21 million coins could never be manipulated by banks, central banks, or governments, in order to bailout broken systems like in 2008-2009. It was created as an alternative to fiat and banks that ultimately have a 3rd party to an individual's wealth, either as a 3rd party custodian of that wealth, or a 3rd party in the form of inflation should the central bank ever create more dollars, devaluing existing dollars. Despite a somewhat slow start, the Bitcoin blockchain had begun, and it would continue to grow over the years. We will touch on some events that happened in Bitcoins past, but there are many more examples, and it's important to understand there have been many exchanges and wallets exploited over the years. These may have involved wealth held in Bitcoin, but they did not affect the Bitcoin blockchain overall, and we will look at a few exploits that actually did affect Bitcoins blockchain in its early years.

Bitcoin Pizza Day:

A little over a year later in May 2010, Bitcoin was used as payment for the first time, 10,000 BTC were used to buy two pizzas from a restaurant in Florida, and at a Bitcoin price of $30,000, these Bitcoin would be worth 300 million dollars today. However, this was back in 2010 and Bitcoin exchanges were not around to convert Bitcoin to dollars, so at the time these Bitcoin were simply considered a unit of account for the Bitcoin blockchain, and as exchanges were set up in the coming years, more businesses would be willing to accept Bitcoin as payment, since they knew they could now convert the Bitcoin into other forms of wealth such as the dollar.

Later that year on the 6th of August 2010, a major vulnerability in the Bitcoin blockchain was discovered, this allowed a malicious actor to create a transaction on the Bitcoin blockchain that spent .5 BTC and created billions of new Bitcoin. Within hours the transaction was spotted, the bug that allowed for the exploit was fixed by developers, and they created a hard fork of the blockchain from a point before the transaction had taken place. The Bitcoin miners updated their version of the blockchain to this fork, and this basically erased the exploit from Bitcoins blockchain, this is why the transaction is not visible on Bitcoin's blockchain today, and this has been the only major exploit of the Bitcoin blockchain to date.

In March 2013 Bitcoin had another issue with its blockchain, although not as impactful as the exploit in 2010, basically the blockchain was temporarily split into two independent blockchains, both had slightly different rules for how transactions were added to the blockchain, and this created two versions of the blockchain. This lasted for about 6 hours, during this time transactions were added to both blockchains, and the core developers then called for a temporary stop to transactions on the blockchain. Normal operation was restored when the majority of the Bitcoin miners switched to an older version of Bitcoin, version 0.7, and this allowed the bug to be fixed before further updates to the blockchain code took place.

The following year in 2014, the CFTC approved TeraExchange to begin listing over-the-counter swap products based on the price of Bitcoin, and this was the first time a U.S. regulatory agency approved a Bitcoin financial product. These types of exchanges and transactions usually deal with commodities, and this is why decentralized blockchains are considered digital commodities under the FIT Act. Put simply, as long as the blockchain is actually decentralized, then there is no one person or group that can manipulate the asset, but if aspects of the blockchain have centralized points of control, then they would be considered riskier for investors, and this is why the SEC wants oversight of these blockchain coins and tokens, or digital assets and restricted digital assets as they are defined under the FIT Act. Whatever rules and regulations are passed in the coming years, it's important to know Bitcoin, or the idea that a blockchain can actually be decentralized, was considered to be a commodity under the CFTC in 2014. However, this does not mean all blockchain coins and tokens are digital commodities, as we have seen there are a lot of centralized points of control for blockchains, and many points of control are not as apparent as others, so defining what blockchain coins and tokens are actually decentralized is a challenge for regulators.

Moving forward to June 2021, the President of El Salvador, Nayib Bukele, announced his plans to adopt Bitcoin as legal tender on the 1st, and on the 8th the legislative assembly of El Salvador voted to make Bitcoin legal tender in the country alongside the U.S. dollar. This made El Salvador the first country to make Bitcoin legal tender, they have plans for a Bitcoin city, and they are also setting up a geothermal Bitcoin mining farm, which we will go over in more detail later when we look at the development of renewable energy sources and Bitcoin mining. *(Reference page 131)*

Obviously, there are many important events in Bitcoins past, these are just a few of the important and memorable ones, and I would encourage further research for a deeper understanding of Bitcoins history. But with these few examples we can see Bitcoins blockchain, like all blockchains, need time and development to work out the bugs, or points of failure in the blockchain as mentioned before. These examples also show a clear path of adoption over the last decade, it may be a slow rate of adoption, but this is changing fast as institutional investors start holding some of their wealth in the Bitcoin blockchain. This will continue to increase as rules and regulations for the blockchain industry are passed by the U.S., and other nations around the world. Adoption and support for the Bitcoin blockchain can also be measured by its hash rate, and the growth of Bitcoins hash rate does not always follow the price of Bitcoin, it has a steeper upward trend, and we will look at this in more detail next.

Bitcoins Hash Rate History:

Bitcoins hash rate is measured by the number of hash's that happen each second, as mentioned before validators hash transactions on a blockchain and reject invalid transactions, and the more validators there are hashing transactions on the blockchain, the higher the hash rate will be for the blockchain. We will use TeraHash, TH/s, as the unit of measurement, but depending on how high the blockchains hash rate is, MegaHash or GigaHash could be used too, basically TeraHash is 1 trillion hashes per second, and GigaHash is 1 billion hashes per second, etc. The hash rate for a blockchain basically shows us how much computing power is being used to hash transactions and secure the blockchain, the hash rate for Bitcoin is constantly changing, this is because the hash rate will increase or decrease as mining farms come online and go offline globally. However, as we will see, Bitcoins hash rate has grown substantially over the last decade, sometimes following Bitcoins price spikes during the 4-year cycle, and sometimes dropping because of laws regarding Bitcoin mining. This is because mining farms are Bitcoin's hash rate, as Bitcoins price increases, more people become interested in setting up a Bitcoin mining farm, and obviously if Bitcoin mining is outlawed then mining farms in that country would have to shut down.

Bitcoins hash rate did not reach 1 TH/s until early 2011, before this the hash rate steadily increased for the first few years of Bitcoin, and around the same time Bitcoin became exchangeable for dollars is when we saw the first big jump in Bitcoins hash rate. *(Reference page 106)* By mid-2011 Bitcoin was reaching its price top for the 4-year cycle, this attracted a lot of new Bitcoin miners, and this led to Bitcoins hash rate reaching 20 TH/s, as mining farms began to be set up specifically for earning Bitcoin and converting some of the coins to dollars to cover their energy costs. Many of these mining farms would remain online even as Bitcoins price fell, although some did shut down, causing a dip in the hash rate, but it had recovered to over 20 TH/s by the end of 2012, and this is also when Bitcoin had its first halving. Bitcoins price would spike at the end of 2013, and during the year leading up to this price top, Bitcoins hash rate would go from just above 20 TH/s to 6,000 TH/s, and even as Bitcoins price fell after the top, Bitcoins hash rate continued to increase to 300,000 TH/s by the end of 2014.

Over the next few years Bitcoins hash rate continued to steadily increase, even as Bitcoins dollar value fell substantially, then the next halving happened in 2016, and Bitcoins price spiked again in late 2017, by this time Bitcoins hash rate was 13,000,000 TH/s. This rate of increase would continue past Bitcoins price top until the end of 2018 when Bitcoins hash rate reached 53,000,000 TH/s, and there would be a dip in the hash rate when Bitcoins price fell from about $6000 to about $3000 at the end of 2018, and the hash rate dropped from 53,000,000 to 35,000,000 TH/s. After this dip the hash rate started increasing again, breaking 100,000,000 TH/s in early 2020, and the 3rd Bitcoin halving happened shortly after in min-2020, leading to Bitcoins next price spike in mid-2021, and Bitcoins hash rate would reach about 180,000,000 TH/s during this time.

Around May 2021 is when Bitcoins price and hash rate dropped significantly, the hash rate dropped because China had outlawed Bitcoin mining, and although some mining farms in China continued to hash transactions and earn block rewards, the majority of them shut down. We will look at this event in more detail next, for now just know that Bitcoins hash rate fell to about 90,000,000 TH/s by July, this was a rapid drop of about 50% in just a few months, and it was somewhat short-lived. By the end of 2021 Bitcoins price was topping out around $70,000, and Bitcoins hash rate had recovered to 160,000,000 TH/s, not quite back to its previous high, but it was a quick recovery and would continue to increase. Even as Bitcoins price fell over the next few years, Bitcoins hash rate would continue to reach new highs, breaking 200,000,000 TH/s by mid-2022, and breaking 300,000,000 TH/s in early 2023. As of mid-2023 Bitcoins hash rate is over 350,000,000 TH/s, with no sign of slowing down as more and more mining farms are set up in the U.S. and around the world.

China's Bitcoin Mining Ban:

China's decision to ban Bitcoin mining in mid-2021 caused a large dip in Bitcoins hash rate, this is because at the time mining farms in China made up a large part of Bitcoins total hash rate, but they did not just shut down forever, and we will look at the migration of these mining farms and why they moved to where they did. *(Reference page 106)* These mining farms were set up in China at first because there is cheap power, either from remote dams with large amounts of electricity from hydro, or abundant energy sources like coal are what fueled many Bitcoin mining farms in the country. This is because the only major reoccurring cost for a Bitcoin mining farm is the power bill, equipment and cooling systems are expensive, but by far what Bitcoin miners look for the most is cheap and abundant energy sources. With mining farms in China forced to shut down, many of them started looking for new locations around the world, and most of these miners would move to a few locations such as North America, and Northern Asia, although some of these farms would relocate to other areas of the planet as well.

The quickest route for some mining farms in China was to move North to Russia and Kazakhstan, energy prices are low and there is an abundance of oil and natural gas in these regions, especially Kazakhstan who has over 10% of Bitcoins hash rate as of mid-2023. However, the majority of these miners moved to North America and Europe, taking advantage of abundant natural gas sources, and even using flare gas as a fuel source to power Bitcoin mining farms, which we will go over in more detail later. There are many energy sources that can power a Bitcoin mining farm, even remote hydropower plants were used in Norway for this purpose, and we will look at Norway's Bitcoin mining farms later as well. For now, just understand these mining farms were moving to areas that had cheap abundant energy sources, some may be concentrated in several areas of the world around these energy sources, and some mining farms built new dams and infrastructure where none had existed before.

As of mid-2023 Bitcoin miners in the U.S. were responsible for over 30% of Bitcoins total hash rate, these mining farms are powered by many different energy sources, and we will go over several of them in more detail later. For now, just understand this event affected Bitcoins blockchain in several ways, it dispersed Bitcoin miners, further preventing a 51% attack or failure as mentioned before, and many of these miners moved to areas with cleaner power sources, basically switching from burning coal to using natural gas. This is important because as Bitcoins block rewards reduce over time, energy sources like coal will not be an option for Bitcoin miners, they would need ever-increasing amounts of coal, and they would see their block rewards reduced every 4 years as mentioned before. Bitcoin mining farms that want to earn block rewards long into the future need to transition to renewable energy sources over time, and this migration of Bitcoins hash rate is a part of that process. Basically, moving away from energy sources like coal, and using natural gas, or even building out new hydropower facilities, either way Bitcoin miners will continue to find cheaper energy sources, and help develop new renewable energy systems. *(Reference page 131)* These cheaper more abundant energy sources would also help the grid, and provide cheaper more reliable power to customers, we will go over this in more detail later. But for now, just understand as mining farms increase their hash rate, the Bitcoin blockchain becomes more secure, and as more validators start hashing transactions, the blockchain becomes more secure, and more decentralized as mentioned before. This increase in hash rate is fueled by more and more mining farms being set up, and new ASIC units that have more computing power than older versions, further adding to Bitcoins hash rate increase over time. These mining farms are the validators for Bitcoins blockchain, and although most Bitcoin miners will stick with Bitcoins original blockchain, some validators could switch to hashing transactions on a fork of Bitcoins blockchain, and we will look at these hard forks of Bitcoins blockchain in more detail next.

Bitcoin Hard Forks:

Bitcoins blockchain has been forked many times before, and it will likely be forked many more times in the future, this is because anyone can copy Bitcoins blockchain, or create a hard fork from Bitcoins blockchain. There are over 100 hard forks of Bitcoins blockchain, 70 of them are considered active, while about 30 are considered historic and no longer relevant, and we will look at a few examples from the several types of forks that exist involving Bitcoins blockchain. About 40 of these blockchain projects are operating and capable of transacting, one of these is Bitcoin Clashic, TNET, there are 21 million coins that can exist, and around mid-2019 the coin was trading for about $3. By the end of 2019 it was less than a penny, and it has remained below one penny ever since, with the only exception being Bitcoins last price spike in 2021, when TNET reached about 5 cents, then dropped back below a penny. This is common for many blockchain coins and tokens during a Bitcoin price spike, many new investors enter the space, and they do not always research the coins and tokens they invest in, and this causes short-lived price rallies in many coins and tokens.

About 30 blockchain projects are not currently operating, they cannot transact on the blockchain, and they are considered still in development. Some of these blockchain projects are hard forks of Bitcoins blockchain, while others are simply copies of Bitcoins blockchain, or even a mix of a hard fork and an airdrop to Bitcoin holders. Bitcoin All, BTALL, is a blockchain that is not directly forked from Bitcoins original blockchain, it has a max supply of 21 million coins, and it has several changes to Bitcoins original code. Bitcoin holders that move their BTC and interact with the Bitcoin All blockchain will be air dropped BTALL coins, there is limited information on exactly how the Bitcoin All blockchain will be developed, and there is no guarantee that the blockchain will become functioning. Another example is Bitcoin DAO, BTD, this blockchain was forked from Bitcoins blockchain in mid-2018, the max supply is 25 million coins, and the fork credits Bitcoin holders that use the forked blockchain with BTD coins.

There are about 45 blockchains that are hard forked from Bitcoins original blockchain, either directly or indirectly, and as we have seen with the last few examples, blockchains that are copies of Bitcoin, or blockchains that are actual hard forks of Bitcoin, do not have the same dollar value as BTC, even if they have the same max limit of coins that can exist. Bitcoin Cash, BCH, is an example of one of these blockchains, it was forked from Bitcoins blockchain in mid-2017 sometimes called a coin split, it has a max limit of 21 million coins that can exist, and during Bitcoins price spike in late 2017 BCH broke $3,000. However, during Bitcoins next price spike in mid-2021, BCH only topped out just over $1,000, and then fell to just a few hundred dollars after. Another example is Bitcoin God, GOD, it was forked from Bitcoins blockchain in late 2017, it has a max limit of 21 million coins that can exist, and topped out around $50 in 2018. Bitcoin God then fell to below one dollar, only to spike up to over 10 dollars in 2021 during Bitcoins last price spike, and since then it has traded for about one to two dollars.

Around 20 of these hard forks involve air drops to Bitcoin holders, basically meaning if you have a Bitcoin wallet address with an amount of BTC in it, then that wallet will be air dropped an amount of the forked blockchains unit of account, or coin. There are several blockchains that are more of a blend between a hard fork and an air drop, but the common factor is that these blockchains use the ledger of accounts on Bitcoins original blockchain, and this makes them a type of hard fork since they rely on the original version of the Bitcoin blockchain. As mentioned before blockchains can be set up many different ways, so there are several types of Bitcoin forks, some may simply be copies of Bitcoins original code, sometimes called a split blockchain or split coins. But some blockchains are actual hard forks from Bitcoins original blockchain, and all of them are not Bitcoin, they may use the same code, or interact with Bitcoins original blockchain, but they are not valued the same, and they have a separate network of validators.

Copies or hard forks of Bitcoin can be made by anyone, Bitcoins code is open-sourced as mentioned before, and this allows anyone to simply copy and paste the original code. Although creating an actual hard fork would involve more than just copying and pasting the original code, but it is possible as long as there are some validators hashing transactions on this forked blockchain, and this is a choice for Bitcoin miners, but most miners stick with Bitcoins original blockchain. It is important to remember the number of validators hashing transactions on a blockchain can affect the security of the blockchain, with fewer validators even an exact copy of Bitcoins blockchain would not be as secure as Bitcoin is today, and most hard forks of Bitcoin do not have anywhere near the same hash power or number of validators as Bitcoin. Although some forks like Bitcoin Cash have seen miners switch to the forked version, and some move their hash power back and forth between the two blockchains as mentioned before, and its hash rate is sizable, but nowhere near Bitcoins hash rate. Simply put, just because Bitcoins code can be copied, does not mean that blockchain will see growth and adoption like Bitcoin has, and just because Bitcoins original blockchain can be hard forked, it does not mean the forked version will be better than Bitcoin. Bitcoin has created an entire mining farm industry, and it rewards those miners with a unit of account that holds and increases in value over time, both from demand for the coin, and from an ever-reducing block reward rate. *(Reference page 103)* Basically, Bitcoins code is only part of the reason for its success so far, the other part would be support from Bitcoin miners, support from Bitcoin holders, and any use case that creates demand for Bitcoin, this along with the reducing new supply of Bitcoin is what keeps Bitcoins price pressure to the upside over time.

Many of Bitcoins hard forks have changes to Bitcoins original code, some have a different limit for the number of coins that can exist, some have different block sizes, and some incorporate air drops in the blockchain code. This does not mean these versions of Bitcoin are bad, it just means there have been some changes made, either large changes or minor ones, but as we have seen, Bitcoin has achieved a delicate balance, and changing even small aspects of the code might lead to major issues in the long term. This basically means these copies, or forks of the Bitcoin blockchain, have many of the same risks that new and developing blockchains have, some might succeed, and others may be more vulnerable to exploits or failures. Either way they have a long way to go before reaching what the Bitcoin blockchain has achieved over the last decade.

Bitcoins Future, Bitcoins Current and Future Developments:

Bitcoin ordinals are similar to NFTs, but there are some important distinctions between the two that we will go over, the first main difference is that NFTs are minted or created with the unique data that makes them a non-fungible token. This data is usually a JPEG, but it can be other information as well, and we will go over NFTs in more detail later when we look at layer 2 tokens. *(Reference page 28)* For now, just understand ordinals are just sats, the smallest unit of account for the Bitcoin blockchain, these sats are all valued the same since they are just a small amount of 1 BTC, and they can be exchanged between wallets just like all the other sats that exist today. The difference between a normal sat and an ordinal is that an ordinal is a sat with additional information held within the unit of account, we will go over this in more detail next. For now, just understand this additional information is held on Bitcoin's blockchain, and in order to attach this additional information transactions need to happen on the Bitcoin blockchain, this requires transaction fees and is what locks the information in the blockchain. We will go over Bitcoin miner fees later, but it is important to understand that once the transaction adding the information to the sat is added into the next block on Bitcoin's blockchain, that information cannot be altered or changed, and holding that sat in a wallet would be basically owning the information, although this information would be viewable, since Bitcoins blockchain is public.

(Illustration, next page)

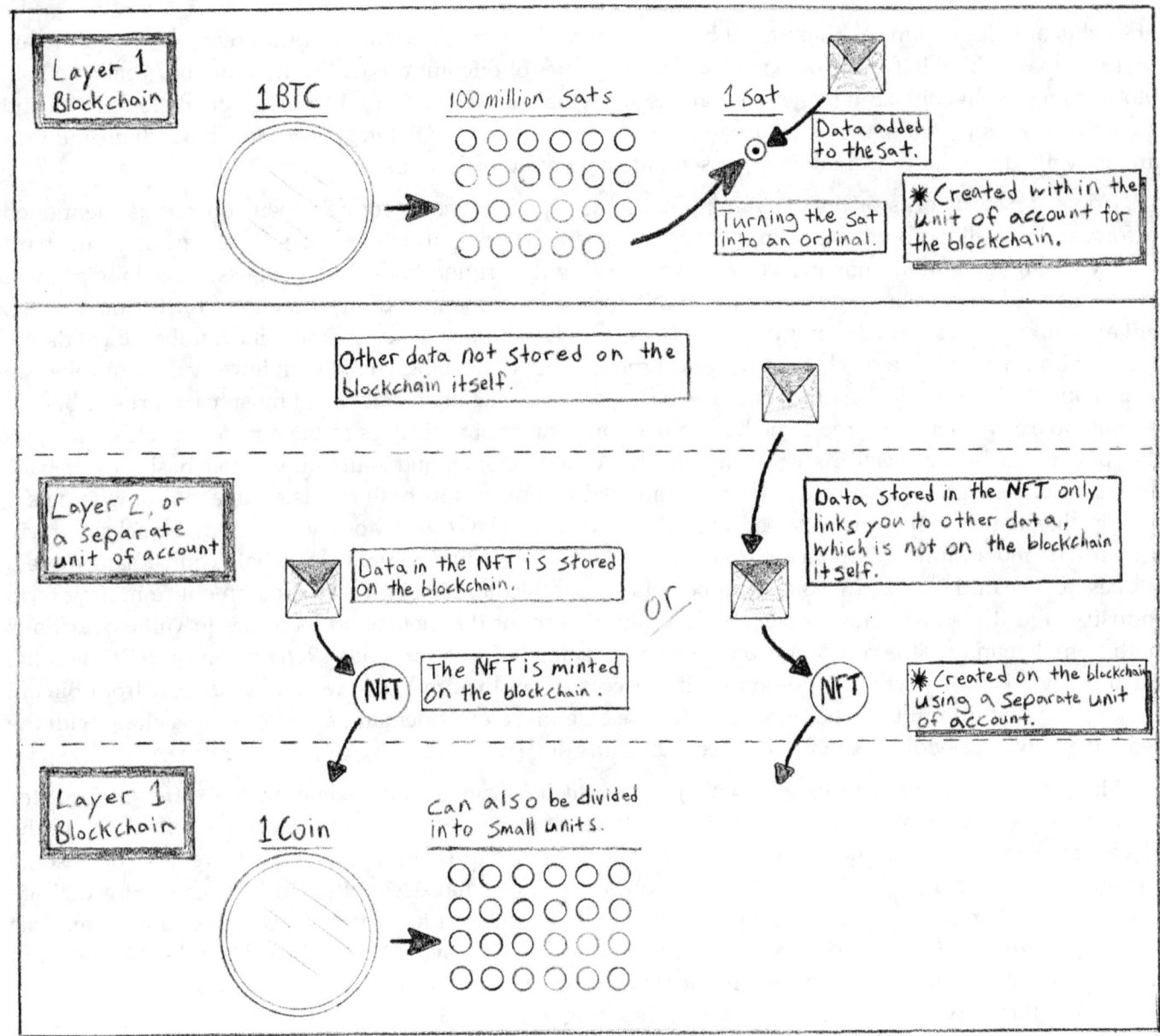

Ordinals and NFTs

Ordinals can be simply thought of as NFTs on the Bitcoin blockchain, however it is important to understand how this unique information is being held in the blockchain, and this actually makes ordinals very different from non-fungible tokens minted on other blockchains. This is because the information is held within the blockchains actual unit of account, in Bitcoins case they are called sats, and other blockchains can also have very small units of account for their coin as well. But the unique information that creates an NFT is minted on the blockchain with a separate unit of account, not within the blockchains main unit of account, and some NFTs will only link you to information outside the blockchain, meaning the information is not locked in the blockchain itself.

Pg. 3, upper section: There will only ever be 21 million BTC, and each coin can be divided into 100 million units of account, or divided to 8 decimal places, making each sat 0.00000001 of a single Bitcoin.

Pg. 39, bottom section: A blockchain can have units of account that are separate from the main unit of account for the blockchain, these can be a single non-fungible token (NFT), or a number of tokens that are interchangeable, and valued the same. Either way, these units of account are not the main unit of account for the blockchain, and they are not equal in value to the coin, or to the token of the blockchain, which is usually created as a block reward for some blockchains.

Pg. 70, upper section: Ordinals are just a sat with additional information held within the sat, this information can only be viewed with a wallet that is set up by a partial node on the Bitcoin blockchain, and in order to create an ordinal, a full node on the Bitcoin blockchain is required.

Pg. 104, upper section: In the year 2132, Bitcoins block rewards will be two sats per block added to the blockchain, or 0.00000002 BTC, and in 2136 the halving will reduce this to just one sat per block added to the blockchain, until the 21 million coin max limit is reached.

Pg. 150, upper section: The information held in a sat can be almost anything, this information could be anything that has a paper or digital representation of the information or asset, and this information would be viewable on Bitcoins blockchain, so sensitive information will not be stored on Bitcoins blockchain. However, other information such as the deed to a property could be stored in the Bitcoin blockchain, and this would mean the information cannot be altered, copied, or foraged, without exploiting Bitcoins SHA, or its network of validators.

Data is added to a sat by using something called an envelope, simply put this means that whatever data is added into the output of the transaction, it does not affect the transaction itself, think of it like keeping the information held in the envelope separate from the rest of the code. This information is held on Bitcoins actual blockchain, and it can be viewed, traded, or held, just like other sats on Bitcoin's blockchain. This is also true for NFTs, the unique information is held on the blockchain, however NFTs can also link to external sources where the actual information is stored. So, it is important to make the distinction between data being held on the actual blockchain, and unique information that may only link you to further information, that is not actually held on that blockchain. As of 2023 sats can only hold one envelope of information, however it might be possible to add multiple envelopes to a single sat in the future, and this is important to understand because Bitcoin has a limit on the number of coins that can exist, this means there is a limit on the number of sats that can exist. Although there would be a very large number of possible envelops that can exist, it would not be infinite, unlike some blockchains that allow for an unlimited number of NFTs to be created, and this would make other blockchains better suited for NFT use cases. But if Bitcoin could be updated to allow for multiple envelopes per sat, then it would be a viable option for use cases involving some types of NFTs, or in Bitcoins case, ordinals.

Ordinals trade through OTC transactions, there is not an exchange for ordinals yet, and this means in order to view and hold the ordinal, users need to create a wallet that is able to easily access the information in the envelope, and this is done using a partial node on Bitcoin's blockchain. A full node allows for ordinals to be created, but only a partial node is required for creating a wallet on Bitcoin's blockchain that is able to access and display the information in the envelope of a sat, and other wallets on Bitcoin's blockchain would not view the sat as any different from other sats. This means if you do not have the special wallet your ordinal could be lost, basically spent as a transaction fee, or sent as a payment. Think of it like having 100 dollars, and only one has a stamp on it, during a normal day of paying for goods and services this single dollar could be spent unknowingly, this is similar to ordinals in a wallet that does not see the unique information held within each of the sats held in the wallet. For now, there are only a few wallet options for ordinals, transactions are done over the counter, basically meaning the user interface is not great for the average person, and if you try to hold an ordinal in a normal Bitcoin wallet there is a good chance you might accidentally spend your ordinal. But ordinals should not be thought of as bad for Bitcoins blockchain, they are just one step in many that will take place in the years to come, these ordinals require full nodes in order to be created, and partial nodes in order to hold and view the ordinal, this will lead to more nodes being set up for Bitcoins blockchain, further securing its consensus method.

Ordinals are still a new and a recent development for the Bitcoin blockchain, it will take time to improve the user interface, and it might not grow to become comparable to blockchains that allow for users to easily mint and trade NFTs. However, being able to lock information in the Bitcoin blockchain will probably have many use cases in the future, we will go over some examples later when we look at the many use cases that exist for blockchain coins and tokens, for now just understand that information held within a sat could be used in many ways. This information would be public since Bitcoins blockchain is public, so sensitive information will not be stored in sats, but if the information was the deed to a property, then holding the sat would be like owning the property, and this deed could not be damaged, stolen, or forged. The information is secured by Bitcoins SHA and its network of validators, in order to change information held in the sat a malicious actor would need to hack Bitcoin's blockchain, and as mentioned before this is impossible without quantum computing, especially for a blockchain with the number of validators and nodes that Bitcoin's consensus method has. Sats could also be used in other blockchains and their use cases, simply put an NFT could be created on a separate blockchain, and this NFT could hold a sat from Bitcoins blockchain, meaning the deed for a property could be information stored on any blockchain, but ownership of the sat is what proves the deed is authentic since the Bitcoin blockchain cannot be changed or altered. There are many more examples of use cases that we will go over later, but ordinals are a good example of Bitcoins development, and as more use cases are created for Bitcoins blockchain, the more demand there will be for BTC, increasing Bitcoins value over time.

Lighting Network:

Another somewhat recent use case on the Bitcoin blockchain is the Lightning Network, and we will go over side channels like the Lighting Network in more detail later when we go over layer 2 blockchains, but a side channel should not be thought of as a layer 2 blockchain. *(Reference page 34)* The Lighting Network started in early 2019, Bitcoin nodes provide a separate settlement channel for transactions on the Bitcoin blockchain, and this basically is transactions taking place between two wallets on the Bitcoin blockchain. A simple example would be, two wallets on the Bitcoin blockchain open a channel between each other using the Lightning Network, each wallet has 10 Bitcoin, and payments or transactions take place between the wallets for a period of time. Then the two wallets settle on the Bitcoin blockchain, with say 12 Bitcoin in one wallet and 8 Bitcoin in the other wallet, and even though many transactions between the wallets could have taken place none of these transactions took place on the Bitcoin blockchain. Only when finally settling, or closing out the side channel, do the wallets get updated on the Bitcoin blockchains ledger of accounts. This allows for more transactions to take place with lower fees, Bitcoins blockchain can handle about 10 transactions per second, while the Lightning Network can theoretically handle millions of transactions per second, and this is what allows for small fast payments using Bitcoin as the form of wealth.

There are dispute mechanisms on the Lightning Network, and it's important to remember these transactions are not taking place on the Bitcoin blockchain, so there can be malicious wallets trying to take advantage of other wallet holders. Overall, the Lightning Network is good for Bitcoins blockchain, again more Bitcoin nodes need to be set up in order for users to access the Lightning Network, although it's important to understand how these transactions are taking place, and the Lightning Network should only be used for smaller transactions that need to be settled fast. For larger amounts of wealth, settling directly on the Bitcoin blockchain would be the safest way to move that wealth. I would encourage further research for anyone looking to better understand the Lightning Network, this is just a simplified explanation, but one important thing to understand is that side channels are not layer 2 blockchains, they are nodes on the blockchain, not an independent and separate blockchain.

(Illustration, next page)

There are many more use cases waiting to be added to the Bitcoin blockchain, as mentioned before improvement proposals for Bitcoins blockchain take a long time to pass and be implemented, and this is why sometimes these updates turn into hard forks if there is enough support for both sides, and an agreement cannot be reached in the Bitcoin community. Bitcoin and Bitcoin Cash would be a good example, and so would several of the Bitcoin hard forks that we went over before, but these hard forks do not always happen, and there have been many BIPs that have been implemented on the Bitcoin blockchain since its start. These updates are what allow for new use cases on the Bitcoin blockchain, Segwit allowed for updates to Bitcoin wallets, and this was required for the Lightning Network to function, this included BIPs 44, 49, and 84. Taproot also allowed for updates to Bitcoins code that brought several new features and benefits to the users of Bitcoins blockchain. As more updates are passed on the Bitcoin blockchain, more use cases will be possible on the Bitcoin blockchain, and although this process may be somewhat sluggish compared to other blockchain projects, the implementation of BIPs is slow and deliberate, and this reduces the risk of failure or exploits on the Bitcoin blockchain.

Bitcoin Block Rewards:

Bitcoins block rewards will eventually end as mentioned before, by this time transaction fees will have substantially increased from added use cases on Bitcoin's blockchain, and these transaction fees will be what keep many mining farms profitable, even after the end of block rewards. These mining farms 100 plus years in the future would have to achieve very high hash rates, the equipment and cooling systems required would still be expensive, and there are some people that believe when Bitcoins block rewards end, all the Bitcoin miners will shut down. I do not believe this will be the case, this is because the number of Bitcoin nodes running in the future will be massive, these nodes will be supporting use cases on the Bitcoin blockchain,

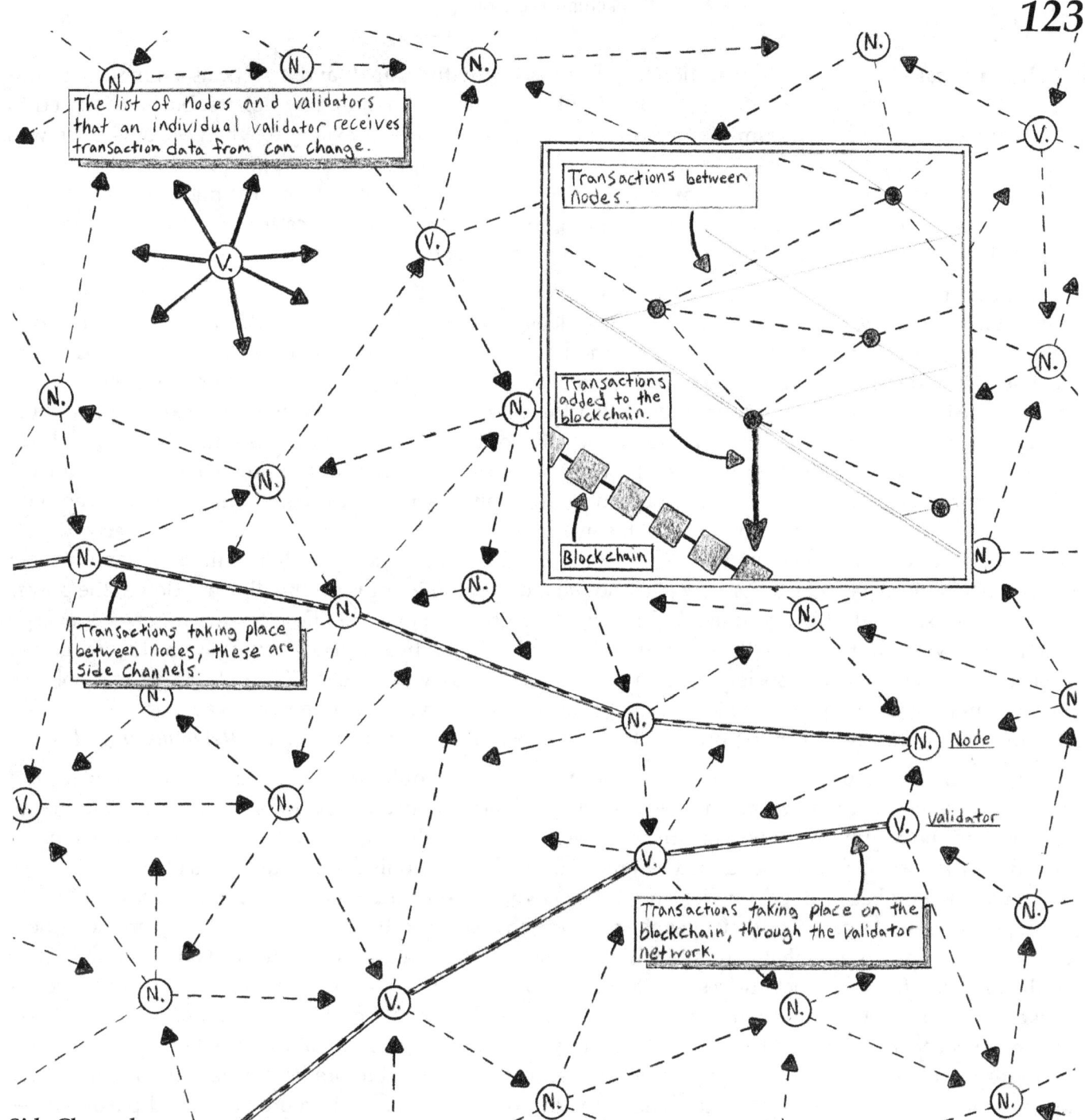

Side Channels

The web of validators and nodes in a blockchains consensus method allows for more connections, simply put, the larger this web is the more decentralized the validator network is, although this depends on who controls the validators, and who is allowed to become a validator. These validators create blocks and actually add transactions to the blockchain, while side channels can be used for faster transaction speed, but it is important to remember these transactions do not settle on the blockchain right away, and the Lighting Network has dispute mechanisms, so it may not be ideal for moving large amounts of wealth.

    Pg. 11, upper right section: Some transactions on a blockchain are involved with a use case on the blockchain, and these transactions do not always need to settle on the blockchain right away, they can settle transactions through the network of nodes similar to the Lighting Network.
    Pg. 49, upper left section: Validators can choose what connections to make, these other validators and nodes are sending transactions to the validator and vice versa, and this is important because it allows the validator to hash as many transactions as possible, while still being able to remove a malicious node that may be pushing invalid transactions.
    Pg. 69, center section: Nodes increase the number of possible connections in a network of validators, basically they create a larger web of individual nodes and validators, and this usually adds to the overall decentralization of the blockchain's consensus method.
    Pg. 109, bottom section: The Lighting Network is made up of nodes on Bitcoins blockchain, and these nodes can settle transactions much faster than settling on Bitcoins actual blockchain through its validators. Although the side channel must settle on Bitcoin's blockchain every once in a while, and it is not an independent blockchain.
    Pg. 151, bottom section: Faster transactions through a side channel like the Lighting Network would be ok for small amounts of wealth, however it is important to remember these transactions do not settle on the Bitcoin blockchain right away, and for larger transactions of wealth it would be better to settle on the Bitcoin blockchain through the validator network, even if the transaction takes a little longer.

and these use cases will involve transaction fees. We saw this with ordinals and their transaction fees around May 2023, average transaction fees on the Bitcoin blockchain are around a few dollars, but they spiked to over 10 dollars for a period of time, and this has happened before. For example, when Bitcoins price was going up in early 2021, transaction fees reached 25 dollars, and spiked much higher for a short period of time. We will go over transaction fees and use cases in more detail later, for now just understand use cases like ordinals do generate a small profit for Bitcoin miners, and as more use cases are created on Bitcoin's blockchain, more fees will go to miners along with their block rewards.

One day miner fees on Bitcoin's blockchain will be larger than the block rewards issued per block, this is an inevitability for several reasons, the first is that block rewards will be zero one day as mentioned before, and the second is that miner fees exist today, although they are small compared to block rewards. As more use cases are added to Bitcoins blockchain, more fees will be generated from transactions that are required for these use cases, and it's important to remember this process will take place over the next 100 plus years, but for now block rewards are still what generate most of the profits for Bitcoin mining farms. Over this period Bitcoin miners will have time to slowly shut down as their block rewards slowly reduce, and as each halving happens about every 4 years, more and more mining farms will become unprofitable, even with cheap or renewable energy sources. Although some mining farms will continue to grow and balance their power costs based on their mining fees. So, Bitcoin's blockchain will not lose all its validators, and we will go over this in more detail next, for now just understand as mining farms eventually shut down, the power sources they use would then be freed up to power the grid. This would allow for the renewable energy systems that were built for these Bitcoin mining farms, to be used by the grid, creating even cheaper power for customers, this is good for society in general, and this process will be slow. We are still in the early phases of Bitcoin mining farms developing the renewable energy industry, and a long way away from seeing those advancements transferred over to powering the grid at near zero cost to customers. *(Reference page 131)*

Not all mining farms will shut down in the future, there would still be transaction fees that would generate a profit for a mining farm, and this will continue the growth and development of renewable energy systems, and the computing power of ASICs, as well as their cooling systems. Nodes do not receive block rewards or transaction fees as mentioned before, these rewards are only for the validators of the blockchain, so even as the number of Bitcoin nodes grow, they cannot receive transaction fees, in fact they will likely be supporting the use case that generates the fee, not what collects the fee. Basically, in my opinion, there will be some mining farms that continue to hash transactions even after block rewards have ended. They will be profiting from transaction fees by this point, and although the reduction of validators on Bitcoin's blockchain would not be ideal today, in the future there will be many more nodes hashing transactions on Bitcoin's blockchain. These nodes would make it even harder to push invalid transactions as mentioned before, especially if the number of nodes was very large, but it is hard to predict this far into the future, for now we can just assume that as use cases are added to Bitcoins blockchain, more nodes and partial nodes will be set up to support these use cases. This process will likely be slow, since BIPs usually take time to be agreed upon, and this is a good aspect of the Bitcoin blockchain, slow and deliberate development of use cases, this reduces the risk of exploits or failures in the future. This increase of nodes on Bitcoin's blockchain will help further secure Bitcoin's consensus method, as mentioned before nodes play an important part in pushing and pulling data to and from other nodes and validators, and as more nodes come online, it will become harder and harder for invalid transactions to be attempted on the Bitcoin blockchain, even with fewer validators in the decentralized network.

It is impossible to know how the Bitcoin blockchain will work in 100 years, but as we have seen, use cases and transaction fees could create enough profit to keep some mining farms online, and even though many mining farms will eventually shut down over the coming decades, Bitcoins consensus method will gain many nodes as it loses some validators. This would at least show there is a way for Bitcoins blockchain to continue after the last halving, the end of block rewards will not be the end of the Bitcoin blockchain, and it's important to remember this will all happen slowly over many years, we still have decades of growth for Bitcoin mining farms. This growth will be in several industries, obviously growth and development in chips and the computing power of ASICs is one, and another big area would be renewable energy sources. Next we will look at how mining farms will develop this industry and how they will play a part in balancing the power grid.

Bitcoin Validators, Mining Farm Quote:

Before we go over several types of renewable energy systems being used by Bitcoin mining farms, let's better understand what a medium-sized mining farm looks like, what equipment is required, and rough numbers as far as energy costs, equipment costs, and block rewards earned. In 2021, I talked two of my friends into helping me set up a small Bitcoin mining farm at my house, and I will go over this mining farm in more detail later, but around mid-2022 we had found a local investor interested in setting up a large Bitcoin mining farm in the city that we lived in. He was part owner of the local mall, and me and one of my partners meet with him to go over an idea to put solar panels on the mall's roof, and run a mining farm out of one of the vacant units at the mall, and I will go over the rough quote we came up with for equipment, cooling systems, and estimated block rewards.

The ASIC units are usually the biggest equipment cost for a mining farm, we looked into two popular models at the time, the S19J Pro, 224 units at a price of about 1.1 million dollars, and the S19XP, we would only need 166 units at a cost of about 1.5 million dollars. The price difference between the ASICs had to do with their hash power, and we will not go over the differences between these two models, there are many ASIC manufactures that are producing newer models every year. The main takeaway is that you are paying more for higher computing power, and some of these newer models are even reducing the energy required while still maintaining higher hash rates. My partners and I had quickly realized our cooling systems were going to be very important since we live in the Mohave desert, this is why we suggested a dielectric fluid cooling system, the oil is able to move and dissipate heat better than air, and we had set up our smaller mining farm with this type of cooling system. Manufactures now make something similar to what we built at my house, but for several hundred ASIC units we would need larger pools, and we found a manufacture that sold tanks that could hold 20 ASIC units each, we would need 10 of these tanks, each one about $7,000. There was another option called the MegaPod that we will go over next, however either way we would need about 700 gallons of the dielectric fluid, and we suggested Bitcool-888, it was designed to not damage the rubber or plastic components of the ASIC units, and would have cost about $25,000.

The oil would be pumped in a closed loop through a radiator, there are many ways to dissipate heat, but with the amount of heat and fluid passing through the radiator we decided the most efficient method would be large cooling towers. Basically a large radiator, the ones we found were 15 to 20 feet tall, cost about $10,000, and we would likely need two based on the number of ASICs that would need to be cooled. Electrical work was going to be a large cost, especially since there were supply chain issues and sub panels were in short supply, the mining farm would have been pulling about 500,000 watts or .5MW, and for this, transformers and a series of electrical panels are needed. This is when we found the MegaPod, it is a popular idea for mining farms since all the panels, pumps, and ASICs are enclosed in a 40-foot shipping container, these can be easily moved, and requires a small footprint compared to warehouses full of air-cooled ASIC units. The container we were looking at would cost about 1 million dollars, but it would come with just about all the other required equipment, electrical panels, pumps, everything but the ASICs and cooling towers, all they need is an energy source and an internet connection, and they are ready to go. This ease of mobility is a huge plus for this type of mining farm, this will become more apparent as we go over some renewable energy sources such as stranded natural gas, and we will be able to see why this type of cooling system is more efficient, especially when enclosed in the pod design. *(Reference page 131)*

This information was from a quote in mid-2022, so obviously equipment costs will vary with demand, and this was all based on a block reward rate that would be cut in half in just about 2 years' time, after that we hoped to mine for the full 3.125 block reward cycle. *(Reference page 103)* But it's important to remember Bitcoins hash rate is continuously increasing, so these would be best case scenarios, and if the mining farm improved its equipment over the 4-year cycle it might be able to absorb the next halving and the next 50%

reduction in block rewards. But I think it's too hard to guess what Bitcoin mining will be like in a decade, ASICs will likely have a lot of computing power, and the hash rate of Bitcoin will likely be far higher than it is today. So, mining farms should focus on being profitable for at least one halving, or about 4 years, if over this time they are able to improve their mining farm or cooling systems then they might be able to survive another 50% reduction in block rewards. If not, they will likely shut down because they will no longer be able to afford their power bill, and this is why renewable energy is so important for mining farms. They either need to increase their hash rate or reduce their energy costs if they are to remain profitable long term, and this will be the driving force behind the development of the renewable energy industry.

This mining farm would have cost about 2.5 million dollars, and this would not include the cost for land or warehousing since it was going to be set up in an existing building, so there is a substantial up-front cost for mining farms. The goal of this mining farm was to earn about .1 BTC a day, this was based on the hash rate at the time, and over time this would become less as more validators came online and started hashing transactions. This is why the goal of a mining farm should be to remain profitable for a full halving cycle, the hash rate will keep increasing over this time, and a mining farm might be able to remain profitable through the hash rate increase. However, this steady increase in hash rate combined with a 50% reduction in block rewards is the balance that the Bitcoin blockchain has achieved, Bitcoin miners need to be constantly improving their systems, or they will no longer be profitable, and this improvement of a mining farm is possible, but it will lead to the weeding out of mining farms overtime. This creates mining farms that are able to hash transactions and earn block rewards for many halving cycles, further increasing their hash rate and securing Bitcoins blockchain at the same time, and it's important to understand what is happening here, Bitcoin mining is becoming a business. The business has no physical product, so warehousing or retail space is not required, except space for a few 40-foot shipping containers, and this means there are no customers for Bitcoin mining farms, no customer acquisition or advertising is needed. A Bitcoin miner's only goal is to hash as many transactions as possible, for as long as possible, Bitcoins code ensures they will be compensated an amount of BTC if they are not pushing invalid transactions and trying to manipulate the Bitcoin blockchain.

There are a lot of factors to consider when going over the block reward numbers that this mining farm could have earned, and this is why mining farms with tight margins have trouble surviving long term, but if this farm had been set up, and had updated its equipment over time, I believe it could have maintained something close to these numbers. So, if the mining farm is making .1 BTC a day, that would be about 3 BTC a month, and depending on energy costs the power bill would have been anywhere from $25,000 to $35,000 a month, based on an energy price of around .07 cents per kWh. We were basing our numbers on a Bitcoin price of about $20,000, this would mean each month the mining farm would earn about 3 Bitcoin, worth around $60,000, and about half of that would be needed to pay the power bill. This is why I had suggested incorporating solar energy, to offset the power bill as much as possible, but these would have additional up-front costs on top of the 2.5 million dollars required for the equipment, and this is why the investor had decided to negotiate with local power plants and pull directly from the grid. The mining farm would have been able to stack up about 1.5 BTC a month, 18 Bitcoin a year, which at a Bitcoin price of $20,000 would be worth about $360,000, and if these numbers could be maintained for the whole halving cycle, then it would earn about 1.5 million dollars, or 72 Bitcoin over the 4-year period.

These numbers would obviously change over the 4 years, so it's important to understand all the factors involved with Bitcoin block rewards, the first one to understand it that by the last year of the cycle the mining farm would not be earning 3 Bitcoin a month. This is because over the years Bitcoins hash rate would have increased, and how much the hash rate increased would determine how much the block rewards would be reduced for the mining farm, assuming the farm did not increase their hash rate with better equipment. Another factor would be Bitcoins price, if the price fell below $20,000 then the mining farm would need to sell more Bitcoin to cover the energy costs, maybe 2 Bitcoin or even more, affecting the number of Bitcoin the mining farm is able to save per month. This was not going to be that big of an issue for this mining farm since I had suggested holding 6 months' worth of energy bills in cash, not in Bitcoin, and this would allow the mining farm to continue hashing transactions and earning block rewards even if Bitcoins price fell below $20,000, and we will look at an example mining farm to better understand this idea next.

Example Bitcoin Mining Farm:

An overly simplified example would be, Bitcoins price is fixed at $10,000 and the mining farm's power bill is $5,000, the mining farm earns 1 BTC a month, and Bitcoins hash rate is also fixed so the mining farm's block rewards will essentially be fixed as well. We will go over two mining farms and two different ways mining farms can use their block rewards to pay the power bill, but first understand these are extremely over simplified examples, and mining farms do not have the luxury of working with fixed numbers. They must be constantly aware of many factors that change in predictable ways, like the Bitcoin halving, and factors that change in unexpected ways like Bitcoins price and hash rate. Over a 12-month period the first mining farm would sell 0.5 BTC to cover the $5,000 power bill each month, after 12 months the mining farm would have 6 BTC. While the second mining farm had $30,000 in an account that could cover 6 months' worth of power bills, over this 6-month period the mining farm will earn 6 BTC, the same amount the first mining farm would earn in one years' time. If the second mining farm was able to cover the next 6 months of power bills as well, then the second mining farm would earn and be able to keep 12 BTC compared to the first mining farm's 6 BTC, but to be fair where would the second mining farm get the dollars in order to keep all their block rewards. To understand this, now imagine during the 5th month Bitcoins price jumped to $60,000, then fell back to $10,000. The mining farm by this point would have 5 BTC, so they would sell 2 BTC for $120,000 that would cover the next years' worth of power bills, and they would be able to keep all the remaining block rewards for the 12-month period, ending up with 10 BTC and enough cash to pay the power bill for 6 additional months. If the same price spike happened for the first mining farm, then for that 5th month when Bitcoins price was at $60,000 the mining farm would be able to keep almost 0.9 BTC instead of 0.5 BTC. After the 12-month period this mining farm would have closer to 6.5 BTC rather than 6 BTC, it is an increase, but nowhere near 10 BTC and a years' worth of power bills saved in dollars.

With this example we can see how holding Bitcoin and waiting for a price spike is the better option for Bitcoin mining farms looking to keep as much of their block rewards as possible, and it is easier said than done, this example does not take into account many other factors that are important for a Bitcoin mining farm. However, with an asset like Bitcoin you should not think in terms of dollars, Bitcoins dollar value is very volatile, and mining farms cannot rely on Bitcoins value for large reoccurring costs like the power bill. For example, if Bitcoins price dropped to $5,000 then the first mining farm would be spending all their block rewards that month to pay the power bill, if the price drop only happened for one month then after 12 months the mining farm would have 5.5 BTC, not 6 BTC. While the second mining farm would be unaffected by this temporary drop in Bitcoins price, but if the price drop lasted for many months then the second mining farm would need to raise money or sell some of their Bitcoin, so there is risk with either method. Although keeping 6 months' worth of dollars for the power bill does protect a mining farm from large price drops, if Bitcoins price say dropped to $3,000 for a month, then the first mining farm would have to come up with the $2,000 difference. Or sell some of their block rewards, or shut down the mining farm, and again this is a simplified example, Bitcoins price does not drop for just a month period like this. This method is used by some mining farms, but not all of them, many smaller mining farms have very tight margins, they need to sell some of their Bitcoin every month or every few months, and they are usually the first mining farms to shut down after a halving event. Some ideas like incorporating solar to offset a mining farm's power bill would help mining farms absorb these block reward reductions, either from the halving, or from the increasing hash rate. Although most small mining farms have somewhat tight margins, and this is why it is hard to include debt servicing costs and even any form of constant ROI into a Bitcoin mining farm. This is because the asset being earned has a volatile price and if Bitcoin needs to be sold to make payments on loans, or as a return for investors, then the mining farm will not be able to stack up block rewards, and we will go over this in a little more detail next.

Do Not Think in Dollars:

Mining farms need to think in terms of Bitcoin, not in terms of dollars, and they need to think in Bitcoin halving cycles, or 4-year periods, where they might only sell their block rewards a few times each year, or each halving cycle. *(Reference page 106)* When debt servicing costs, or ROI for investors is added into the mining farm's costs it eats away at or destroys the mining farm's ability to earn and stack block rewards, and this does not mean an investor cannot gain a return on their investment, or that debt cannot be used to fund the construction of a mining farm. But these companies would need to understand the asset they are earning as a block reward, ROI would not be predictable, and if measured in dollars the mining farm would lose out on the possible wealth gain they could achieve if they simply held the Bitcoin. A mining farm's goal should be to earn as much Bitcoin as it can, basically having as high of a hash rate as possible, and to hold on to the block rewards earned for as long as possible, or until Bitcoins price has reached a level the mining farm is comfortable selling the Bitcoin at. As mentioned before sometimes large mining farms will sell large amounts of Bitcoin at a premium to exchanges or anyone looking to get a large quantity of Bitcoin, but for small mining farms their block rewards are sold at exchanges for market value, or that Bitcoin could be used as an investor's ROI.

If investors are to be paid in Bitcoin and the mining farm is to remain profitable long term, then the dollar amount of Bitcoin they will be paid back will be less than the dollar amount they invested in the mining farm, and none of this is set in stone, this is just what I have learned through my research and firsthand experience with Bitcoin mining. A good example of this would be the mining farm quote from before, over 2.5 million dollars for the mining farm, but even with the best-case scenario as far as hash rate increase goes, the mining farm would only earn 1.5 million dollars' worth of Bitcoin over the halving cycle, or over the 4-year period. But it's important to not think in terms of dollars, because that 1.5 million dollars is actually about 72 Bitcoin, and at a Bitcoin price of about $40,000 that 72 Bitcoin would be worth about 2.9 million dollars. Simply put, holding on to Bitcoin is a form of return for investors in a mining farm, as long as they are able to hold on to the block rewards they earned, and they are not forced to sell them to cover the power bill. There are many ways to set up a profitable long-term Bitcoin mining farm, this was just an example of a mining farm me and my partners looked into setting up, but there are many factors that cause many mining farms to shut down, and we will look at these factors a little more next.

Weeding Out of Bitcoin Miners:

Mining farms have many factors that affect their ability to stay online hashing transactions, many of these are normal and routine issues that a mining farm deals with, a few examples would be, having a reliable internet connection, repairing ASICs that break down, and keeping the hardware cool enough during the changing seasonal climates, depending on the farm's location. While some of these factors might cause a mining farm to go offline, most of these routine issues can be fixed, and this would not keep the mining farm offline permanently. Although, major factors could cause the mining farm to shut down completely, and both small routine factors and larger factors play a part in the weeding out of mining farms over time, and the block reward reduction every 4 years is what accelerates this process. ASICs require more than just plugging them in and keeping them cool, the same is true for GPUs that hash transactions on a blockchain, and I would encourage further research for anyone looking to set up a mining farm. Knowledge on how to send your hash rate to a mining pool and how to connect your wallet are somewhat technical, and the same is true for downloading the blockchain in order to begin hashing transactions, so we will just be focusing on the larger issues that affect mining farms overall.

Small mining farms with only a few ASIC units might not be able to afford to repair a unit, this would be a sizable part of their hash rate, and might lead to the miner shutting down, while other mining farms might not invest in efficient cooling systems, and they might have to shut down during summer months if the temperature becomes hot enough. These smaller factors alone would not be much as far as weeding out Bitcoin miners, most mining farms are able to deal with routine issues, and most mining farms would be able to remain profitable if not for other factors. However, the continuously increasing hash rate is a problem for smaller mining farms with a low hash rate, over time their block rewards become less and less, while their power bill remains the same. This plays a small part in the weeding out of smaller mining farms over time, they either need to increase their hash power, or they will become unprofitable. The Bitcoin halving also affects smaller mining farms, they are usually the first miners to shut down after the 50% reduction in block rewards, and this is why the halving is an important factor that leads to the weeding out of mining farms over time.

Medium to large sized mining farms are less affected by the continuously increasing hash rate, these farms often have hundreds of ASIC units with a somewhat high hash rate, basically this means they can last longer than smaller mining farms with lower hash rates, and they will eventually become unprofitable, but it will take more time. These mining farms could increase their efficiently and hash rate over this time, allowing them to remain profitable for even longer, and these larger mining farms often have better funding that would allow for these improvements to be made over time. However, the Bitcoin halving can affect these larger mining farms as well, it depends on the price of electricity that the mining farm is paying. Some might be able to absorb this 50% reduction in block rewards, while others will not be able to, and they would have to shut down, or reinvest in better equipment in order to become profitable again. The Bitcoin halving ensures even the largest mining farms must be continuously improving their efficiency and their hash rate. New ASICs with more computing power are being created each year, and these large mining farms cannot simply keep hashing transactions with the same ASICs for decades, they would eventually have such a small portion of the total hash rate that they would earn very little block rewards.

The Bitcoin halving and the continuously increasing hash rate are major factors in the weeding out of Bitcoin miners over time, and there are other factors that can affect a mining farm's ability to stay online and hashing transactions at a profit. But these are smaller issues that might not affect every mining farm, while the Bitcoin halving is something that is hard coded into Bitcoins blockchain, and it will affect every mining farms profitability. The total hash rate also effects a mining farm's profitability, although it effects smaller mining farms more than ones with higher hash rates, and the hash rate increases as more mining farms come online, so this is a factor that varies, and not one that is predictable like the Bitcoin halving. Think of Bitcoin mining farms like baby sea turtles hatching on the beach, the odds are stacked against them, and many will not make it, the same is true for Bitcoin mining farms, over time many will become unprofitable and will be weeded out. But many others will overcome the obstacles, and they will be able to hash transactions and earn block rewards through many halving cycles into the future. While some mining farms are able to remain profitable with debt servicing costs and ROI payments, many smaller mining farms cannot take on these additional costs, and this is a big factor in maintaining a long term and profitable mining farm. As mentioned before, energy costs are the biggest reoccurring cost for a mining farm, and as we have seen this can be balanced out with block rewards, but when other large costs like debt servicing costs are added into the equation, the mining farm would have an even harder time remaining profitable. The obvious way for a mining farm to remain profitable is to reduce its energy costs by using renewable energy sources, but avoiding debt to fund a mining farm would be best practice if possible, it only adds another cost to a reducing block reward. Another way to reduce energy costs is to incorporate Bitcoin mining farms into the power grid, we will look at this in detail next, then we will look at how these ideas are being used today in places like Texas.

Balancing the Grid with Bitcoin Mining Farms:

Balancing the grid with Bitcoin mining farms is possible, and we will go over the basic idea in detail before looking at some examples in Texas, and some examples that incorporate renewable energy sources like solar. *(Reference page 131)* Let us look at an example grid and power plant to understand where Bitcoin mining farms could help balance the energy demands of a city, first we have a grid that powers a small city, and it requires different amounts of energy depending on the time of day and outside temperature. This example city requires 50 watts of energy during the night and most of the day, except during peak hours in the afternoon when the city is pulling 60w, and the power plant has the ability to generate up to 200w, but it runs at peak efficiency around 120w. This is important to understand, because the equipment in a power plant is constantly being adjusted to the needs of the grid, this puts wear and tear on the equipment from being spun up and down throughout the day, and running the power plant at 50w or even 200w would also put added stress on the equipment. The power plant also does not know how much energy the city will require in advance, it depends on the 1000s of people in the city and how much energy they are using at any one time, and this is what causes brown outs or rolling black-outs in a city, the power plant requires time to increase its energy generation, and in the meantime some people are without power. Simply put, when demand increases on the grid, someone has to cut back on energy use, they can do this voluntarily by working with the power company, or they can simply lose power, either way there is not enough energy to go around, and it will take time for the power plant to increase its output.

Now imagine if the power plant did not need to be constantly adjusting its power generation, let's say it runs its equipment at its ideal efficiency 120w, instead of bouncing back and forth around 50-60w adding wear and tear to the costly equipment, and having to do so at a moment's notice should the grid require more energy. This would mean there is about 60-70w of additional power depending on the time of day and the grid requirements at the time, and this power cannot simply sit in the grid waiting to be used, if this energy is not used it will likely burn up power lines or sub stations. In order to prevent overloading the grid a Bitcoin mining farm is set up at the power plant, its ASICs require 20w, this leaves 100w for the grid, and other mining farms in the city could be set up using about 50w in total. This is ideal since the city generally only needs 50w of energy for most of the day, and during peak energy usage around 60w, some of the ASICs at the power plant can be shut down. This would mean 60w for the city, 50w for mining farms in the city, and this leaves 10w for the mining farm at the power plant, meaning only half of them would need to be shut down. Shutting down an ASIC unit can be done with a flip of the switch, much faster than a power plant can be spun up to meet additional energy needs, and this is what allows the power plant to meet all demand from the grid at any one point in time, ASICs are simply shut down allowing for that energy to be used by the grid when needed. This would allow for mining farms in the city to run 24/7 without having to shut down and lose possible block rewards, and the city would have uninterrupted energy despite the small normal variations in energy demand that can be offset by the ASICs at the power plant.

(Illustration, next page)

However, what about times when grid demand is even higher because of extreme heat or cold, let's imagine the city is experiencing a heat wave, and during normal peak energy usage the city is now pulling 80w from the grid. First the mining farm at the power plant would be completely shut down, this would allow the power plant to generate 120w for the grid, and mining farms in the city that normally pull 50w would shut down some ASICs reducing their energy demand to 40w. This would allow the grid the required 80w without interruption, these mining farms can be shut down fast and would have contracts with the power company to do so if ever required to. In this example we can see the mining farms in the city would still be running 4/5 of their miners, meaning the power plant could meet grid requirements all the way up to 120w before having to increase its energy generation. These events that require large amounts of energy for heating or cooling do not happen often, and as we saw with the example grid, the mining farm at the power plant would usually be the only one that needed to shut down ASIC units. But the additional mining farms in the city can also be used to absorb these peak energy times on the grid, preventing brown outs or any kind of grid failure. These mining farms are considered the first and last buyer for power plants, when there is extra energy that needs to be used now, Bitcoin mining farms are turned on, and when energy demand is at its peak, Bitcoin mining farms can be quickly shut down allowing for uninterrupted power on the grid.

This is a very simple example, and power plants have many more factors involved in balancing the grid, but Bitcoin mining farms allow them a way to absorb energy from the grid at a moment's notice, and it is this ability that makes mining farms valuable to power plants, their ability to be turned on and off with the flip of a switch. This ability is very important when you start to look at other factors like renewable energy sources such as wind or solar, these cannot be relied on because sometimes the wind is not blowing, and sometimes the sun is not shinning, and this adds stress to power plants and the grid. Using the previous example, imagine the city had windmills that generated 10w of energy, this would mean the power plant would only need to generate 40w during most of the day, and 50w during normal peak energy usage. However, the wind is not always strong enough to generate 10w, so the power plant would need to increase its energy output when the wind stopped, and reduce its energy output when the wind was strong enough

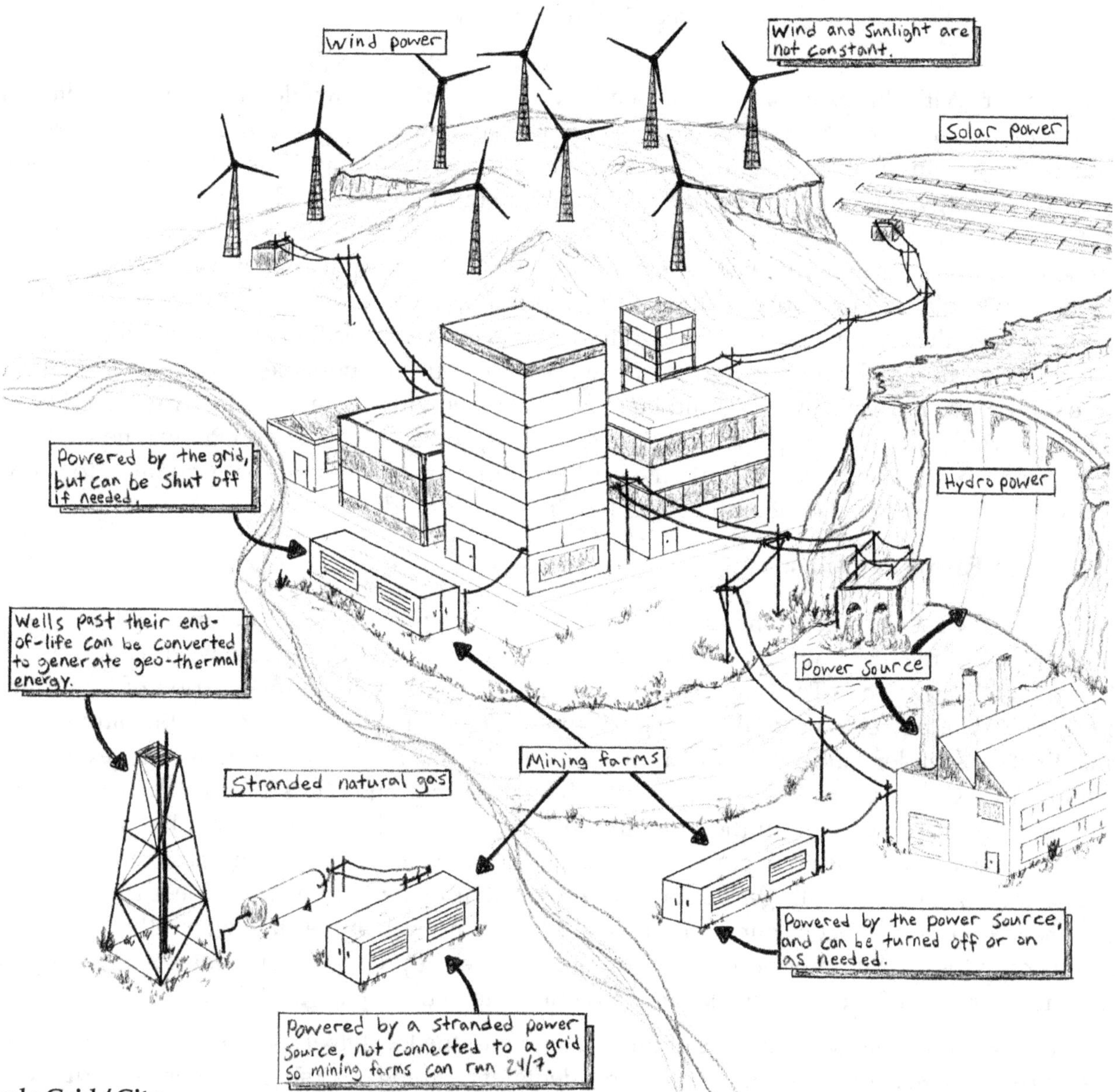

Labels in illustration:
- Wind power
- Wind and sunlight are not constant.
- Solar power
- Powered by the grid, but can be shut off if needed.
- Hydro power
- Wells past their end-of-life can be converted to generate geo-thermal energy.
- Power Source
- Stranded natural gas
- Mining farms
- Powered by the power source, and can be turned off or on as needed.
- Powered by a stranded power source, not connected to a grid so mining farms can run 24/7.

Example Grid / City

This example grid incorporates many different types of renewable energy systems, and ones like wind or solar would not be able to power the city continuously, this is why they must be incorporated into grids with other forms of power generation. However, these other power plants need to be constantly adjusted based on how much energy is being generated by the wind or solar, and this is where Bitcoin mining farms could be used to help balance the grid, as well as being the long-term buyer of energy that power plants are looking for.

Pg. 116, left section: Geothermal energy can provide constant power for a mining farm, or for the grid, depending on how much heat is captured and converted to energy, and this can be achieved by drilling into the earth, or by converting oil wells past their end-of-life.

Pg. 118, right section: New dams can be built in remote areas where large amounts of energy can be generated, and normally there would be no demand for this amount of energy in the area, but Bitcoin mining farms could be set up at the dam's location. Existing dams that are not generating energy at their full potential would also be an ideal location for Bitcoin mining farms, and these hydropower plants can be incorporated into a grid or not.

Pg. 124, center section: Over many years more and more renewable energy systems can be incorporated into the grid that powers a city, and for now Bitcoin mining farms will be the buyer of that energy, allowing for power plants to be expanded, and providing mining farms and grid customers with power. After many halving cycles some mining farms will become unprofitable and have to shut down, but some of the renewable energy systems will remain, and they would be able to provide cheap power for grid customers, since the infrastructure is already set up.

Pg. 125, bottom section: Bitcoin mining farms enclosed in shipping containers can be set up in almost any location, all that is needed is power and an internet connection, and depending on the climate at the mining farms location, these ASICs can use air or fluid cooling systems.

Pg. 129, right section: Solar energy alone cannot generate power continuously, but it can be incorporated into a grid in order to offset a mining farms energy demand, although this depends on the size of the mining farm and its energy requirements.

Pg. 132, center section: Large amounts of energy can be generated in some areas, this is often more than what the grid requires, and these are usually somewhat rural areas, or a small city, with little energy demand.

Pg. 136, left section: Any power source that cannot be used by the grid could be considered stranded, basically the energy potential exists, but it either exceeds the areas demand, or there is no demand for energy in that area. Stranded natural gas is one example, but other energy sources like flare gas can also be used to power a Bitcoin mining farm, and these mining farms would not need to shut down because of high grid demand, this is because they are not connected to a grid.

Pg. 137, bottom section: Bitcoin mining farms are set up in the city, they are also set up at the energy sources connected to the grid, this allows the power plant to balance the grid by turning on or off ASIC units, and this becomes even more important when some forms of renewable energy are incorporated into the grid, such as solar.

Pg. 153, bottom section: Bitcoin ASICs set up at the power plant could be turned on or off as needed, allowing most mining farms on the grid to hash transactions 24/7, and when a natural event causes extreme grid demand, these other mining farms can be shut down as well, preventing grid failure in the city when power is needed the most.

to generate power. With this example, we can see how the power plant would be constantly adjusting its energy generation based on how much power the city needed at any one point in time, and based on how much energy the windmills were able to produce at any one point in time. This is why the idea of using some renewable energy sources to power the grid might sound like a good idea, but in practice it is very inefficient and adds wear and tear to power plants that are picking up the additional load, and depending on the renewable energy source, power generation can stop almost immediately, adding more stress to the grid and power plants. Now imagine the same windmill added into the grid that incorporated Bitcoin mining farms, when the wind was strong enough to generate energy more Bitcoin ASICs could be switched on to absorb the additional load on the grid. Or the opposite could be possible, in the event the windmill stops producing power, Bitcoin ASICs could be shut down, allowing the grid uninterrupted energy even though the renewable energy source was no longer generating power. We will look at how renewable energy sources like solar could be incorporated into the grid without causing stress to that grid later, for now let's look at how girds in Texas are incorporating Bitcoin mining farms today.

Bitcoin Mining Farms in Texas:

In 2022 Texas had about 40 Bitcoin mining farms, 10 of which were large Bitcoin mining farms, and this number does not include the many smaller mining farms usually set up by individuals with only a few ASIC units. During the heat wave in Texas in 2022 these mining farms shut down for a period of time, allowing for about 1,000MW of power to be used by the grid, and this has not been the only time Bitcoin miners have done this. First let's understand why so many Bitcoin mining farms decided to move to Texas, many of them coming from China as mentioned before, and the reason they chose this state is that Texas generates more energy than any other state in the U.S., an ideal area for mining farms. Texas has wind and solar energy sources that cannot be used to power major cities, they are too far away from these renewable energy sources, and the power they could generate is more than what many local girds in these rural areas need. *(Reference page 131)* Many Bitcoin mining farms were set up in areas of the state where they could absorb additional energy the grid did not need, this promoted the development of new renewable energy power plants in rural areas, and Bitcoin mining farms also contribute to these local tax bases.

Some of these rural areas saw millions of dollars flow into the local tax base, some of the larger mining farms created employment opportunities for local residents, everything from site managers, security workers, and technicians to install and monitor the mining farm's computers are needed. Some of these mining farms are able to provide lower energy rates to customers on the grid they are connected to, and although this might not affect every grid customer in Texas, let's look at how these mining farms are able to do this. Bitcoin mining farms lock in contracts with power companies, these deals can be for just a few cents per kWh while other grid customers pay far higher rates, and sometimes these mining farms have contracts for more energy than the mining farm requires, allowing some of the energy to be sold back to the grid. During times of extreme heat or cold the mining farms will shut down, however they are still getting paid, just not in block rewards, and when the mining farms shut down they sell that power back to the grid. Even for short periods of time that the mining farms are offline, they can still receive millions of dollars, and this compensates them for the block rewards they would have earned if they had stayed online hashing transactions. Although most Bitcoin miners would rather earn block rewards, so they only shut down during periods of time when the grid is stressed do to abnormally high demand, and this helps prevent grid failures that would cause customers to lose power when they need it the most. Mining farms that have contracts for more energy than they require could also sell that power back to the grid, and this would not only be done during peak energy demand, but on a regular basis, allowing for grid customers to have lower energy costs, let's look at a simplified example to better understand how this works.

In this example there is a small city and a local grid connected to a power plant, because the power plant does not know how much energy the city will need at any point in time they charge 10 cents per kWh, and this cost might increase or decrease a little based on demand at a point in time or during a certain season. The power plant could invest millions of dollars to reduce the price per kWh, but if in a year or two there is no longer demand for that additional energy then that investment would be a loss for the company, and this is why power plants want long-term contracts that guarantee there will be a buyer of the energy. Since most grid customers are not able or willing to commit to lengthy contracts they have higher energy rates, however a Bitcoin mining farm works out a contract with the power company to buy energy for 10 years at a rate of 2 cents per kWh, and they agree to sell energy back to the grid if they have excess, or if there is an emergency and the gird needs additional energy for the city. This mining farm's contract is for twice as much energy as the mining farm requires, this means they will be able to sell half of that energy back to the grid regularly, and their cost for that energy is 2 cents per kWh, meaning if they charge more than 2 cents, they will be making a profit. The regular customers rate is 10 cents per kWh, so as long as the mining farm charged less than 10 cents, customers would be saving money, and this allows the mining farm to charge 5 cents when selling their additional power back to the grid. The city now has cheaper power than they would have without the mining farm, the mining farm has the large amounts of energy required to run its ASICs, and the power plant has a reliable long-term contract that will allow them to invest in additional costly infrastructure and equipment, without the fear of energy demand in that area falling over the coming years. This is a simplified example, and the only grid customers that would see cheaper energy costs would be ones on the grid that the mining farm is connected to, so this would not help reduce energy costs for everyone, but it would help the small city and local grid.

    Not all mining farms in Texas are connected to a grid, off-grid mining farms are ones that get their power from energy sources that are somewhat remote, a few examples would be using flare gas as a power source, or using natural gas without having to transport it, because the Bitcoin mining farms would be set up at the natural gas source. We will look at both of these examples in more detail later, for now just understand Bitcoin mining farms can be connected to a grid and work with the grid in order to ensure customers have uninterrupted power, or they can be set up directly at the energy source and not connect to a grid. Either way energy is being used to power the mining farms that hash transactions and secure Bitcoin's blockchain, sometimes these are set up using existing infrastructure, and some mining farms are funding the expansion of existing power plants in order to generate more energy. These are costs that would usually need to be subsidized since no company is willing to invest large amounts of money unless they know there will be demand for energy in that area for a long period of time. Bitcoin mining farms are that long-term demand for energy that will allow for the development of new power plants and improvements to existing grids. We are starting to see this happen in several states on a small scale, and in Texas they are just getting started, as more mining farms are being brought online each year, and some of them are using renewable energy sources, which we will look in more detail next.

Renewable Energy Sources Being used Today:

    Bitcoin mining farms are using many different energy sources around the world, and we will look at a few examples like, nuclear, hydropower, geo-thermal, natural gas/ flare gas, and solar, in detail next. These are energy sources that being used today, but there are many other energy sources that can power Bitcoin mining farms, and these could be further developed in the coming years. Things like methane could be used to power mining farms, and this methane could come from several sources like, landfills, or manure from farms, anything that creates methane could be used. Any source of continuous energy would be ideal for Bitcoin miners, something like ocean wave power generation would provide constant power, and even small amounts of energy could run a few ASIC units, although the more energy produced the more attractive it would be for Bitcoin miners. These power sources do not always come from nature, waste treatment plants could incorporate a Bitcoin mining farm, and they would use the heat generated from the ASIC units in the sewage treatment process. They would then create biofuels that could be used to power the mining farm, and the block rewards earned by the mining farm could help offset the high costs necessary to construct and manage the waste treatment plant. Hydropower will be detailed next, but this usually involves large dams, while small whirlpool hydropower is less damaging to the environment, these can be set up in remote areas that are off-grid, and although they would not generate large amounts of energy, it would be enough to run a small mining farm. All that is needed is a large enough stream of water, and a few feet in elevation drop along the stream's path, and depending on the stream this could produce continuous energy that could power a small mining farm. There are many more examples of power sources that could be used to run a Bitcoin mining farm, but for now let's look at somewhat larger power sources, ones that are being used to run mining farms around the world today, and ones that will likely be used for many years to come as the renewable energy industry is developed.

Nuclear:

Nuclear power has become a popular option for Bitcoin mining farms, in 2021 the Mayor of Miami invited mining farms to come and use the cities ample nuclear power, although as mentioned before, many mining farms decided to set up in Texas instead. But other states understand the benefits to nuclear power and mining farms as well, and during 2022 and 2023 the Susquehanna nuclear power plant was built and brought online in northeast Pennsylvania, along with the Cumulus data center. The nuclear plant will eventually generate 475MW of energy, and a part of phase 1 of its construction was a 48MW data center that covered 300,000 square feet, with about 2.5MW directly connected to the power plant. This allows the mining farms to stay online hashing transactions 24/7 without interrupting the grid, while the power plant sends the rest of its energy to the gird, and provides customers with cheaper energy rates. This is not the only nuclear power plant, or modular nuclear power plant, being planned in the near future, and we will not go over this power plant in detail, however we will look at how the Cumulus data center could set up Bitcoin mining farms, and how they could affect Bitcoins decentralization.

Power plants that can generate these large amounts of energy are ideal for large scale Bitcoin mining farms, but these data centers could also host medium-sized mining farms, or even a few ASIC units owed by an individual, and we will go over how these different mining farms could affect Bitcoins consensus method. A single nuclear power plant would not be able to gain the majority of Bitcoins hash rate, but as more nuclear power plants are built their energy could become sizable compared to other forms of energy generation, and this might lead to Bitcoins hash rate being concentrated at several locations, or controlled by several people or companies. However, if the power is divided between several or many mining farms, then this centralized risk is reduced, and again Bitcoin mining farms are located around the world, so even if a few nuclear power plants are built for Bitcoin mining, they would only be part of Bitcoins total hash rate. Instead of powering one mining farm with 10s of megawatts of electricity, medium-sized mining farms could be set up like at the Cumulus data center, and these mining farms would have 100s of ASIC units with a high hash rate. Several of these mining farms could be powered by the nuclear plant, each would be independent of one another as far as their hash rate on the Bitcoin blockchain, and they could send their hash power to different mining pools. Basically, they would be different validators in Bitcoins consensus method, even though they are powered by the same energy source, and could be located in the same building.

This leads into the next option for power plants with large amounts of energy, hosting services for Bitcoin ASICs, these ASICs can be bought by individuals, and they pay a fee to the host for keeping their units online and hashing transactions. Sometimes this is called selling rack space, and it is great for someone who wants to mine Bitcoin, or earn block rewards, without having to set up the equipment and monitor it, the hosting service takes care of the maintenance, and the ASIC owner receives the block rewards. Individuals can own several ASIC units, or just one, but the important part to understand is that the owner controls the ASIC's hash rate, they can send it to whatever mining pool they want, and they can change mining pools if they no longer agree with the mining pool operator as mentioned before. This basically means a power plant selling rack space could have 100s of ASIC units, each with a different owner, and many sending their hash rate to several different mining pools, this adds to the decentralization of Bitcoins blockchain overall, even though all the ASICs are in the same building, and getting power from the same source. While digitally these ASICs are decentralized, their physical location is not, and this would be a concern if eventually all Bitcoin mining farms were getting power from several large nuclear power plants, but there are other sources of cheap energy, and it is not likely Bitcoin miners will ever become this concentrated. This is because nuclear power is good, but it is expensive to build and operate, while hydropower can also generate large amounts of energy, and we will look at how they are doing this in Norway next.

Hydropower in Norway:

In Norway as of 2022, there are about a dozen large Bitcoin mining farms, most using hydropower as their energy source, and this is because hydropower makes up about 90% of the energy generation in the country. These mining farms used over 100MW of power in 2022, this made up for about 1% of Bitcoins total hash rate, and these numbers are expected to increase in the years to come, as more mining farms are set up in remote areas in the northern part of the country. These mining farms are not only earning Bitcoin block rewards, but they are also producing large amounts of heat, and this heat could be used in many different ways, like heating fish farms, greenhouses, and providing heat to residential districts. One large Bitcoin mining farm, Kryptovault, has one of its operations ducting heat to a local lumber mill, the heat is used to dry the lumber, and this is important in a cold environment, since if the heat from the ASICs did not dry the wood, some other fuel source would have to be used. While dissipating heat and keeping the ASICs cool is a challenge in warmer climates, it is easy in colder climates like Norway, and the heat they generate is a valuable resource for local residents and businesses, especially in the very cold winter months.

Most of Norway has the ability to generate hydropower, however most of the country's energy demand comes from southern Norway, and northern Norway does not have the ability to send some of its power south because of the distances involved. This is why more mining farms are looking at utilizing these energy sources that simply cannot be used by major cities because of their remote locations, making northern Norway more attractive to Bitcoin mining farms, but there are Bitcoin mining farms that are being incorporated into grids as well. Just like in Texas Bitcoin mining farms are being used to balance the grid, they are working with grid operators in a balancing market that allows them to be the demand side for grid power, basically this is what Bitcoin miners and grid operators did in Texas as mentioned before. There are many more examples of Bitcoin mining in Norway, and I would encourage further research for anyone looking to better understand how heat from the ASIC units is being used, and how these hydropower plants are generating power for both mining farms and gird customers.

Geothermal:

Geothermal energy is being used to power Bitcoin mining farms in El Salvador, geothermal power plants are similar to nuclear power plants in that a very hot source is used to turn water into steam, and this steam is used to spin generators that produce electricity. With nuclear power the heat source comes from the nuclear chain reaction, while with geothermal the heat comes from within the earth, and this heat provides a constant supply of steam, which provides a constant supply of electricity for the Bitcoin mining farms. El Salvador is ideal for geothermal energy generation, and they have been mining Bitcoin since 2021, at first, they had a very small hash rate, however they have continued to increase their hash power by expanding the power plant and adding more ASIC units to the mining farm. This is an ongoing project with 241MW of renewable energy planned, from both solar and wind, the project will cost about 1 billion dollars, and with funding they will continue to develop the geothermal power plant. El Salvador has decided to focus on the debt-free approach, with the first investment of about $250 million coming from Bitcoin industry leaders, and collaboration from top manufactures of renewable energy technology. The block rewards from the mining farm are to be split up, rather than paying investors a dollar amount, they will get a percent of the total Bitcoin block rewards, 27% is to be divided between investors, 23% will go to the government of El Salvador, and 50% will be reinvested into expanding energy production and improving the Bitcoin mining farm. This mining farm is still growing, if it reaches the goals set by the government, then this Bitcoin mining farm will be one of the largest in the world, and this is just a short description of what El Salvador will be doing in the future. From Bitcoin Beach, to their "Volcano energy," and plans for a Bitcoin city, I would encourage further research for anyone looking to better understand how El Salvador is adopting Bitcoin, Bitcoin mining, and renewable energy generation systems.

Geothermal power is also being considered in the U.S., with several companies in California and Texas offering what they call a "GreenFlash" service that retrofits oil and gas wells to generate geothermal energy, and they set up Bitcoin mining farms at these well sites that are no longer active, allowing well-owners to generate a profit even after their oil or gas well has reached its end-of-life. However, as mentioned before, Texas and many areas in North America, attracted Bitcoin mining farms because of their abundant energy sources, natural gas is one of those energy sources, and it is a popular energy source for many Bitcoin mining farms. So, while using oil and gas wells that are past their end-of-life is a good way to generate geothermal energy, many Bitcoin miners are using that natural gas as their energy source instead, and we will look at this in more detail next.

Flare Gas / Natural Gas:

Flare gas is the venting and burning of natural gas that comes from an oil well, these gasses are a byproduct of the oil well, and burning the gas or venting the gas is the only option for some oil wells. These gases are basically methane, a greenhouse gas that is more environmentally damaging than CO_2, and this is why the gas is burned, it prevents the more damaging greenhouse gases from being vented into the atmosphere. Depending on the oil well these gases can make up almost all the greenhouse gas emissions for a well site, and when the well site is close to a pipeline the gas can be sold to power plants, however when there is no pipeline the gas cannot be sold, and it is usually burnt or flared. This energy source could be used by anyone that needs somewhat large amounts of continuous energy, however piping the gas to a city is not possible at every well site, and anyone that wanted to use the energy would have to be physically located at the well site. Bitcoin mining farms that are enclosed in shipping containers have the ability to be moved to many remote well sites, all they need is an internet connection, and the natural gas or methane powers generators that provide continuous electricity for the ASIC units. Sometimes natural gas wells are considered "stranded" basically meaning it is too costly or impractical to build a pipeline, and this prevents the gas from being sold to power plants, but these stranded wells can be used to power Bitcoin mining farms. **(*Reference page 131*)** This gives stranded well sites a buyer when before there was none, and the same is true for flare gas from an oil well, this natural gas or methane can now be sold to Bitcoin mining farms, usually at cheaper rates since the gas cannot be used for anything else.

This type of remote natural gas powered Bitcoin mining farm is popular in several states such as, North Dakota, Montana, Colorado, and Texas. Texas being the largest state as far as oil and natural gas wells, many of which use flaring because they are too remote to transport the gas to buyers, and this has created a new source of profit for oil drilling companies, and the owners of wells past their end-of-life. Bitcoin mining farms are fairly mobile, all they need is power and an internet connection, and as mentioned before, when in the pod design these mining farms can be set up in just about any location, making them ideal for remote well sites. This energy source is great for mining farms, allowing them to hash transactions 24/7 without needing to shut down because of extreme grid demand, and this is because these remote locations are usually not connected to a major grid, otherwise the natural gas would be used to power that grid, and the well site would not be "stranded." Flare gas is a part of most oil wells today, all of them could be earning block rewards instead of just wasting that energy, and I would encourage further research for anyone looking to better understand how Bitcoin miners are tapping into previously unused energy sources such as flare gas or stranded natural gas.

Solar:

Solar power is another renewable energy source that can help power a Bitcoin mining farm, solar alone is not able to power a mining farm 24/7, but solar power can be used to offset a mining farm's energy cost. Although large batteries could be used to store some energy when the sun is not shining, this is another large cost in addition to the solar panels, and the ASIC units with their cooling systems, basically it can be done, but the costs to set up the mining farm would substantially increase. This is why solar power is usually incorporated into a grid with other sources of energy generation, and as mentioned before energy sources such as wind and solar are good, but they cause wear and tear on power plants as they increase or decrease their power generation based on grid demand, and whether the sun is shining, or the wind is blowing.

Bitcoin mining farms allow for power plants to keep the grid balanced even when energy sources such as solar are incorporated into the grid, these mining farms are basically a buyer of first and last resort for power plants, and they are ready to turn on to absorb additional energy on the grid, or turn off when the grid needs additional energy. There are other grid customers that can cut back their energy consumption if needed, but many can only reduce their energy usage, they do not stop using power completely, and they cannot do this with the flip of a switch like mining farms can. Many businesses could turn off their heating or cooling systems, but they would generally still need basic things like lighting, and without someone reducing their energy usage by a substantial amount, the grid could experience blackouts, causing businesses to lose power, even ones that reduced their energy usage. This is how Bitcoin mining farms can help every type of grid, not just ones that incorporate solar power, and next we will look at a simplified example to better understand how solar could be incorporated into a grid that also powers Bitcoin mining farms.

The example grid and city would be similar to the previous example, the city requires about 50w of energy for most of the day, with afternoon spikes to 60w, and the power plant can produce up to 200w, but it runs at its optimum efficiency around 120w, with Bitcoin mining farms using the additional energy on the grid. *(Reference page 131)* This city is located in a desert where afternoons in the summer cause even higher energy demand, the city also has very few cloudy days, and this is an ideal location for solar power since the city receives well over 300 days of sun a year. Although solar can be set up in just about any location, if that location has more sunny days then the grid would not be as stressed from solar panels producing energy then stopping, then starting again. But this does not mean solar should not be used in some areas, it just means the solar panels in this example city are in the ideal location for solar. The Bitcoin mining farms in this city have contracts with the power plant, they also set up solar panels near the mining farm, and during the night or off-peak hours the mining farm pulls energy from the grid. During the day when the sun is shining the mining farm would not need as much energy from the grid, and this would depend on the number of solar panels set up by the mining farm. But either way the solar would be offsetting the mining farm's energy needs from the grid, and this reduced demand from the mining farms would happen at the same time the grid is at peak demand. Simply put, in the desert when the sun is shining the city needs more energy to run air conditioners, this creates peak demand for the grid, and this sunlight is also what creates energy for the mining farm, allowing them to reduce the amount of energy needed from the grid. These mining farms would also be able to shut down during emergencies, allowing for the solar energy to be used by the grid if needed, and as mentioned before this would only be done in coordination with power plants when there was extreme grid demand. This is a simplified example, and it is similar to how girds in Texas and Norway are incorporating Bitcoin mining farms into the grid, and although large scale Bitcoin mining farms might not be able to create enough energy from solar alone, smaller and medium-sized mining farms could use solar as a way to offset their energy costs. The small mining farm I set up at my house incorporated 27 solar panels, and we will go over how this Bitcoin mining farm was built, its hash rate, cooling systems, and how much the solar was able to offset our energy bill next.

Our Bitcoin Mining Farm:

After about a year of researching Bitcoin and blockchain technology I convinced two friends to pool our modest Bitcoin gains and set up a small Bitcoin mining farm, in 2021 our three ASICs arrived, and we spent the next year or so setting up the mining farm and testing the cooling system's efficiency. Before we go over this process it is important to understand the mining farm was set up at a house I had just bought, with the intention of setting up a small mining farm so we could learn how it all works, and then moving on to set up a larger mining farm at another location once we knew what we were doing. This house had been a rental that had depreciated in value to a point where the owner either needed to reinvest in the property, or sell the home at a lower price due to the work that needed to be done, and after we were done with the mining farm, I would remodel the home. This was around the time when asset prices were increasing, the stock market, housing prices, and crypto prices were all going up, and at the time I had a rundown mobile home that I had just finished fixing up. I was able to sell the mobile home for more than 10 times what I paid because of the flood of buyers coming from California during the lockdowns, and I wanted to buy a house with the money while I could still lock in an interest rate around 3%. With the amount of quantitative easing being planned by the Federal Reserve at the time, I believed inflation was going to drive interest rates on mortgages higher, and many other things were happening at that time that further pushed me to learn about Bitcoin, invest in Bitcoin, and eventually set up a Bitcoin mining farm.

The main takeaway here is, the process of setting up this mining farm was full of trial and error, as we will go over, we started with an air-cooled system, and eventually set up the fluid cooled system. During this time, we put holes through interior walls and external walls, we ran the 220v electrical lines, and everything else needed, like Ethernet cables and thermometers to name a few. Basically, the house was a mining farm, 2 of the 3 bedrooms had hardware set up in them, the internet cables were run through the living room, and the garage became the workshop for building the fluid cooling systems. As we will go over, these ASICs and GPUs put off a lot of heat, with the doors closed the mining rooms were around 90-110 degrees depending on the time of year, and during the two winters we had them running I never had to turn on the central heater. The house was always around 80-90 degrees, even in the summer since the central AC unit I had was not enough to cool the house with the ASICs putting off the amount of heat that they did, although once we had set up the fluid cooling system the heat inside was not as bad, and I opened the door to allow the mining rooms heat to warm the house for the second winter.

The only reason we were able to set up this mining farm in a residential area was because we had the ASICs inside the house, when using an air-cooled system the fans are extremely loud, and if they had been outside the neighbors would most likely have complained, but the house insulated the noise pretty well, although obviously it was very noisy for anyone inside the home. I lived in the home with the mining farm during the entire process, the heat did not bother me, I enjoy the hot summers in the desert, but the noise was intense, and we did everything we could to reduce the amount of noise in the rest of the house. After switching cooling systems, the noise was no longer an issue, and the last 6 months of mining was not that bad, however it took a long time to get to that point, and next we will go over the process of setting up this mining farm and its cooling systems.

GPU Mining Rig:

In early 2021, before the ASICs were delivered, me and my two friends built a GPU mining rig, and we used it to hash transactions on the Ethereum blockchain. This mining rig had 6 GPUs with a combine hash rate of about 240 MH/s, Megahashes are one million hashes per second, and as mentioned before TH/s is one trillion hashes per second. So, you can clearly see the difference in computing power between GPUs and ASICs, although our GPUs were not top of the line, and there are GPUs that have higher hash rates. We will not go over how the mining rig was built, there are many resources that go over the process in detail, everything from the type of CPU required, to the power supply units that would be needed, and the noise and heat put off by the mining rig is not much compared to the ASICs, although these factors will increase as the number of GPUs is increased. With this hash rate, and the block reward rate from the Ethereum blockchain at the time, we were earning about 0.1 ETH every two weeks or so, and this payout period became longer as the hash rate increased on the Ethereum blockchain, by the end payouts were about once a month. We had the GPU rig running for a little over a year, during this time we stacked up ETH, and we used this ETH to help pay the power bill for the Bitcoin ASICs once we had them set up. The energy required for the GPU rig was next to nothing compared to the ASICs, just 10s of dollars a month, and the price of ETH was going up around this time, so we would sell the ETH each time its price had a sizable increase. We will not go over the GPU mining rig in detail, we had only set it up to learn how crypto mining worked before investing in the more expensive equipment, and we shut down the mining rig in 2022 when the Ethereum blockchain switched from POW to POS, we could have earned block rewards on another blockchain, but we decided to sell the GPUs instead. I would encourage further research for anyone looking to set up a GPU mining farm, if set up at scale GPU mining can be profitable, and these mining farms have the ability to switch between blockchains unlike ASIC units, this can increase the mining farm's profitability if they move their hash power to whatever blockchain has the best block rewards at any one point in time.

ASIC Hash Rate:

The 3 ASIC units we had were Canon Avalon 1146a's, they would usually have about 190 TH/s, and we had payouts of 0.01 BTC about every 2-3 weeks. This would vary depending on Bitcoins total hash rate, when we first set up the ASICs Bitcoin was at about 180,000,000 TH/s, with payouts about every 2-3 weeks, and then China banned Bitcoin mining as mentioned before, dropping the hash rate to 90,000,000 TH/s. During this short period, we saw payouts every 10-12 days, however as mentioned before Bitcoins hash rate recovered somewhat fast as mining farms moved from China to other areas of the world, and by the time we shut the ASICs down in late 2022 Bitcoins hash rate was over 200,000,000 TH/s. *(Reference page 106)* By this time our payouts were happening about every 4-5 weeks, and as mentioned before, it is important to understand we were not getting paid less block rewards, it just took us longer to reach the 0.01 threshold for a payout from the mining pool we were sending our hash power to. If we had added another ASIC unit our hash power would have increased, and our payout periods would become shorter, but instead we went from 2 payouts a month to about one a month, and this is how an increasing hash rate affects smaller mining farms, our power bill was fixed, but our block rewards were fewer and fewer each month.

Solar:

I had half of my roof covered with as many solar panels as possible, the 27 solar panels generated about 9000w, the same amount of energy required for the 3 ASICs, and they offset our power costs by about 25-30%, the amount of power drawn from the grid at night made up about 75% of our bill. These numbers varied since some months we would have the ASICs off for several days or weeks while we were working on the cooling systems, during those months the power bill was obviously less, and for the several months that we were running for the entire month our power bill was over $1000. We had the ETH block rewards to cover most of the bill, and I would pay for any difference with dollars, some mining farms will sell some of their block rewards to pay the power bill, however we decided to hold on to the few hundred dollars' worth of BTC for the several months we were short. Basically, our margins were very tight, if we did not have 9000w for about 8 hours a day from the solar, our power bill would have been even higher. The area the mining farm was located in is an ideal area for solar, with over 300 days of sun a year, meaning if this same mining farm was set up in an area with more cloudy days its power bill might only be offset by 20% or 10% depending on the location. We looked into getting batteries so we could store energy from the solar panels and run the ASICs at night too, meaning we would not be pulling energy from the grid, but the cost was not worth it in our opinion. The solar set-up cost about $33,000, and the batteries were estimated to be over $60,000, so this was not an option for us at the time, and the gird power we have comes from the Colorado River. So, even though the solar only generated energy when the sun was shining, hydropower is what powered the grid, meaning technically our mining farm was run on 100% renewable energy, and we will look at our mining farms energy requirements in more detail next.

ASIC Cooling:

Each ASIC unit required about 3000w, we had 3 in total, but we started with 2 ASICs using the fans that came with them as our cooling system, and we later added the 3rd as we improved our air-cooled system. We knew the ASICs were hot and loud from our research, but we were not prepared for the amount of heat that these ASICs put off, and the AC unit we had bought was not even close to what we would end up needing. The AC unit was able to cool a 1500 sq ft garage, the bedroom was less than 100 sq ft, we cut a hole in the bedroom wall to install it, and even with it running continuously the mining room was over 90 degrees. We opened a window when it became hot enough to cause the ASICs to go offline, but we could not always do this because of the noise, and because the outside temperature was increasing and sometimes hotter than the room. During the first winter we could keep 2 ASICs cool enough with just the AC unit by ducting the cool air directly to the ASIC units, this worked for a short period, but as the outside temperature increased, so did the mining room's temperature, causing them to overheat and go offline. This caused our hash rate to drop and affected how many block rewards we would earn, so we cut another hold in the wall, and instead of ducting the cool air to the ASICs, we ducted the heat directly from them to the outside. The fans on the ASICs are about 5 inches in size, and our units had four of them, two of them pulling in air, and two pushing air out of the computer, running the cool air over the circuits. So, we had 6 pipes running through the hole in the wall, this vented most of the heat out of the room, however the room's temperature was still somewhat hot, the ASICs themselves radiate heat, and even with the AC unit running, the room was still about 80-90 degrees, and very loud with their 12 fans running.

These fans were moving the air from inside the bedroom to outside the house, when we just had the AC unit running, that air was being recycled within the room, and these new air ducts were creating a negative pressure in my house. At first, we opened the window a little and this allowed for outside air to come into the room to replace the air being forced out by the fans on the ASICs, and this only worked for a few days, the outside temperature was getting hotter, causing the ASICs to overheat and go offline. When the window was not open the bedroom door would not stay closed, I used a bungee cord to try and hold it shut, but the negative pressure in the room forced it open a few inches, and so I had to cut a few four-inch holes through some interior walls to allow for air flow to replace the air leaving the mining room. During this time the sound was intense, the door and interior walls with a little sound proofing were all that cut down on the noise, and the high pitch of the ASICs was tough to deal with, but the heat dissipation was the bigger issue, if the ASICs overheated, they would go offline, while the noise only affected me, not our block rewards. As summer approached it became obvious all air-cooled systems would not be an option for us, the AC unit also needed power, so adding more AC units would only increase our power bill, and this is when we started looking into fluid cooling systems.

Dielectric Fluid Cooling:

During the several months that we were changing the air-cooled systems I was researching dielectric fluid cooling, it seemed to be the answer to our cooling problems, but we were not sure if it would work in the extreme desert temperatures. At this time dielectric fluid cooling was somewhat new, the fluid we used was developed in 2017, but there were few people building cooling systems like this, and although we could have bought a prebuilt tank and pumps, the few manufactures there were at the time were not great. Some cooling systems had many of the same problems we later discovered, and when bought from China refunds or customer support was nonexistent, so this led us to building the cooling system ourselves. But in just the last few years several manufactures have started selling something similar to what we built, so there are now better and cheaper options for dielectric fluid cooling systems, and I would not recommend some of the equipment we used, although it did work. Before we go over the several set-ups we had, let's get a better idea of what a dielectric fluid cooling system does, and how it is able to cool the ASICs that are putting off a lot of heat.

First, the liquid is an oil not water, oil does not conduct electricity, and it is more efficient than air when it comes to dissipating heat, technically vegetable oil could be used, but we went with Bitcool-888, it was designed to not be corrosive to the rubber and plastic components in the ASIC units. This oil fills a tank with several ASIC units in it, as they hash transactions they create heat, the hot oil rises to the top of the tank and overflows into a smaller tank where pumps force the oil through radiators. These radiators act like car radiators in that a fan moves air across the radiator fins removing the heat from the liquid being moved through the radiator. After passing through the radiator the cool oil is pumped directly under the ASIC units, this cool oil quickly absorbs the heat coming off the ASICs, keeping them cool, and then the hot oil overflows into the smaller tank and the process repeats. This is the basic concept, and our set-up was similar, however we had to redesign our system a few times through trial and error, we would set up the system and see how the ASICs did, monitoring their hash rate and temperature.

Our first set up was a horse trough, a car radiator, and a small pond pump, we put the horse trough in the mining room, and the car radiator was on the other side of the wall outside. At first, we had built a false bottom with holes to allow for the cool oil to enter the tank, but we decided on directly piping the cool oil to the bottom of the 3 ASIC units instead. After our cooling issues with the air-cooled setup, we wanted to

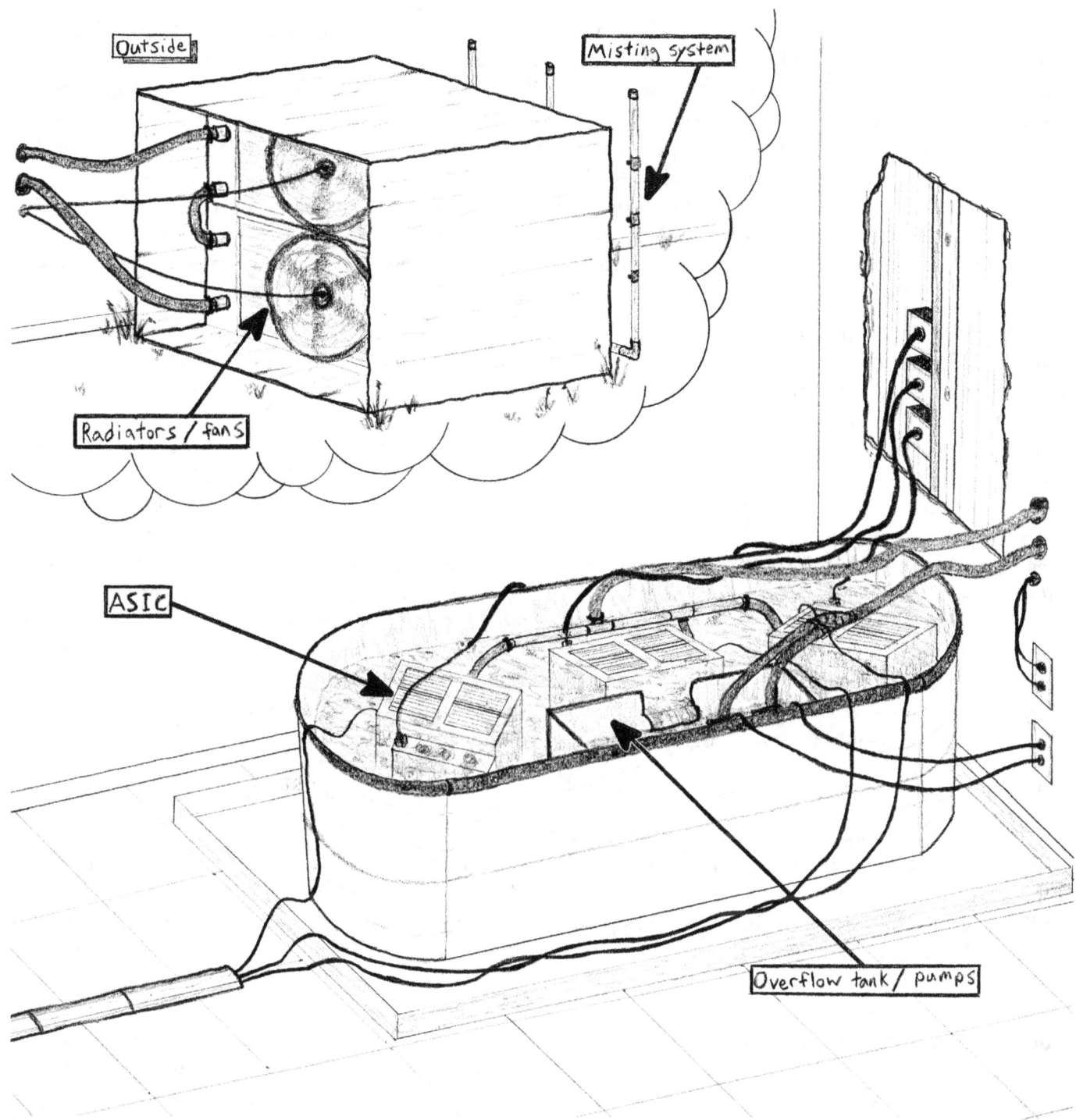

Our Bitcoin Mining Farm

This is the mining farm I had in my house, we had a pan under the horse trough that held the dielectric fluid, and inside the trough we had the overflow tank and the three ASICs. We opened up the exterior wall so we could run the power lines, we also punched through the wall to run the piping outside, and the internet cables ran into the next room where the router and GPU rig was set up. The fans on the car radiators required power, as well as the pumps in the overflow tank, and this was the set-up we had that allowed us to run all three ASICs with few issues. The misters were located on the other side of the radiators, and they are what kept us hashing transactions for some of the hottest months in the Mohave desert.

make sure we were using the cool oil as efficiently as possible, given the materials we were working with. I soldered copper piping linking the radiator to the tank and ASIC units, we used sheet metal to make a small overflow box and put it in the tank with the ASICs as well, and in the overflow box we put about 50 lbs. of weight to keep the box from rising to the top of the tank, as well as the pond pump. The pump was also connected to the radiator with copper piping, basically the hot oil in the overflow tank was pumped through the car radiator, and the cool oil went back into the horse trough directly under the ASICs, this was a continuous loop that keep the ASICs cool and heat was dissipated outside through the radiator. This system worked with two of the ASICs hashing transactions, but when we turned the 3rd one on the tank's temperature would increase to a point where the ASICs would go offline, cool down and restart again, and this affected our hash rate and block rewards.

We had a thermometer in the overflow box, the hot side, and one inside the pipe of cool oil coming into the tank, the cold side, as well as a thermometer outside, and I would record these temperatures every few hours during our testing. Also during this time, we researched on Reddit to try and find out what the issue was, simply put we need a certain number of gallons per hour, GPH, flowing through the radiator in order to cool our 3 ASICs, and even thought the pump was strong enough it was not able to keep them cool. We soon found out the 90-degree angles in the copper piping was reducing the GPH, we had over a dozen of them and each one reduced the pump's efficiency, and we had noticed that during the afternoon high temperatures the two ASICs would also go offline for short periods of time. Basically, the outside air was hotter, and not able to cool the oil in the radiator as much, meaning the ASICs would overheat in the afternoons more often as summer got closer, and this was when we decided to do our first rebuild of the fluid cooling system, since summer temperatures were only getting hotter and hotter. Completely removing the copper pipe I had just soldered a few months before, only to spend more money on new flexible piping was discouraging, but it is part of the process, and failures will happen. If they end the journey to your goal then they are bad, however if they are but milestones along the path to reaching your goal, then they are good, and can be used to measure your progress, as long as you have learned from them.

Dielectric Fluid Cooling 2.0:

We wanted to make sure we were not right at the temperature threshold for the ASICs, so in addition to removing the copper piping, we added a second car radiator and second pond pump, and we ran flexible piping that could withstand the high oil temperatures and did not restrict the pump's GPH. The second radiator would allow for more heat to be dissipated, and the second pond pump was needed to force the oil through the additional radiator, this worked overall, and we had all 3 ASICs hashing transactions, until the summer temperatures started reaching around 100 degrees. Even when outside temperatures were high, we would not shut down all the ASICs, usually just running 2 of them instead of 3, but after the new piping, additional radiator, and additional pond pump, we were running all 3 ASICs with few issues, until mid-2022 when the outside temperature started to increase. This increase did not cause the ASICs to go offline right away, anything under 100 degrees for the outside temperature was no problem for our cooling system, the oil temps would increase, and so would the ASICs, but these temperatures were still just under the threshold to knock them offline, and we will go over these numbers in more detail later. For now, just understand we were able to keep the ASICs cool and hashing transactions, and we were making small minor adjustments to the cooling system during this time. But as summer approached, we started seeing above 100 degree temperatures, and it was clear we would need further cooling if we were to keep the ASICs online.

Our two car radiators had fans on them running continuously, this is what cooled the oil passing through the radiator, and as the outside temperature increased the air flowing through the radiator was hotter, reducing its ability to cool the oil. This is when we added a mister system to the radiators and fans, by spraying the radiator with water for just a few minutes, the cool oil temperature would drop drastically, and at first, we had them misting water for 5 minutes out of every hour during the daytime, and we soon realized if we ran the misters at night we would get higher hash rates too. By misting the radiator with water heat was removed from the oil much faster, and this very cold oil temperature allows the ASICs to increase their computing power, basically allowing for higher hash rates, and that means more block rewards for the same amount of power. At first, we used the misters sparingly, they did cause a mineral buildup on the radiators over time, we have very hard water in my city, and I had to use a pressure washer to clean the radiators of the mineral buildup. However, as daytime temperatures started reaching 100 degrees and the night barely dropping below 80 degrees, we started using the misters more and more, and this was not that bad, it just required some cleaning, and it was keeping the ASICs cool and online hashing transactions.

As we got into summer the misters went from 5 minutes out of every hour, to 5 minutes out of every 30 minutes, and at peak summer temperatures of about 120 degrees we were running the misters 5 minutes on, and 5 minutes off. The hottest outside temperature recording I have was 117 degrees, and during these nights the outside temperature was still around 90 degrees, meaning our ASICs were still online, but not running at the higher hash rates seen during the cooler evening temperatures in the earlier months. These extreme temperatures only last for a month or two in the summer, and I would adjust the misters based on the ASIC temperatures, keeping them in their ideal range. This mister system, along with the other components of our cooling system, allowed for us to keep the ASICs online hashing transactions for about 3 of the hottest months of summer, and as outside temperatures began to fall in September 2022, keeping the ASICs cool was no longer a problem. Although, Bitcoins total hash rate had increased by then, meaning our cooling systems were working, but even with the ASICs running 24/7 our block rewards were only paying out about once a month, and this was not enough in dollar terms to cover the power bill. With the ETH just about all sold, and our block rewards reduced because of the ever-increasing total hash rate, we decided to shut down the mining farm, and I began remodeling the home.

Education:

Throughout the process of setting up the mining farm we learned a lot, and each improvement increased the mining farm's profitability, for example, the AC unit used about as much power as one of the ASICs, so when we switched to the fluid cooling system, we actually saw our power bill reduced a little. Even though the radiator fans and the pumps require power, it was far less then what was required for the AC unit. However, the equipment required for the dielectric fluid cooling system was expensive compared to the air-cooled systems, the AC was about $750, while the horse trough was $200, the car radiators were $750 each, $60 for replacement fans, and the oil was just over $2,000. Meaning the fluid cooling system had a high up-front cost, and this does not include the many other additional onetime costs of flexible piping, pumps, power converters etc. but once set up and running efficiently, this cooling system eventually allowed for us to run all 3 ASICs with no issues, and even allowed for higher hash rates when outside temperatures were cooler.

Even before the summer of 2022 we knew we would most likely have to shut down by the end of the year, this was based on the increasing hash rate, even once we had perfected the cooling system the amount of block rewards we earned each month was fewer and fewer, and we would need to sell most of the block rewards just to cover the power bill. We realized this before summer, but we wanted to see if we could keep the ASICs cool enough in the extreme desert temperatures, so we kept working on our cooling system, and we started joking the mining farm was an experiment now. There was no way this mining farm would be profitable after the Bitcoin halving in 2024, we had hoped to remain online until then, but the increasing hash rate sped up the process, and this is normal for small mining farms that are not able to scale up with the increasing total hash rate. During this time, we would joke about how we could just buy Bitcoin, we would get more BTC than we could possibly earn from the mining farm, but we already had the equipment, most of it was set up, and we decided to just go for it and continue building the cooling system. The education we were gaining from the process of building the mining farm was now more valuable than dollars or block rewards, although we were still earning BTC, and we continued to slowly grow our small stack.

If we had investors that were looking for any kind of annual return on their investment we would not have been able to keep the mining farm online for as long as we did. As mentioned before it is best to think in terms of BTC rather than dollars, and if an investor has a dollar amount they hope to get from their investment in a small Bitcoin mining farm, then the mining farm will have problems remaining profitable. As block rewards are sold there is more risk of Bitcoins price falling and the mining farm not being able to afford the power bill, requiring further capital from the investor, or the small mining farm would have to shut down. However, we had a goal of holding onto as much BTC as possible, and after one of our partners finishes his contract with the Navy in 10 years, we will split the block rewards we have earned, basically the amount of dollars we put into the mining farm is greater than the current value of the block rewards we earned. However, our plan going in was not to require a return on that investment for several halving cycles, other mining farms might need to compensate investors sooner, and if paid in dollars then the block rewards would need to be sold. But if payment was in BTC, then simply holding the coins on a self-custody wallet for long periods of time could be the investors return on their investment.

By the time we shut down the mining farm we had proven our cooling system worked by keeping the ASICs online and cool for the hottest months of summer in the Mohave desert, and we had stacked up a small amount of BTC in the process, but the greatest thing I gained from this experience was knowledge. I was now better able to understand how POW blockchains work, and not just the digital side being a validator in the blockchain's consensus method, but also the physical side, dealing with the hardware and the systems that keep them cool and online. We could now take this knowledge and move on to scaling up to a larger Bitcoin mining farm, knowing the temperature thresholds for ASICs, and knowing how to efficiently remove that heat allows for mining farms to be scaled to any size, and this later led to the quote for the larger Bitcoin mining farm that was mentioned before. Next, we will go over some of the temperature numbers we had, how they affected the ASICs and their hash rate overall, and how these numbers were affected by the several improvements that were made to the cooling system over this period.

Temperatures and Noise:

We started with an air-cooled system, as mentioned before this was just one ASIC in my spare bedroom with the wall mounted AC unit, and this worked in the cooler winter months at the time. However, when we turned on the second ASIC the room's temperature would increase to well over 100 degrees, and the ASICs would overheat and go offline. This was when we started ducting the cool air directly into the ASICs, doing this and slightly opening the window would allow the heat to leave the room, and we were able to keep the two ASICs cool. We tried turning on the 3rd ASIC, but it would heat the room to a point where the ASICs would start going offline, and at this time the outside temperature was increasing into the high 80s, this ment that keeping the window open a little was no longer an option. This is what led to us ducting the hot air out of the room as mentioned before, this allowed us to run all three ASICs without over heating them on a constant basis, and this cooling system worked for a few months, but the ASIC temperatures were increasing as the outside temperature slowly got hotter. The AC unit was not as efficient as the outside temperature increased, and soon we could only keep two ASICs running without overheating, until we decided to switch to the fluid cooling system as mentioned before, and this completely removed the noise from the ASIC fans. We had put up some foam sound proofing squares, and we hung a heavy blanket over the door, this helped reduce the noise from the ASIC fans, but it was not great, and once we had the fluid cooling system set up the sound proofing was no longer needed, and we started to test this new cooling system.

The fluid cooling system worked for only 2 ASICs at first, turning on the 3rd ASIC would cause the oil in the horse trough to increase and cause them to go offline, this is when we replaced the copper pipes with flexible tubing and added the second radiator and second pond pump as mentioned before, and the room was now much cooler and there was next to no noise. The car radiators made a little more noise than a few AC condensers that run 24/7, and in the desert, everyone is used to the noise that these condensers make. The bedroom was also much cooler, about 80 degrees or so, and this heat came from the oil in the horse trough that was always around 100 degrees or more, and this heat was radiated out into the room.

Rough Temperature Numbers:

Most of the temperature numbers are in Celsius since this is the unit of measurement the ASICs used, we switched our digital thermometers to also use Celsius, and this made it easier to make our cooling adjustments, below is a rough conversion chart from Celsius to Fahrenheit for those that need it.

C = F
15 = 59
20 = 68
30 = 86
40 = 104
50 = 122
60 = 140
70 = 158

We will go over some rough temperature numbers for days that we saw the ASICs overheat and go offline, and we will also go over some rough temperature numbers when the outside temperature was cooler, and we were able to keep them online. The cooler outside temperatures were obviously in the winter months, and the hotter temperatures were in the summer months, and the misters played a big part in allowing us to adjust the amount of cooling the oil received from the radiator in the summer. These two examples will have rough numbers as far as the temperatures, I found it easier to just check oil temperatures rather than checking the ASIC temperatures, and once we had the misters set up, I could adjust the cooling based on these numbers. This was needed in the last few summer months when we were hugging the upper temperature threshold for the ASICs, we were keeping them just cool enough to stay online hashing transactions, and this was possible because the misters once turned on would cause the cold oil temperatures to drop almost 10c instantly. Although this would depend on the outside temperature, in the cold winter temperatures this was about 10c, and in the extreme summer temperatures it would only reduce the cold side by about 5c. And this was only for the oil temperatures, the ASICs would only be cooled up to 5c or so in the winter, and during the summer it was even less. The misters allowed me to monitor the oil temperatures throughout the day and if needed I could knock down the high oil temperatures by running the misters for a 5-minute period on top of their set schedule. This would usually only need to be done in the hot afternoon temperatures of early summer, until we set the misters to 5 minutes on and 5 minutes off during the few weeks of near 120 degree temperatures in mid-summer.

According to the Canaan Avalon 1146 operating manual, the ambient temperature cannot exceed 35c, and the chip temperature cannot exceed 85c. We found these numbers to be conservative and inexact, and the following numbers came from my own personal observations and recordings. These rough oil temperatures for the cold side were, anything above 40c and the ASICs would start to lose hash power, and as the temperature got close to 50c the ASICs would start to go offline. While on the hot side, we found that we would start to lose hash power around 50c, the ASICs would start to go offline around 55c, and when the temperatures reached 60c all ASICs would be offline. The cold oil temperatures were pretty accurate, the thermometer was inside the pipe between the radiator and the horse trough, although this does not mean the ASICs were cooled to this exact temperature, and the hot side was accurate as far as the oil temperature in the overflow tank, but the ASICs themselves were usually hotter than this temperature. We could monitor the temperature of each ASIC through our dashboard, they would usually drop in hash power around 60c, go offline around 70c, and these numbers lined up with a hot oil temperature of about 55-58c. I found it easier to make adjustments based on the cold and hot oil temperatures rather than checking the ASICs through the dashboard, this is why both examples only refer to oil temperatures. It is important to remember we were working with what we had available, the horse trough worked great as a tank for the oil and ASICs, but it allowed for a lot of extra oil to sit around the ASICs, retaining heat and not flowing through the radiator in a fast cycle. This is why custom-built tanks are made to exactly fit the ASIC units, this prevents additional oil from retaining heat, so our oil temperatures might be slightly off compared to other dielectric fluid cooling systems that were purpose built, but either way, these are the numbers that would keep our ASICs online, or cause them to go offline.

Temperature Recordings:

With an outside temperature of about 39c, the cold oil side would be in the low 40s for most of the day, and in the afternoon the cold side would reach the high 40s, while the hot side would be about 50c for most of the day, and in the afternoon it would reach about 55c, this is when we would see the ASICs go offline, usually one or two at a time, and they would come back online once they had cooled down. On days like these I would check the temperatures about every hour or two during the day, during the night we did not have overheating issues as much. Once we had the misters set up, during the hottest hours of the day I would make adjustments to them if needed, usually just running them for a 5-minute period when the hot side got above 53c. This would drop the oil temperatures, and the hot side would usually fall back to at least 50c for an hour or so, but this depended on the outside temperature, when we were at the extreme summer highs the misters were running 5 minutes on and 5 minutes off as mentioned before, and this would only keep our hot oil temperatures in the mid-50s. Just below the threshold keeping the ASICs online and hashing transactions, although at a lower hash rate then during the summer nights, when the oil could be cooled to lower temperatures.

With an outside temperature of about 20c, the cold oil side would be about 30-35c for most of the day, and in the afternoon the cold side would reach about 40c, while the hot side would be about 40c for most of the day, and in the afternoon it would reach into the high 40s. Well below the threshold to knock the ASICs offline, and during these temperatures we would have a higher hash rate, nothing big, just over 200 TH/s during the colder nights in late 2022. During this time there was little maintenance required, I still checked the temperatures a few times a day since it was easy for me to do in-between the research and writing I was doing at the time, but it was not really needed, we had the fluid cooling system up and running efficiently by this point. This is also when we started to notice the higher hash rates we could get at night if we set the misters to go off a few times, but it was cold outside temperatures, high winds, and the little light rain the desert gets that saw our highest hash rate. We would only achieve the 230 TH/s rate for periods of time with cold temperatures and the few storms that happened towards the end of 2022, one of these cold nights we saw outside temperatures of 9-10c, with a cold oil temperature of 27-28c, and a hot oil temperature of 33-34c. The desert does not stay cool for long, and these outside temperatures around 10c only happened a handful of nights, but for the rest of the winter months in 2022 there was a noticeable average increase to about 200 TH/s from the normal 190 TH/s we saw during the early months on the air-cooled system. During the extreme summer temperatures, our hash rate varied a little, and they would have a hash rate closer to 150 TH/s during the days, and then increase a little at night.

Mining Farm Conclusion:

We spent about as much BTC on the ASICs as we earned from them over this period, but we also had other equipment costs, and in hindsight it would have been better for us to just buy Bitcoin and hold it rather than set up a small mining farm to earn block rewards. However, much like gold mining, sometimes small mining farms are profitable, and sometimes they are not, it just depends on the price of Bitcoin at the time along with many other factors, and this is similar for gold and gold mines, their profitability is determined by the price of gold at the time. Overall, Bitcoins increasing hash rate means that smaller mining farms will be weeded out and will not be profitable unless they have very cheap energy costs, basically it's all about scaling up a mining farm, or increasing the total number of ASICs and their hash power. If this is not the long-term goal, then an investor would be better off just buying and holding Bitcoin rather than mining it, unless the cost for energy is very cheap, and in that case small mining farms with low hash rates could still be profitable, but they would have very long payout periods. But I am glad we took the time to understand the technology rather than just buying Bitcoin, we gained knowledge, we even earned a little Bitcoin along the way, and I will have a newly renovated home ready to put up for sale in the near future.

Being a part of Bitcoins consensus method was a very fun experience in hindsight, although it was a lot of work, and I now have a better understanding as to why this type of consensus method is called proof of work. It was stressful when we had to redo work that we had done on the cooling systems, it took a lot of time, and a lot of money to eventually keep the ASICs cool in the desert temperatures, but looking back I believe the experience has added to my overall understanding of the Bitcoin blockchain. I might not know how to do the coding, but I know the importance of mining farms and their hash power in a POW blockchain,

Bitcoins code will not be changed or updated without support from mining farms like ours, and it made me feel like I was a part of the Bitcoin blockchain. Although our mining farm was just a very small part of Bitcoins consensus method, only about 200 TH/s of the 200,000,000 TH/s that Bitcoins hash rate had reached by the time we shut down the mining farm, and this is similar to my small part in the overall military. These mining farms require hard work, no matter how small of a part they play in the consensus method they are important, and just like in the military someone needs to do the hard work, even if it is tough and no one else wants to. The military pays it soldiers for their hard work, and so does Bitcoin, anyone that puts in the work to hash transactions on the Bitcoin blockchain will be compensated in block rewards, as long as they are only hashing transactions and not trying to push invalid transactions as mentioned before. If someone does not want to do this work, then they can just simply use the Bitcoin blockchain to hold and increase their wealth overtime, or utilize Bitcoins use cases as they are developed and implemented in the future.

Small mining farms can be thought of as small data centers, except these data centers are not owned by a large company, these smaller individually controlled mining farms allow the Bitcoin blockchain a resource that other networks do not have, and this is individuals that are independently incentivized to hash transactions and keep the blockchain going. *(Reference page 88)* Simply put, this is because as validators go offline the remaining validators earn more block rewards, and this is constantly happening on the Bitcoin blockchain, however if the hash rate ever dropped by a large amount many smaller mining farms would want to start hashing transactions to earn the higher block reward rate. This is something that is not possible in a traditional network of data centers, if the network had a few data centers go offline then information on the network would slow or stop completely, and there would not be other individually controlled data centers coming online to keep the network running. However, Bitcoins consensus method allows for anyone to set up a mining farm and hash transactions on the Bitcoin blockchain, and it compensates them in the form of block rewards as mentioned before, this is the incentive for the mining farm. This type of compensation is not possible for traditional data centers as we know them today, where companies own and operate their own hardware, and this is what prevents individuals from being a part of the network, also preventing them from coming online to help the network when it needs it most. An example was mentioned before when China banned Bitcoin mining, many smaller mining farms were somewhat like minutemen for the Bitcoin blockchain, coming online when they were needed most, and this makes it very hard to stop the Bitcoin blockchain. As long as there are block rewards to be earned, there will be individuals around the world setting up small mining farms to hash transactions if their energy costs are low enough, and as transaction fees increase on the Bitcoin blockchain, these rewards will increase as well, ensuring Bitcoins consensus method will be secure for many decades to come.

Bitcoin Conclusion:

The Bitcoin blockchain has many aspects, as do many other blockchains, and the Bitcoin blockchain is valued in several ways, at the end of the day Bitcoins price is agreed upon by buyers and sellers, in many marketplaces globally. It is also valued by users of the Bitcoin blockchain, this value can also come from Bitcoins price, or it can come from the use case on the Bitcoin blockchain, and we will go over use cases for blockchains in more detail later. For now just understand, some people find value in the Bitcoin blockchain based off the value of its unit of account, some people find value in use cases such as ordinals, and some people find value in setting up a Bitcoin mining farm that earns Bitcoin block rewards. Basically, some people will trade Bitcoin, some will use the Bitcoin blockchain, and some will be a part of the Bitcoin blockchain by either setting up a node or a few Bitcoin ASICs, and it is all these factors together that drive Bitcoins adoption, growth, and increasing value. If someone finds value in the Bitcoin blockchain, in whatever aspect of the blockchain, then they will interact with the Bitcoin blockchain, and as they do, there will be fewer and fewer Bitcoin available in the circulating supply, further pushing price to the upside, and this increasing value drives other aspects of the blockchain such as the miners earning block rewards that are paid in BTC.

This upward price pressure will continue for the next 100 plus years, although there will be ups and downs over each halving cycle, as Bitcoins price increases more mining farms become profitable as mentioned before, and the block rewards these mining farms earn is the only new supply of Bitcoin, this supply is reducing as demand globally is increasing. Even if one country bans Bitcoin, other countries will continue to buy and sell Bitcoin, and this means there will always be some form of demand for Bitcoins unit of account. As mentioned before Bitcoin is used alongside the U.S. dollar in El Salvador, and other countries banning Bitcoin would not affect its use by people in El Salvador. The Bitcoin halving plays a part in this price pressure to the upside as well, if supply was constant then a price balance could be reached since there would be no major supply increases or decreases. Although Bitcoins price could still rise as more individuals start holding some of their wealth in Bitcoin, this reduces the circulating supply, and is what creates price pressure to the upside. However, Bitcoins supply is in not increasing at a constant rate, the halving reduces the block rewards by 50% every 4 years, and this creates a supply shock that is a factor in several types of cycles on the Bitcoin blockchain.

Bitcoin Cycles:

Bitcoins halving and difficulty adjustment create cycles for the Bitcoin blockchain, the more noticeable cycles are created by the Bitcoin halving every 210,000 blocks as mentioned before, and these cycles do not always directly line up with having event itself. As mentioned before, Bitcoins price cycles tend to peak many months after the actual halving date, while smaller mining farms feel the effects right away from the reduced block rewards. While some aspects of the Bitcoin blockchain are barely affected at all, like Bitcoins total hash rate, which has continued to increase and seems unfazed in the long term by price drops or the halving event. *(Reference page 106)* Many of these cycles play a part in Bitcoins overall adoption cycle, each time Bitcoins price has a large increase more investors become interested, the same is true for people interested in mining Bitcoin, and both of these benefit the Bitcoin blockchain. It brings many new people into the space, some might sell Bitcoin as the price starts to decline after the peak, and many mining farms will be weeded out by the reducing block rewards and increased hash rate over the 4-year period. But with each new wave of individuals interacting with the Bitcoin blockchain, some will decide to be in it for the long term, further adding to the number of long-term Bitcoin hodlers, and mining farms that will increase their efficiency allowing them to hash transactions and secure Bitcoin's blockchain for many halvings into the future.

The adoption cycle for Bitcoin is made up of these waves of new users, these users can either come from investors chasing the price tops, or from new use cases on the Bitcoin blockchain such as ordinals, even new ways to invest in Bitcoin such as Bitcoin ETFs, and all of these will create more demand for Bitcoins unit of account. This is why Bitcoins max limit of 21 million coins is so important for it to have steady price pressure to the upside over time, all new demand could be absorbed if the new supply of coins was increased or at least set to a constant fixed new supply. But Bitcoins halving creates the opposite effect, and this means even if Bitcoins demand was not growing, price would still be able to hold or increase because of the reducing supply over time. *(Reference page 103)* However, as mentioned before there are over 8 billion people on the planet, about 4 billion have access to the internet, and that is all that is needed to access the Bitcoin blockchain. Over the last decade Bitcoins unit of account has been dispersed through many individuals buying and selling the coin, basically this is a fair launch, and it allows for the price discovery of Bitcoins unit of account. The Satoshi wallets could pose a short-term risk to this price discovery as mentioned before, although this is unlikely and would not affect Bitcoins price in the long term. So as more and more people hold their wealth in the Bitcoin blockchain, and as more use cases allow for more people to interact with the Bitcoin blockchain, there will be fewer Bitcoin in the market of buyers and sellers, leading to the upward price pressure over time.

An example of this is some BTC that I hold on a self-custody wallet, I never plan on selling this BTC, and I will pass it on to my sister and nieces regardless of its value in dollar terms. I also have other BTC, on several types of wallets, that I would be willing to sell back into circulating supply, when the dollar value of the Bitcoin has reached an amount that allows me to invest that wealth into something I want like real estate, and until then I will hold the small amount of BTC regardless of its price in the short term.

Basically, as more people start to hold their wealth in the Bitcoin blockchain, there will be more people that decide to hold that Bitcoin for long periods of time, and with larger numbers of people doing this, Bitcoins circulating supply will be further reduced, keeping price pressure to the upside. It's important to remember his takes place over long periods of time and requires holding Bitcoin, not trading it or trying to time price tops. While these actions might allow the investor to increase their wealth in dollar terms, this buying and selling does not create the same price pressure to the upside as long-term hodling does, and most investors usually do not gain wealth from trying to time the markets, unless they dedicate a lot of time to studying the charts. Eventually with enough time, this idea of holding long term in order to increase an investor's wealth will become a self-fulfilling prophecy, simply put, as more people hold long term, there is fewer Bitcoin in circulating supply, and over several halving cycles that Bitcoin that was held long term will be worth orders of magnitude more in dollar terms. Again, this takes place over long periods of time, and there are other ways to increase your wealth faster by trading Bitcoin, but there is added risk in doing so. This means each individual should decide how their wealth is stored on the Bitcoin blockchain, and this long-term wealth storage in the Bitcoin blockchain allows for individuals to pass on generational wealth, if they are patient enough.

Long-Term Wealth Storage:

If someone was able to hold an amount of Bitcoin over several decades, then they would want to make sure that BTC was on a self-custody wallet. As mentioned before exchanges or 3rd party wallets have control over their account holder's wealth, and even if the 3rd party wallet does not use an account holders wealth today, they have the ability to, and over several decades companies and their platforms can change. Someone that was able to save up Bitcoin over many years on a 3rd party wallet, might eventually lose that BTC if the 3rd party to that wealth fails in some way, and this would prevent the individual from creating generational wealth, although it might not if the 3rd party did not fail in some way. Basically, there is a possibility that the wealth in the 3rd party wallet could be lost over long periods of time, either by mistake or intentionally if the exchange is exploited, and there are risks for self-custody wallets as well, like forgetting or losing the seed phrase as mentioned before. Ultimately it will be up to each individual to decide how to hold their wealth held in the Bitcoin blockchain, self-custody wallets, 3rd party wallets, or even in the form of an ETF, there are many options, each with pros and cons based on the individual investor and their plans for that wealth. Self-custody wallets would be the best option, because of the long periods of time involved, no one knows what the future will be like, so keeping as much control over your wealth as possible would be best practice, and let's look at a simple example to understand how holding wealth in the Bitcoin blockchain can allow for generational wealth growth.

In this example, a single mother working two jobs saves the little she has in the Bitcoin blockchain, even if it is just a few dollars' worth of BTC each week or month, and she holds this Bitcoin on a self-custody wallet that only she has access to. Over the years the stack of BTC will grow, the dollar value will rise and fall, but the amount of BTC will continue to increase, and in an emergency she could still access the wealth, although her goal is to pass the wealth on to her children, so she tries not to sell the BTC if at all possible. Think of this like buying a lotto ticket that never goes bad, instead of spending $10 each week on a piece of paper that becomes worthless as soon as the numbers are drawn, and they do not match the numbers on the ticket, that $10 could be used to buy Bitcoin, and this ticket can be redeemed at any time, but the longer you hold it the more it is worth in dollar terms. Basically, the value of the Bitcoin she is able to stack up over many years depends on her desire to pass that wealth on to her children, if she is able to take the little spare money she has each month to buy Bitcoin, and move that Bitcoin to her self-custody wallet, then over a period of 20, or 30, or 40 years, that Bitcoin would be worth far more than what she invested in dollar terms. Depending on how much BTC she is able to accumulate over this long period of time, she will be able to pass on generational wealth to her children, and this could be enough to buy a car, a house, or even pay for college, obviously depending on the amount of BTC she is able to buy over the decades, and this would provide opportunities for her children that she never had growing up.

The main thing to understand in this example is that she has control over her own wealth, there is no 3rd party to that wealth, and that wealth was being held in the Bitcoin blockchain, not in other assets or currencies, since most currencies will be devalued over these long periods of time, and not increase in value like Bitcoins unit of account. Her investment allows her to directly pass on that wealth to her children, there might still be an inheritance tax, and transactions using this wealth would be public since Bitcoins blockchain is public, so it would not be wise to try and avoid any of these taxes. However, the important thing to understand is that there is no 3rd party to that wealth, and no 3rd party to the transaction of that wealth. She could directly send it to them, or she could just give them the hard wallet and seed phrase, meaning there is no transaction on the Bitcoin blockchain showing the wealth has been transferred, until the children start to sell the Bitcoin, creating the taxable event. Self-custody is important for some people, and not as important to other people, meaning some 3rd party wallets will remain popular, and new ways to invest in Bitcoin such as Bitcoin ETFs may become popular too.

Forms of Demand for Bitcoin:

Bitcoin ETFs exist today in several countries, and they will likely be approved in the U.S. sometime in 2024, this will be a new way for investors to buy and sell BTC, but it's important to remember exactly how the Bitcoin is being held. A Bitcoin ETF would not be anything like a self-custody wallet, an investor's wealth can be frozen or confiscated with a court order, and this is because the Bitcoin would be held in one or several wallets that the ETF issuer has control over. However, allowing this 3rd party to an investor's wealth allows the investor to easily buy and sell Bitcoin through the ETF, and this convenience is what many traditional investors are looking for, they do not care about self-custody as much as other investors might. Basically, a spot Bitcoin ETF that allows for the investor to withdraw the BTC to another exchange wallet or self-custody wallet, would not necessarily be a bad thing. Bitcoin would need to be held by the ETF, creating more demand for Bitcoin, and as long as the BTC can be moved between different wallet types, then the investor has the ability to choose how their wealth is held, giving them financial freedom, even if they end up choosing to hold that wealth in a Bitcoin ETF. However, if Bitcoin in the ETF cannot be sent to other wallets, then this would be a centralized point of control for investors holding their wealth in the Bitcoin ETF, and this is because the only way to realize any wealth gain, or transfer that wealth, is to convert the Bitcoin back to dollars. This creates a taxable event, for both investors simply realizing their wealth gain, and for parents trying to pass wealth on to their children, both would involve the 3rd party which is the ETF issuer, and the ETF issuer could restrict transactions of the investor's wealth if they were ever required to. *(Reference page 94)* Going back to the prior example, the single mother trying to pass on wealth to her children could do this through the Bitcoin ETF, but she would be relying on the ETF issuer to make the transfers, while if she held the wealth on a self-custody wallet, she could directly send it to them, or just give them the seed phrase as mentioned before.

A Bitcoin ETF will create a lot of demand for Bitcoins unit of account, but other use cases on the Bitcoin blockchain will also create demand for BTC, as mentioned before ordinals are basically NFTs on the Bitcoin blockchain, and as these inscribed sats begin to represent real world assets like real estate, there will be even more demand for BTC. *(Reference page 120)* These use cases could be solely on the Bitcoin blockchain, or involve other blockchains, either way nodes will be needed for many of these new use cases involving the Bitcoin blockchain. Both full and partial nodes will be needed, and as mentioned before nodes play a part in securing a blockchain's consensus method, so the more that are set up the more secure the blockchain becomes. Nodes are also a way for large investors to further protect their wealth held in the Bitcoin blockchain, rather than trust another node's version of the ledger of accounts, large investors would be able to have their own copy of the blockchain, and this again adds more nodes to Bitcoins blockchain, further securing its consensus method.

As more individual investors, companies, and governments hold a portion of their wealth in the Bitcoin blockchain, Bitcoins price in dollar terms will continue to increase, and this wealth can be used in several ways. Although Bitcoin could be used like a currency, basically used for everyday payments of goods and services, in order for these transactions to settle fast they need to be made through other methods like the Lightning Network, and this would be ok for small amounts of wealth. But as mentioned before the transactions taking place between Bitcoin nodes do not settle on the Bitcoin blockchain right away, meaning this type of Bitcoin transaction would not be ideal for moving large amounts of wealth between wallets on the Bitcoin blockchain. *(Reference page 123)* These large amounts of wealth held in the Bitcoin blockchain would be similar to stores of wealth like gold, and this would be a better use of the Bitcoin blockchain, rather than using BTC as a currency, using it as a way to store wealth over long periods of time. As more investors around the world start holding some of their wealth in BTC, it will become the common factor used to measure value, even between very different countries and peoples. Bitcoin can be used as the neutral method to transact wealth, and these transactions would even be able to take place between adversaries without fear the other side will be able to reverse or freeze the transaction.

The need for this became even more apparent when several countries that had accounts with the Swift platform had some of their wealth frozen and seized after the Russian invasion of Ukraine, and I would encourage further research for anyone looking to understand how Swift payments work, and the alternative payment platforms being developed by several countries, including the BRICS nations. Basically, the Bitcoin blockchain allows for transactions of wealth that cannot be stopped or manipulated by a country or its sanctions, these transactions are public but not directly connected to an identity as mentioned before, and although large Bitcoin mining pools or large mining farms could prevent their blocks from containing a transaction, this would not be the same as restricting the movement of wealth. The Bitcoin mining farm, or mining pool, only has the ability to approve or reject transactions in its version of the next block in the Bitcoin blockchain, and as mentioned before every Bitcoin validator and node is hashing the same transactions. The official next block is basically chosen at random, so trying to prevent a certain transaction would only be possible for validators with a sizable percent of the total hash rate, and even then, if the next block was issued to another validator, then the transaction would likely be added in their version of the blockchain. *(Reference page 5)* Simply put, they are technically ways to restrict transactions on the Bitcoin blockchain, but they are not easy to achieve, and the decentralization of large validators on the Bitcoin blockchain prevents this. Because even if they are able to prevent a transaction for several blocks, eventually it would be added to the blockchain by another validator. This would make the Bitcoin blockchain a safer option for transferring large amounts of wealth between countries or companies, the alternative Swift platform must comply with sanctions that might restrict an account, and this would make the Bitcoin blockchain more like a form of payment similar to gold, it is trusted, it can be verified, and it can be exchanged between individuals without a 3rd party.

Bitcoin and Gold:

As Bitcoins price increases over time, more and more investors will hold some of their wealth in the Bitcoin blockchain, and they will do this to protect their wealth over long periods of time, as well as realizing their wealth gain along the way trying to sell tops and buy bottoms of the Bitcoin price cycle. *(Reference page 106)* As the number of individuals, companies, and countries that hold Bitcoin increases, Bitcoins unit of account will be an easy way to measure wealth across the many different holders of Bitcoin, and this would be similar to gold and how it is used to determine the value of two currencies or assets between countries. Basically, gold is a metal that is commonly accepted to have value that people are willing to use when buying or selling goods, and this is why gold has been used for thousands of years, because it could be traded between countries that may be very different from one another, or maybe even in conflict with each other. The Bitcoin blockchain has some of these abilities as well, transactions on the Bitcoin blockchain can be made between anyone, even countries in conflict. This is because they would know the other party could not manipulate the transfer of wealth, and this is important in a digital economy, since now countries must not only trust the asset they are invested in, but also the network that allows for the transfer of that asset. This would make the Bitcoin blockchain a better option for transactions between countries, and as more countries hold Bitcoin it will become an easier option for them, and wealth held in Bitcoin would only be a portion of a country's overall wealth, they will likely still hold and trade gold, bonds, commodities like oil etc. However,

Bitcoin could become the common asset between many nations, basically it will be similar to gold in that it is something most countries trust, and this idea will continue to grow as more people start to hold some of their wealth in Bitcoin.

This is where the "digital gold" reference comes from, basically as more people invest in Bitcoin, then Bitcoin becomes the common form of wealth between more countries or groups of people, and this makes Bitcoin similar to gold in this aspect. Using Bitcoins blockchain in this way would be better than using it as an everyday payment method, although it can be used in this way, and long-term wealth storage, or the ability to transact without a 3rd party, will likely be Bitcoins main use case in the near future, although this could change as new use cases are developed on the blockchain. This makes Bitcoin the gold standard that all other coins and tokens can be measured off, and this is already the case for many blockchain coins and tokens today, their value can be represented in terms of Bitcoin. The same is true for fiat currencies, they can also be used to value Bitcoin or other coins and tokens, and in some countries Bitcoins price is at all-time highs when measured in the local currency. This is because the currencies value is falling, not because Bitcoins value is increasing, and having a stable agreed upon unit of account for transactions of wealth is why gold has been used for so long, and why the U.S. dollar has been used in more recent times. The unit of account used by the majority of the world is called the global reserve currency, for the last few hundred years paper currencies that usually represented an amount of gold, would be used for transactions of wealth. But even before this use of paper currencies gold was widely accepted globally, and it filled the reserve currency status, basically meaning it was valued and accepted by most people and countries globally.

So "digital gold" is not suggesting the physical metal is similar to the digital unit of account, gold and Bitcoin are very different in many ways, but similar in that they can be used to transact wealth in a secure way that does not involve a 3rd party to the transaction. I would encourage further research for anyone looking to better understand the similarities between gold and Bitcoin, for now let's just look at the basic 4 elements of value to better understand why gold and Bitcoin are similar. These essential elements of values are; scarcity, how much there is of it; transferability, can it be traded bought and sold; utility, can it be used in some way; and demand, does anyone want it. Gold is scarce, there is only a small amount mined each year, however gold is a naturally occurring metal in the universe, so there would technically be an unlimited supply of gold that exists, it is just beyond the reach of miners for now. The metal can be transferred by using bars or coins valued by their weight, this is ok when transacting in small amounts of gold, but larger transactions would require the storage and transport of the heavy gold bars, and this means the cost to transfer wealth in gold goes up substantially depending on the number of gold bars involved in the transaction. Gold's utility and demand come from things like gold jewelry, or from industrial use in chips or computer hardware, demand for gold will continue to increase in several industries, and this demand should keep golds price to the upside over time.

The Bitcoin blockchain has a max limit of 21,000,000 coins that can exist, this limit cannot be changed even with a hard fork as mentioned before, and this would make Bitcoin scarcer than gold, since gold exists everywhere in the universe. Transferring Bitcoin is easy, it can be moved anywhere on the planet relatively fast, depending on where your Bitcoin transaction is taking place, either from a hard wallet or between two accounts at a centralized exchange, and as mentioned before faster transactions would be better suited for smaller transactions of wealth. While larger transactions would likely be done on Bitcoins actual blockchain, sometimes taking several new blocks to be created before the transaction is accepted. This means some Bitcoin transactions can take longer than other transactions, but the fees for transactions and storage of Bitcoin is far less than gold, and this is because it is costly to store and transfer actual gold bars, while setting up a self-custody wallet is somewhat inexpensive, especially when compared to storing any amount of gold bars in a vault.

Bitcoins utility is growing with every new use case on the Bitcoin blockchain that requires BTC as a transaction fee, as mentioned before this will be a slow process, and this steady growth will create demand from investors that want to profit from this growth as well. We will go over other use cases that can drive this demand in more detail later, not all of them will be possible on the Bitcoin blockchain, but many of them will be, and these new use cases will be what drives continued demand for Bitcoin in the future. This adoption of Bitcoin globally, and its price pressure to the upside over time, is just my opinion, it is what I see possible based on blockchain technology and its capabilities, and it is slowly happening as more institutional investors and countries begin holding some of their wealth in the Bitcoin blockchain, further increasing demand. However, not every good aspect of Bitcoins blockchain is digital, there are several good aspects of Bitcoins blockchain that are physical, and things like balancing the grid with Bitcoin ASICs is already happening in several locations around the world, and it is also my opinion that these mining farms will drive the development of the renewable energy industry in the future.

Balancing the Power Grid:

Bitcoin mining farms can help balance power girds, they are also able to use energy sources that cannot be used by the grid, and as mentioned before Bitcoin mining farms are the long-term buyers that power plants need in order to justify investing in new equipment for their plants. These mining farms can be incorporated into the grid in several ways, they help reduce the wear and tear on expensive equipment, and this happens when renewable energy sources go back and forth between generating power and not generating power as mentioned before. *(Reference page 131)* Mining farms are able to help balance the grid by turning off or on when the grid needs them to, and during emergencies or extreme grid demand the mining farms can be completely shut down, allowing that energy to be used by the grid when it is needed the most. As mentioned before, these mining farms can also regularly sell power back to the grid, allowing for cheaper energy costs for grid customers, and locking in long-term contracts for that energy with power companies, allowing them to invest in further development of the power plant. Bitcoin mining farms can also use oil wells that are past their end-of-life for geothermal power, or stranded natural gas sources that cannot be reached by pipe, as mentioned before any cheap, abundant, and continuous energy source could be used to power a Bitcoin mining farm, and this demand for energy will drive the development of the renewable energy industry. This is happening for a few reasons, the first is that Bitcoins hash rate keeps increasing as new mining farms come online and try to earn block rewards globally, and a higher hash rate means more energy is required. Another reason is that other energy sources such as coal simply cannot keep up with a mining farms demand over long periods of time. Most Bitcoin mining farms need large power sources, and these power sources need to be able to scale, or they need to be renewable, since Bitcoins hash rate will likely only keep increasing overtime. This would mean fuel sources like coal are not ideal for long-term Bitcoin mining farms, basically they would eventually run out of coal, while hydro, geothermal, or nuclear are continuous energy sources. Transitioning away from energy sources like coal is better for the environment, and Bitcoin mining farms will help society shift away from these fuel sources in favor of other energy sources such as natural gas or hydropower as mentioned before, and this search for cheaper abundant energy sources will continue as Bitcoins hash rate continues to increase.

Bitcoins hash rate is continuing to grow each year, with slight dips as miners are weeded out through the halving event, and after large drops in Bitcoins price, which force some mining farms to shut down, although this is usually temporary since the hash rate has recovered somewhat fast and has continued to reach new highs after such events. *(Reference page 106)* This massive increase in Bitcoins hash rate will likely continue until ASIC units reach some kind of computing limit, and this would not stop Bitcoins hash rate increase since new farms could continue to come online. It would just reduce how much larger mining farms would be able to increase their hash rate over time, and this is usually done by upgrading ASIC units. Mining farms that are able to consistently rotate their ASICs to the newest models with the highest hash rate will be able to earn more block rewards for longer periods of time, although every halving those block rewards will be cut in half. So, increasing a mining farm's hash rate is important, but the same ASICs hashing transactions at different energy prices can also affect the mining farms profitability. Basically, Bitcoin mining farms are fighting the constant increase in hash rate, as well as the 50% reduction in block rewards every halving, they need to increase their computing power or reduce their energy costs, ideally both. But not every new mining farm will hash transactions long term, and this is what creates the Bitcoin mining farm cycle as mentioned before, or the weeding out of miners over time. This balance ensures there will always be people willing to hash transactions on the Bitcoin blockchain, based off Bitcoins hash rate and the potential block rewards earned, and based off Bitcoins price, both affect the mining farm's profitability. The other major way to improve a mining farm's profitability is to reduce the energy costs, and cheaper power would mean a mining farm could run more ASIC units for the same dollar value. Or more mining farms could be set up at the power source if possible, either way this adds to the number of individual ASICs and larger mining farms, both of which add to Bitcoins total hash rate, and further secure its consensus method. As long as there are block rewards to be earned, there will be people ready to hash transactions on the Bitcoin blockchain, if the total hash rate is low enough, or if Bitcoins price is high enough. They are incentivized to make a profit, and this profit comes from Bitcoins POW consensus method, but there are other ways to make a profit involving blockchain technology, staking coins to a POS blockchain would be similar, and we will go over other use cases like this in more detail later.

(Illustration, next page)

Alternative Blockchains:

Many use cases for blockchain technology currently happen on blockchains other than the Bitcoin blockchain, these other blockchains are sometimes referred to as alternative coins, or Alt-coins, and this is because these blockchains are the alternative to the original blockchain which is the Bitcoin blockchain. There were other blockchains and other SHAs that existed around Bitcoin's creation in 2009, but only the Bitcoin blockchain has seen major adoption. This growth can be seen in the overall market cap, or the amount of wealth being held in the blockchain, as well as the network of validators and nodes that support the Bitcoin blockchain, and both of these are continuing to increase with each halving and the cycles it creates. These alternative blockchains and their units of account are not necessarily bad, or worse than the Bitcoin blockchain. It just means most blockchains have not been around for as long as the Bitcoin blockchain, and as mentioned before it takes time to develop new blockchains, centralized points of control or failure can exist, and they need to be identified and corrected by developers. This is not impossible for developers, and there are several other blockchains that could be considered decentralized in similar ways to the Bitcoin blockchain. This along with a use case there is demand for would make that blockchains unit of account valuable, and it would make other tokens issued on the blockchain valuable, depending on their use case.

It takes time for improvement proposals to be implemented on the Bitcoin blockchain as mentioned before, and while these use cases are being developed on the Bitcoin blockchain, other blockchains can fill in where there is demand for a use case. Basically, some use cases are possible on the Bitcoin blockchain, but it is easier to create a new blockchain to fill the need for that use case rather than pass and implement a BIP that would allow for that use case on the Bitcoin blockchain. These other blockchains can be set up in many different ways, their consensus methods can be POW or POS, the network of validators can have voting power on the blockchain or there can be a separate governance structure as mentioned before, and these blockchains can have many different types of use cases. These Alt-coins and their use cases can help the Bitcoin blockchain by testing out new ideas, and their development could be used as a blueprint for similar use cases on the Bitcoin blockchain. Ordinals or Bitcoin "NFTs" would be an example of this, although not all use cases are possible on the Bitcoin blockchain. So, until Bitcoins blockchain is updated to allow for certain use cases, other blockchains will fill in where there is demand for these use cases, and this demand will come from more users interacting with the blockchain and its use case, driving growth and development for the entire blockchain industry.

Decentralization is Important:

While not all Alt-coins are centralized, many of the ones today are, or they at least have one or two centralized points of control as mentioned before, and it's important to remember how this technology works at its foundation, basically decentralization is important, it is what protects the blockchain from manipulation or malicious attacks. Investors that hold some of their wealth in the blockchain of an Alt-coin, or users that

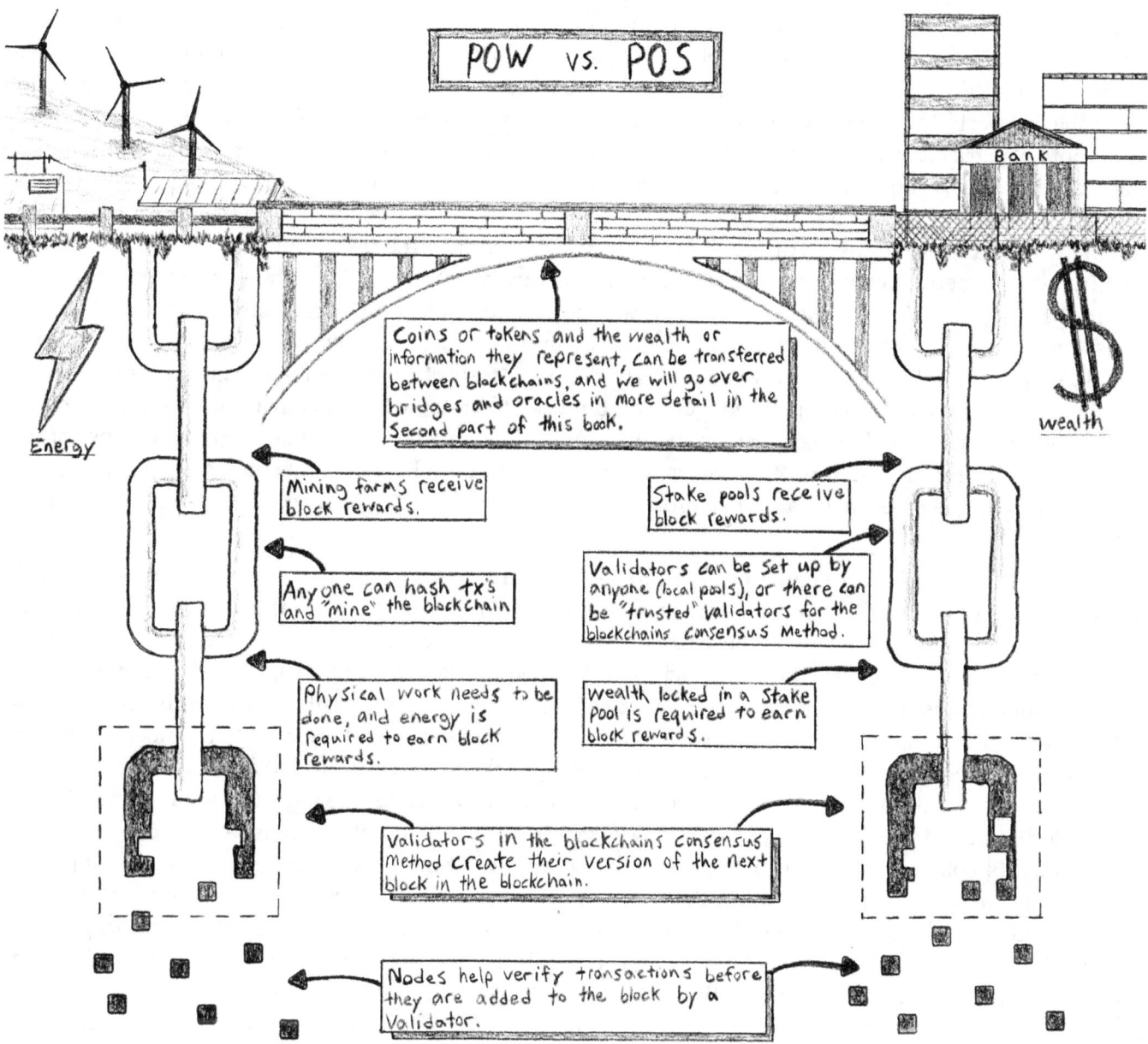

POW vs. POS

There are many different consensus methods, each have their own pros and cons, but it is important to remember there must be a cost for the validator in the blockchain's consensus method, otherwise these validators might try to manipulate the blockchain as mentioned before. That cost to participate in the consensus method comes in the form of equipment and energy costs for a POW mining farm, and for POS it comes in the form of the wealth required to become a stake pool operator. Either way it is wealth that helps secure a blockchain, basically this wealth can be invested into developing the renewable energy sector, and the computing power of new ASICs. Or the wealth can be locked in the coin of the blockchain, giving investors a steady interest on their wealth in the form of block rewards, with little effort required from the investor. As we have seen there are many aspects to a blockchain, and the validator network has a great deal of control over a blockchain and the transactions on it, ultimately these validators are what keep the blockchain online, and investors holding wealth in the blockchain should trust and understand that blockchains network of validators and consensus method.

Pg. 15, center section: Proof of work blockchains require energy in order to hash transactions on the blockchain, and validators are compensated with block rewards. While proof of stake blockchains use wealth locked in stake pools to hash transactions on the blockchain, the validators are compensated with block rewards, and there is far less hardware needed with this type of consensus method.

Pg. 27, upper section: Blockchains can be connected in several ways, basically wealth or information can be moved between two separate blockchains, and a simple way to think of this would be as a bridge between the blockchains. However, oracles can be set up in many different ways, and we will go over them in more detail in the second part of this book.

interact with a blockchains use case, need to understand how the coins and tokens that represent their wealth are being held, and this includes the type of wallet holding that wealth, as well as smart contracts that involve that wealth, which we will go over in more detail later. *(Reference page 96)* Basically, even a decentralized blockchain like Bitcoin, can involve a level of control or 3rd party access, but it is based on how the investor chooses to hold their wealth on the Bitcoin blockchain. For example, Bitcoin in a 3rd party wallet would allow the 3rd party to prevent transactions of that wealth, while transfer of Bitcoin in a self-custody wallet could not be restricted. *(Reference page 94)* The Bitcoin blockchain is simply a tool, just like any other tool in that it can be used in good ways and bad ways, it comes down to each person and how much they care about 3rd party's that have access to and control over their wealth. If this is a concern for the investor then Bitcoin and many other coins and tokens offer self-custody wallets, but they require a little work, and they are not as user-friendly as many exchange apps that can be simply downloaded by users. These exchanges offer many features that investors are looking for, and we will go over them in more detail next when looking at use cases. For now, just understand the Bitcoin blockchain allows for a secure method of storing any amount of wealth, in a way that does not involve a 3rd party that may restrict or prevent a transaction of that wealth, and this wealth is just information in a ledger of accounts on the Bitcoin blockchain as mentioned before. This information can also involve use cases on the Bitcoin blockchain, such as ordinals or transactions through the Lightning Network, and this other information is locked in the Bitcoin blockchain once it is added into the next block in the blockchain, and this information cannot be changed or manipulated after it is included in the next block.

Bitcoins blockchain can be copied or hard forked as mentioned before, but this does not mean Bitcoins decentralization has been "copied," we have seen there are a lot of factors that can affect a blockchain's decentralization, one of them is the network of validators, or Bitcoin mining farms, and these cannot be simply copy pasted. However, Bitcoins blockchain has been forked many times, and these are not always hard forks of Bitcoins actual blockchain as mentioned before, but they are possible, and the Bitcoin blockchain will likely be forked or copied many more times in the future. Eventually there might be a blockchain that is developed into something that is better than the Bitcoin blockchain, but until that actually happens Bitcoin will remain the standard, the original blockchain that started over a decade ago, and it has grown into the secure decentralized blockchain that it is today. There will always be other coins and tokens claiming to be "the next Bitcoin," or claiming to be decentralized, but over time most of these blockchains have failed in some way, and even the blockchains that have seen growth, have not seen the same level of adoption, growth, and development that the Bitcoin blockchain has seen over the years. Bitcoins amazing growth over the last decade is hard for newer blockchains to replicate, and this is because many of these blockchain projects are rushing their development. Basically, it is hard to replicate something that took over 10 years, in just one or two years, and many of these new blockchains projects have new ideas for certain aspects of the blockchain. Such as the type of consensus method, or the blockchains voting structure, basically many new ideas come and go, but the Bitcoin blockchain remains. A blockchain can be set up in many different ways as mentioned before, now that we have seen how the Bitcoin blockchain works, we will look at other ways to set up a blockchain, some are good, some are not so good, and we will look at Alt-coins and their use cases in more detail next.

Alt-Coins and Use Cases...

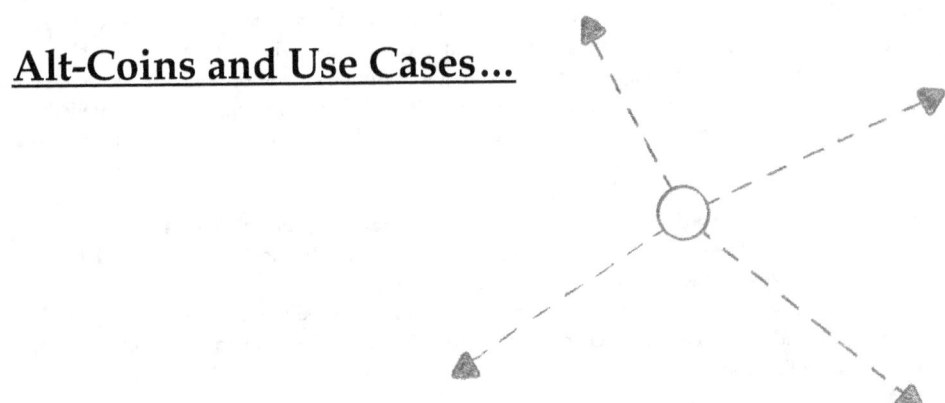

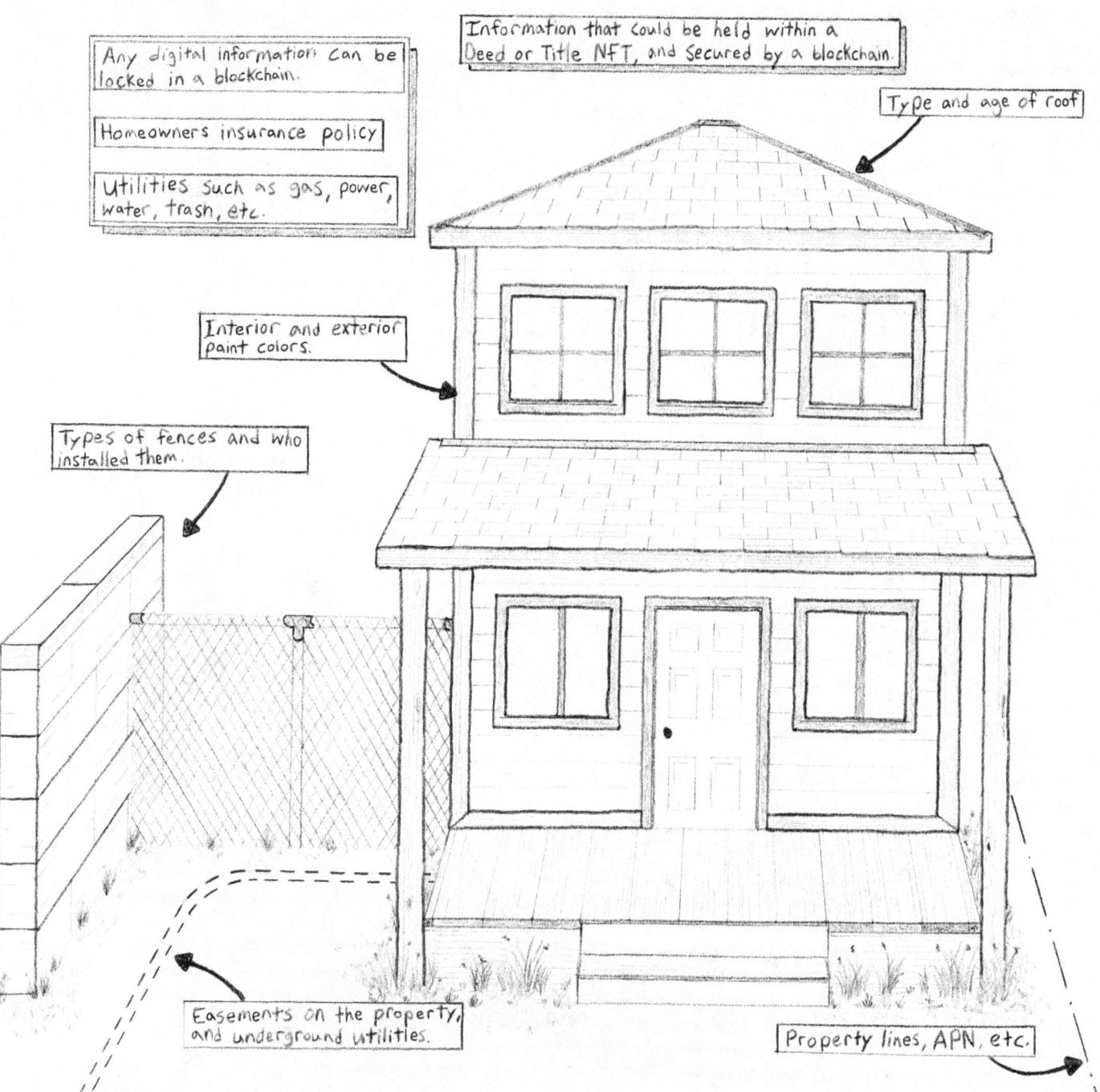

Blockchain Use Cases

There are many use cases for blockchain technology, and as we transition to a tokenized economy, we will see blockchain technology involved in more areas of our lives. As traditional industries incorporate blockchain use cases they will become faster and more secure, an example would be real estate transactions, and the deed or title to a property. Blockchain technology would allow for faster more secure transactions, although it will not replace every aspect of the transaction, and there would still be the need for some things like real estate agents and home inspections. Blockchain technology would also allow for the property to track and secure other information as well, basically anything that has to do with the ownership of the land and the structures built on it, it would make some things easier for a homeowner, and could be updated overtime.

However, as convenient as some of these use cases are, it is important to understand the blockchain that supports these use cases, basically; how is the information held on the blockchain, how is that information transacted between wallets, and who has access to the information during this process. Understanding this is important because centralized points of control could be used to manipulate or prevent some transactions on the blockchain, and this will depend on how the blockchain is set up. Understating what a truly decentralized blockchain is, and understanding what self-custody is, will allow individuals in the future to better understand the risks associated with their digital wealth or information, and blockchain use cases will likely be supported by many diffrent blockchains in the future.

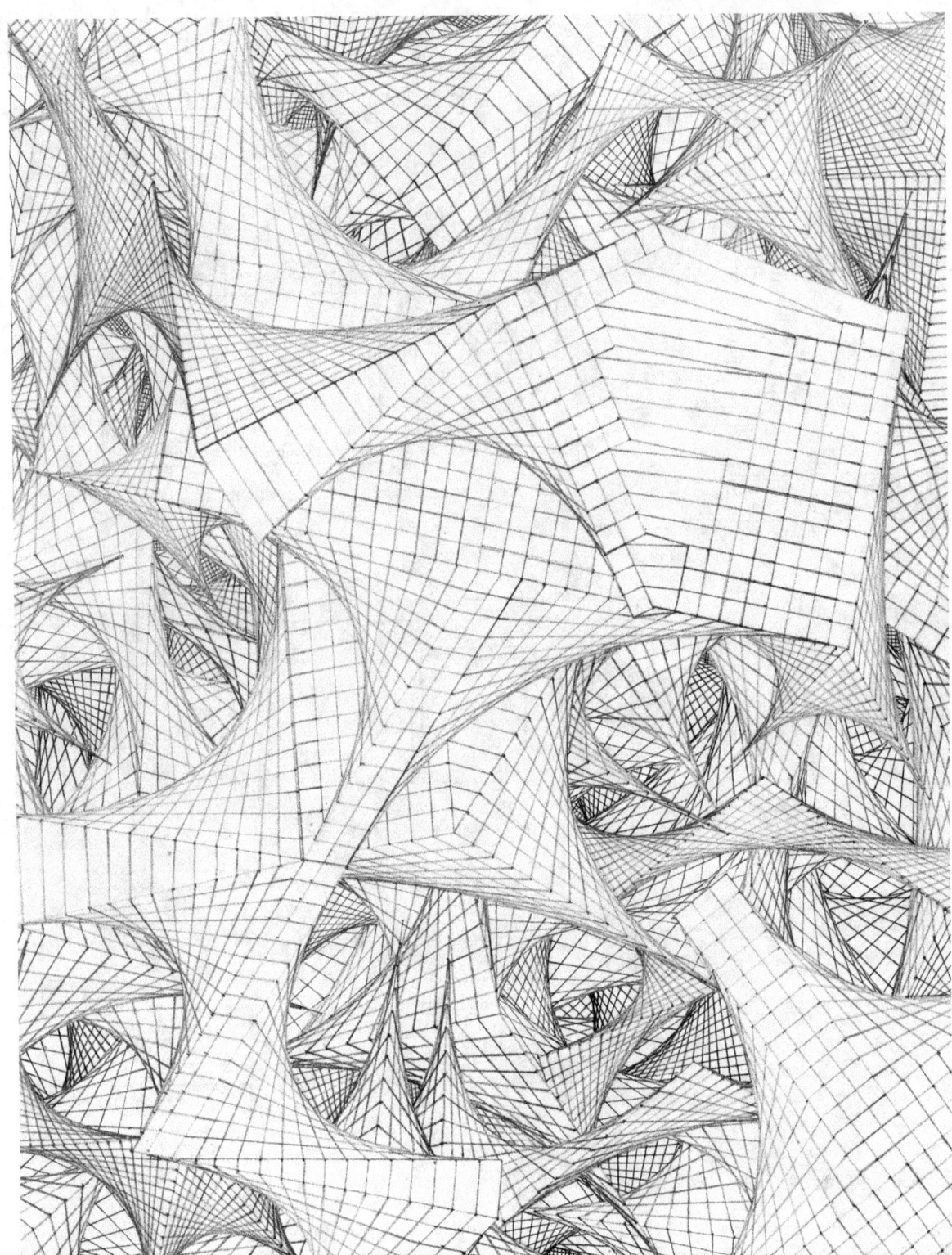

My Proof-of-Work

It took me over a year to finish this book, and during this time on average I would only be able to write for a few hours each day, although some days it was tough to write anything. Whenever I had trouble writing I would stop and draw something to help me relax, nothing complicated, just two lines with marks at varying intervals. I would then offset by one, and connect the two points, doing just a few sections each time. This drawing was not originally intended for the book, it was just random lines meant to help me relax, however over time it became more and more intricate, and I started thinking of it as my progress on the book, slowly being added to over time. Each night when I got to a point where I could not write anymore, I would add to the drawing, and although I could have gone back and fixed the few mistakes, I left them unchanged. This drawing had become the proof that I was still working on the book, it was proof of my time and energy in the book, and like a blockchain, there is no going back to change the past. I am a fan of cheesy jokes, so this drawing can be thought of as the "proof-of-work" for my book, it took time and energy to create, and it cannot be altered, much like blockchains with a POW consensus method.

My recommendations for those looking to continue their research:

General resources:

Coin Bureau   www.youtube.com/@CoinBureau

DAN teaches crypto   www.youtube.com/@DigitalAssetNews

Mining resources:

Son of a Tech   www.youtube.com/@SonofaTech

VoskCoin   www.youtube.com/@VoskCoin

Make that hope a reality!

I volunteer at the DACC, a consumer-based advocacy group for blockchain technology. We have supporters in many states and we are working towards the adoption of realistic rules and regulations for blockchain coins and tokens. Join the DACC if you are interested in helping make that hope a reality!

www.joindacc.org

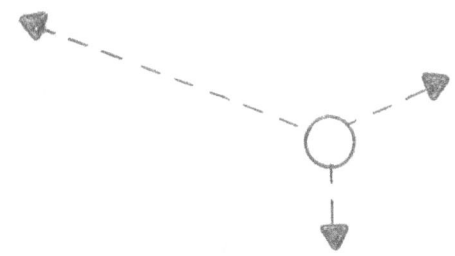

www.ingramcontent.com/pod-product-compliance
Lightning Source LLC
Chambersburg PA
CBHW082329220526
45470CB00008B/2452